Y0-BRH-220

Presented to Lenoir-Rhyne College Library

in appreciation of the help of

Mr. Burl McCriston

A gift from
Dr. Fred & Mildred J. Ebersole
June 1991

WITHDRAWN

DEAR CRAIG AND BRIAN
*A Space-Age Grandfather
Shares His Faith*

FRED EBERSOLE, Ph.D.

CARL A. RUDISILL LIBRARY
LENOIR-RHYNE COLLEGE

VANTAGE PRESS
New York

BV
4501.2
.E230
1991

153392
May 1992

FIRST EDITION

All rights reserved, including the right of
reproduction in whole or in part in any form.

Copyright © 1991 by Fred Ebersole, Ph.D.

Published by Vantage Press, Inc.
516 West 34th Street, New York, New York 10001

Manufactured in the United States of America
ISBN: 0-533-09036-9

Library of Congress Catalog Card No.: 90-90088

1   2   3   4   5   6   7   8   9   0

This book is dedicated to *Mildred*, my loving wife and sweetheart, who sustained four years of its writing, and to *Marian*, our faithful daugher and loyal teacher of youth, and her devoted husband, *Dr. Karl*, together with the grandsons *Craig* and *Brian* and to the memory of dear *Carolyn*, our older daughter, who was received into heaven upon leaving us her gift of *Renée*, our only granddaughter. We also take this opportunity to thank her father, *Richard,* and *Evelyn*, a most faithful surrogate mother, for safely parenting her into adulthood.

This family page is the appropriate place to share a special tribute to my dear wife who has catered to me for sixty-two years and is still at it. Elsewhere I have pointed out that it was she who actually sparked the idea of writing this book. She, from Evangeline's Village in Nova Scotia and I, a North Dakota prairie lad, met at a Halloween party in the First Baptist Church in Cambridge, Mass. It had to be God's will. I met her pastor later and learned why the mothers of teenaged girls had him appoint her the leader of their Canadian Girls in Training. Later on, her endowed "motherhood training" was still her forte when, in Elsmere, N.Y. (Albany), the Brownie Scout bigwigs chose her as the number one Brownie mother for dozens of the young girls of the village. This "family" was added to our own two daughters for the next five years before moving to a suburban Jersey town where she taught another five years in the fifth-grade section of our church school. Family tragedy in the case of our older daughter and failing health (severe tinnitus and now 90 percent deafness) have taken their toll but Love is still the name of the game. Her life and mine are bound and melded together as one, in the pages of this book.

Contents

Foreword

"How do I gently discourage this eighty-year-old gentleman without breaking his vibrant spirit?" The man before me is a new member of the congregation having just taken up residence at a retirement village. Bit by bit he has been feeling me out about his project, but the full impact of his undertaking is staggering me: "I plan to publish a book of my views on the Christian faith to guide my grandsons on their pilgrimmage and the church as well. . . . "

Rather than try to deflate him with the realistic horrors of writing for publication (especially in a field other than one's own expertise), I offer gentle encouragement knowing full well the probability that the project would never reach completion, much less publication. After all, here stands one of my strongest encouragers, supporters, and critics (in the best sense of the word), one of those few church members who is always looking forward and not afraid to let go of the past to move into unchartered territory on faith. The least I can do is to keep my new friend excited about his newfound calling.

For my lack of complete honesty, I was soon inundated with section after section of this book in its rough form. Since I have been living with the text for some time, let me suggest some thoughts on the question that struck me initially: "How should I read this book?"

The most obvious answer is "personally"! It is conversational in style, addressed not only to two grandsons but also to the other children of the Christian church which is equally beloved by the author. It is impossible to escape being drawn into this intimate conversation of faith.

Like the accent derived from living in a certain area of the country, the author has his own vocabulary and style. Using a unique combination of words old and new, the author above all seeks to communicate the ancient faith to a modern world, the theological to the scientific, the inherited faith to a people who must learn to adopt it as their own personal belief. His thrust, I believe, is essential in a time when the chasm has widened between what is heard in the pew of churches and in the streets of the city. The bridges offered are not only fresh language, but also challenging thoughts.

The lay person will find a surprising freshness of expression. However, one might feel lost at first trying to follow this fast-paced pilgrim. Press on, though, and I believe you will receive a blessing. For here is a layman who by his own admission began to grow spiritually only after long stints of faithful church leadership and when retirement afforded him the opportunity to apply his scientific training (Ph.D. in chemistry from MIT) to an analysis and expression of the Christian faith.

Those professional clergy may be tempted to look down upon such "non-guild" utterances of a novice. It will be clear from the outset that the author, while well read in some areas, is not totally immersed in the whole stream of theology. He will offer ideas which seem novel though many clergy have toyed with them for years.

The chemistry of this author's faith combines so many seemingly diverse positions that labels of "liberal" or "conservative" just will not fit. Instead, the reader will sense the emergence of a new compound, a new creation, inspired by a mind trained in the scientific world and a heart tuned by the living Word.

The resulting brew is volatile. Views ranging from the heretical to the conservative abound. Readers will be challenged an annoyed, encouraged and uplifted. A potential explosion like the Reformation might well occur if individuals and churches are moved to take seriously this challenge to Christian Education which is long overdue, this push to move beyond secular evolution to a thoroughly Christian understanding of development, this insistence the the nature of God and prayer be expressed and understood by the scientific mind of today.

An overarching principle is the passion of the writer who knows that his eighty-seven years have been extended for the purpose of writing this book. It is "preachy" at points, but strong words are necessary. It sounds "Presbyterian" almost exclusively at points until one discovers the intense commitment to ecumenical endeavors coming out of the author's background in Methodist, Baptist, Congregational, and finally Presbyterian churches (not to mention Bible and theology under Lutheran professors during undergraduate days). There is no subtlety offered, no "sugar coating." Time is too short and precious. The Gospel faith must be understood by the modern mind. The Word must not only be heard but also done.

It is this passion that I did not fully understand when inadvertently encouraging this book. But it was also this divine compulsion that would have brought this important word to print in spite of my efforts or lack thereof.

How should I read this book? Carefully, for it is the essence of Christian Education which is loving. Prayerfully, for it is not only an author's communication, but also inspired by the author. Joyfully, for it is a timely expression of the timeless Truth of the Gospel.

Traditions and traditional understandings of the faith are meant to be "passed on" from one generation to another. In part this means handing the content of the Christian faith to the Craigs and Brians. But it also must mean to "pass judgment on" what we have received as the persistent Word is constantly reforming the church. This book has done both in a fresh way that can only be described as inspired and "passed on" by a passionate man who can only be called "faithful." Thank God he was not discouraged or dissuaded!

Charles M. Durham
Senior Pastor,
First Presbyterian Church,
Tuscaloosa, Alabama

Excitement—a Preface

This book asks you as a Christian, or one who wishes to be so, to learn the definition of a word which does not appear anywhere else in this manuscript. Yet this entire book has been written to inform you how to become *excited* and in turn become an *exciting* agent in a mission for God. As an initial step, may we share in studying the verb *excite*, as defined in the Random House dictionary (1971).

> **excite** *v.t.* **1** to arouse or stir up the emotional feelings of; **2** to arouse or stir up; **3** to cause, to awaken; **4** to stir to action, to stir up, *physio.* **5** to stimulate, to excite a nerve; **6** *elect.* to supply with electricity for producing electric activity; **7** *physics* to raise (an atom, molecule, etc.) to an excited state; syn. stir, awaken, stimulate, animate, kindle, inflame . . . **2** evoke; **3–4** agitate, ruffle.

The pauperism of our English language is apparent when a verb has so many variable meanings. Subtract from the above a child's excitement at Christmas or the preparation of a family going off on a vacation. You may then realize that definitions 4 through 7, especially 5 through 7, plus the synonyms, denote the emphasis in recounting this pilgrim's progress and experience.

We propose that God and energy are inseparable. The Divine system for communicating, i.e., radiating, God's way of transferring His energy to us, leads us to recognize that we are under the influence of a Spiritual Field of Force akin to His magnetic field of force. At birth He gave us each a wireless receiving set, our conscience, by which we are able to receive His throbbing, quickening Power, and the force to do spiritual work if we also learn a bit of new vocabulary. His messages are beamed to us each day but we do not excite our lazy systems. *We must choose* to be excited and take the church of Christ off the endangered list. Our American churches have become a minority influence. The polls say that less than 15 percent of the salaried employees in charge of producing our TV programs of news and entertainment attend any form of church worship. Lecomte duNoüy, the devout Christian biologist, saw forty years ago the possibility of God's remnant having "to take to the desert" to preserve its leaven for a different and more receptive new age.

This book challenges Christians in this Space Age to open the circuits to God, daily exciting via prayer through old channels and newly excited with the power and energy they will find in the Spirit. It also emphasizes the need for teachers and pastors of our teenage confirmation classes to generate a new curriculum that will be able to increasingly excite themselves and others. Expressing the message in today's adoption of scientific terms seems obvious. And the myriads of neutral, passive, lazy, encapsulated families and those infected with the Milquetoast virus will learn what they can do with God's Spiritual Field of Force.

This Pilgrim submits that he is excited by God for the sake of his grandchildren; may you join him and become exciters for your families!

Author's Note

The reader is advised, as the illustration on page 209 simplifies it, to realize that he is a part of the total universe, and is immersed within God's Spiritual Field of Force. We suggest that His Gift of our Mind and Conscience enables us to connect with this Force in a fashion similar to that of the activated compass needle which responds to our planet's field of magnetic force. We admonish you to rethink your own situation each time you encounter one of the Pilgrim's auspiciously placed *capitalized* terms. They are a signal that the Divine Presence is knocking at the door of your heart.

Take a journey with Dr. Fred. See life and times that brought about a faith so strong that it casts a beacon illuminating for us a pathway through some of the inconsistencies that plague modern Christianity. On these pages science and religion are woven into a smooth, strong line of thought that reinforces the "Seeker" and "the Doer."

I've known this man for a long time—35 years. I've seen the prayer and study that would produce a book like this. To me, it is a natural outcome of his pilgrimage into faith that he has something to tell, and you will be the richer for it.

The discipline that he applies to doctoral studies, teaching at MIT, and scientific endeavors at General Aniline & Film, is immersed in Bible study, prayer, and the pursuit of a theology, and is worth much reflection on the part of the reader. It is especially inspiring for the new pastor who enjoys the vigor of youth and the enthusiasm of fresh learning.

The human condition is a mystical experience, clouded by materialism and the forces of evil so strong that most of us are in desperate need of guideposts to point the way. This book is a distillate and I bid you to drink from this cup: "it runs over." This man is truly a disciple of the Lord. I know it.

A friend, Robert

In Appreciation

Assisting in bringing this book into being was a group of friendly, supportive people, both lay and ordained. Portions have been read and commented upon by the following ministers of the Gospel: the Reverend Dr. Hal Hyde, Jr., the Reverend Mr. W. W. (Buddy) Olney III, the Reverend Mr. Dean Overholser, and the Reverend Mr. Theodore Dixon. Especially appreciated for their unbounded enthusiasm and encouragement are the Reverend Dr. Charles M. Durham, my present pastor, and the Reverend Mr. William E. Griffiths, our chaplain at Abernethy Village.

Special appreciation is extended to Mr. and Mrs. Robert Provost, friends of thirty-five years. Rose was a most talented and kindly colleague during many years when we were fellow employees of GAF Corporation. She faithfully typed the early scripts but due to traumatic illness in her daughter's family was unable to work on the final one. Robert is a devout Roman Catholic layman, the product of a full four-year parochial high school. Special recognition is due him for bringing a copy of Lecomte duNoüy's *Human Destiny* to my attention and proving his ability and interest in discussing important sections of it. He is an exceptional layman in his understanding and appreciation of the spiritual nature of the universe and mankind within.

And finally, very warm thanks for the cooperative spirit and ability of Mrs. Barbara Mitchell, our church secretary in Newton, who under pressure to produce the final script for the publishers did a magnificent job. She was a kindly Christian helper in a time of need.

DEAR CRAIG AND BRIAN

Chapter I

Orientation: Making a Road Map for You, the Reader

PROLOGUE: WAITING ON THE LAUNCH PAD . . .

Let us accelerate our getting acquainted. If you care to flip back for a glance at the foreword and table of contents, you see the making of a pilgrimage, and usually pilgrimages require some sort of map. The map is useful whether the journey is purely physical or wholly mental and spiritual, or a mixture of all three, which mine tries to be. Of course my map is an after-the-fact historical listing. I did not know I was going to be a pilgrim until after I had retired from my vocation. Check out the sketch on page 35. At this moment it may seem a bit complicated but I invite you to be my companion in review. Perhaps my experience may help you on your private journey. Note that my diagram reflects the continuity of youth, middle life, and retirement years to date. It underlies the later discussion of the Growth Curve in the next chapter as more than an academic approach. What does your curve look like?

A special comment regarding the autobiographical aspect of my curve is necessary. The historical overtone as reflected in the abscissae i.e., denoting the passage of time, the years of a man's lifetime, is a convenient fact. However, the perpendicular coordinate which denotes the measure of the Quality of that Life is an entirely different matter. How good am I? So I must be very careful. The quality of any one life is usually apt to be judged quite critically by others. Therefore, there is no mathematical unit on that scale; I have attempted to keep my ego in restraint. Higher simply implies better quality and Lower means lesser. The steepness of the curve at points may be open to some criticism since the speed with which one gains *knowledge* is always greater than the

1

process time, during which it is transformed into consistent *action* of character. Only Almighty God registers the truth on His complete file cassette of my life. Note the flattened character of the mid-life period. It indicates that despite my busyness in church educational work, I was not rising to God's expectations.

Although ten letters to grandsons in chapter 3 will reveal something of myself, the real personal basis and motive for this pilgrimage through most of the twentieth century comes early on in the conclusions of chapter 4 dealing with my identity. It is important that you learn to use some new vocabulary. Most are not actually new words. They are words that most of you use each day, but they have been endowed with expanding new meanings, which I feel are demanded for the twenty-first century. These words, tinged with a degree of modernity, will be necessary for helping to gear up Christ's Church for its fulfillment in the Space Age.

This is not a theological treatise, but you will need to swallow some theology in small doses. I hope that I am able to make the medicine go down easily. It is the kind of theology I believe the lay person in the new church will seek to absorb so that he or she can remain in communication with a more expectant God, pulsating at higher energy levels toward His disciples of A.D. 2000, far in excess of what we have been able to comprehend hitherto. How else in this age, when the modern mode changes so drastically with each generation, are we going to be able to "put on the armor of God" the way Paul was able to do? Your grandfather or great-grandfather, dropping off his heavenly plane today, would never recognize the place. Software replaces hardware as a topic of conversation, six-foot dishes stand on edge in back yards, and a few of the preachers who, sorry to say, actually needed to be invited by parishioners to a Sunday dinner when I was young, now live in million-dollar homes equipped with more amenities than they can manually operate without hired help.

Christ's Church in America has in general allowed itself to deteriorate in places almost to the point of stagnation, or so the statistics tell us. It has become so since the period of fervent evangelistic zeal in the latter part of the nineteenth century. How and when can there be another "haystack meeting"[1] when soldiers of the cross will surge out to combat our malignant, modern, pagan culture, which has forced the church into a minority position? How and when can the apostles of A.D. 2000 write a new creed? For I am sure that God expects us to recognize

2

the obsolescence of the framework of the A.D. 385 edition for the Space Age. How and when will our churches begin to act upon the premise that Christian education must actually become Christian nurturing (i.e., parenting); and that now is the time to excise the remains of Robert Raikes syndrome and cast it into utter oblivion? This will take differently equipped seminaries and an improved brand of pastoral teachers and pulpiteers; these people must be professional leaders able both to proclaim the Word and to DO the word as ACTION. True, this will be at the risk of not raising the church budget without real effort and quite occasionally becoming suspect under the laws of our land; it may even entail taking to the streets now and then and inviting the chance to go to jail.

Allow me also to share a private, almost secret thought with you. Looking back, this pilgrim was a real sinner during thirty years or so of constant Sunday-by-Sunday church-school educational activity. He fooled himself into thinking that he was doing a good job for Christ and His Church by immersing himself in and overloading himself with such duties. In fact he kept so busy that there was little time or no time beyond his professional vocational obligations for the personal reading and praying (meditation) that is absolutely necessary for establishing and maintaining a warm relationship with God Himself. God had given him a special three-year college major in Christianity, had equipped him with a spiritual receiving set, and He now waited for the pilgrim to make use of it. Finally, in much later life, he got around to writing some letters to his grandsons and then realized that he had written himself into a bigger job than he had anticipated. The only decent thing to do was to try to finish the project. Apparently, his Spirit-Enabler had had a more demanding challenge in view all along. Reading and meditation, with a growing concept of the POWER and ENERGY of Almighty God, called for pilgrim sorties into new and unplumbed areas. I, as that pilgrim, really had to learn to pray, at least clumsily, and establish an I-You relationship with our Redeemer-Enabler, which could honestly be attested to as more than going through the motions of make-believe.

I have used two terms above: Power and Energy. Allow me to suggest that by capitalizing them I convey a sense of divinity to them. If there is one word beyond LOVE that you should absorb from this book it is ENERGY. For me, it is the one word above all others, except LOVE, that epitomizes the infinite activity power of the Divine Presence we name God. It labels the probable first thing in existence

3

before anything else was made. Discussing this in detail in chapter 9 will disprove the view of some of the saints who liked to talk about the universe as having been made *ex nihilo*, i.e., "out of nothing." I suggest their "nothing" was God Himself. Can you imagine that God's energy powers both the prosaic manufacturing plant out there on the edge of town as well as that thriving community of faith, the church next door? In the writing of this book I have come to view that possibility as quite reasonable. Now let's be on our way.

SECTION 1. WHY DID I WRITE THIS BOOK?

How does an octogenarian, born at the late edge of the horse and buggy days, have an ability to communicate with youngsters in the Space Age whose daily experiences are Star Wars and TV violence? Children who, perhaps, as the polls say, may not be able to write a cogent paragraph about a thing (an object), or anything intelligible about an idea or an emotion. Nor does the English language supply words of such specific intensity and longevity of meaning as to override the generational quirks of teenage adaptation and invention. Could I, an elder, hope to convey a message so that it might reflect the truth of my actual experience in terms of today's comprehension?

Since time began, God's answer for such problems has been the family. Fathers and mothers have always been charged with guaranteeing that education shall be their ever-present responsibility. Our Judeo-Christian background also makes certain that within the family a special fount of knowledge shall be erected. This fount is blessed of God so that everyone in the family shall be instructed "in heart, in mind, and in Spirit." The members of that family shall realize that mankind is built upon such a sturdy tripod: a body of flesh and of mind fashioned in the image of God's Spirit.[2] The ideal family shall be monotheistic with God in charge everywhere. So I appeal to you who are fathers and mothers to accept your roles as translators of my words, a number of which will deliberately be made new in application.

There is a word, an outstanding key word in human life, that cannot be adequately described by merely using other words. Its translation into understandable terms must come via *actions* and *behavior*. It demands demonstrations, and often demonstration does not fit hand-in-glove with the full idea of the word. The word is "love." We use the term

4

"love" or "to love" to express such a wide range of emotion and affectionate action as to be both pathetic and confounding. We use it to run the gamut from animal instinct to Divine Grace; it describes extramarital sexual intercourse with a prostitute or unfaithful spouse to the other extreme of the mysterious Divine Love of God for His creatures. It thus embraces actual opposites: lust, which takes, and the love of God, which gives.[3] Beside which, we love any *thing* as well as a person, be it a car, money, a new dress, or that morning's anthem at church. It must also reflect the effect on me of the relationship of a Sunday school teacher[4] with his boys in a prairie village in North Dakota in pre–World War I days; the teacher was the kind of a man who could introduce the idea of organizing a troop of Boy Scouts in that raw, primal culture within months of the transport of the British origins of scouting to this country. Likewise, it was apparent in the relationship nurtured between a college freshman and the medical director in charge of physical education at Saint Olaf College. He taught two of us of college age every Sunday in the little Baptist church in Northfield, Minnesota, quite disconnected from the official Lutheranism at the college.[5]

So why did I write this book? The answer comes, which would not have been possible a decade or two ago. The twenty years since my industrial retirement have afforded opportunity for continued teaching within the church, which resulted in extended private study including a considerable amount of theology (as published for the layman).

I must pause a moment to pay tribute to the influence of my dear wife. I firmly believe that God acts at times through the principle of the Eternal Triangle, which is discussed in the final chapter. Thus, He operates at times through the agency of individual humans with whom we associate in daily life. My wife, coming across the packet of letters, kept raising the serious question: Why not expand these into a full length book? It took earnest discussions on several occasions before the trigger was pulled. Yes, I do feel that God was behind it. His prolonging of my years could well mean that He was waiting for me to complete my assignment. He was aware of the awakening response I was registering against an obvious decline in the authority of Christ's Church in the culture of our land. He surely saw me as a pretty uncertain example of discipleship, but perhaps with possibilities. I was all talk in enclosed conclaves of the community of faith, but not doing much as a channel of His energy in affecting the public domain. Perhaps if I woke up and diligently labored, I could help Him get the message out on His Spiritual

Field of Force, for general broadcast to EVERYONE. I could not exhibit the scholarship of a John C. L. Gibson or a John Powers, S.J., but I could do the very best I could. He would sustain me through the difficulties if I were on the right path.

Conveying ideas generated in one's own life over into the idea-generating department of another's life is most difficult. We must toss a word, or a term, back and forth and around a group in a number of passes before we are sure we are well understood. I have a growing compulsion to share some of my experiences with you on a two-way street before it is too late. In this increasingly secular, materialistic, litigious, violent, and sexually promiscuous culture it seems as if Christ's true Church in American may be encapsulating. A Christian majority has already become a minority, and within such a remnant a further inner core or *remnant of remnants* must be kept alive and vibrant, ready for the "fullness of time" in the advancing new century. Under God's direction we will be called upon to leaven a new era in His ancient and eternal rescue plan. I invite your comments and corrections of my ideas. Hopefully, you now understand why this book was written. I *had* to do it—for Christ's sake.

SECTION 2. VOCABULARY FOR THE SPACE AGE

"When I was a child, I spoke as a child, I thought as a child." So said St. Paul almost two thousand years ago.[6] He does not mention any special teenage coinage, but it would be interesting to know if "nerds" existed in A.D. 50 and how the Greek language handled them. Paul advises us that in due course he advanced in knowledge and wisdom characteristic of an adult. Paul was honest about it. He reached a stage of adult understanding but conceded that in tackling certain problems of life and seeking desirable conduct after his Christian conversion, he still saw some things rather dimly and darkly.[7] He hoped that God in Christ would eventually get him straightened out and things would become clear and concise with age and experience.

So we, too, as infants, begin with objects we see, or can hold in our hands or put into our mouths. We learn the words for them by the inflective sound of a parent's voice, even before we learn to pronounce them vocally ourselves. Day by day a whole vocabulary is rigged up centered around the basic needs of food, bodily comfort, and body

6

waste elimination. Especially as regards the latter item, considerable baby talk addressed to personal hygiene lingers on even to adulthood. Many of us do not try to use the proper physiological terms for the private areas of the body, long into and after midlife continuing a modified infantile vocabulary. In a similar fashion, childish practices of speech in the religious realm are apt to develop and be even more permanent. Millions of "Now I lay me down to sleep" prayers have been taught to children by loving parents, but at the prepuberty level of ten to eleven years they have failed to graduate the child into a higher and broader concept of God's love. Perhaps the parent retains a religious childishness and refuses to grow out of it.

The teenager who has not been subjected to a family situation entailing an extraordinary, traumatic experience of deaths or sicknesses is very apt to retain an infantile religious vocabulary. These infantile concepts and words are not easily moved to a higher level even in the hearing presence of a devout Sunday school teacher. We wonder if parents are a little too laissez-faire between weekends?

During the process of learning newer and higher-level vocabulary, the young individual gradually builds a store of two kinds of words. Some deal with exterior facts, or news that means little to him and which he easily forgets. Others deal with his own firsthand experiences. Thus the admonishment not to hurt others is meaningless, or nearly so, until he himself is hurt. (Later on we will discuss content versus nurture in the Christian learning process.)

Also, words having much the same sound or identical sounds often have multiple meanings, all real and in good order in the dictionary. As a rather too simple example take the word "grip." The youngster wrestling violently with his dad on the living room carpet is playfully seized by the father in a strong, firm grip (no doubt the tactic by which Dad regains his physical equilibrium and a few quick moments of rest). The word "grip"—to hold any object tight—is thus easily learned both as a verb and as a noun. But puzzlement enters the picture when the lad hears his father upon a later occasion tell Mother he will bring his grip downstairs and stow it in the car. That evening on the phone he overhears his father telling someone that Jack could not make it to work that day because he had a bad case of "grip." No matter that the medical term is actually "la grippe," the sound he heard was identical to the others. Some time later, Big Brother appears on the scene in company with some of his pals. What funny stuff are they up to this time? It develops

7

that they are practicing a sort of handshake in which certain fingers are placed in a particular position and with a certain number of repetitive motions of the hand clasp. They tell Bobby they are practicing the secret grip of the club they were initiated into that week. Bobby may think he has seen it all, but even concerning the definition "to hold," he has yet to see a certain modification of it. That evening Dad reports back to Mother that his Stillson wrench is of no avail in correcting the trouble in the basement; he does not have sufficient room to maneuver the wrench into a position where it can grip the pipe. The next Sunday at church Bobby pays better attention than usual to the pastor's sermon. The preacher keeps talking about a wonderful feeling when one is gripped by an idea, or a thought, or an emotion. What's that about being gripped by a high resolve to do better in Christian conduct? Bobby does not know how, but apparently when one is overwhelmed by wishing to do something the way Jesus did it, he has either gripped an idea, or an idea has gripped him. Bobby concludes that an idea can be as important as a firm handshake, a contract; probably more so, since he has heard that men and women actually have given up their lives in helping a neighbor in need.

Recall our earlier reference to the word "love," which is an example revealing the bankruptcy of the bare English language.[8] When we use this word we usually accompany it with descriptive or leavening terms so that we build up a specific context. In establishing the context, we are apt to overlook that which *we* take for granted. We are apt to overlook the fact that he with whom we are communicating often does not know what we really mean. We agree that the choice of words is most important and especially so in those instances when ideas are being developed and communicated. Direction in the choice of appropriate words is the role of a teacher, be he friendly or antagonistic towards his subject.

Let us place the word "love" in a religious context. One is reminded of a situation at a communion breakfast to which the Easter confirmation class has been invited to be the guests of the deacons or elders, or the official board, or whatever. A rather sketchy and very brief response is heard. When later one of these young persons stands in public and makes a statement such as "I love Jesus Christ," we as listeners receive the statement in terms of what *we* wish the statement to mean. If, in a commitment service, the questions and responses are being read from a printed page, we are even more certain to insert our own meanings into both questions and answers, because the usually mumbled responses of the inductees do not provide telltale clues on an individual basis. One legitimately wonders if the new communicant understands the question in the first place and, second, wonders whether the young person making the response is using his own words or is merely parroting the words of the pastor who has been drilling the class in the preceding periods of class work. Ideally the youth, the middle-aged, and the older person will have legitimate differences in meaning, else there has been no spiritual growth during the lives of those making up the congregation. Some churches, willing to admit that attainment of physical age is not a guarantee that growth toward God has taken place, *are beginning* to strengthen the curriculum and the sharing activity of the confirmation service. New programs tend to enhance spiritual growth of both the inductee and pew member. It is a nurturing, sharing process far exceeding bare factual education. See chapter 6, which details such a program.

Some vocabulary changes take place within a few decades. Consider the word "charismatic." In my youth and middle age I knew a number of charismatic people. They wore friendliness on their sleeves and had a warmth and PR radiation that was unmistakable. Today I almost dare not use the adjective because the specific branch of the Church that has developed about the person of the Holy Spirit seems to have appropriated it rather exclusively for themselves (or the rest of us have done it for them).

Some words do resist change for a long period. To fear God in 1000 B.C. is no longer to fear God in A.D. 2000, but many Christians fail to see such metamorphosis when they study the Old Testament. Perhaps this was caused by a slow loss of memory, a disease, or disuse of the term, or a conclusion that it is not relevant to the Space Age. It is almost as if we were saying, "Move over, God, we don't need you for everyday life. We won't bother you until we run into real trouble." But more on that later. Tradition, like the balancing control on the great ocean liner, keeps us from making too many aimless turns and twists; but keeping the status quo can lead to passivity and a laissez-faire atmosphere. The Christian faith suffers because it tends to put a brake on its dynamism whenever we fail to develop new meanings for its ancient words of tradition. The Space Age demands this revision.

Ever so often some noble character delivers an impassioned oration on behalf of the beautiful Elizabethan English of the King James version of the Bible. The professor of literature may be left to its enjoyment, but why do you suppose that three are literally dozens of translations of Holy Writ on our bookshelves today? Carry out an experiment such as I am wont to try several times during a unit's teaching assignment for an adult class. Take your J. B. Phillips testament along and turn to the announced reference text for the lesson; then, without further ado, read the pertinent verses with emphasis. Even that chap in the back row, whom you know occasionally takes a snooze on you, will be wide awake when you finish. "What's that you are reading?" "The Bible," you say, and after class he and a number will come up to examine the volume. Only occasionally, however, does one ask you where he can buy a copy, which response, of course, speaks for itself.

Change, or an enlargement of the definition of a word, is in itself not a guaranteed improvement. Care must be exercised and, of course, a certain degree of logic must be evident. One attempting to enhance the basic or traditional use of a term must be sure he is not creating a suspiciously heretical change in a religious theme that has sound roots. An exciting experience was at hand the day I taught my men's class what I thought the Bible was telling us about the salvation offered us sinners through the love of Christ. I resolved to present SALVATION as described biblically, without once using the word "salvation" itself. I avoided any direct quotation of a verse that contained it, and of course this included the verbal form: "to save." My title for the day was "God's Rescue Plan," and I have used this phrase constantly ever since. God's Rescue Plan is an exciting story that is like a strong nylon fish line running through the Old and New Testaments; from the moment of God's gift of *free will* to His human creatures it runs on into the mystery of God's spiritual heaven and our everlasting life, which we claim at our mortal death.

SECTION 3. ANALOGIES (SPECIALIZED VOCABULARY)

When poets and other spiritually sensitive writers are faced with describing an experience taking place at a point where the secular senses of seeing, hearing, feeling, tasting, and smelling cannot be relied upon to furnish their usual data, such description may be put in the form of some sort of an analogous comparison. Rather than be called to account for mislabeling it an allegory, or simile, or a metaphor, we can employ symbolic language—this or that is "like unto," but not "identical to."[9] An analogy must employ symbolic expressions that leave a margin for interpretation by the listening or reading party. Now the cynic may say, "When the writer chap doesn't know what he is talking about, he falls back on an analogy to make it sound as if he did." Faith says God beams his human creatures with messages in the form of analogies. Seeing the everyday things we are familiar with, how could He talk to us via old Hebrew, but in such fashion? We do not know much about the spiritual kingdom, but God, our Creator, surely knows all about us and our difficulty of understanding. He forgives our inability to agree unanimously on what His analogies really mean. It is possible that He may enjoy our disagreements on the analogy, for they are the basis of our eventual communal growth, arrived at democratically.

A very basic analogy employed by the old Hebrews, and their poets who wrote the Old Testament, is the description of the Ark of the Covenant, God's dwelling place. Read Exodus 25:10–22 carefully and you perceive that the Ark becomes, at first glance an empty cube—exceptionally beautiful to be sure—fitted with handles so it could be carried at the head of the line of march. "God is a Spirit and those who worship Him must worship Him in Spirit and in Truth."[10] God as a Spirit was not perceivable by ordinary human senses, so the Ark became a fitting abode for Him. It became a strong, very explicit backup of the God Moses was teaching them about.[11] Moses had said, "Look, men, you cannot go out and cut down a tree and fashion God out of it. You cannot stop at the next water hole and surreptitiously scoop up some clay and fashion Him with you hands. God is Spirit." How beautifully the Ark in its inside physical bareness and cleanness symbolized the nature of their spiritual God. The Ark, except for a short period of desecration at the hands of the Philistines, came back to the Holy of Holies in the Temple. The Holy of Holies, in succeeding restored temples, continued to proclaim God as a Spirit. The rending of the Veil released that Spirit to the whole world at the time of the crucifixion. Thus, analogies are stepping stones that symbolically lead us toward the "front door of heaven." Faith makes the leap to the threshold. Of course most analogies have their limitations. They are not completely descriptive of the given situation. The Ark was a magnificent symbol for that time. Its shortcoming was that it confined God to one place and to one chosen people. At that moment of writing the "chosen people" had no conception of their God as our God of the total universe.

Magnetic field of force, a basis for a Spiritual Field of Force: From our early childhood, and certainly no later than early scouting days, we have been aware that our planet Earth has a property that operates twenty-four hours a day but which most of the human family never give a thought to. Not so of course for the car buff on an official car rally as he darts about the countryside, or the fully outfitted wilderness trail hiker, a man in a boat safari, or a navigator of the seas. The compasses they carry let them in on the secret. Earth is immersed in a magnetic field and the terms North and South poles, though not absolutely identical to the geographic poles, give the general direction and placement to the lines of magnetic force running generally in a north-south direction. Important aspects about this phenomenon are that: (1) a force exists that can move a compass needle (i.e., do work); (2) the true nature of magnetism so far cannot be described by the physicist as a substance, but it is energy, not mass denoting weight; (3) a similar magnetic force is created when a coil of wire is revolved in the close proximity of a second coil that is stationary; (4) the needle of the compass is a magnet and responds to the magnetic field of force.

A problem that troubled my own meditation periods from youth onward was the inability to generate a feeling of the energy nearness of God on an everyday basis. We are reminded that the theologians keep pressing on the fact that God is both transcendent and immanent; He is the creator and sustainer of the Universe reaching outward to infinity, but He is "closer than hands or feet";[12] if so, He must be very finite in close personal quarters, in the home, on the street, in the lab and office, in every work place. I would read of Rufus Jones's[13] experience with his vacation Sunday school class on an island off the coast of Maine. Asking the scholars if they had heard of the Atlantic Ocean and perceiving their ignorance, he always got a big charge out of discovering with them that they were *in* the Atlantic Ocean day and night and had not known it. Of course, when he had made the Atlantic over into God's care and concerned love he made even the grown-up point of God's immanence.

Dwell on the idea of a magnetic field of force. There exists a power[14] we cannot fully describe. Our bodies are immersed and bathed in it but we do not perceive it sensually. Does this not allow us to grasp the idea of the spiritual portion of God's Universe being in us and over

12

us constantly? And wonder of wonders, God has even provided each person with a compass needle, the conscience. The needle is tied into us as through ESP[15] were turning us toward God. Perhaps one senses the spiritual power in our Universe, i.e., God's power, as a kind of magnetism. There is a drawing power. He is actually in our body in a mysterious way and has implanted within us the extrasensory perception towards God's spiritual Power. The Holy Spirit, our Holy Comforter, can be our daily companion and guide. He is the Enabler. He gets things done. As we open our hurts and needs to Him, we perceive that He has already seen our predicament. We immediately feel there is a Power, there is a Force. He moves us. He does spiritual work in us if we yield to Him. His close companionship is our strength even though He may decide to answer our prayer via a route that we may have to patiently wait to open before us. (See chapter 11 on prayer.)

As we ponder over the constant close and intimate relationship with God as the Holy Spirit and Comforter, we may be tempted to lay aside this analogy of the enveloping magnetic field when we wish to go our own evil way. Should the Christian find himself in the midst of evil, overt sinfulness, be it in a drunken stupor at the saloon, explaining a sequence of violence, or selling nonexistent real estate, or rigging a stock market deal, or in the act of marital unfaithfulness, God's presence is still the all-enveloping Presence. The persons in the evil scene have flicked off the compass needles, their consciences, and so they sin in what they suppose to be secret. But God has been there all along and later when the sinner comes to his senses in a prayer begging for forgiveness, he is confessing his shame and is all the more humbled because he realizes that God has observed the act and known his guilt from the start.

This analogy of God's Presence has been very helpful to me personally. If at the end of the day one makes certain that he has turned his compass needle on, i.e., by a confessional prayer and praise for His love, one awakens the next morning in full preparation for the new day. Lo and behold, God has left a nugget for him during the night. Yesterday's problem is largely overcome or a new idea has been laid at his doorstep. (At another point in this book I have said that most of it was written before breakfast—the morning after.)

Electric power versus the mystery of spiritual power: This discussion is introduced with a word of caution. Since Electric Power is immediately recognized as the symbol of the heavy industrialized productive activity behind our acquisitive, economic system, there may be an immediate repulsion of any use of it as a possible avenue toward the appreciation of spiritual nature. To affirmatively perceive the suggested analogy of this electric power, let us think of the analogy of the first step only, namely the *power source*, as the limit of our consideration. In other words, consider that a source does not necessarily negate itself because both good and evil end results may be obtained from it.

I trust it is possible for you, Dear Reader, as you stand or sit before any gadget or machine powered by electricity, to pause before pushing the button or flicking the switch. If possible, remove any thought of mechanical power and concentrate only on heat and light, for these can be related to God's attributes quite easily. Then begin to meditate on the source of the power you are about to appropriate for yourself. Consider the source of this power God given, as when He formed the Universe. It has hidden within the natural resources He lavishly poured into Man's lap. God can be the source of power, both mechanical and spiritual, with mechanical application left to Man's free will subject to both good and negative results as per human nature.

For even God's good gifts may be dealt with immorally and unethically. A simple example of source is a sparkling spring of water gushing up in a clean and protected environment. That flow of water may be drawn off into a system that dispenses it to the thirsty traveler, or it may be piped to a distillery that brags about the quality of its water source. In the first case the spring is actually a life-and-death essential, while in the second, excluding the possible production of medicinal alcohol, it may become a partner in America's greatest narcotic problem with untold examples of broken lives and homes and wrecked automobiles and dead bodies on the highway. Detailed discussion of other aspects of water power lies ahead on page 177.

Those who may object to my discussion of the analogy are skewed in that negative direction by any number of theologians and preachers of the Gospel who never had any significant amount of physical science in their educational background. They are a bit touchy on the subject of science and technology. They note the exploitation of the end products of scientific research in our economic system and see the seemingly overwhelming tide of nuclear armament, modern weaponry with its built-in pressure toward active war. They see the whole gamut of the secularizing manufacture of *Things* intended as amenities of life. They are inclined to slighting reference to "scientism," which they make out to be an enemy of the spiritual nature of God's creation.

To me, such a view overlooks the original injunction of God directed toward His human creation. He enjoined Man to use His gift of a Mind in taking charge of the physical planet.[16] Man in the twentieth century has succeeded beyond the wildest expectations in His domination of the physical universe. It is true that in this process he has been guilty of moral crimes against his Maker, as a brief listing reveals. He has polluted the air, quarreled over and disregarded a wise control of underground resources. He has diverted a portion of the unlocked power of the atom in what so far appears to be a suicide pact for the end of life upon the planet; and he seems to have forgotten how God defined Love as He surveys that portion of the world not so favored in the original distribution of resources. The hungry and the wretched nations look at the rich, well-fed ones and say, "How come?"

Perhaps the spiritual professionals may come into their own in the advancing century and by the power of God bring the spiritual development of mankind up to a level comparable to the secular. Perhaps they will be able to answer for the seeming failure of the Kingdom of the Spirit to implant in science programs a suitable bridle and control toward more worthy end points. And in the process we must pray that the former mistakes may be recognized as sins to be forgiven only as their causes are recognized, eradicated, and the sores healed.

Dear Reader, we are now back at the point where hopefully we may more specifically consider the analogy of the electric power and spiritual power. We will not penetrate the mystery of His Spiritual Kingdom until we shed our mortal clay and join Him eternally. Perhaps another manner of speaking will help clarify my objective. We claim with fervor that God is Love, and may we not also say simultaneously that God is Power,[17] the majesty of His physical universe reflecting His Power as does the overwhelming nature of the Power of His forgiving grace as He deals with us as both individual and communal souls?

Electric power shares mystery with Spiritual Power. After a century of science our physicists are still unable to define electricity except to state that it is a flow of energy in a conducting medium. As everyone knows, energy cannot be weighed, measured with a ruler, looked at, or handled as a concrete, hard, material object. We know briefly that many metals have an atomic and electron structure facilitating the carrying of the flow of energy. They all somewhat resist carrying the energy and hence become warm. Unexpectedly we now find that certain very un-

15

likely chemical compounds, some special ceramics, will conduct the energy with no warming up, i.e., with no resistance, at a very low temperature. No doubt scientists for years to come will be discussing what really happens within the atomic structure of the molecules when the temperature is manipulated and what was once a nonconductor becomes a conductor.

Electric power and Spiritual Power are both great mysteries. We know them both by what they do. Electric power comes from God via His physical universe. Spiritual Power is the divine basis of God's Spiritual Kingdom. They are both mysteries. And without any sense of blasphemy, when Jesus exhorted us to overcome evil with good He was presaging the period of the sixteenth century when spiritual savants would extend the Power of God, making it a vital force of Reformation within the lives of all common men. So, on a lesser scale, was He presaging the year 1989, when presumably we begin building that fifty-six-mile ringed behemoth, the atom smasher. Professionally there would seem to be little mutual respect between the theologian and the scientist, but there is hope that the former will now make himself a more able representative of God, learning how to make his approach to the scientist. We may yet rejoice at the sight of a mutual love feast, seemingly impossible within human powers. But God may yet bend our wills to His.

At the risk of redundancy I wish to restate the simplicity and mystery of the nature of Power at its origin, i.e., energy in the natural physical universe. This energy exists when one body of water, whether in a lake or stream, is found to be at some height above the level of a second body of water. When water at the upper level is allowed to flow down to the lower level, this mysterious energy can be drained off by appropriate methods. You and I and our families have enjoyed innumerable happy picnic episodes at such sites in nature. How absolutely vacant were our minds of the mystery of the energy (except perhaps in the mind of an early father at one of those picnics who wondered if the force he saw before him or at his feet was great enough to operate a future water-powered mill).

A simple water wheel, activated by the flow of water over it, carries the energy from that flow directly to the physical mechanism of the desired process, usually a grinding surface or sometimes a set of interlocking gears. There appears to be little mystery to energy at that point. However, if the energy is required at some distant site, it is harnessed by allowing the water to flow through a turbine. Thus we witness industrial power being born. The mystery is now before us. The turbine is essentially one coil of wire whirling inside a stationary coil. What is this flow of energy in the conducting wires leading from the stationary coil? Perhaps it is sufficient to state that the electron structure of the conductor is activated in such a manner that the energy fed into one end of the wire almost instantaneously appears at the other end, which, in the case of a motor, is similar to the point of origin, merely coiling in reverse. Fed into one stationary coil, the adjacent moving coil is the mechanically energizing wheel of the motor in question.

Science analogy for updating the Apostles' Creed: A basic analogy remaining to be discussed at this point relates to the monotheism of our Christian concept of the Trinity. (See page 177.) Our Hebrew brothers have a legitimate source of suspicion when they hear us speaking of three persons in the Godhead as one. They are confounded when they hear the terms of "son," "father," and "begotten" used freely in a quite mortal, sexual, family manner. When we add to this the third person, or the Holy Spirit and Comforter, and still claim unity in the Trinity, they question our allegiance to the one great God of Abraham. Though we believe, with Paul,[18] that our Jewish friends will, in a future day, be attracted to Christ's Church, a more urgent challenge faces us now in the Space Age. If we religious people, as Christians, wish to reach the secular scientist and his resultant agnostic, secular culture that is enveloping us, *we must enter his mind through language that is more attuned to his.*

Theologians, so far, do not appear willing to help much. Barth, in explaining the Trinity, speaks of three "modes," as translated from his German. This term, to me, carries a flavor of capriciousness or arbitrariness, possibly even the assumption of a role, as by an actor. Furthermore, Barth infers that in addressing God it must be to Him in terms of *one* of the three persons exclusively in a particular period of prayer. If the translator had chosen to use the word "manifestation" instead of "mode," I believe English-speaking persons could better grasp his idea.

For a more helpful approach to the unity of the Trinity, let us start with the mentality of a high-school graduate who has had a year of chemistry and a year of physics. In the Space Age, a high-school graduate without this elemental science will be considered a cultural illiterate. This goes too for the B.A. who has yielded himself to God's call and plans to enter a seminary in preparation for the pastoral ministry. The seminary should insist that he or she earn academic credit in elemental science. If lacking that training, the candidate should be sent to a summer school prior to seminary enrollment. Remember that the pastoral candidate is preparing to carry God's message to a secular population growing more agnostic generation by generation. The candidate should be able to appreciate the "three states of matter," which the chemist/physicist uses as a basic term.

God gave us 100 basic elements when He built our universe. While a few remain as free elements, most of them are combined into specific chemical compounds. These compounds are made up of precise proportions of their elemental constituents and they exist normally in one of the three states of matter, i.e., as a solid, a liquid, or a gas. Some exist in all three simultaneously. Let us choose a simple example; it contains two kinds of the elemental building blocks; it is made up of sixteen parts of oxygen by weight combined with two parts of hydrogen by weight. Its scientific names is hydrogen oxide, but because it is so essential to *all* biological life we give it the common household name "water." This compound is inside our bodies, in the bloodstream, within the plasma and inside every single cell of our bodies as a liquid. It is present as a vapor (gas) within the air breathed into the lung cavities. It is reflected by the humidity figure given by the meteorologist on the TV evening news. The air taken into the lungs is more or less damp, depending on external environmental weather, i.e., humidity. Can you possibly think of a more apt analogy for the immanence of God in our everyday experience?

What an advantage such a new age high school teenager has as he reads Scripture or hears his pastor expounding on the multiple facts of God's spiritual nature. That spiritual substance has power to create, i.e., expend itself in new forms. Some of it can dwell in a human like it did in Jesus, some of it stays near me or within me during the entire day while I am in class or practicing with the team in the afternoon or having an evening of fun. What was that in last Sunday's sermon about God being nearer than breathing and closer than my hands and feet* and *always* being the same God? Hey, I get it. Last fall one of our early chemistry lessons showed us how water, a chemical compound, can exist in three different states, yet it was always of the same composition, sixteen parts oxygen and two parts hydrogen, no matter what. Why can't God be like hydrogen oxide, i.e., be the spirit in three forms just as

*See note 12 at end of this chapter.

water exists in its three physical states? The student glances sidewise at his parents. Dad does not seem too interested. Mom is politely attentive. Say, I'll bet if the preacher were to talk a little more like Mr. X—— in chemistry class, I know Dad would spruce up and pay attention. And when we got home to dinner, Dad and I would have something special to talk about.

The reader is referred to page 177 which deals with the upgrading of the Apostles' Creed, a creed written several hundred years after Christ, based on a primitive three-layered world with a side chair for Christ near a heavenly throne. Now that the young teenager has learned about the three states of hydrogen oxide, he is all set to appreciate the revision of that statement the Space Age demands.

SECTION 4. ATTEMPTS AT DEFINING A MODERN PILGRIM

Every Christian is a pilgrim through life if in a dedicated laic sense he does his best to intensify the loyalty that he continually professes to God in Christ. A pilgrim is empowered to do so, not on the basis of his own strength, but through the leading of God as His Holy Comforter and Enabler, the immanent Spirit of God. This Spirit is the daily catalyst, opening new doors and revealing a fresh vision for the pilgrim, the successive challenging areas for his investigation. Such a pilgrim, busy in Christ's Church, will feel reassuring impulses from time to time to try it in some new fashion. He presses on to the top of the next hill for a better view, a new perspective. And if the pilgrim, as in my case, has some background of science and technology, the chance to engage in experimentation becomes a working model. I offer apologies to John Bunyan, whose pilgrim of long ago was led by God toward a higher level of living. But I am only a single pilgrim among many Christian pilgrims of the late twentieth century with some doubt and questioning in our stance. Changing metaphors, are we really carrying the torch of Christ into the new century or are we, as I suspect when at low ebb, merely flickering candles?

The dictionary definition of the word "sortie" reflects a type of military venture in which either a detail is sent out on a special mission or a U-2 plane is dispatched for surveillance. Though not militarily inclined, I find myself in good company. Paul, living in another age, never hesitated as a Christian soldier to put on the proper armor against sin. The enemy is all about me in strength. He is power over another individual, selfish pride and arrogance, acquisitiveness, lust and greed. If you would like a complete list, turn to William Barclay Daily Bible Study, the Book to the Romans, chapter 1, and see the contemporary list of our sins in modern English, as compared to Paul's Greek in his first chapter of Romans. Paul's list of sins of the greatest political power on earth on the eve of its demise seems rather appropriate as we contemplate the world situation today. The pilgrim must be vigilant in the face of the sins within his own heart as well as those without.

I have selected six experiences that I consider sorties into unknown terrain, during which one is likely to encounter inimical situations. They are listed as follows:

Sortie I   The 1970 Presbyterian Celebration of Evangelism in Cincinnati, Ohio.
Sortie II   Christian sharing groups, the real Christian experience.
Sortie III   Learning to sing the Twenty-third Psalm.
Sortie IV   Revising the Apostles' Creed for the Space Age.
Sortie V   God's evolution process.
Sortie VI   Prayer, without which there would be no personal god or personal spiritual life.

A sorry commentary on the above is that for the adventures in numbers one through four, I had to wait for retirement from industrial life. The reason, surprisingly, perhaps, to those who may simply think I was slothful in early Christian life, was the possible misapplication of total time devoted to church activity. In Christian workshops we learn that the fault with many of us is that we become so busy with the details of daily and weekly church programs that literally little time is available for personal study and development. Looking back, I can see that this fits my case. Beginning at age seventeen I had a weekly responsibility in young people's fellowships both local and countywide, and while yet a graduate student still busy with my doctoral work I was pressured into the general superintendency of a church-school with an enrollment of 800, fully departmentalized, but without teacher training discipline. This introduction into the field of Christian education, beginning with my attention focused on Paul Vieth,[19] lasted until our second daughter finished M.Y.F. in 1956 and left for college. Thereafter, continuous service in both local and ecumenical Christian education projects, together with several changes in my vocational environment, as well as the death of our older daughter at the birth of our granddaughter, were exercises in living in which I was totally engrossed. Yes, I may hopefully testify to some spiritual growth during this maturing period, but only God knows to what actual degree. Retirement afforded the first opportunity to really calm down and listen to what God was trying to tell me about what He was waiting for me to do during the remainder of mortal life. As you will perceive, this paragraph becomes the suitable introduction to our next chapter, "The Growth Curve."

Chapter II

The Growth Curve

A UNIVERSAL STATISTICAL TOOL

Growth means life. When a plant or an animal grows we say a vital force is present. When a surgeon cuts away a foul point in our bodies, cleans up the localized mess, and sews us up again, this vital force knits in enough new tissue to make us well again. My physician friend puts it this way: "We clean up the damage, and then we wait for God to mend it." But more than botanical and zoological tissue grows. Our brain is the site of the mind. We believers feel that in a mysterious way God is the generator of the thinking process. He consummated His two-billion year (current theory) life-creating process by making man a three-dimensional creature of body, mind, and spirit. All three aspects of us grow. When we are young we have childish ideas and we express them with a limited vocabulary. As we mature into adulthood, we put this childishness aside. Our minds, energized by the Spirit, then function at higher and higher levels and an image (idea), once as dull as the facial expression of one of Caesar's soldiers reflected on his polished brass plate, springs forth with new clarity and meaning as the God-given gift it is.

The religious person rather easily accepts the idea that the vital force is an attribute of God, or is God. I gather that when Father Teilhard de Chardin spoke of such a relationship it was quite appropriate for him to look at the reproduction of new cells in both plant and animal life as the expression of the power of God in all life. Hence the feeling on the part of some that perhaps he was a pantheist instead of a spiritual monotheist. Tell me why our Almighty God cannot hold His man/creature/servant to be a pantheist, also, as long as he views all God's *nature*

22

as a part of God Himself? (See chapter 9.)

As this pilgrim describes his experiences in his sorties into life about him, he is aware that the adoption of new vocabulary (chapter 1), cannot be merely a mechanical exchange of new words for old. A good example is the learning of the vocabulary in the process of developing effective use of a foreign language. Our memorization of the sight and sound of the new word is not sufficient, and the definition of the English word may have to be changed along with the word in the foreign tongue. Even identical words do not retain identical meanings. On the Isle of Jersey in the English Channel, the average person will think of "cow" as specifically a Jersey cow, because that is all he knows about. He does not think about any of the dozen or more breeds or types of cows. The word "wife" has a meaning quite different from ours in a polygamous culture, where there may have to be an added syllable to denote whether one is referring to number one wife or so on down the line in favor.

Paul Tournier relates that English translators of his French language books had difficulty translating his references in his use of the word for "spirit." Apparently, in French, the word for "spirit" is more synonymous with "mind," and he confesses to his difficulty in explaining his ideas comprehensibly for English-speaking readers. Consequently, we hear that one does not really master a foreign language until he has learned to think in it. We may follow through by saying that one of our goals in the Christian life is to become able to speak and use God's spiritual communication, which we learn to partially decode. (We are prevented from saying we can learn to think in God's language because we humans cannot think as God.) We really cannot use His language of the Spirit except as we pray constantly for His help in making His purpose plain to us. Our understanding is aided by observing the success our neighbor has in his living with God. I strike a chord here that you will meet throughout the book. *We are of communal faith. We must have each other.* That is an essential element in the metamorphosis of a Christian. The change from "I" to "You" is not complete because a change in attitude must accompany the use of the word. We grow in our ability to make this change as we associate with other persons.

We began with the assertion that *growth means life*, but that is not enough. Life also means Purpose. There can be existence without growth and life, but such bloodless existence is miserable. Today we hear less and less of rocking chair retirees. Those physically capable have to turn to something to do. Affluence and idleness are still classed as sin: foundations, special help projects, charitable giveaways in volunteer activity all must be added to provide some flavor in living. Purpose gives organization to life. Some of us may not examine our purposes too clearly as regards the return on the effort, but I believe most of us wish the goal of that purpose to represent a quality of life at a higher level than we are on now. And as we move from a lower to a higher level, it is an interesting observation by the professionals that we do not travel in a straight line from here to there. We move on a Growth Curve. Let us investigate it.

Growth is appropriately expected of a Christian. He has to be careful in defining personal growth, for in getting from here to there, i.e., from a lower to a higher level, some quantum of that quality has been apprehended, but we suspect that some goes into an unknown "bank." The danger is that one's ego gets in the way by distorting or exaggerating that increase in quality. God's Truth coming into focus upon it may find that we are not so improved after all. As a matter of fact, at one point I considered deleting this chapter after having scribbled the first draft, feeling somewhat as Ben Franklin in his attempt at deliberately attempting to cultivate the idea of the Christian grace of Humility. In his essay he reported that he worked out a daily regimen of certain acts of meek servanthood. It was of no avail. He was working deliberately toward his own sense of rapture and reward and he was not thinking of his neighbor except secondarily. He was becoming more unchristian than he had been previously.

I do not know whether Franklin ever arrived at a satisfying experience, but in today's language we can write him a more viable prescription. *Do not aim at a high mark for yourself, aim at giving a higher-level attainment to your neighbor.* To be sure, you may be temporarily messing up a plan that God has already set before your neighbor in his need, but that is to be preferred to being myopic to all else but your own virtue. If there is any virtue for you in a given situation it will probably be recognized as a by-product, the "Peace of God." I believe in my case I, for a long time, was confusing knowledge gained by general reading and study with actual spiritual growth. You will note further on that I describe some of my experiences as the Sorties of a Pilgrim. I was gaining much in the way of knowledge, but was I really strengthening my actual conduct as a Christian? I hope I was—was I loving my wife the way I should be if Jesus were around; was I really succoring my neighbors in distress? I must leave this judgment in God's hands. I finally decided that there were helpful features about upward growth curves for all persons in general that allowed me to include this discussion but on less than the large technical scale I had originally set upon. Suffice it to say by way of introduction that the professional statistician (i.e., mathematician) has found that the growth in weight of your newborn child, the increase in volume of your new business venture, the growth of the new church that started from scratch, the beginning of a new procedure in almost any area where people are involved, can be plotted (i.e., drawn or sketched by diagram). Characteristic of that picture, special important points can be observed, which practically demand helpful outside influences be brought to bear if the upward climb is to be realized.

First let us draw a picture of how an alternating electric current looks as it pulsates its way into the transformer that probably hangs on a pole in your backyard.

The statistician calls the curvature between point A and point B the Growth Curve. Now let us lift this theoretically perfect curve out of the electric current setting and place it nearby, where two lines meet at right angles. These two lines are called coordinates. The flat horizontal one is the x coordinate, and the y coordinate is the upright perpendicular line. When two related properties of a procedure are plotted in the area to the right, we produce a graph. Choosing the two related properties is quite simple. Since we are studying Growth, we naturally realize it takes place over some period of time. We could take readings of Growth every day or week or month or year or decade. Months or years would seem most appropriate for our lives; we label the base x coordinate in these units of TIME. There is almost a limitless idea of the unit of measurement to be laid out on the perpendicular y coordinate, depending upon the subject being analyzed. Of course it must represent some factor we accept and recognize as growth.

In a business, dollars are a very common unit, and it may be used to represent any number of the descriptive activities of the business; for example, gross sales, net sales, inventory, profit, et cetera. For the newborn baby the unit of growth might well be ounces and pounds of weight as each time unit of a day passes. An organized group such as a church tends to measure its growth by observing how the members grow in number.

The church may at times be justified in the use of arithmetical

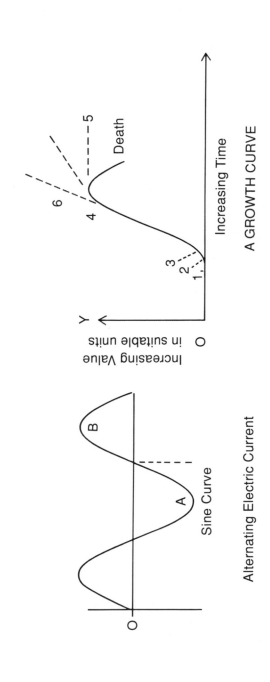

Sine Curve

Alternating Electric Current

A GROWTH CURVE

Increasing Time

Increasing Value
in suitable units

Death

numbers, but humanly we tend to cover up many failures of performance when we expect the observer to assume that those single memberships are all of equal merit. We intuitively realize that if we are to discuss growth individually in terms of spirituality, we have no quantitative data that is acceptable to all. We know the church is interested in the Quality of the spiritual life of each individual, so we will have to adopt some arbitrary unit. Jesus Christ is, after all, the perfect template for measuring the quality of our membership. But it would be absurd to strive for a percentage of His perfection, which is God's perfection. The best we can do is to adopt a way out by falling back on the term Quality of Life, i.e., value. We will have to make do with a unit of growth that no two persons will agree upon exactly. The Quality of Life will be interpreted as growing when there is less and less evidence of overt sins and more and more evidence of service and selfless love for our neighbors. Private sin and selfish secret greed will be assumed to be simultaneously lessening, but how much is impossible to tell. I believe we can all agree that as a *qualitative* term we are at liberty to use INCREASING QUALITY OF LIFE as a goal toward which all church planning and individual development is oriented. It will always be both objective and subjective in nature; the latter being left in God's hands. Let us now label the perpendicular y axis with this term and place the portion of the curve from A to B inside the upper triangular space in such a fashion that the beginning of the graph begins with point A on zero.

Our picture now looks like the following: Instead of leaving TIME on the x coordinate as a general term, we can define it as the average mortal life span and mark it off in decades. You will also note that six locations on the curve have been pinpointed for discussion. The universality of the curve is now in evidence because much of the same monitoring will apply no matter what the specific process. Keep in mind that the curve says that at point 5, death is likely to ensue. Being able to set the goal at point 6, instead of allowing 5 to develop into disaster in the case of the church, means steering straight to God. In the case of Mom and Pop, below, it means an agreeable business success.

Let us start with Mom and Pop on a little practice run. We have changed the units on the Time line to months and have replaced the Quality of Living with actual figures of dollar signs. Mom and Pop own a small building in a small city. They sell their home to generate capital and create living quarters in the rear of what they plan to be a small grocery.

Point 1 for them is the usual slow point as things are getting organized and the customers are becoming aware of the store's presence. Perhaps several weeks or more are required to pull through the initial flat stage. Then the business begins to take off at 2 and it lifts off the launch pad in great shape. In the period between 2 and 3 there is a large yield of insulin absorbed in the development of the business. Enthusiasm runs high. The test, however, arrives at point 3, at which place the longer-range question of repeat business must be answered. Newcomers and onlookers make a business only as they are enticed into becoming repeat and regular customers. After the period of original push, the danger point, 4, is arrived at, perhaps sooner than expected.

If no *extra effort* is now planned there is a usual slackening off of trade. I, personally, do not deliver this opinion. It is the behavior of practically all businesses as analyzed by hundreds of statistical experts. In this particular store it may mean that a refrigerated case must be added to take care of a small basic line of meat. The product line *must be increased* as surely as the sun rises tomorrow. In other words, what we are saying here is that *new growth factors must be added at point 4* or the normal downward cycle of the curve takes place and at point 5 the business is headed for oblivion. To maintain the upward thrust of the operation and to arrive at point 6, a number of successive efforts must be invested. We list just a few to clarify things.

Soon after the basic fresh meat products have been added, there will no doubt be under consideration addition of a fresh vegetable line, not necessarily spectacular in nature but nevertheless making it possible for Mr. and Mrs. Customer to avoid a trip to the competitive super-market every time they want a head of lettuce. Perhaps the original grocery line did not carry many household cleaning and scouring aids, or paper products used in the home and at the picnics. Pretty soon the operations cannot all be contained in that lower floor. They vacate the living quarters and can reorganize the whole operation; perhaps they add a little snack bar for the kids, operating it after school, et cetera.

The and-so-forths are absolutely a necessity if the business is to grow and remain profitable. It may be true in the case of a Mom and Pop store that an end point in volume of business must be anticipated. But innovation as to the content of the product line and the manner of doing business must be *continually* upgraded in order to keep it there or soon the customers begin to fall off, the operation begins to fade, and Mom and Pop decide they will sell out and let someone else do the worrying.

APPLYING THE CURVE TO TWO YOUNG CHRISTIANS

We now approach a much more difficult task. How do we record the history of growth that pertains to Christian life? We have already discussed the impossibility of choosing a concrete unit for the measurement of quality. Nevertheless we do recognize life on a low level and on higher levels. We will recognize the differences of life for the two examples below. The base line, of course, will remain *time*, and we expect that this will be a lifetime for two young teenagers who live on our street.

The Sunday school has brought these two to a very important time of their developing Christian lives. They are members of Christian families in good standing in the church membership. Thus they have a fair notion of what a Christian is and does by the spirit and actions of the older members of their families and their church. They have their Bibles, received via the church's Christian educational program. Their confirmation class is enrolled by the pastor for special instruction in the duties and responsibilities of church membership. They are average good kids, from average good families in an average church. (Note that I omitted the plus adjective—the word "good"—in the term "average church." God will have to suggest the proper adjective for our particular church.) After the pastor has devoted the given number of weeks of special instruction, the confirmation worship service is held and the young teenagers stand before the congregation to make their vows. In some instances such candidates may have come from a breakfast session with their deacons, or elders, but in the open part of the breakfast period they did not respond when the pastor asked if any would like to give a personal testimony. So now as they stand in the sanctuary they are a bit uncertain as to what is expected of them. The pastor has allayed any fears, however, for in prior sessions of the class he has gone over the vows they are to answer to. They will not even have to read a statement of their own vocalization. The affirmative response of one young man and one young woman will be indistinguishable in the group huddled together as all murmur "I do." Afterward they will receive good wishes from many oldsters and special hugs and kisses from Mom and Dad and perhaps a special Sunday dinner in their honor. In many public school schedules they will be back in regular regimen on Monday, by the latest, Tuesday morning. Life will continue in the usual pattern of the family and nothing extremely exciting will occur until school is out later in the spring.

Humanly, judging from what we have heard and seen them doing up to this point, we suspect that they have not been charged with an overwhelming desire *to do* things differently that could be interpreted as lifting them off the slow point (1) on the growth curve. Later, in chapter 5, you may discover why this could be. They could be the product of Encapsulating Families, i.e., "good families" that after a couple of generations have smoothed out their pattern of life into pale, smooth, middle-of-the-road passivity. There are no signs of an *Incendiary Fellowship*[1] because the pastor and the local "saints" have not created an impression that there ought to be such a fire-making goal.

Before school is out that year the church has announced some summer activities: vacation Bible school in a neighboring church, weekly schedules of camp activities supported by the denomination, and a special two-week camp for high school boys. Mary, our young lady, is solicited by a teacher in the vacation Bible school to help as a special teacher's aid; and our young man gets to go as a freshy to the boys camp. Next year, at school, Mary joins the Junior Red Cross group and experiences her first personal lessons about those in need. Her growth curve is definitely rising. In his junior year Tom has a chance to go on his church's summer support work group somewhere in the Appalachian area and gets a thrill out of the older group camaraderie and the evening meetings. His curve rises also. We might say that both are at point 2 on their curves. There may be a slight flattening of their spiritual growth curve the next year when they go away some distance for freshman year at two different colleges. They adopt a new, freer lifestyle and make new friends and contacts. They are interested enough in the campus religious groups to join. They are back to more or less regular church attendance with these new friends. In her locale, Mary is accepted readily and is chosen on a committee now and then for various student retreats and conferences, and at the church she attends she is looked upon as one of the supporters of the Christian Life on campus. At his school, Tom does not show initiative in leadership in any of the religious activities but is content to be an occasional attendant. The two curves definitely begin to diverge at point 3.

At point 3, Mary is actively on her growth curve, while Tom is going out on a plateau, just holding his own. His point 4 was premature. Two years out of college with a job and a new wife, he maintains a spiritual plateau only stimulated upon the birth of their first child.

Mary, in her senior year, attended a national campus youth assembly as the representative of her class. She is not a "career girl" and after graduation and a three-year stint as a bank teller finds the right young man with whom to begin her family. Mary is definitely active in several places in her new church and becomes the youngest woman elder in the church. She teaches in the Sunday school and no doubt will take a turn at running the Women of the Church before too many years. Mary is definitely at point 4 on her growth curve, and headed for point 6. She will still have to face a phase in her church attendance when, in the midst of her business with many things, she will not take time to read the spiritual literature and begin specific meditation periods within her own person. She will be so busy with the Lord's work that her own personal development may temporarily run out on a plateau. She will know the Bible as a teaching text without thoroughly demanding of herself that she follow its precepts in earnest belief and practice. She may recover this in later life and shoot for the stars.

Why have we spent this much effort to bring the Spiritual Growth Curve to your attention; and why were Tom and Mary presented as actors? Their story has brought us to the basic problem in developing Christian life, no matter where in this wide world of God's we find ourselves. Intuitively we recognize that mere statistical memberships in churches and religious groups galore, of one kind and another, all with the intent to be good moral and ethical people, are not really a wholly satisfactory basis for determining the spiritual quality of life. God has commanded us through Christ's teachings not to judge one another. However, if the quality of life can only be estimated by memberships, we are back at the difficulty of equating quality with numbers. These outward activity signs are a slight indication of growth but are not substantive. God's record of our growth may not look at all like ours. We cannot draw our own curve of humbleness before God. Only God searches our individual being and knows the truth. He is aware of the facade we wear, the false mask, which covers, not the overt sins other people can see, but the greedy selfishness and overt pride of our private selves. Thus God sees us on two curves, one of accomplishment of education, position, and powerful places in business and industry, or whatever is public; while the other is the path with Jesus as the true template toward the growth of the heart and love of neighbor. When you and I resolve on starting a new life-style closer to God, which involves building affirmative values into our behavior, we join in producing a spurt upward in our flattish Growth Curve.

In the case of the wheat plant, the organism comes to full fruitage and then *it dies*. However, life is nurtured through the new grains of wheat, which under suitable interim conditions again germinate and emerge in new plants which start the cycle over again. It is a cycle of renewal via death.[2] You and I have a God-given property He did not bestow on that wheat plant. He gave us free wills and we do not need to die of the Spirit prematurely, unless we *will to*. GROWTH itself must now be defined in terms of PURPOSE. Education, training, reading, discussion, and meditation now take on some of the aspects of fulfillment of divine purpose. Not only do we perceive that educations are gained conventionally in preparation for a specific vocation, but God is giving them as a gift, a device by which we are enabled to share in the course of His larger plan. Of course I have now painted myself into a corner. So how do I know if I am on a *True* growth curve? With an attempt at honesty, I may not be on much of a curve after all, but I do see a bit brighter sunrise in each of the retirement years. Perhaps I am justifying my longer-than-common life in order to give me sufficient time to write these words to you. I feel that God is encouraging me, in the midst of my daily sinning, to keep on plugging in His behalf. As with the wheat plant, I too die to sin, as Paul declares, but can rise to a new day because I will it in response to a merciful and forgiving God.

We have referred elsewhere to the fact that church membership statistics show that Christians are a minority in America today. We shudder at the probability that within the membership itself, really active support members may likewise be a minority. Tom, our attempt at a live example, represents that great number of Christians who spiritually do not grow meaningfully beyond the level of their youthful experience. As a matter of fact, I have taught adult classes in which the apparent spiritual level of the members appeared to be that prevailing when they had joined the church as teenagers. Tom represents the great number of our members who are content to let the church baptize us, marry us, and bury us, supporting it with very modest financing and with intermittent attendance at its worship services. Very definitely this portion of the membership does not yield much, if any, priority to the church's calendar of events when it conflicts with family self-interest. Did you ever try to set up a summertime training conference at your well-known church center only to soon discover that the church has no priority above their own ideas of a plan for leisure vacation time?

Have you been aware, Dear Reader, that if the minority situations mentioned above were optimistically left near or at the 50 percent level, i.e., that half of adult Americans are outside the church and that within the church only half of those on the church roll are actually spiritually supportive, then the true minority cannot be higher than one-fourth? (One-half of one-half is one-fourth.) Thus, even at optimum conditions, only a fourth of our population constitutes the major roadblock before the Russian Communist party and today's secular world culture. Note well that use of the term "Russian" does not imply that that people is an enemy. It is the pagan totalitarian bureaucracy therein that we must combat. In reality the struggle is between two minorities. We wonder in private whether the three-quarters of our nation that wears a borrowed Christian ethic or none at all will act to make a righteous peace for us all. We need God's help. We must believe that He is the only source of righteous power to do the job. He has given America a remnant of remnants by which to leaven the total world now so clearly characterized by agnostic violence and disunity. Can God depend on American Christians to deliver the goods? Or must we wait in agony for His plan to include the true awakening, the real leaven to be developed by His national churches in the Third World? To drive home the importance of getting us all back on God's Growth Curve, the one He intended for us, the words of Elton Trueblood in his *Incendiary Fellowship* rise up to haunt us. "Committed Christians do not represent the mainstream of Western culture." What Trueblood refers to is a "mild middle of the road Christian syndrome," which gives way before "an articulate and arrogant paganism." A few years ago, some of us were rather shocked when a promotional splurge appeared for the book, *Europe in the Post Christian Era*. We assuaged our feelings with the thought, *What else does one expect from a group of state-supported churches?* Is America sending a similar devastating signal? Is our nation under God choosing point 5 on our spiritual Growth Curve or are we in secret building the launch pads that can shoot us straight to Him via point 6?

God's MIRACLE of the 1980s

It was the appearance on the world scene of Mr. Mikhail Gorbachev as one of His angels. On the evening of August 30, 1989, the McNeil-Lehrer TV broadcast really confirmed it. "Godless" Russia and the world got a jolt it never expected would or could happen. Communism fell apart at the seams, leaving Castro at this date as the only disciple still in need of a new pair of glasses. A great unforeseen cooperative effort on the part of the Russian bureauracracy made this TV Program authentically possible. The depiction of southern, rural Russia at the time of Mr. Gorbachev's boyhood was most enlightening. It indicated that his mother had remained a baptized member of God's church and further revealed that he had never embraced the brutal totalitarianism of Stalin, even as a young Communist trainee rising in the ranks of the party. Neighbors, elementary teachers, and professors of law at the University of Moscow thought him to be a specially gifted, hardworking young man, well liked by everyone. Though care had been taken to avoid all direct reference to the church and religion, one got the impression that the grandchildren would probably be challenged by God's outreach. This film is blessed of God, I am sure. The media, both ours and theirs is to be congratulated for this cooperative venture. God's miracle, Mr. Gorbachev, has already changed the face of the world. Today, Russia and the U.S., and the nations of the world are united in a campaign to cancel the brutal efforts of the Iraqi madman.

MY GROWTH CURVE—IF ANY

I am willing to risk being misunderstood by attaching here a biographical note reflecting some of the points made above in the discussion of the Growth Curve. This sketch reveals the continuity of experience that produced this book. It will be noted at once that my questionable period of mid-life, which I criticized in my description of my fellow church members generally, is here exposed. How much we miss by being absorbed in the busyness of the church and damping down our own personal growth is for God to say. Possibly there is background growth and interaction of which we humanly are not aware, but I cannot claim it. (Such is the period between age forty-seven and retirement at sixty-five, the point at which I became a Pilgrim.) The dotted line is a superimposed theoretical Growth Curve. The area between it and my own slow development curve to the right carries the concerned implication that I have accomplished but a fraction of the mission God must have had in mind for me. I have been a "slow bloomer."

a. Baptism at 17, followed by high school, college, graduate school
b. Marriage and abrupt assumption of superintendency of large metropolitan church-school
c. Teacher, later dean of ecumenical Albany (N.Y. School of Religion followed by a decade as superintendent, junior department of 100 fifth and sixth graders, introduced by our two daughters
d. Midlife plateau: Sunday assignments giving way to committee assignments in Christian education, self-satisfaction beginning to slow me down

Retirement was followed by challenges to renewal via the six sorties:

1. Sortie to Cincinnati, Ohio, Celebration of Evangelism, 1970
2. Sortie into Church Sharing Group experience
3. Sortie—Learning to sing the Twenty-third Psalm
4. Sortie into Revision of the Apostles' Creed for the Space Age
5. Sortie—Evolution, God's Method of Creation
6. Sortie—Learning to Pray, neophyte still continuing

This pilgrim is now prepared to begin his journey. He invites you to be his close companion as he explores the basis of his faith. Those early monthly letters to the grandsons are now unfolding before us in the next chapter.

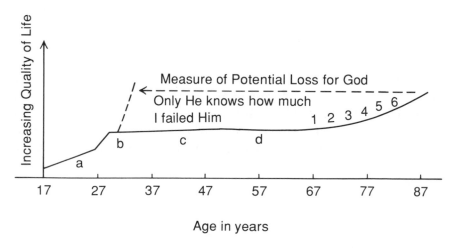

Chapter III

Ten Letters to My Grandsons

When the number one grandson began his confirmation class work in the pastor's hands in the fall of the year he entered junior high school, one of God's seeds germinated and took root in my mind. Intergenerational fellowship was a theme here and there emphasized in Christian education literature. The loss of patriarchal influence in steadily deteriorating American culture was being called to attention. Well, just somehow, this grandfather might be able to write out and develop a line of advice, based on his experience, that would help a couple of grandsons wake up to their spiritual challenge. Only God knows the answer to this grandfather's effort. I did not allow myself to become too downhearted when I did not receive a direct comment from number one, but via his parents, I got his message: "Grandpa is too preachy." It met with heartier acclaim from his parents who joined Grandma in seconding the motion to enlarge the subject matter of the ten letters into a full-fledged book.

Our one and only granddaughter was not intentionally slighted. In the course of our human timetable she was ahead of our grandsons in her part of the family by a decade. She was already melded into her church membership and was well on the way to a fuller life when the boy cousins came along. Nevertheless, as the book was conceived and developed, her youthful entry into early mid-life at age thirty-one helped me to expand the concept of the full row of church pew members before me. She is the Renée on my dedication page.

The initial group of eight letters followed the months from fall to Easter and has been called part one. Part two became a necessary postlude in my mind as we approached confirmation together. These last two letters speak for themselves and, as you will see later, were the originating leaven which led to chapter 9—on God's creation as God's plan of evolution.

SKELETON OUTLINE OF THE LETTERS

Part I—Getting Started

Part II—A Demand of the Space Age

THE LETTERS

Letter I

Dear Craig and Brian:

This is the first day of our new adventure together. It is a breaking point of new ground; and such beginnings have a purpose. To develop our purpose in this adventure, imagine a track meet in which an important event is the relay race. Relay races are team efforts and the baton must be passed to each succeeding runner. The exchange must ideally take place smoothly and without loss of stride. Your grandfather has already been on the track for quite a spell. He is running hard and is closing in on the end of his lap. He hopes that God will give him enough time to prepare some messages about his experiences, and pass them on to you just as the baton is passed between members of the relay team. *You* can expect to be a grandfather someday and have some thoughts to pass on to *your* grandson.

These messages will not be of equal merit in your eyes. Some of them as first reading may even appear to have no meaning at all. Perhaps at a later time and in a different mood, after an additional experience of your own, you will read it again and understand what Grandfather is trying to get at. We call this growing into maturity. (Hopefully your grandfather is also still growing.)

One of God's creative acts was His gift of MEMORY to His human creatures. No person remembers the details of his own birth and the first several years of his infancy. He relies on the stories from his family. So, let me, your grandfather, absolutely reassure you both that we, your parents and grandparents, looked upon you as gifts from God; gifts we have loved and cherished ever since the day you came to us. Please *remember* that in periods of correction and discipline we still love you. And it is in the warmth of that continuing love that these letters will be shared with you.

So until next month, with love,

Your Grandpa

Letter II

Dear Craig and Brian,

Today we take a first step together. What a challenge lies in the word FIRST. Do you know what the most important FIRST in all the world is? Here it is. It is the phrase:

"IN THE BEGINNING, GOD . . . "

You may ask, "Grandpa, how do you know that God was the beginning?" I cannot answer that question without introducing another word, FAITH. And that raises another question which deals with the meaning of words we use when we talk or write about IDEAS to another person. We are never quite sure that the other person thinks the word holds exactly the same thought that we have in our own mind when we use it. And even we ourselves often do not have the same meaning in mind every time we use a word!!! (Example: grip—a handhold; grip—a suitcase; grippe—a sickness; grip—a mechanical hold as with a pipe wrench.) With IDEAS it is even more difficult. How good is good and how bad is bad? Do love and hate go together? See what I mean?

Back to our magnificent FIRST, above. "How" and "know" in the question above are words that indicate that a factual explanation follows. They usually imply that we can feel, hold, measure, weigh, see, smell, or hear something that the scientific world calls data. These data when put together in a sequence of causes and effects lead us to a conclusion. We call such a conclusion a fact. On the other hand, philosophers, those who ponder and study IDEAS, also use the words "How" and "Know" for their conclusion making; but they can *never* be one hundred percent sure that the other party completely understands them. (The cause and effect relationship is partially retained within the mind and is not readily demonstrated.) The IDEAS remain partially hidden. It is therefore very difficult to talk about FAITH. I believe a good way to start is to tell a story. It is about a man who became God's hero. His name was Abraham and he was neither a scientist nor a philosopher.

Abraham and his family lived in or near the city of Ur on the Persian Gulf, almost four thousand years ago. Abraham, like all God's human creatures, had been given the ability to go beyond hard facts that the mind usually likes to work with. God gives each person a special receiving set. It is a very individualistic set—as much your very own as your fingerprints are your own. You have your own wave length and must fine tune your own set. Most of the time you may not be catching the message that God is sending but every once in a while it breaks in on you suddenly and then you realize that you 'know' something very special. You feel differently about your parents and your brother and your friends in the church and in the community. As a matter of fact, you now have feelings about who you are yourself as a person; and where you belong in this existence we call 'life.' We then realize that we not only have our usual mental ability but we awaken to the existence of *spiritual* abilities in ourselves. We look around and we begin to compare notes. We don't have exact words or enough words to describe what is going on between God and us. It is best illustrated by Paul, who said that "faith [in God] deals with things we cannot feel with our hands and measure, but it is the substance [stuff] of life itself and assures us of its meaning for the future." Some of Paul's exact words on this subject may be looked up in your Bible as follows: Romans 4:18–25; Hebrews 11:1; Hebrews 11:8–10.

God had been beaming messages to Abraham for quite a while. Finally He began to get through to him. Abraham had broken God's code sufficiently to realize that the worship of the Moon-god and his family of lesser gods was for the birds. The main thing that burned up Abraham was the big annual worship service held up on the flat top of the artificial hill where the big altar was erected. Thousands of people gathered every year to watch the ceremonies performed there.

The priests carried out a bloodcurdling act, when a beautiful teenager, a girl one year, perhaps a fine athletic boy the next, was slain with a knife and offered up on the altar as a gift to the Moon-goddess or the Moon-god. In early life, perhaps before he married Sarah, Abraham had begun to feel uneasy about this, and then suddenly, God got through to him. *He knew this was absolutely wrong.* He did not know just what to do. One problem was that his own father, Terah, remained devoted to this old-time religion, and he loved his father, even though he kept little idols (man-made gods) all over the house. One was a god who supposedly looked after the vegetables that grew in the garden; another was the god who ruled the fire in the kitchen; another blessed the water they drank; and he had an assistant who controlled the rainfall; another god operated the wind system which provided fresh air. Actually, another god saw to it that every female sheep and goat in the family herds had a little lamb or a kid each year without fail. And then ever so often, Terah insisted they attend that awful human sacrifice ceremony up on the big hill. He said he must represent the family and pay homage to the number one god who was the king over the whole family of gods. Anthropologists who study ancient religions are of the opinion that in the beginning, pagan, uncivilized people carried out such sacrifices to bribe the god so he would be good to the people and keep them from starving and getting hurt in the months ahead.

God's message to Abraham did not all come at one time. God knew that Abraham would be unable to understand what He meant for him to do if He laid all the heavy instructions on him in one session. So God gave it to him in easy stages. "Abraham, your father is growing old and is turning more and more of your family's supervision and daily work with the herds over to you. I, your God, have a better place for you and Sarah, which I will tell you about later. For now you make plans to move the entire family away from Ur and graze your animals westward a few hundred miles toward the Big Sea. I will help nudge Terah into consenting to your taking charge." Abraham did as God has instructed him and after a whole year of grazing the flocks forward a few miles each day, he reached a nice spot called Haran. This was so attractive, with plenty of water and grass, that he decided this was the place God promised him to live in forever. But at that point, Abraham didn't know half of it. We will find out next time what God really meant.

With love,
Grandpa

Letter III

Dear Craig and Brian,

So there was Abraham in Haran doing his thing. Terah had died and now Abraham was in complete charge. He thought that he had it made (except for one thing). He hadn't any children of his own as yet. His flocks were getting so large and he was getting so rich that he was even thinking about dividing up the animals and giving some to his nephew Lot. And then the bombshell exploded. God was sending messages again and they were coming in loud and clear. First, God reminded him of what had developed in their good relationship. He told Abraham how much He appreciated Abraham's understanding of Him as the ONE TRUE GOD, the creator of the universe, the Giver of all life's gifts. He knew that Abraham was now more constantly turning to Him for advice as to how to act and how to be a good patriarch of an ever-growing group. Distant relatives of the family who had been attracted by Abraham's reputation came to live with him. They were a little clan or tribe. They saw in Abraham a very honest man who dealt fairly with all persons. This enlarged family had quickly noted that idols and idol worship were now tabu. Abraham had decreed on behalf of Jehovah, the one God, that there was to be no more worship of objects made of wood, or stone, or metal, by human hand. His larger family was to look upon Jehovah as being so just, and so good, and so mighty and powerful that no human would ever be able to describe Him completely with words. (Later, after many hundreds of years his descendants tried to describe Abraham in his new relationship with God, and called him *righteous*.) Of course we humans speak of God as being righteous too, but we must be careful to remember that when applied to God it is a *super* righteousness and even includes things we don't fully understand, like "Why did God make us?"

41

Apparently God said, "Because Abraham has been the first man to break away from idol worship and to try to understand Me and come close to Me, I can depend on him. I will charge him with the full responsibility of working with Me." Abraham was dumbfounded when God called him and broke the news: "You are to 'pull up stakes,' [remember that they all lived in tents then], and move westward, closer to the Big Sea and then southward into a Promised Land which I have selected for you. It will be more wonderful for you than Haran has been. And furthermore, Abraham, you are going to be the founder of a great nation. The leaders of other nations and their peoples will be blessed because of you and your services to Me." Abraham found himself in a tough predicament. How could he become the father of a great nation when Sarah and he did not have a child and they appeared to be past the child bearing stage?[1] He did not hesitate for long. He made the false move of playing around with Sarah's servant girl. He was not a perfect man but retained human faults just as we do today. However, he came to his senses. If God was such a great God he would not expect Abraham to do it on his own. Somehow God would perform a miracle. And He did, and Isaac was born to Sarah. You know the remainder of the story. Abraham's life is therefore a very fine example of what we mean by FAITH. He is remembered to this day for it. He left Haran and struck out into the unknown, depending entirely upon God. By that act of complete and absolute faith, he put his signature to God's contract (covenant) with him.

You are now studying with your pastor in preparation for becoming a member of your church, one of the institutions which God expects to be the cradle of faith. Keep in mind that though it is God's Church (i.e., Christ's), it is also very human and the kind of faith you bring to it as a young man can make it better or make it worse. It will become your community of faith. Initially, your main feeling about it will no doubt center around your hero worship of Jesus. You will think of Him as a brave man who was falsely accused of a crime and was executed in the common and brutal manner of the times. You will think about some important assertions that Jesus made. "I and my Father are ONE" and somewhere along this line of thought it may come to you that Jesus and God are probably just different words for the same Person.[2]

Our discussion of faith should also remind you that you will become a member of the same community of faith in its larger dimension, in which the black boy, Calvin, lives. You remember how much you liked him when you met him at Grandpa's. You had never talked to a black person before in your whole life. Likewise, it will be the same community of faith as that described by the missionary when he visited your church and told you about the Chinese boys and girls halfway around the world. Do you think Abraham has blessed you? Will you be a blessing to someone else?

With love,
Grandpa

Letter IV

Dear Craig and Brian,

Before we leave the story of Abraham's faith we will do well to understand how the idea of God's love came to be associated with it. Bible scholars seem to have an idea that the attribute of LOVE in respect to God's character was not recognized until much later on in the period of the Prophets. But this is not really so. Even before Abraham we know that God is a God of Love. You, of course, in your confirmation class, are focusing on the sure testimony from the life of Jesus who is number one with us Christians when it comes to demonstrating what Love is. But we should not be misled. The ancient Hebrew poets were spiritual storytellers of the first rank and tell us a lot about Love.

They tell us about love in the creation stories found in Genesis, right at the beginning of things. To begin with God had created a wonderful universe. He looked around at it and called it very GOOD. The way the story is told surely implies that God wished for a human family to live in it and enjoy it with Him. So, along with this magnificent gift of a nice place to live, He gave us the equally stupendous gift of LIFE, our origin. Thus we humans were made His children with this wonderful world as our home. That surely was a sign of the great love of God toward us. And do not forget. He did not create us as a group of store mannequins or mechanical robots. No, we were given the Will to choose our manner of conduct, good or bad.

We call this story of creation in the Garden of Eden a 'symbolic' story. Some people have trouble with the word 'symbolic.' Actually, the ancient storytellers had a scoop on the greatest story the world has ever known. By using a descriptive term like 'symbolic' we do not mean that it is a make-believe story or a 'fairy' story entirely imaginary and

43

without fact. They had to invent words or use everyday words as best they could to describe an event about which they actually knew next to nothing in detail, except *one* important fact: *the true Author had to be God*. God had been beaming his spiritual shorthand to them for some time and they were the brightest, sharpest, most sensitive-minded members of that clan that God had chosen for His special task in the world. They did not know it at the time but they were really the first seminarians of God's very first seminary. Ask your pastor for the course bulletin from the seminary he graduated from and you can tell what a seminary is. They study about God there. He is a special God, not like the gods that the pagan civilizations filled heaven with. The latter had a full range of all kinds of characters, some hardly different from humans except that they had powers of invisibility, controlled time, space and travel, and had charge of nature.

Our God is the One all-powerful Person who has his human children at heart. His concern for them is shown in His first lesson about how to live together. It was to love one another always, as a reflection of a Father's love for his children. The storytellers themselves had a hard time explaining what the word love represented, but they pointed out many examples of what they meant. Let us list a few:

Item 1. The loving gift of life meant a loving family with a loving Father-God.
Item 2. God gave everything in His good earth to Adam and his family. They were to manage it and enjoy it to the fullest.
Item 3. The high value God set on human life; of which examples are:
    (a) unlike other civilizations in which disobedience was punished by instant death, God gave Adam and Eve a second chance; and
    (b) in the Cain and Abel story, normally Cain would have been killed immediately for having killed his brother Abel. Instead God saved him for a useful life's work, that of a good blacksmith.

With such an inherited storytelling background, Abraham and his clan in daily lives grasped the idea of the majesty of their God. It strengthened Abraham's idea of monotheism and he came to worship the ONE TRUE GOD who was supreme in righteousness, justice, good will, and LOVE.

Abraham's example of faith and his personal love toward God is one of the most important stories in the Old Testament. I am going to tell it with a different twist from that which you received in your Sunday school class. When his son Isaac was a young boy, possibly not yet twelve, Abraham had a dream one night which he attributed to God. He thought that God was telling him to take little Isaac out into the wilderness and there offer him up to God as a sacrifice. You must remember that he was only one generation beyond his own father Terah's participation in observing the annual worship service of human sacrifice on the hilltop altar back in Ur. Though Abraham had revolted against that, a trace of the old way of thinking remained in his blood. It meant that to pay the ultimate homage of faith to one's god, you offered up the most valuable thing you had, namely a blood and flesh member of your own family. He now resolved that he would show his supreme love and loyalty to Yahweh by offering Isaac as a human sacrifice. This was a monstrous, staggering thought, for Isaac was to be the path by which this chosen family was going to be able to fulfill God's promise to Abraham to become a blessing to all the nations of the earth. Of course you remember that the storytellers had a happy ending in mind all along, and Isaac's life was spared when the wild ram was slain and sacrificed in his place. So animal sacrifices were established as the main feature of public worship thereafter for a thousand years or more. Boys, your grandfather does not believe that God actually set out to TEST Abraham's faith, love, and loyalty. God knew Abraham, inside and out. He did not need to be tested. As you become older you will realize that by our mistakes and misbehavior we work ourselves into dangerous situations. "We paint ourselves into a corner," from which there seems no way of escape. *We set up our own tests* against which we must then prevail by confessing to Christ and imploring His help. No doubt God looks on at times, in commiseration if not downright sympathy. Of course His love has been present all along.

In our letter next month we will enjoy a complete change of scenery. We will fly halfway around the world from Palestine to the prairies of North Dakota. See you there.

With love from
Grandma and Grandpa E.

Letter V

Dear Craig and Brian,

Are you aware that your grandfather has a first cousin named Stella who spent forty-five years in Burma as a missionary and who now lives in the Bethesda Home for retired Christian workers in Cincinnati, Ohio? Her father and my father, as two brothers, homesteaded in North Dakota when the land was opened up for settlement in 1898. She was my Uncle John and Aunt Lucy's first child, having been born in Ohio, as well as her younger sister. Uncle John and his family lived one mile south of us on the broad, rolling Dakota prairie. Even in such a far-off lonely place, God called people to Himself, just as He spoke to Abraham so long ago. He gave Stella a different task to prepare for and she later became the head of a girl's school some miles north of the City of Rangoon. She is writing her autobiography, and I hope she includes a detailed account of the moving of her school (on foot) to escape the Japanese bombing in the early part of World War II. For her conduct in this trying episode she was decorated by King George of England.

There is a boyhood experience of mine involving Stella which ties into the theme of faith which we have been discussing. It is a memory which dates back to a very long ago childhood. I was perhaps not over four or five years old and had not yet started to school. One Sunday in the summertime after our family had been to services at our mission Methodist church, and much smaller than your church in Coldwater, I was overjoyed to learn that after dinner we would all get in the carriage again and go for a drive. From the comments of my father and mother I could feel that something *very special* was to be the main event that afternoon. It was soon apparent that we were to join with Uncle John's carriage; and also surprised that the young preacher of the morning was with them. It turned out to be quite a drive, and because the pairs of horses were also work horses on the morrow, neither driver pressed for speed. Six to seven miles, as I learned later, made for quite an extended jaunt. On the way a few curious remarks passed between my father and mother which I could not fathom at all. They had to do with a slight wonderment as to whether the young Methodist preacher would become so flustered that he would forget his lines when he did whatever it was that everyone expected him to do. More heightened mystery with a reference to the 'water.' What in the world was this all about? In my own fashion I soon became a real participant in this strange and wonderful happening. Having arrived at a wide spot in the creek which served as a watering hole for grazing cattle put in this faraway summer pasture, we climbed out to stretch our legs. One noticed that the preacher was conferring with Uncle John and Aunt Lucy together with Stella at the edge of the water. I remember that my cousin was dressed in a simple cotton gown, probably one of her nighties. For the life of me I could never remember a thing about the preacher's attire (but thinking about it when I grew up, I am sure that Uncle John did not allow him to wear probably the only suit the young man owned into the water). The preacher made a little speech of which not a word registered with me, probably explaining how strange it felt for a Methodist momentarily becoming a Baptist. What did register was his act in dipping Stella lightly under the surface after they had waded out to a deeper spot and some words that were only half audible from both. Were they Father, Son and Holy Ghost? But the thing I do remember, and very vividly at that, is the glowing smile Stella flashed toward her father and mother and sister and later at the rest of us. I knew something mighty important had happened there that sunny afternoon in the water hole. You may suspect that eighty years later, I am using words to describe what took place within me at four as therefore subject to exaggeration, but I am positive that we were aware of the descension of the Spirit of God upon that scene and into the heart of my cousin. One did not really need a white dove from heaven to testify to that.

Driving home afterwards was a happy occasion and I plied my parents with the questions as to what all this meant. It was simple. Here was a young girl dedicating herself to Jesus Christ and pledging her life to one of service for Him. I did not know it at the time but she had already decided for the foreign field of service. The dipping under the water had something to do with helping to change bad habits into good ones and starting a brand new life. Of course the true, fuller symbolism was to come to me as I grew into young manhood and took my own next step as an actual participant; but let me say that on that day so long ago, your grandfather entered into *his first* conscious spiritual (religious) experience. It was a first small baby step toward God. The only misleading point of the happening was that for a decade thereafter, I associated a public stand for Jesus as meaning that going to a far and distant land was the only way one could serve Him. Stella went on to finish school and college and under her Methodist Mission Board she labored among the Burmese for over forty-five years.

Today I know that service for Jesus Christ need not take us far beyond our front door. The moment of commitment whenever or wherever it happens begins with improving your relation with every member of the family. The family is God's basic spot for nurture in all aspects of living. In the daily hassle of getting up and off to public school the child is instructed in the courteous conduct of a home (especially to his mother who is the queen of the home) and continues to practice helpful relations to his brother and dad and all his schoolmates and teachers. When he does it badly, parents show him a better way and when he is deliberately mischievous or disobedient, he is appropriately punished. To begin with he gives his parents the benefit of the doubt. As he progresses through high school, differences of opinion on conduct will be expected, but remember one thing—in the pow-wow that ensues, never forget that Jesus ought always be present as THE THIRD PARTY.

With much love,
Grandpa

Letter VI

Dear Craig and Brian,

In my last letter I described an early family baptism in the homesteading days of North Dakota. In view of your own preparation for possible church membership, I felt it would be worthwhile to pursue the subject of baptism a bit further. Be prepared to listen to some ideas you have never heard before.

For the young person, as a starter, we may define Baptism (as a Christian) as follows:

(a) The young person first recognizes Jesus' high ideals of living but also acknowledges that he is unable to live up to them, and this is answered by

(b) his imploring (i.e., opening his heart) so the Spirit of God can enter and take charge, thus making his life one of purpose in God's plan.

You notice something lacking, like where is the pastor and why is not the 'water' mentioned? Look at it again very carefully. We will add some implications which are at first not so obvious. You see right away that the above definition calls for certain *outward action* involving one's relation to all other people—as well as an *inner* belief as to what should be happening in him. It is quite obvious that a baby a few weeks old who is 'baptized' in an adult ceremony is not baptized at all.[3] The baby isn't able to know Jesus, he cannot take a position towards others (except to cry for food and attention). He is unable to make a prayer and is unable to ask God to take charge of his life. The imploring is done on the basis of faith on the part of the parent implorers who believe God is present and ready to bestow His blessing; and also faith that God truly wants him despite his selfishness and poor performance and will carry on with him through thick and thin. Now read the above a few more times and then get Dad and Mom to comment on it too.

Who should the 'implorer' be? Your church says that a ceremony of baptism can be carried out on the baby's behalf, by a special agent that God has appointed to take His place, namely, your pastor. But this puts the cart before the horse. The pastor cannot speak for the baby, for that baby must retain responsibility for his own individual actions. All the pastor can do is offer a prayer to God on behalf of the child pledging the care and teaching of the parents and the church members, hoping that the oversight provided by them will eventually lead him to a knowledge of Christ. They can never, however, speak for him in the actual acceptance of Christ. Such a ceremony has comfort in it for some parents but *we ought not to call it baptism* within the biblical concept. There is another careful act of nurturing called dedication, which we discuss a little later.

You have rightly concluded that your grandfather does not believe in the baptism of infants. You have also concluded that he believes that such a ceremony is an empty symbolism because the subject cannot exercise a mental concept of what he is doing. Even the churches practicing infant baptism realize that something is missing until at about the sixth or seventh grade minimum; there must be a concluding act of faith on the part of the prospective member. You boys are examples of such a system as well as your daddy who was baptized as a baby in the Lutheran Church. Both your Ebersole grandparents are examples of baptized church membership after attaining an age of 'reason.' As a matter of fact I was not baptized until I was 17 years old. Now whether the actual ceremony for the public declaration is carried out in a tankful of water or your head is touched with a hand moistened in an ounce of water really does not make a bit of difference. Jesus allowed his cousin to lead him out into the stream and pour some water over his head

49

chiefly, I suppose, to honor and support John's preaching. It was a sign that John's message was coming from God.

Christian fathers and mothers who do not believe in baptizing babies usually present their babies for dedication to God. This happened with both your mother and her sister. The child does not know what is going on but the parents are being charged with the heavy responsibility of maintaining a Christian home. The parents are not guaranteeing that the child is going to serve God when he grows up, but they promise to do everything they can to challenge their child to that action. They become aware that when seemingly impossible burdens and problems arise in the home, God is waiting to help.

You may think of asking your grandfather this question: "Do you think your experience of baptism in water makes you a better Christian than those of us who are sprinkled as babies and then 'confirmed'?" That is a loaded question. Paul points out the danger of making this kind of comparison. Many Christians excel me in the practice of their Christian lives.

I am just as sure that many of them were baptized as infants. The important test is the quality of our individual performances. To support and renew life, some folks eat steak and potatoes, while others do just as well on rice and fish. Personally, I don't believe it mattered to God when I was baptized or even if I was baptized. He was concerned about my desire to become His son and whether He could count on me after He adopted me. In other words, would I be a dependable, hard working member of His family? That shifts the value of my experience to something very unique. Am I (the real me) following through on His plan for me? I don't believe He busies Himself making comparisons between us. If we are *mature enough* at the time we take this important spiritual step, any special emphasis that we absorb, like the step of baptism, will make for a stronger sense of commitment. If a certain person wishes a dramatic happening, like immersion to start with, so be it—but he must realize that life is then just beginning. He must learn to pray and he must learn how to hang in there. No matter in what manner your desire for baptism was carried out, you *can* be better Christians than your grandfather.

The act of baptism is only as important as the person asking for baptism makes of it. Did you know that our brothers, the Quakers, do not baptize either their infants or the adult members? They are excellent practitioners of Christian faith.

With love from Grandpa

50

A P.S. to you, Dear Reader: I trust I have not offended you good people who conscientiously discharge your obligation to your children in a different fashion of baptism. But without the above letter my own personal story would be incomplete and inadequate. F.E.

Letter VII

Dear Craig and Brian,

It is a bright, sunny winter morning. I am in an upbeat mood and have just finished rereading the book of James in Dr. Phillips' translation. This book would have a modern title if written today; something like "Daily Regime for the Practice of the Christian Faith." James may be misunderstood by some people. He doesn't claim that the way to get to heaven is by doing good deeds in abundance. One does not gain the favor of God with works. Rather, James says, if you love Jesus and try to follow His pattern, the good deeds that result are just the overflow of gratefulness for the good relationship. In other words, the good deeds are a result not a cause.

After a little meditation, sadness begins to creep into the picture since in the world at large such a very small percentage of people really know Christ. One-third of the world's population (1981) have never even heard of Him. Here at home in the U.S., less than 50 percent of them are members of a Christian Church. And many of those names on the rolls are probably not really practicing Christians either. For them God remains in the background, fuzzy and indistinct and perhaps only appealed to in times of very serious trouble. They do not know God as Christ revealed Him. I am at once sobered by the feeling that *He is grieving because of us*. He must be disappointed in His human creation; such a lying, stealing, killing, gossiping, lazy bunch of procrastinators. All of us do not engage in such direct, outward, violent things but there are plenty of us who put on a good outward show and yet inwardly shut out Christ and keep to our selfish inner selves. In other words, we may claim a loyalty to Christ which, when all is said and done, is *a matter of all talk and no action*. God must feel very hurt about this lack of action on our part. One area is a particularly sorrowful one. God sees millions of His Children starving to death and many of the rest of us are not paying too much attention to their sorrowful condition. We say, "Will God let things continue as they are?" But at the same moment He is asking us, "When are you going to do something about it?" The hunger problem is only one of the world's evils. Watch TV news and you will be swamped in evil happenings. God asks, "I gave you a gift when I made you. It was the gift of freedom to make your own decisions. You know what is right. Why don't you see and hear and put my Love to work. I can only accomplish a cure through you, my loyal servants."

The last sentence above contains the answer. God has a Rescue Plan (see footnote [at the end of this letter]) but we fail to recognize that we are the Rescue Team. You boys know something about Rescue Squads and Units. We see them operating today in most communities. They can be helpful in illustrating how God's Rescue Plan works. You and I and Grandma and the rest of the folks who are members of the church make up His Rescue Squad. Some of us on this team are not too well trained. We have not done all our homework on the Bible that we should have. We ought to crack that special textbook more often than we do. We fall down in another department. We can't always recognize the sick patient. In illness of the body we usually recognize the symptoms of a sick person. When it comes to illnesses of the mind and the spirit, these are not so obvious. But we are generally smart enough to recognize two kinds of patients:

(1) There are those who have already pledged themselves to the Jesus way of life but have allowed themselves to become rusty in the practice of LOVE. Life has become just one big bundle of problems which they can't cope with anymore. They have lost both God's address and His code call.

(2) And there is the worldwide group, those who have never met Jesus at all. They are ignorant because we on the Team have not gotten around to visit them or tell them by TV or radio. So we must fit ourselves to recognize these two kinds of patients: those who may be as personally close as our family members in the home and those who are impersonally distant but are bound to us as bothers and sisters wherever they are.

Now how about the one we think is the patient but who then refuses to admit he is the patient? He cannot bring himself to admit that *he* is the patient because he considers himself absolutely okay. All okay. This example is important because you and I may make the mistake of thinking it is *always* the other fellow who is in need of a doctor. Let us carry on a bit with this patient who still claims he is not a patient. He may be and probably is a very self-centered person who is so wrapped up in himself that when the Rescue Team (the church membership) get him into the hospital (the church) and he meets the intern (the minister) and sees all the nurses around (the members of a class or other group), he still says, "I am not sick. What are you making all this fuss about?" Actually the patient might even be a high school student who thinks everything is okay since he is just sliding by on the skin of his teeth. Just enough homework to keep from flunking, and lots of time with the kids just goofing off. Not an ounce of extra effort being exerted. Using less than half the brain God endowed him with.

What do the members of the Rescue Team* then do? Can they persuade the patient to let the Great Physician prescribe? The easy answer is to overlook the problem near one's elbow because that is the too difficult one. (Remember the priest who looked the other way on the road to Jericho? Many of us pass by on the other side.) We go for the heathen who is far away, write a check for benevolences a little larger than usual, and take a nice nap. I believe that in the next letter, which concludes Part I, we should come to some conclusions touching on the confirmation ceremony as a part of the Rescue Plan. Until then,

With love,
Grandpa

*Rescue Plan: In a much later letter we talk about a more adult concept of God's Rescue Plan. New young members of the church do not really understand the terms used by pastors, deacons, and elders when they refer to 'salvation,' 'original sin,' 'hell,' 'heaven,' 'repentance,' and so on. You will grow into an understanding of them as you continue to study your Bible, attend Sunday school and church worship and discuss questions with your parents and pastor.

Letter VIII

Dear Craig and Brian,

You have now made the most important decision of your private life and have taken the first public step in Christian faith and practice. I have chosen the words of that sentence very carefully as describing you experience. They help to divide this letter into two natural parts. The first has to do with the *privacy* of your experience and the second *deals with all other people*. Thus you have had an *inner* and *outer* happening. Your grandmother and I are overjoyed that you have joined the community of faith. We congratulate you for taking these first two steps at the side of Jesus. They match in mind and spirit the physical changes now taking place in your body. You are now *three dimensional*; body, mind, and spirit. *God's plan for your life is three dimensional.* Exercise thoughtful care in all three. We love you and we pray for you, hoping that you will let God be Number One in all three areas. You then will be a complete MAN.

First we will discuss that matter of the private decision you finally made in joining the church. You did not start out on this definite step last fall very enthusiastically. You may have resented giving up the time from your personal schedule to begin the unit of study with your pastor. His broken and uneven schedule, classes, and assignments added to your displeasure. You were probably not too happy to discover that preparing to join the church was to involve a lot more than sliding through a hit-and-miss 'study,' finally dressing in your Sunday best and appearing with a group of friends at the church altar upon an appropriate Sunday morning. I have a side remark at this point. I have not personally seen the printed text and other material used. But the idea behind such a long and expanded study indicates that the United Methodist Church saw the importance of doing more than has been the custom in former years. Many denominations have depended largely on the recommendations of Sunday school teachers and a brief six or eight sessions with a pastor as sufficient preparation. I praise the effort required for real homework which you were asked to perform. If you rebelled at first, you changed your mind and saw that if joining the church was so important then the cost in time and effort getting ready for it was worth it. Otherwise when you said, "I will work with You" to Jesus, you would be making an empty promise. You wouldn't know what the basic requirements were all about. A question when you finished the course: was there a definite point in your private inner thought when you actually said to yourself, "Yes, Jesus, I would like to be your partner," or "Yes, Jesus, I'd like you to be my new scout master," or if you didn't actually use words, did you have a strong feeling of admiration of Him in His heroic life on earth? Did you feel sorrow over the fact He was so cruelly put to death for the sake of other people (He being innocent all the while)? Did you have a feeling that you wanted to do something in company of other people to make a better world for us to live in? Sometimes we older members of the church suspect that when a group of young people join the church in one ceremony there is a good deal of 'peer pressure.' That means, "I will join because Tom, or Dick, or Harry, or Mary, or Elsie, or Betty is going to join and I like being with them. I don't want to be left out." It could mean that in such an approach the importance of Jesus is overlooked completely or [that He] at best remains just an historical storybook person instead of becoming one's personal hero and savior. I am sure that you understand the point we have covered so far; that the prime requirement is that in your own secret heart and mind you have said, "I have decided for being a partner of Jesus from here on. I will do my best in adopting LOVE as the basis of living."[4]

The second phase now comes into focus. Studying in the company of Dad and Mother, brother and friends, you 'go public' with your decision. That is very, very important and there is a certain aspect about sharing your decision with others that I suspect many young church members never experience (or they pick it up very much later in life). Not only is your public declaration a method of having sharing witnesses to your inner spirit and thus strengthening your resolve to follow through, but down the road you should expect to receive help from them in the practice of your own Christian faith. Jesus as your savior can keep you on the right track. The church is supposedly a Mutual Self-Help Society in which a special partnership exists. You are a special partner to the other members, just as you are a special partner of Jesus. No doubt some young people look upon such help (if coming from an older person), as a parent or older busybody 'telling off' the younger one and feeling critical of his performance. This makes for rebellion and resentment when misunderstood. Ideally, it should be difficult to distinguish between 'help' and 'discipline' for LOVE and CORRECTION ought to be made out of the same stuff—care for the other person. If you learn to accept discipline, you have it made. You receive discipline from Jesus, from your parents, and your church membership partners as you *will* it.[5]

Another point. Having joined the church, where do we expect to learn the most about Christian practices? We have previously pointed to the Bible as our textbook and therefore our Sunday school classes and the sermons on Sunday are necessary for better understanding. However, this 'classroom approach' has to be supported by a lot of laboratory work. The lab periods in the home are by far the MOST IMPORTANT LEARNING PLACE for Christian practice. There one certainly learns by doing. And in doing we make mistakes. But we can learn by mistakes. The object is to become able to recognize our mistakes and be *honest about them*. Know where we are wrong and take steps to correct our behavior. No cover ups. No blaming the other guy. Another point is mighty important in the home lab. That's courtesy and respect especially as regards men and boys, towards mothers and girls. Jesus kept demonstrating that *caring* relationships count above everything else.

Learn to practice love in every one of your daily contacts at home and school; and when you slip and allow a bad moment of temper to cause you to say something that 'digs' at the other person, calm down and in your heart search for forgiveness. Your search for forgiveness is going to be helped by thinking of Jesus. When you have learned to go to the offended person and tell him you are truly sorry you will feel a healing power. It is God who has touched you in that moment.

Happy days, partner.

With special love today,
Grandpa

Letter IX

Dear Craig and Brian,

How do you suppose we tell time when we study the ancient history of our earth? Your experience as a student would perhaps suggest that a calendar might tell us. For instance, a calendar tells us when school begins, when Christmas will arrive, the time of your next birthday party, and, best of all, when school is out!! But even if we looked at the oldest museum calendar anywhere in the world we probably could not read it without the help of an archaeologist. It would be in the form of a mud-brick tablet or a piece of engraved stone. We must push backward in our thinking about TIME until we realize that there must have been some point at which we humans could not read and write. No one had invented an alphabet as yet, writing and reading were out of the question. The record of what had happened and what was happening had to be memorized and had to be passed on from parents to children in each generation by telling stories by word of mouth.

Now think back to the first chapter of your Bible. God did not create His human family until He had shaped the more or less solid earth and prepared it for habitation with its plants and animals. How about the time lapse from the formation of solid earth to the point of its first human inhabitant? Be careful with the answer because you must use that wonderfully intricate brain that God has blessed you with. God gave it to man that he might become the "master of the earth and subdue it." A group of scholars and engineers with a great interest in the creation of the earth and the changes that have gone on within it and upon the crust of it are called geologists. They have given us the calendar we are searching for. It is the rock of the earth's crust. Some of these geologists are also chemists who have found one hundred different substances out of which rocks, plants and animals, and humans are made. Two of these are named lead and radium. You will learn about them in more detail as you complete your education. You will then know how radium slowly transforms into lead and by carefully determining the amount of each we can calculate the age of the piece of rock we hold in our hand. Thus we learn that the earth's crust is *four thousand million years old*. Look at it again, 4,000,000,000 years, i.e., that is the same as saying 4 billion.

This reminds me of an experience when I was a freshman in college way back in 1921. A required course was a year of Bible study and the professor was an elderly ordained minister nearly at retirement age. I give this estimate of his age because I want you to have a feel for the views held by religious folks at the turn of the century or just before. We had to learn the chronology, that is the time table, of the Bible story. The authority was Ussher's Chronology, still referred to by a few traditional students today. There it was in black and white. The exact date of creation was 4004 B.C.!!! I was just eighteen. I had an uneasy feeling that something was wrong but in those days a green freshman did not undertake to differ from his professor too strongly. And I myself didn't know enough about it to want to get into a discussion. He did not invite office consultation and I was a stranger of a different denomination with no early courage. So I wrote the same test answers that everyone else did. Actually, both the Egyptian and Chinese civilizations were already in full swing by 10000 B.C. or before. The rocks of the earth's crust are not only God's calendar of time. Digging down into the crust we discover a part of God's historical storehouse. We find the fossil remains of many kinds of little plants and the giant rushes from which coal was formed. Also there are the skeletons of animals, many of them strange in shape and of giant size. We find the bones of big apes and gorillas and in five special places scientists have discovered bones and/or skulls which appear to be almost human. The specific rock calendar in these areas says some of these fossils were embedded at least two billion years ago!!! A million more or less when we speak of such happenings

57

is not very significant. And we will have more to say about this in our last letter.

Now we go back to the Bible story of creation and understand that the writers, truly men of God, were faced with describing something of which they really knew nothing about firsthand. They knew only that God was responsible. The men who wrote the final edited account about 2500 years ago (i.e., about 750 B.C.) didn't have a geologist or a chemist to help them. They figured that a week was a pretty good working period and so they divided up the creation effort into six 'days.' We do not blame the final editor for including at least two descriptions; in one, the writer did not feel he had the insight to add a detail on how God made man like the other writer did. He did a wonderful job in a simple, logical, straightforward fashion. *We call his story an 'allegory' and honor him for it.* Especially do we appreciate his description of God's work on the sixth day when humans were fashioned and he made the point that *both* males and females were absolutely necessary. *Fathers and mothers* were to be mighty important in God's family. Later on we will speak again about the important finishing touch of God's, when in His own way He added Memory and Mind to the brain machine, and then installed that special receiving set so that a human could tune in on God's wave length. We label this receiver Conscience, since if tuned in properly, we are able to tell Right from Wrong. All these gifts from God will be the subject of later discussions.

This is pretty heady stuff, partner, and it is time to relax.

Much love from Grandpa.

P.S. Grammy has just brought out the Mayan Calendar made of brass. You will examine it when you come next month.

Letter X

Dear Craig and Brian,

We have discussed God's rock calendar of the earth's crust and accept it as a fact which all persons regardless of their religious beliefs must adhere to. We must also accept the fact that the fossils found embedded within the rocks show that the life of plants and animals has existed on earth for about two billion years. Further, it is in order that we respect the scientific work of botanists, biologists, and zoologists which has resulted in a system of classification. This starts with the simplest ones like single cells, and proceeds step by step through the complicated ones. When the fossil remains of an animal are of such a strange shape or size we conclude that these specimens belonged to ancient orders, families, genera, and species which became extinct. They disappeared and others took their place. *How* this happened is not the subject of our letters. The names of possible theories about this will be mentioned later. They will be interesting reading. You may even go into a course of study in science which will present a number of theories. The most important thing to remember, however, is that we believers have faith in the certainty that whatever took place *God willed it and is in charge.* God was the mind, and the force and power behind it all. *He was the Creator and is still creating.*

Now we arrive at a most important point. He is our human creator as well. Many Christians and other religious believers will accept the things above in reference to the plant and animal kingdoms but they stop short of placing their human ancestors at the end of the line of the highest order, the mammals (those who give birth to live young). They violently refuse to even look at this possibility. I will try a high level term on you. We can say that they find such an idea 'traditionally repugnant.' They refuse to use the word 'animal' to describe any part of a man's body. This unwillingness to associate the word 'animal' with human creation comes about, no doubt, because we stress the fact that "God created us in His image" and so the animal suggestion is almost insurmountable in their minds. Now what about the 'animal component' of a man's body? Need we go much farther than to recall that our medical doctors and our researchers in medicine recognize, in the bodies of the animals, the organs, performing the same physiological functions as in the living tissues of our own bodies. Indeed the actual extracts and secretions of certain animal organs can be prepared and used in our bodies to overcome a deficiency that has caused human sickness. We also know that various substances which are being considered as new medicines or drugs are tested for a long period of time on laboratory raised animals from mice to monkeys on the assumption that the experimental results on humans will be the same.

As you and I ponder over these things, we naturally ask ourselves a very direct question. If our rock calendar contains the skeletons and fossil remains of ancient animals of both simple construction and complicated ones like the mammals, what are the very latest (i.e., the most humanlike skeletons) to be found? To date, five skeletons or parts of skeletons have been found which appear to have a number of physical human features. We will list them briefly. One has been uncovered in central Europe and another in England; one in southern Asia (Java); another in north China (Peking); and one in southern Africa. Paleontologists (scientists who study prehistoric fossils) tell us that although these discoveries show quite humanlike characteristics, they are not classified as man, that is as belonging to Homo sapiens. At least one of them is now thought to represent an extinct species. Now you may well ask, if God supervised such a process over a period of several billion years why in the world did the Bible story say He took just twenty-four-hour days? We must remember that the Bible writers faced the same handicap we do today when we try to describe God who is a Spirit. And God is a very special kind of Spirit to whom we are related.

An allegory is a story in which the characters described and their immediate actions are used to express a truth which came about when there were no human eye witnesses. In this case the action took place before there were languages and words; indeed, even before there were ideas which are the background of words. Actual description as we know it is impossible. But God, being a Spirit, had implanted the spiritual receiving set alongside or in the human mind. Thus it is not really a make-believe story like telling a fairy story to a classmate. It is a bit like trying to describe a brave man without using the word 'brave.' You describe things the character does which are truly brave but the listener's imagination puts together the idea of what bravery really is.

So, under the prompting of God's spirit, men did the best they could with the words at hand. And what a wonderful story it is—just as meaningful today as it was so long ago. We immediately recognize that the Rock Calendar of the age of the Earth makes the creation story an allegorical, spiritual story. We feel that this is past arguing about. Yet the so-called literalist (Fundamentalist) refuses to accept the geological fact. A modern example shows how truth sometimes is very hard to come by. You already may know from your general science that Copernicus in 1543 challenged the science of astronomy in his day by finding out that the Earth both revolved on its axis and rotated around the sun, accounting for our yearly seasons with the lengthening and shortening of days. Only a few fellow scientists believed him. He was thrown out of the church by the Pope on the grounds that he was defying the Bible. It took a full generation of 35–50 years for other scientific people to accept the demonstration of this truth; and probably that many more to convince the mass of the uneducated who tagged along later. Little wonder that in 1989 we still have a body of Christians who will not accept the rock calendar of the geologist (. . . pulling down a black veil between themselves and the botanists and zoologists).

The tendency to brush this all off is easy to come by. We look at Jesus Christ and may say, "Why get so uptight and disturbed about the Genesis Bible story when all we have to do is unite in our acceptance of the meaning of His life. Can't we hold vastly different ideas of God's creation and still make out alright in the end?" For your grandfather this is not enough. To maintain our self-respect we must use the brain power and mind that God gave us. When we 'learn' a truth we must fit it into a pattern for living. When these truths do not fit into the jigsaw puzzle clearly and solidly, we may have to rock along with *various* theories for a time but let's remember that theories are blessed by God too. He expects us to wrestle with problems for a while. It indicates we are learning how to use His gifts. In the meantime there will be some friction between geological, biological, and zoological theories. So be it as long as one group does not become self-righteous and claim that it has the only pipeline from God.

With much love to my partner,
from Grandpa

POSTLUDE COMMENT

Although the theme of creation is taken up in Chapter 9 under the title "God's Evolution," it seemed necessary to print these letters as we originally wrote them. I advise the reader to withhold judgment until he has read the whole story. Chapter 9 is written at a fully adult level.

It may help to repeat my simple stand at various vantage points. This is one. Educated people today realize that despite what one wishes to believe about the way our Bible was inspired, we must separate the facts and fancy as to the age of the physical world. It is approximately four billion years old. Note that the unit of man's time is in the billions, not millions. When the reader erases the six twenty-four hour days out of Genesis, he still has to read John C. L. Gibson's *Daily Bible Reading*, Volume I, Genesis 1–11 and see what made the old Hebrew poets tick. Those storytellers were not writing a secular history or a book of science. Based on the relationships existing in the earthly family, they did their best to bend a secular vocabulary to describe a Spiritual Power, a Person the likes of which no man has ever seen until the manifestation of that Power in Jesus. In the next chapter I pay homage to the sensitive imagination of those early storytellers.

Chapter IV

Finding My Own Identity

IN THE BEGINNING

After writing the entire first draft of this book, I reviewed the impression created chapter by chapter, beginning at this point after the ten letters. I tried to imagine myself a stranger meeting me for the first time. Realizing that a number of my views may be found to be controversial at first reading, I concluded that this section on my basic beliefs should be brought forward in the telling. Thus you, the reader, would perceive that we have more common ground between us than you at first may have suspected.

I trust that my basic concept of our common faith will not sound too naive. I find that the New Testament is not completely understandable without the background supplied by the Old Testament being kept firmly in focus. I am absolutely certain about this today. We must see the Old Testament as what it truly is—our record of the beginning of Christian faith, though we dub it Judeo, for such it was "in the beginning."

Because I conclude this early chapter with a summary statement of my faith, I do not slight God's incarnation in Jesus Christ in any way. Christ was a fulfillment—but a fulfillment of what? It never quite seems answered, head on, by us as Christians. Try to see in these few pages ahead that we are the inheritors of a covenant people. We are not misled by realizing that a good deal of the early history of the covenant relationship has to be expressed in the language of a religious myth. It is a spiritual story expressed in human, sometimes rather secular, language, and though inspired via sensitive human spirits in tune with the Master Spirit, it nevertheless contains evidence of some human fallibilities. Our faith today, in the Space Age, must be allowed some reinterpretation of its original symbolic language. Language itself changes, as we have discussed in chapter 1. The only way that I accept "Fulfillment" today is to be allowed to add new meanings to the basic traditional language of A.D. 350. These are still nurtured by its root system originating in primitive cultural history. Allow me to say it again, if it has not yet become apparent: I hold the religious myth of the Garden of Eden to be second to nothing in the Scriptures except the appearance of God among us in the person of Jesus of Nazareth.

HOLY WRIT FOR GOD'S CHILDREN OF ANY AGE

Our spiritual growth knows no physical age though on the average it may be said to quicken approximately after the seventh grade. Men and women of any physical age range from "babes in the wood" to mature saints of the faith when the windows of God's light are opened upon them. Thus does God in His gifts, both of spirituality and the purely fleshly attributes of His human creatures, supply the mysterious medium by which He will communicate with them from birth.[1] God constantly beams His messages to us and a babe receives his share. Of course, in our varying maturity we perceive, as did Paul, that a number of childish perceptions will be replaced later on by more effective knowledge of the Truth.

The point I make is that since we vary in our spiritual perceptions, which are perhaps as numerous as our physical fingerprints, so we vary in the ability to understand and decode God's messages to us. Though skewed in the direction of maturer physical age, there are many instances wherein children have received and followed God's thrust in life's mission. So we see (in the fifth letter) my prairie cousin, Stella, who committed at twelve, spent forty-five years in Burma as Christ's ambassador.[2] Nor does this communication from God cease automatically because we may retire at a certain age, physically. Our medical world now knows that brain power has its own fullness of time and can become more active as the heavy cares of physical life are shed. Then comes the startling surprise that one's soul power even exceeds the brain power and seems to be operating at times in a totally different system; like a bit of yeast in a great mass medium of dough, it continues to leaven the whole; and being transferred to new situations and problems it continues to enlighten us ad infinitum. The retiree may find himself experiencing such spiritual recreation as to literally feel himself becoming a new person. Both Jesus and Paul spoke of this.[3]

Whence comes this soul's creative urge? Who, what, and where is the dynamo behind such power? Humanists claim that the brain power of Homo sapiens is all that is required for fulfillment. It needs no outside help. Faith tells us more: that God is that dynamo under full power waiting for us to make the connection. Dear Reader, do not be alarmed by the use of the word "dynamo." God is not a machine, but just as you cannot describe electricity, so also is the term "dynamo" mysterious, not in its form and structure but in its origin and its output of power.[4] Only via God, the source of resurging spiritual power, can we accept and acclaim the selection, training, and fruition (not yet completed) of that clan of nomadic sheep and goat herders who lived just beyond the far edge of the written history of civilization in that land between the Persian Gulf and the Mediterranean. Nowhere in the history of mankind has such a phenomenon of continuity in a spiritual growth, decline, and rebirth of a people been so apparent. A sweeping statement, you must admit, but Jesus Christ affirmed it.[5]

We began by saying that spiritual growth knows no age. But I am ashamed at the lateness of the hour. My effort at recovery has been a shared communal one, for we do not undertake to teach an adult peer Bible class without keeping the individuals therein in focus as we prepare. In this instance the teacher does not have the stance of an elder talking to a less-experienced younger. He is confronted with self-satisfying expertise in successful vocations of life, with a built-in resistance to acceptance of a new thing and likewise with a basic skepticism that a teacher is going to be anything more than an articulate entertainer.

To break through the multilayered veneer, the teacher tests his own ability to pray, absorb, and experience as equally important to his reading and studying all resources. His preparation must do much more than enable him to merely intellectually parrot the thoughts of his favorite Bible commentator. He must humbly contribute of himself, and to do this he must hope with all his heart to enter into God's presence for the guidance he cannot find within himself. The challenge he meets is to become able to present the solid traditional truth in any but the traditional vocabulary. He points backward to expose and apprehend the saints' commitment and motivation, but he must point to the present and the future to make meaningful applications to the modern materialistic mind. It is vital that he be prophet as well as priest even though only a lay person.

So, to put myself in the proper mood to write this portion of the chapter, I go back many years to the group of middle-aged couples who searched for some answers under the title "How We Got Our Bible." Our study dealt with the problems of reducing a Semitic clan's vocal folklore and culture to a written form. That occurrence took place in a millennium roughly defined as beginning with Hammurabi and his codification of governmental laws and reaching to the height of the Davidic brand of theocracy, thus approximately 2000–1000 B.C. Absolutely no known originals of these writings exist now. A nomadic tribe of herders could not be bogged down with the weight of writing materials. Hammurabi's lawyers wrote on clay tablets by impressing characters into the surface of the clay with styluses. This was much too cumbersome for nomadic desert life. We know that at the end of the land, the Egyptians introduced papyrus as writing material during the same millennium. We have no exact data for its introduction into Hebrew writing and worship. The Hebrews later made a contribution to writing by introducing a parchment made of sheep's hide. No doubt that during the later third of that millennium, during the period of the Judges, some parchment was used, but no remnants have been found of that age.

Bible scholars[6] tell us that choice of language and details of word construction reveal the evidence of at least three strains or groups of associated writers who worked on the Pentateuch. Not only were their writings recognized (Jaweh-Yaweh, Elohim, Priestly), but there were at least two precursors of J (Yaweh), designated by the titles J-1 and J-2. I mention these variations to challenge your attention to the twelve-volume *Interpreter's Bible* (written by 146 scholars), which becomes an absolute necessity in enlightening the teaching of the Old Testament. We are reminded of the inadequacy of words in describing a quality of life which by its spiritual nature involves emotional abstractional facets. Indeed some of them may not be reduced to words at all, the emotion being conveyed by the rhythm or manner of the speech, as in poetic renditions. Many parts of the Old Testament are presented in poetic form, substantiating the quality of sensitivity that we attribute to poets. Perhaps we more readily concede that art and music also really escape the finite restriction of definition in words. Since I am neither poet nor artist nor musician, I must choose the limitation of words, and it is with some expectation of being misunderstood that I share with you the following sketchy outline of our approach to God through the creation stories and patriarchal adventures. Nor can this sharing be final, for the wonder of living is growth. Tomorrow, next month, next year, your experiences and mine will have moved on to new power on new wave lengths and, tuning in on each other and on God, we will find new challenges.

These stories of the first eleven chapters of Genesis were first sung around the desert campfires of many generations of Semitic, nomadic herders. On special occasions no doubt the stories were skillfully dramatized and accompanied by music and dancing.[7] A mighty God, so awesome and pure, and so powerful that His name could not be pronounced outright, was in charge of His people day and night. In the midst of the polytheistic religions of the pagan world civilization, we give credit to Abraham for receiving the message from God that reflected his absolute, monotheistic nature. Next to the creation of humankind, God's mightiest act was to convince humans of his ONE-NESS and his HOLINESS. Abraham conceded this and exhibited the learning of his first lesson in his righteous living. He would not openly rebel against his heathen father, Terah. *No*, they would move to a new locality, Haran, and Abraham would care for him in love until he died, honoring him as a son should. Only then would he collect the camel load of household gods Terah had brought with him and throw them out on the trash dump. Many years and many generations later, after Abraham's people had experienced four hundred years of servitude in Egypt—God delivered this particular remnant of His people into the hands of brothers Moses and Aaron, who ran God's reform school in Sinai. This boot camp actually developed into a forty-year plan so that a fresh young generation could be equipped by Moses with God's law. A high-level, eager idealism and a conquering spirit were developed to replace that of the oppressed slave. Even aging Moses, one of God's favorites, was to be left behind.

They entered the Promised Land. Some two hundred years passed. Samuel became chief of priests at worship. A delegation of the clan families came to him and asked him as God's representative to set up a monarchy. They looked at the Baal cult kingdoms around about and thought it would be nice for Israel to have a king and a queen and all the trappings of a court just like the neighbors. Wise old Samuel resisted them as long as he could. "Look, men, I'm warning you, you will start out honoring God but soon the socializing among yourselves will become socializing among the neighboring nations. Your armor and war chariots will become more important than your soup kitchens. Our God will tend to become a God among other gods. You will sin and God will have to punish you." You know the story. After the high point under David, when Solomon's sons and heirs ran out on God, there followed a period of several hundred years in exile under Assyria for the northern tribes, and later, Persia, for Judah and the south. No doubt some attempt at writing Israel's history had begun under the later years of the Judges. The changeover from a nomadic to an agriculture civilization made for a basic stabilization of social relationships. An educated class, chiefly priestly, probably now had the leisure for meetings, studies, lectures, et cetera.

We briefly sketch the scanty resources for such a venture: no libraries, no written biographies of leaders and past saints, no skill in the mechanics of writing, which was probably originally left in the hands of a few scribes. In many instances there was uncertainty as to how special words, used only as a vocal sound hitherto, were now to be reduced to a written alphabet. Indeed, it would appear that a major difficulty would be the establishment of a language later recognized as having a peculiar use of consonants, leaving the vowels to be added mentally as the words were perceived either by sight or as a sound. We must remind ourselves that we have no original writings of record representing the period before the monarchy began to fall apart, approximately 900–800 B.C.[8] Sumerian type clay tablets are unearthed today in archaeological diggings in the general Near East area. Thus was found the story of the pagan Noah, who was adopted by the Hebrews and made over into a servant of our God.[9]

Imagine this earliest writer on the nature of his God and God's universe. It is the springtime of a new year and he has temporarily moved out of the cramped inner winter quarters of the village. He has taken from the storeroom a tent and some of the camping paraphernalia that the herding members of his family used in summer as they helped watch the village sheep. He had encamped on the fringe of the desert, seeking solitude for meditation, and as he greeted the morning sun after a night of prayer, his thoughts were these: *God has made this beautiful world and God the Creator has made me. I am his creature. Why did He make me? Who was God's first man? . . . He must have made a woman to serve the man and to bear him children . . . but I am confused, why did God really want a human family? Did He have a certain task that He planned for us to keep busy at?* This early historic writer may not have gotten beyond the firm feeling that somehow God had made the human family, that he himself was a child of God, and that God in His creative nature was of unlimited power. He took pleasure in His human family and wished them to have association with Himself.

Another similar writer in another tent, in another spring, made a very bold decision. He thought, *Today I feel very close to God. I am going to talk to Him about that very first man He made.* And so came a story of Adam and Eve. And finally after a number of other neophyte writers had tried their hands at it, there came the self-appointed chairman of the committee who tried his hand at describing the arrival of Adam and Eve. But this story proved to be very difficult. No one seemed to have the right answer as to what made Adam tick. The writers, very sensitive men of God, talked this over for years, perhaps for generations, with other new groups of writers. Then, wonder of wonders, one day a disheveled man came rushing in from the desert. He had been out there without food and water for several days. "God told me a secret, God told me a secret," he kept repeating, until a couple of closer friends took him aside to restrain him and satisfy their own curiosity. "When God made Adam and Eve He gave them a special gift. It was the privilege of making decisions themselves."

Such a group of beginner writers, with the sensitive spirits of the more poetic minds, were headed by a ringleader editor. Such as J-1, a real pioneer scribe and storyteller of the first rank, who was followed by J-2, a more spiritual soul. No doubt these two chaps had helped superintend the dramatization of the Garden of Eden episode in the Friday evening campfire periods of song and dance that ushered in the weekly attempt at Sabbath origins of the worship rites. The only character they could not actually put on the makeshift stage would be God Himself. A strong clear voice from the wings or background would be sufficient to portray Yahweh, the ONE true God. The real cut-up in acting ability was the one who volunteered to impersonate the Talking Snake. The body and eye language could be carried to extremes. He was sneaky, cunning, sly and smooth talking. Men could act that evil part because they themselves had become sufficiently evil and so knew what it was all about.

These folks in the northern area knew that another section of the extended family was concentrated at a place called Beersheba in the south. One day the man who played the Talking Snake in that camp came traveling through and dropped in to see his relatives. He reported that the stage director of the dramatic Eden in Beersheba was called E, because the folks in that camp called their version of God by the name Elohim instead of Yahweh. E picked up some pointers from J-2 and went back south to share his good fortune. This dramatic competition between Talking Snakes even spread to the eastern side of the Jordan River, which is called Transjordan. In this section of the clan, the Talking Snake had profited by his contacts with his peer character at the other two locations and he developed what he thought was the Super Talking Snake.

Sometime later, after the monarchy had been established, there was quite a group of priestly literary minds who came to the conclusion that it was about time to get the whole God-Act from the beginning of time put together in an orderly fashion. They had the leisure time to run down the leads and interview everybody whom they thought could throw any light on the subject as a whole, i.e., Creation from the beginning. The chairman editor who superintended this job was P. He put out the first five books of the Bible we call the Pentateuch. It was not essentially changed in the authentic translation later put out as the Septuagint in A.D. 100.

Not only was individual Free Will bestowed as an outright gift, but the following Life which flowed from the Garden of Eden thereafter (even after the breaking of God's commandment about the fruit), was to be interpreted as one of concern and love despite the Sin. The strong implication regarding family life was that the family unit was going to remain as the important unit of life. Despite the sinning, Adam and Eve were to be God's agents for nurturing the future of mankind. God has given Adam the right to choose the proper method of disciplining the family. All of the fellow writers must have appreciated that step forward. At that very instant these writers themselves became in a sense partners in Creation. They realized at last that God had given them the gift of Free Will, but they did not immediately understand that as humans they had at that moment also begun to create evil by their failure to decide what was good in God's sight on every occasion.

You can now see the later possibilities of what happened as the result of the gift of free will, but let's leave this to the theologians for now. We will state at this point that this was a supreme gift from God, our noblest asset, but simultaneously the means of our self-destruction.

With our Will we make decisions daily. The self-esteem so easily becomes self-importance and self-interest, and before we realize it we have become ingrained with gross selfishness.

The writers and editors of the ninth to eighth centuries B.C., who finally polished off the book of Genesis and the remainder of Pentateuch, were the product of spiritual growth of many centuries during which the patriarchs of Abraham's clan appeared as mountain peak performers in a long chain of receivers of God's revelations. I feel that it is imperative at this point to insert my private opinion relative to the actual historicity of the first eleven chapters of Genesis. Rather than become confused with figures of speech—similes, allegories, metaphors, fables, myths, parables—let us adopt the term already in use by a number of our more realistic preachers and theologians: "symbolic language." When we speak of the spiritual nature of God, whom no man has seen, and since there were several language metamorphoses involved as spoken communications became written communication, the term "symbolic language" appears to be a very excellent one indeed.[10]

OTHER OLD TESTAMENT THEMES FOR THE MORE SOPHISTICATED

We cannot expect that our imaginations will match the imaginations of all of the Old Testament writers. Others have cautioned us to be aware that the Oriental mind and the Occidental mind are not always in synchronization. Perhaps the word "imagination" is not just the word to describe the difference. We must leave this to the more subtle probing of the psychologist. Albeit, we do concede to the East a facility in expressing the experiences of life in more suggestive and perhaps in more mystical and emotional shades of meaning. Previously I have suggested that there is a realm of experience at the point where words are inadequate to portray them, a realm where emotions and perceptions arrive via poetry, art, and music. Perhaps this is where the Oriental minds of most of the writers of the Scriptures shine with greater brilliance than those of the West. Be that as it may, we do not know exactly what the Tree of Life and Tree of Knowledge were supposed to represent as they grew in God's oasis, the Garden of Eden. We have a right to assume that these two trees have to do with the perfect attributes of God Himself. The writing scribes and editors had no better way to indicate the eternity of God the Spirit and the enormity of all knowledge which is Truth.

Other writers indicate that the Tree of Life may have referred to the matter of Eternal Life. This is questionable because life after death was not dwelt upon in the Old Testament era of the life of God's chosen people. Only upon Christ's resurrection was the invitation extended to be with Him in eternity. The Tree of Knowledge is more of a mystery because before the story is over, the "knowledge" was of shame for man's nakedness. Despite this, God gave to Man His logical mind and the command still stands that he is commissioned to subdue the Universe. The original meaning in the mind of the first storyteller is not clear. Perhaps we might conclude that the Mind of God, which is not to be approached by impatient, discourteous humans demanding immediate full fruitage, is meant. No, God was to dispense knowledge and His essence of Life in His own fashion and at His own good time.

The trees were not to be rated for their fruit by crude and discourteous humans who were impatient to sample them. No, God was to dispense His mission of Life in His own fashion, and *adamah*, Humanity, on that early Judgment Day of birth, was to learn in sorrow that a life of hard labor was to be forever. That eternal life could not be claimed at Adam's origin, it could only be claimed at Adam's mortal going—his departure into the spiritual kingdom of God. Likewise with the attribute of Truth, the final distillate of all Knowledge. We are quite sure from the later life of God in Jesus as a culmination of the Old Testament prophetic teaching *that no doubt the major ingredient of Truth is Love*. Love was God's antidote for the possible EVIL that man was going to create when His gift of Free Will was programmed toward SELF instead of toward Neighbor and God. In A.D. 1990 language, God gave Adam the Free-Will freedom gift but wrapped up in the same package was His Truth-Love recipe, so that when Man struck out for himself and ran out of gas in No-Man's-land, he would have in his knapsack, hidden all along, the manna, the power, the ingredient LOVE, which would put him back on the track of God's Rescue Plan, should he choose to avail himself of it.

In a moment we will have more to say about the Love of God as it was manifested in His treatment of His new human family. But first let me add a word on Eden's temptation to disobey. We have all at one time or another shied away from the slithering animal we recognize as a snake. The reptilian level of existence is so low in our mammalian minds that the snake instinctively is looked at as an object of disgust.

We must be careful in our castigation of the snake. He is one of God's creatures, a scavenger by nature, and as a common garter snake or black snake he is truly the gardener's friend. We likewise give him due respect as he appears upon the physicians' symbol of professional services. The symbol is interpreted as representing triumphant life in the face of danger.[11] The herpetologists love him, or at least respect him, and study his life habits in great detail. Perhaps we should not be too hard on him in the Eden story. The spiritually minded storyteller needed such a quiet penetrator of the undergrowth of life, a very sly and patient representative chosen to represent the evil of our hearts, which arises when our self-interest rises to overshadow life in general. Let us also remember that Creation dealt with raw life everywhere. Only a later, more sophisticated culture could produce the symbolic devils which flourished magnificently and cunningly under the pen of a C. S. Lewis. They took the place of the Talking Snakes in the preceding cast of characters.

In the symbolic language of early Genesis, God treated Adam and Eve with mercy and forbearance. This is rather surprising, since Bible scholars are given to delaying the addition of love to the attributes of God until Hosea came along. In the case of Adam and Eve we note that the punishment meted out to them was not so terribly severe after all. If God had reflected the oriental culture of Asia in that long-ago time, He would have summarily put Adam and Eve to death, cleaned up the laboratory bench as it were, and washed all the debris of the negative experiment down the drain. Would He make a new creature for a new plan? *No*, we underestimate the supreme, mysterious wisdom of God. He had a Rescue Plan. He would save Humankind for a hard and difficult sweat-of-the-brow kind of existence as penance for the crime. But down the road, after some discipline and chastisement under cyclic growth and rebellion, He would eventually bring them to a level of spiritual attainment *where He could step in Himself* and take a personal hand on a more human basis. Forbearance of rebellion is a chief burden of love. As a parent patiently deals with the tantrums of a child or the anarchisms of a rebellious teenager, so God deals with us. God is a Spirit and we worship Him in Spirit when we respond in sincere imitation of Him, and treat all His creatures with forbearance. He had a future with a purpose in mind.

Patience, forbearance, and mercy, as divine attributes, are noted in two additional sequences represented by Cain and Noah. In the case of

Cain and his brother Abel, God wishes to make the point that His gift of human life is precious and that no human really has the right to deliberately take the life of another. The Bible literalist accepts the two brothers and their parents as a family freshly created from scratch over a two-year period. But they actually enter the stage as the product of *prior vocational expertise*, that is, sheep herding for Abel versus farming for Cain. Current analysis of man's cultural development points out that at least a generation or more may be required to establish such a solid vocational difference in the history of tribal development. From nomadic wandering on one hand to agricultural stability on the other took some time, as, perhaps, did the practice of offering a sacrifice to God. It is most likely that the gifts of Cain and Abel as "sons" of Adam were chosen by the editors of Genesis so that the Hebrew audience would get this historic message that nomadism came first in God's plan. The herder-nomad stood higher than the farmer.

Sunday-school children and young people, not to mention adults, from the day they first read the account, have pondered over the basis of favoritism that God appears to have granted Abel, the sheep and goat herder, as over against Cain, the farmer. In our American West, though sheepmen and cattlemen fought through their grazing rivalry, they combined in their hostility toward the farming homesteaders. One may be suspicious of the private prior family life of the J-1 or J-2 editors in describing the choice of the nomad's sacrificial gift as superior to that of the farmer's; perhaps this choice sprang from loyalty to the Semitic origins of the Js' people in comparison with the Baalic culture of their Cain—the farmer neighbor. Gibson[12] leaves the favoritism up to the Grace of God, but my view satisfies the curiosity. God did not require the "tooth for a tooth" or "eye for an eye" penalty of the ancient culture and instead punished Cain by exiling him to the outer reaches of Palestine where his descendants became good blacksmiths and artisans of metal. God rebukes the murderer for taking a life but treats him with mercy and forbearance for a period of rehabilitation. A special mark protects him.

Another example of the establishment of the value of life is the episode of the intended sacrifice of Isaac by his father Abraham. In this matter of Abraham and Isaac, we are told that God sent Abraham to sacrifice his son as a test of his loyalty to Him. I do not believe that God orders or deliberately initiates such a test of His human creatures. It seems entirely out of character with the examples given in the Creation scenes. "Test" is a very human word. We *test* the machines we use. We work objectively to discover degrees of performance by notation of observable data. God, who knows us inside out, knows our secret heart, has absolutely no need to require a test. He allows us to test ourselves.

God, in my humble opinion, did not order Abraham to commit that act, for it was completely opposite to the nature and character of our Lord. The ingrained Sumerian worship employing the sacrifice of human life as a supreme gift of piety was an inherited part of Abraham's prior pagan culture. Abraham did not become a 100 percent man of God in righteousness and deed overnight. Abraham still had a hunch that morning when he started out with Isaac that he was going to make the sacrifice because it was the supreme gift to God he had covenanted with, no matter what it might cost him. I hold that Abraham was human and spiritually mistaken. That morning, the true God was immersing Abraham, mind, heart, and soul, in His own loving spirit. Before the day was over He would find a way to break into Abraham's consciousness with a new sense of the value of human life. He would institute a brand new concept into the worship of Himself. He would be completely satisfied with an *animal* sacrifice, until such time as it was suitable to offer Himself in Christ once and for all. His humans must be spared to become active and loyal servants in the future. His chosen human partner must be led to approach a new measure of faith. He would reveal to Abraham that an animal should be henceforth offered on the altar as more acceptable than the human. The latter would offend Him. Scripture reveals that God will accept a human life poured out selflessly to Him in conscious love and loyalty. Such circumstances are totally lacking in Isaac's case, for he would have been an innocent victim of cruel circumstances over which he had absolutely no control, and father Abraham would have been forced into the role of murderer. God saved him with the ram. (Reread Letter IV in chapter 3, pp. 43–44, for prior juvenile version.)

Another instance where Genesis editors revealed God's compassion is in their treatment of the Noah story, the Great Flood Episode. Ancient traditions from a number of historical cultures, apart from our Semitic one, have established the fact that in the distant past a flood disaster had indeed beset the human race somewhere in the Mesopotamian region. Our science would indicate that by the time humans had appeared, the Earth's crust would have developed a relatively stable condition, and a forty-day rain would limit the catastrophe to a relatively small portion of our planet's surface. As the *Interpreter's*

Bible points out, this no doubt prevailed no farther than the valleys of the Tigris and Euphrates rivers. It took the more spiritually sensitive Hebrew forbears to lift the physical tragedy from a Babylonian pagan/polytheistic setting to one more closely consistent with the Holy Yahwehistic one. One such pagan Sumerian historical note of the event had already been set down in clay tablets similar to those used for Hammurabi's Code of Laws. The pagan hero was named Utnapishtim and his exploits are related in a poem described in the *Interpreter's Bible*, Volume I, page 536.

The Genesis editors could not let this remain unnoticed. They adopted the pagan hero and transformed his motivation into a religious theme. Noah was a faithful man of God submerged in the wickedness of Man. With him and his family as the survivors of wickedness, the writers of God's Scripture began a long system of successive declines and rehabilitations under divine supervision. The idea was that of a specially preserved remnant of the hard-core faithful, which could afterwards emerge again and grow up into fruitage with their spiritual qualities enhanced and permanentized. Such a part in God's drama was to be filled by Noah and his family.

Noah, as an imaginary hero of God, became the servant and saviour of the human race (that portion, at least, that was in covenant with God) and a worthy agent in God's plan to salvage his best people. Perceptive exponents of the awareness of God always being in charge have pointed out that from the beginning He has worked through REMNANTS: small segments from the threatened society, faithful to God, who have been selected to survive. This remnant keeps the leaven warm and in safety until once more it can, under favorable new conditions, expand and grow so that God's presence can again be felt in high places. America and the world can in the twenty-first century be confident of Great Expectations.[13]

An interesting facet about the Noah story is that no details of Noah's life are given as the reason he and his family were chosen beyond the solid pronouncement that he had heard God's command and in faith acted upon it. There is no suspicion of how he may have followed details of a religious regimen to have earned his status, except that he was a man of righteousness. To be such he had remained close to Yahweh. We can be thankful to the aforementioned editors for leaving the statement unadorned.

God alone knows the secrets of the heart and has His own good reasons for blessings bestowed upon his individual children. God was giving humanity another chance at going straight. In His mercy he chose Noah and his family as the surviving servant. It seems too bad that Noah must be relegated to Hebrew folklore and imagination. But we are grateful to the storytellers that in the midst of their Baalic, polytheistic neighbors, they could perceive such a good beginning of God's Rescue Plan. He will bring out of Noah's descendants a strain of people from which Abraham's family will emerge to nourish the faith. Disciplining and training will take another millennium to bring them to the fullness of time. Surely an attribute of God is His patience and mercy.

We feel compelled to cover an additional episode in a later chapter of Genesis in order to round out the superior force in spiritual writing which the Hebrews gave us. This traumatic spiritual episode, perhaps more than any other single story of the older Patriarchal period, reveals a timeless, amazing truth, God's divine power to transform a human life. He took a crude human clay instrument, devoted to selfishness, and so rebuilt it and refueled its motor in such a fashion that it could be the agent to nudge untold millions toward a path of righteousness. It was a refocusing of the conscience into the delicate sensitive guidance mechanism that the Creator meant it to be for His human creatures. God took a self-centered, conniving, thieving, rascally Jacob and by the magic of His power made him Israel, the father of a great nation which had been pledged through Abraham "to be a blessing to all the nations of the earth." Bible students and theologians have pondered the situation by which God chose such an unlikely character from this clan of nomads, if you will, and make him into a channel to nourish His own Incarnation plan. We have to conclude that "all things are possible" through the recreative process of God the Creator.

And the overwhelming thought and conviction is that He can do the same with me if I remove my stubborn will as an obstruction. As Paul said, "I die each day to sin but I arise each morning in the hope that I shall be a new man in Christ." The story of Jacob contains a secondary action as important as the first. It results from a condition imposed by God which we have not yet fully apprehended as disciples of Jesus. It is that the reestablishment of the personal relationship between an individual and God is not complete until a new relationship has also been confirmed *between the individual and his fellow humans.* No better term exists for this than "triangular reconciliation." It is the Eternal Triangle. (See page 294.)

Jacob had no sooner become a true son of God than he felt the inner compulsion to patch up things with Esau. Some skeptical or ironical student may wonder why Jacob did not rush out pell-mell, saddle up his camel, and ride off to hunt up Esau without any further ado. In the wild and woolly "East" of 1700 B.C. Palestine, Jacob's personal safety was no sure thing. We may excuse him for not having a faultless intelligence agency in the persons of his field hands and herders, who could not be sure just how many men Esau had in his employ in an area some days' travel distant. We are initially suspicious of the manner in which his intended presents for Esau were deployed. There were a number of successive parties of men—servants and goods—each of which was to advance along the road toward Esau only as each party ahead had in turn reported back to the following group the possible climate of Esau's reception of them. With Jacob's prior character in mind, it appears as if he were prepared to buy back his brother's favor, yet unwilling to pay more than forced to under the circumstances. We are happily reassured by Esau's spirit. "Forget it, Jake," he said, "I have more than enough for my own. Why not take these animals back to your own flock?" And then we have the magnificent replay of Jacob, "Esau, I insist that you keep the presents, for I am trying to make amends to you for my unjust treatment of you."

Reconciliations is the basic theme of the remainder of the Creation story. The writers of the Patriarchal history must get the clan down to Egypt, for at least a portion of Abraham's people was destined to spend the next four hundred years there in servitude. But the writers had an opportunity in their treatment of Joseph and his brothers to develop the spiritual growth of Jacob and his whole family. The sins of favoritism, jealousy, quarrelsomeness, lying, and conspiracy against human life for financial gain were all realistically dealt with. Even Joseph in his job as Prime Minister of Egypt played games with the family which at times looked suspiciously like revenge. But the objective sought, Rubin and Judah growing into reputable manhood, Joseph being accepted once more, the reunion of father and son, the adoption of Joseph's half-Egyptian sons, and, finally, the burial of all the family including Joseph, symbolically projecting Canaan as the Promised Land, was a magnificent story of reconciliation between God, His people, Jacob and sons, and they in return with God and with each other. Again we may have to bow to Miller and Hayes.[14] The possible destruction of this story is hinted at in our discussion of Miller and Hayes's new book on the Ancient History of Israel and Judah. (See page 144.)

This chapter has been subtitled "In the Beginning." It is a story of a search for identity as recorded in the book of Genesis. My quest for my identity may be summarized in the following outline, which is based on the preceding discussion. Basically I begin in the belief that I am "made in His image and must worship Him in spirit and truth." What are these attributes of God, which I can comprehend and then attempt to reflect in my character if I am really and truly made in His image? The sorry imperfections of my response due to my human fallibility and the negative force of my contrary will and self-interest are there for you to see. But I must keep trying, and that is my thank-you to God. The following section presents my own situation as a reflection of Israel's situation. I trust that I will not be misunderstood as an obstruction to your faith. Paul had mountaintop experiences. I cannot have his full conception of rising each day, a new man in Christ, but I can try, and the Holy Spirit, my Enabler, will supply my deficiency as He sees fit to do so.

MY IDENTITY—A STATEMENT

As indicated in the beginning of this chapter, the importance of the Old Testament is not only reflected in the spiritual history of a chosen people, but for the individual Christian it may become the very solid foundation from whence comes his concept of God's spiritual attributes, enabling the student to gain a fresh hold on the matter of God's even-handedness and His tolerance of man's imperfections. Thus, we conclude with a statement that one may label a bit of laic theology. It is expressed in a vocabulary that ordinary men and women use in this modern age. This is not a finished summary, for I hope to remain on a personal Growth Curve, but this is a last meditative thought on the subject for the moment. I hope that you are able to see in it stepping stones for building your own faith. It will surpass mine as God opens new windows to you. Now, take these steps with me:

GOD MUST BE ALL-POWERFUL . . . "In the beginning, God . . . " This universe does not appear to have been created by a committee. God's singleness did not allow for a compromise in any way. This God was so different, so powerful, and so infinite that our Judeo forebears had difficulty agreeing on a name for Him. They beat the Greek philosophers by about 500 years. God was a single God and far above ALL other gods; and they could not really describe Him because He was all SPIRIT; representing Otherness out to infinity, but close enough personally to talk to about the day's work.

1. To begin with there was simply a mess of unrecognized something that the storytellers called chaos. (See chapter 9; it was really *Energy.*)
2. God "separated" and "put together." There was no reason to ask how. He just did it. (Again, see chapter 9.)
3. He made lightness and darkness, firm land, oceans, marine life, plant life and land animals.
4. Now the original early Hebrew two-level world was just about ready: above, sun, moon, stars, firmament, heaven; lower level: grassy earth, rivers, birds, animals, and flowers. The storytellers had also decided where there were to be a couple of trees, dominating a nice garden spot. They were needed in the plot of the unfolding drama. (Death as yet was not in focus of course, so Sheol had not yet come into being.)
5. Summary: up to this point, the attributes of God were plainly seen; review them with me as follows:
   A. His *All-powerful singleness*;
   B. His *ability to handle infinite detail* (He could number the sparrows);
   C. A *Sense of purpose*: He was making this Creation to be used.
6. Thus they were prepared to introduce the special Garden hinted at above. It was to be the nub of the Creation story. The storyteller with no words but his ordinary, everyday language made do very simply. So God reached down, grabbed up a handful of His earth and from it shaped a human (or humans—*adamah*). He breathed some of His own Spirit into that clay and Adam was born. Of course a procreative helpmate was in order. The storytellers were not exactly unanimous as to just what God did to make that helpmate, Eve. So one view was that Adam's rib yielded her. After all they were to be as one. The other storyteller left it up to the mysterious power of his Elohim. (Today, in the Space Age, we listen to the gynecologist who knows of a different order of origin. In the development of the human fetus, the male is made from a female embryo, an outstanding reflection of

an attribute of God, for He is the unified parent and contains within Himself the total category of male and female nature.) All the attributes of both sexes are His.

A further attribute of God: He *bestowed a portion of Himself in each human*, thus, antedating Paul, *man enjoys a three-dimensional being: body, mind and spirit.*

7. He places His humans in the Garden He had prepared with the two mysterious trees. Special instructions: DO NOT EAT THE FRUIT. God did not leave the notice merely wired to a branch for them to overlook. He presented the garden to the couple and specifically instructed them: *Do not eat the fruit.* This reveals another attribute: *God's loving concern and interest in His human creatures.* He wishes them to enjoy the resources of His world, but with discipline. Furthermore, we notice *God's willingness to play fair: He gave them the gift of free will.*

8. Enter the Talking Snake. Next to God, the leading character on stage, he represented the Evil of mankind which we made by perverting the *Free Gift.* This storyteller was a 2000 B.C. pre-edition of C. S. Lewis. Adamah chose not to obey God. The snake represents us when we tempt others.

Forbearance in the midst of evil is God's next very evident attribute.

9. Punishment for disobedience: *For Adam,* "Sweat, blood, and tears" were in order as he would labor to take care of the resources God handed over to him. After all, Adam did just fine for labor and exercise he needed and the taming and husbanding of the earth gave him purpose. *For Eve,* the pain of childbirth, but always with the pledge of God's standby help. Human motherhood was to bless the earth.

This illustrates God's *forgiveness and mercy.* God did not destroy them and start over on a new experiment. No doubt His Rescue Plan was already on the drawing board. He would inaugurate it the moment His human family showed signs of getting lost.

Allow me to suggest that the eight attributes of God reflected by the Garden of Eden story as noted above may be arranged in a fashion pleasing to the individual's choice. The following rearrangement discloses some of my meditation upon it.

Genesis reflects the following attributes of our Creator:

1. A sense of purpose.
2. All-powerful singleness (100 percent monotheistic)
3. Contributes His own spirit in the makeup of His human creatures (makes us three-dimensional)
4. Willingness to elevate human wills—the gift of free will
5. Forbearance of evil created by His family
6. Forgiveness and mercy, outstanding
7. Loving concern and interest in His family (We are to enjoy it)
8. Ability to handle infinite detail (both infinite and immanent): "And God saw that it was good."

I am stressing the importance of the Garden of Eden story because whatever develops from the scholarly Bible criticism of the Miller-Hayes work on the secular history of Israel and Judah, we can still feel that the nondescript melting pot origin they describe is the womb from which springs our Christian faith. If, after the scholars agree that what we were wont to call the Mighty Acts of God did not actually occur in secular world history upon the scale described in the Pentateuch, we will still be able to fall back on the symbolic language of the first eleven chapters of Genesis. We can then agree, with John C. L. Gibson, that they are the most beautiful and powerful religious myths the world has in its ancient heritage.[15]

It is well that this statement of my identity appears at this early section of the book. It will prepare the reader for tackling some theory and other points in chapter 9, with no doubt at all concerning the solid base of my personal Christian belief. Second, it should help Space Age Christians realize that they ought not to slide quickly past the real spiritual heritage we all carry from our Judeo past. Actually we should perceive that it is impossible to be devoted to the study of the New Testament without its rock foundation, the Old Testament. The two ought not to be grafts to one another; they are one and the same vine.

I FIND MY IDENTITY

1. God, the Creator, made me and sustains me; I am His creature, I belong to Him.
2. God gave me a tremendous gift: my will to choose my action. I must attempt at all times to make my choices in conformity with His wishes. I sin against Him when my will succumbs to my greedy self-interest.
3. God called my creation good even though in His omniscience He knew I would fail Him. God chooses imperfect humans as His instruments. His power can flow into and through me even though I am encumbered by my resistance as a clay vessel.
4. God values human life even though it is imperfect and expects me and others to preserve it. I so declare and accept it.
5. God treated humanity—part of His creation—with forbearance and mercy. He expects me to do likewise to others. Yes, I am my brother's keeper.
6. God calls all humankind to reconciliation with Him and with each other. Upon that reconciliation He gives us a new start. The dynamic power of God, working through Christ and His Holy Enabler, the Holy Spirit, keeps me headed Godward.
7. Thus I gain my identity as a child of God; and I thank him daily.

I perceive a question rising in your mind, created primarily by the development of such a statement on the basis of the *Old* Testament. Except for point 6 above, the New Testament is not directly referred to. Fundamentally, I wanted to show that our faith needs the complete undergirding of the solid foundation that is supplied by the entire experience that mankind has had with God, the Spirit. One might say I have leaned backward in showing the common ground my Hebrew brother has with me. I regret that he avoids adding Jesus of Nazareth as the Messiah he is searching for. I wonder whether the devout Hebrew, in the secret of his private closet, is tempted to appropriate Jesus fully in his gratefulness to God for His manifold gifts. I hope so.

In the concluding sections of chapter 5 dealing with Old Testament themes for lesson writers, I have referred to what I discern as the major attributes of God. I refer the curriculum writers to the above list and the points made in "My Identity." Please bear in mind that the stance in chapter 5 is hopefully academic and objective. I tried to give future lesson writers a more complete picture as presented in the ancient history of the Old Testament. In this present chapter, I take for granted that you will have perceived me as working through my very private, personal, subjective search for that which has actually come into focus in *my own* experience.

Chapter V

Christian Education—Gearing Up for the Next Century

SECTION 1. DEFINITION AND CURRICULA

Christian education cannot be defined in any terms except those which are pertinent to the Christian Church. Therefore its definition must include a Hope and a Purpose. In the Christian's view this is to say he recognizes it as a Mission of Christ's Church. Indeed, some of us will say that it is the mission of the church. Properly defined, Christian education *is* the church.

Many older saints will object because, in terms of traditional vocabulary, it will be stated that the chief mission of the church is to proclaim the Word of God, thus placing the crown of glory upon the pulpit Bible preaching. May the Traditionalist liberalize his terms a bit and he will admit that simply to learn about Christ is pretty shallow unless the idea of commitment in response to a challenge is involved, the evidence of which is *action* and *conduct* by the disciple. The preacher *is* the chief teacher in Christian education, but when he paints a picture of our Master, he has to exert himself to be as much of a prophet as he is a priest; and this calls for correct conduct and action in the home, in the shop, in the store, in the office and in the board room, in our legislative halls, and—yes—in the *street* when occasion demands it. We so easily forget that Christ was a Revolutionary: we sidestep Elton Trueblood's call for incendiary fellowship.

All that we have so far said is that after we have learned all the facts that we assemble in cause-and-effect relationship, our mission of education also has to include the relationship we enter into in order to get the job of the church done. It is hard for some of us teachers to finally have to admit that after soaking up all the Content, we do not know how to follow through. Simply *knowing* does not insure *doing*. Family-type relationships help shape up some curricular material for the children, and on the whole if we can keep up with the dramatizing of the Bible stories and role playing and can insist on good relations at play and other social activities, we may be doing a fair amount of real parenting. Today's main problem here is the lack of cross-town experience in differences of skin color and economic status. Without this a child automatically grows up to be a candidate for caste snobbishness.

Family, the Easy Role for the Children

If Christian Nurture were in force, how would the traditional idea of a Sunday school class be changed? A basic concept would be to attempt to develop a relationship like that characteristic of a family, i.e., Christian parents taking charge of God's family. Thus, parenting is a Role Model for Christian education. What do we really mean by that statement? Perhaps not too much change in the elementary grades, but certainly some brand new elements for the Youth Division. For preschoolers, creation of the friendly feeling in the preschool group is basic, of course. Church atmosphere is an extension of good family home atmosphere. Storytelling and games predominate and the guidance of the teachers provides a general order that is basically low key and peaceful. Dominant things to develop are courtesy, the right of ownership, or temporary assignment of ownership, correction of wrongdoing with forgiveness catalyzed by the teachers, keeping things put away and tidying up. Attention to the physical comfort of the child, his nutritional and body elimination needs, will be pretty much like home. "Church is like home, only there are more of us, and we sing a lot." Love abounds in every relationship.

The church for this age needs to act and speak as though God is always very near. I dare say that many families at home overlook this except at "Now I lay me down to sleep" at bedtime. Grace at meal times is expected and is regular practice at the refreshment periods. The teacher will introduce the idea of talking to God as frequently as possible. Teachers may have to be reminded of this. The praying life of a Christian must become obvious to the child through the example of the adults around him. It is reflected in songs and poems. These are offered as links to God. The child should feel this comes naturally. There is good relationship all around, between peers, between teachers, between pupils and adults. Except for the added emphasis on the nearness of God, contemporary kindergartens of our churches are probably not too far from par in this matter of nurture.

On grades 1–6: Nurture in these grades will be more centered on group action as over against the individual. The group learns to plan, build, draw, paint, dramatize in a communal effort. Working together is difficult at times, a tremendous teaching point for the teacher who must be the referee. These pupils will attempt to demonstrate what the lesson means. Dramatization may go beyond the Bible story itself. Plays children perform in may suggest real family situations at home, incidents of daily living. Teachers are constantly on the lookout to develop forbearance, kindness, and insistence on order. An emphasis is placed on how people feel, how they react. There is now discussion as to *why*? The answers are given in the advancing idea begun in the preschool age. God is near. He is pleased when boys and girls do things for Him. They help keep His world in order. Praying becomes a reality, again by observing the example of the teacher.

Let us consult together for a moment over a restatement of what we need to do *extra* in the new Space-Age church. The mainstream denominations have, without saying so publicly, arrived at the point where their recruitment of new membership is dependent on the new blood introduced via Confirmation from the youth of the congregation. The challenge of Christ for the Adults on the street corner is left for the Salvation Army. For the rank and file of backsliders, sinners of the lower and upper economic scale, God establishes evangelicals like Billy Graham. Graham also does a great clean-up job for the mainstreamers by reactivating their fringe membership; when it peters out, he lifts back the laggards as reactive participants for God. Still, total membership declines overall.

For a better answer, we need to go back to Jesus. To be sure, He expected that everyone know His Scripture (then the Old Testament) thoroughly as the establishment of God's law. All of the concomitant features of His daily living, however, fleshed out the template for His disciples to follow. He made very plain a caring, sharing, loving, praying community was expected by God. Life was not a slavish following of a rigid set of rules; it was creating a relationship between persons; tolerance, healing, and helping were stressed. More action, more execution of principle, was called for. *Such action is Christian Nurture* in which education, per se, becomes the handmaiden of nurture. The generational family still provides the most excellent setting for its perfecting, especially if applied to the family of the church, the community of faith.

Looking at the Nurturing Teacher

In the past when approaching the subject of learning to be Christians and attracting others to do the same, we have always started with the ideas of stating a goal to be reached. The committee reports back with a glowing picture of the new child, new youth, or the new adult. Everyone lists books to read, lesson materials to buy or make. Essentially we are looking for new tools to put into the same hands, which suffered the decline we plan to combat by the new approach. We miss entirely the question as to whether the teacher/leader who will implement the new plan needs to be reevaluated and retrained too. Will the "new tool" be any more successful in the same hands? Of course, you immediately point to the high number of qualified public school teachers working diligently in your church and wonder why I question their proven abilities. All I am raising is the basic question never really faced up to previously. The Church will *have* to ask it of our staffs if the new century is really going to be "new." Do our expert public school teachers know that Christian nurturing and Christian teaching in the Church demands better Christian expertise than we have had hitherto? Will we all come to realize that the family with its guiding parents is the role model for Christian nurture, which means loving the person into church membership instead of trying to teach him into it? Your rebuttal is, "Don't you think you are being too idealistic?" No, I do not accept that conclusion.

Back in the '30s and '40s when our two daughters were elementary school participants there came the mighty surge of "progressive education." I am not taking sides on any specific plus or minus value. I simply point out that great numbers of teachers proved incapable of carrying out much of the new teaching procedure. Many master teachers had to go back to summer school and brush up in order to change their approach and be able to guide other teachers. I am saying in a similar fashion the Christian Church needs to be examining the demands that true nurturing will make upon next generations' children. I believe that curricular writers would do well to take up this neglected area and aim at improving the approach. Christian history and facts must be translated into actual individual commitments via methods garnered from many sources. There should be units precisely set up for teacher training, and in this respect, I sincerely urge you to closely read pages 107 and 261, where I am emphasizing the new educational roles of the ordained preacher/teacher as the dean of education for his church.

Steps Leading to Faith

The old time church school teacher who has been reprogrammed into a more complete acceptance of the commitment to Nurture will review and revitalize the steps that are taken to reach a state of faith. We can fill in facts but we must keep in mind that beyond these facts the Spirit of the one being nurtured must make the final leap on his/her own accord. How can one best be the parent/teacher who, through love, helps that person evolve from birth into faith? The basic steps to faith are:

1. Birth
2. Learning—by firsthand experience (facts discovered by the senses)
3. Learning—by communication with others (depends upon vocabulary)
4. Knowledge—more of the same, but now
   a) understanding relationship between facts
   b) thus making logical choices, i.e., choosing values
   c) abstract thought begins to have influence
5. Wisdom—higher level of analysis and connecting objective with subjective thought
   a) can handle more serious complications of good and evil
   b) increased ability for abstract thought process
   c) makes existential choices with God's help
   d) becomes conscious of the *worth of all other individuals*
   e) *humbleness* becomes a reflection of the degree of wisdom attained
6. Belief—a solid platform of thought governing most actions: A code of conduct in agreeable tradition has been established covering most common situations, however one may have a Christian belief short

of the actual commitment required for discipleship
7. Faith—the leap from belief and logic into an I-You relationship with God; all talking *about* God is now flavored by trying to learn to pray to Him; thus Faith waits upon God to reveal His purpose and plans for the individual.

The new age church school teacher/leader is able to pray as follows: "Dear Father-God: I am today a nurturer of the persons [by name], who I am associated with. They are my friends. With Your help, I will do my best to love and nurture each person into the discipleship of Jesus Christ. Help me through my own deficiencies as I offer myself to You as a servant parent in Your family. Amen."

Comments on Adult Curricula

The general adult curricula for the denominations depending upon the International Uniform Lesson topics and Scripture, in my opinion, share one general weakness. The lesson materials go back to a Bible situation and tend to keep the discussion focused upon a bygone culture. If the discussion ever gets around to contemporary Space Age life, it tends to shallowness. The deeply personal, spiritual convictions which are characteristic of a real Sharing Group experience remain submerged. The more recent Shared-Approach publishers and writers try to overcome this by posing a group of questions at the close of the lesson in an attempt at focusing on life's currently harassing problems. But the average teacher, mentally programmed to old-time Bible emphasis, slides over them without raising any temperatures. The class member with his class quarterly left at home in most instances does not even know that there were questions. It appears that, decade by decade, the attendance of the congregation's adults in class has shrunk to a very small fraction of the actual membership.

I am convinced that rather than abandoning such lesson material abruptly and disruptively, thereby incurring a critical reaction by the "elderly," who have been programmed by a lifetime habit, we ought to definitely shift our emphasis to new ways of challenging the mid-adult section of the membership. This younger Space Age–oriented adult should be approached on the basis of the everyday life of members of both sexes. Some increase in interspouse support would be expected, but the most promising aspect will be the attendance expected of the heads of single-parent families. All members transferring into a new church home, as well as those younger ones coming in via confirmation, ought to be immediately pressured into *participation* as the lifetime expectation of church life; else why are we now refurbishing the maturing program if not to point out that there is so much more expected than passive listening to a sermon in the new University of Life? This thrust is particularly aimed at the saints in high standing, members of the session, official boards, et cetera, who piously chitchat in little knots here and there in the morning "campus grounds," while regular class groups are busy in class or upon projects? Do not tell me that picture is absolutely foreign to *your* church. If perchance it is, I will help you shout Hallelujah and use you as an example throughout the Kingdom as the new promise of the future.

An effective approach to study material might well be to scour up materials pertaining to moral/ethical problems of this era, A.D. 2000, and then go back to the Bible to find a variety of answers. It could be productive of real effort in getting to know what the Bible says under various approaches. You will need to find or develop a capable leader for such study projects. Timing and approach to a given social or religious problem will always have to give way to the expertise of both lesson writer and teacher. There are just not sufficient Isabel Rogerses and Albert Winns to go around. Their kind of leadership wrote the sparkling, top-level material for the upper high school youth in the old Presbyterian Covenant Life curriculum. It was more than the run-of-the-mill church-school teacher could master, so the two approaches may have to be synchronized, i.e., teacher training and lesson writing. It is about 500 years since Luther. Do you not think it may be time for another spiritual revolution? Perhaps we need to rebuild the structure of Christ's Church from inside out. If we don't, God may have to wait for the national churches of the Third World to lead in His evangelization goal of His whole family.

The Space Age curriculum will call for reemphasizing some old and definitely adding the researched new. In another section I point out the advantage of doing a good deal of our Bible study, in which we soak up missed content. This can be gained at ecumenical community religious schools, set up on a regular recurring schedule. (See page 109.) For the younger adult, who is a product of the youth curricular process to be discussed a bit later, he or she will be rather completely counseled, analyzed, tagged, and placed in training by the associate pastor or, where one professional prevails, the pastor (the old-fashioned kind, but, reprogrammed). While they are getting their legs, the fellowship class and special study under the eye of the pastor will keep the fire burning. For the truly elderly and physically limited, the church's efforts will pay more dividends in happy lives by seriously attending to day-care service for the ambulatory and home visitation care and fellowship for the shut-ins.

You may have guessed it. We oldsters are not quite up to the requirements of the Space Age. As grass, we have already withered, and the fire is lit for tomorrow's burning. Currically the church ought to go all out and marshal every force possible in rebuilding the Twenty-first-Century Adult.

Would it not be acceptable at this point to insist that we get to the heart of the matter by defining Christian education and establishing the master curriculum in one sentence? It could read as follows: Christian church education is engaging in a lifelong process of Christian nurture, which is the practice of Love in every human relationship throughout God's universe as exemplified by the Incarnate God in Jesus Christ, who showed us the way of Love; and as we reconcile ourselves to Him, we know that His Church, the community of faith is built and rebuilt!

SECTION 2. NURTURE IS LOVING

As indicated in Chapter 1, the attempt to define the word "Love" out of context is next to impossible. Such context runs the gamut of human and supposedly divine relationship. The word becomes an umbrella for ideas and actions ranging from selfish, promiscuous sexual lust at one end of the arc to the majestic and sublime worship of God and His care for us at the other. Thus two persons of dissimilar backgrounds may well discover that the English word love fails utterly as a communicative link. In such cases *actions must take the place of words.* Love ought always to be a *verb.*[1]

The use of the verb form, of course, shares some of the mutual difficulty in the use of the noun. However, the verb implies that we actually *do* something in the way of illustration. "Do actions always speak louder than words?" We enter into what we think are loving acts of kindness, but cannot take it for granted that the recipient immediately accepts this as the real thing. Sometimes there may be a period of such acts necessary before a suspicion of acting or make-believe has been set aside. As C. S. Lewis so honestly insists, one can *learn to love even the unlovely* if one *wills* to love. He suggests that the initiator of the acts of such love may feel a bit embarrassed because he has only gone through the sham motions, but—lo and behold—there follows shortly such a euphoric feeling of accomplishment that the real thing begins miraculously to emerge. I must add, this is God's miracle.

The Good Samaritan was not conscious of being an instructor in lexicography, but Jesus made him so as He asked the rhetorical question, "Whom do you observe to have been recognized as loving his fellow man?" Hosea lived his love. No abstraction or acting there, in his forgiveness of a wayward wife; so did God love His wayward people and still does; and they in turn learn to live righteously in loving Him. Twelve men left everything that had given them security and in their insecurity were sustained by Jesus' love for them and theirs for Him. A few blemishes in the group testify to the quality of that love. Also, Saul, doctor of Jewish law, initially a murderer of Christians, became Paul; and by the labor of his hands and heart, he lived his love and made his supreme sacrifice in payment for Stephen's death. We hold the example of Christ as our supreme example of total love, which every act of his adult mortal life testifies to.

If there be anyone who, dwelling on that awful day of Crucifixion, is tempted to cancel some of the suffering because "Almighty God could somehow in the strength of His divinity have negated some of Jesus' human hurt," let him at once recall that Jesus the man was flesh and blood born of woman as well as God. That mortal flesh suffered as with ours. Some three or four ministers ago, one especially eloquent and dramatic in the pulpit undertook to describe the trauma of that occasion. He dwelt on the spurts of blood as the large rough-forged nails pierced His hands; the raising of the rough timbers, with Jesus nailed fast to them, to an upright position so that the cross dropped into its hole with a heavy thud, at which point human feces scattered over everything; the coarse shout of the execution soldiers as their job was completed and they snatched His clothes to one side; leaving the gaunt, bleeding, lonesome, and deserted figure silhouetted against the sky. Many of us left that worship with the vow, "I love you, Lord Jesus, help me to be as brave."

Of course I cannot really completely define the action of true loving because I cannot be a true lover, no matter the degree of effort. To claim to do so would be presumptuous. I can only respond in part, a very small part. My human fallibility stands in the way, otherwise it would raise implications that I speak from some special vantage point not shared by others. But I do know this: My loving must be done by action, not ostentation, but in many simple ways, even as the tone of voice with which I speak in unlovely situations. Who is the "I" in "I love"? I must shift from an objective stance to a completely subjective one. I have heard others speak about loving; I have read about loving and how others love or have loved, but now I love. I am now vulnerable, as others compare what I say with what I do. The New Testament tells us that it is not good policy to begin comparing our performances in loving with others' performances, especially when it gives us a feeling of satisfaction in doing so. This may be said of all self-comparisons with others in any kind of moral behavior. Human nature so easily becomes judgmental in such comparisons and my ego provides me with a sliding scale always skewed in favor of ME. With the Spirit's help we grow in our ability to focus more exclusively on our own performance today, compared with what it was yesterday; thus the relations of spouse with spouse, and of saint with saint within the church, are learned with tolerance and mercy. I cannot know what God knows about the other person and therefore I cannot become judgmental of him. I can only look at my own record today against what my record was yesterday and attempt to improve it bit by bit, bearing in mind of course that one's memory of one's own faulty record slips so quietly and completely into the unconscious. If you doubt this, ask an uncle or aunt or a cousin about past happenings in your youth and they can relate many things you wish they could forget too.

This discussion brings us to Paul's famous love letter in Corinthians. Those who have clung exclusively to the King James version may be caught up in ecstasy by the cadence of the familiar words. But one can profit be a reading of the Revised versions—Moffit, Philips, Montgomery, the New English, and Living Bible, and others—and be rewarded by shades of meaning the Spirit will reveal to him. All of these versions have attempted to update the meaning of the original Greek, Aramaic, and other sources. Just as you and I back in Sunday school at nine or ten sensed our first interpretation of Paul's words, we now find in our vintage years how all-inclusive and expanding they are. So too do those contemporary scholars reveal the change that has taken place in our English language as a whole. No doubt each scholar does his best to observe objective values but without question his choice of words has roots in his peculiar personal Christian experience. We can rest assured that the common denominator of the meaning of First Corinthians, XIII, though seemingly brought up to date by the list of translators, *has not yet yielded God's fullest intentions for you and me.* The inexhaustible and inexpressible love of God toward us, which He wishes us to adopt toward others as we are able, will never be fully comprehended until we graduate from this mortal shell and stand in His presence.

More needs to be said about the public devotional use of Paul's chapter. I have already referred to the eloquence and poetic measure of the language, which most persons may unconsciously respond to. In the setting of communal service, within the physical beauty of the sanctuary with its light and warmth, in the midst of the body "of the congregation and saints," the emotional response may be even greater than in the purely private meditation within one's own closet. I now realize at a later period of life that the beauty of the language was making a high-level dramatic impression on me without triggering a sense of absolute compulsion or commitment on my part. I could be said to have been basking in the beauty of the moment without the spiritual barbed point actually touching my will. I could say I was enjoying the vehicle of the message instead of the message itself. I was merely in love with love.

Let me try to further illustrate this point by listening to two friends with a common gardening interest. One of them is enthusiastically presenting the good points of the holly genus. He is discussing the beauty of its characteristic growth and foliage and fruits, and points out the adaptability of its various individual species and varieties for the home landscape. The second friend, who likes to grow dwarf fruit trees, or cabbage, or sweet corn as the case may be, is intrigued by the description of the horticultural details, which make sense to him and strikes a responsive chord in his own work in the world of soil, climate, and plant life. But the chances are that he will continue to grow his own special hobby plants, though happy to accept the gift of a holly plant, which the donor plants for him. The recipient genuinely looks forward to its development. He will unconsciously conclude that he is fortunate indeed to have such a holly-giving neighbor. He will to a degree enjoy the holly environment as a bonus in his own yard *without really having to do any sacrificial personal work about the matter.* Just so can Paul's chapter be a gift holly plant, enjoying some appreciation from the neighbors but never quite demanding their allegiance to it. It may remain a nice exterior bonus, not a necessity of the recipient's inner life.

In an attempt at self-analysis, I read First Corinthians, XIII, one day not too many years ago and suddenly a great sense of shame engulfed me. This may have been the first time in my life that it caused the phrase "Forgive me, Lord Jesus" to really boil up in my stiffened consciousness. Thereafter, each time I read the chapter I was overwhelmed by my shortcomings. I carried this sense of guilt for some time. My attempt at confessional prayer did not give me real assurance that God was hearing me. Perhaps Paul Tournier's book on Grace and Guilt was helpful. After some time it became clear that this Corinthian chapter was in the identical spirit with the Sermon on the Mount. Jesus' demand at the conclusion of this sermon was "Be ye perfect as your Father in heaven is perfect." Mortal mankind cannot actually be as God. But at that summer school on the mountain, Jesus laid out some principles of action that would provide eternally expanding goals for spiritual growth. In effect, He said, "Love is the Law of Life and there is sufficient room for your expanding growth, even until eternity."[2] Realization of the free, unearned gift of God's mercy and forgiveness supplies the answer to my own inability to love more perfectly. Though slippage and failures repeat themselves in my attempt at loving, I am now sustained and a fresh tomorrow appears as a brighter promise. I read again Paul's description of his own private problems and failures, his struggles against the flesh, and his re-creation each day in Christ. He admits that he himself has been unable to fulfill his thirteenth chapter. He has taught me to share in his experience and his love.

A generation ago the Overstreets, Christian psychologists, wrote as follows:

> It is in the capacity to care—to care intently about something beyond a limited self that we seem to find our best clue to what mature individuality is. For it is through our caring that self knowledge and self acceptance are brought into creative collaboration with the form of love we call devotion; self forgiving. Here is vocation in the truly religious "sense." This then, is the essential thing to seek for; not the least common denominator among religions, but the greatest common denominator. The greatest is love; the principle that unites man; the power that moves him to outgrow his childishness in mind and spirit and to become happily and responsibly mature.[3]

I suspect that some of you readers are wondering why I perhaps ran off, on a seeming tangent, on the subject of Love. Why take so much time and space for it in a discussion of Christian education? If you are a sophisticate in the use of a computer Word Processor, you may have suspected that either the author or his typist had a bad night and allowed a section of stored material in inventory to be picked up in error. If the latter *had* happened I would still unhesitatingly claim that the Holy Spirit in His enabling oversight had done this to make sure that my chapter on Christian education was properly undertaken. If we in the Space Age church are going to learn to be disciples and learn to nurture others into discipleship, in some way we have to translate "educate" into "love." *That is why this subsection is here.* It is a new synonym for church educators to meditate and pray upon. Just remember that to say, "To educate is to love," is not quite as strong as saying, "Educating is loving." For me the participle is very warmly subjective. The infinitive is a bit formal. With C. S. Lewis's backing I will again remind you that even in the most trying and unlovely of teaching situations it is a righteous thing to exercise the "the will to love." Constant practice will lessen any concomitant trace of hypocrisy as we inch on toward God's perfection. Since enlightening hypocrisy is loving, we can safely proclaim that it transforms abstraction into action.

SECTION 3. THE ROBERT RAIKES SYNDROME

Identifying Its Lingering Traces in American Churches

We begin in the mid-eighteenth century in England. Its Industrial Revolution was in full swing. Factories were soon scattered throughout the countryside. The slums of English cities were being developed and coming into view for Charles Dickens to pictorialize. It was soon evident that the scourge of that early industrial age was the abundant child labor for the textile mills. Children were put to work at the tender age of seven or eight and worked twelve-hour days. Robert Raikes, a layman, observed these exploited lives, weakened bodies, and blocked, illiterate mentalities and compassionately rose up to do something about it. Using Sunday afternoons as the only available time and the Bible as his textbook, Robert Raikes began the Sunday school program in 1754. The clergy was not initially involved. But so began the innovation which was to develop into the right arm of Protestantism.

For two centuries the Sunday school program has remained almost entirely a layman's movement. Responsibility for supervising and teaching has remained essentially the laymen's function up to very recent times. It is an anomaly within the Christian Church that it should have remained so for such a long period. Indeed its stepchild status kept it outside official churchdom until its transmigration to the American shores. Here, the official church, through the clergy, very early saw the advantage of adding the catechism to the Bible, making two texts. Many nonliturgical churches depended almost entirely upon miscellaneous sources of printed helps, again without direct church connection. The International Sunday School Association was organized and though clergy was included, mainly to help prepare the lesson topics, the organization has always been in lay hands. The circuit rider, a visiting preacher, was infrequently present in many primitive communities, and laymen took charge of week-to-week gatherings.

Setting up a Sunday school was an important way to start a new church in the wilderness. But these denominations did not have financial budgets for much publishing action, and gradually a strong group of publishing houses took over practically all the curricular printed lesson helps available. Clergy helped their lay teachers select what each church subscribed for, but since the loyalty of lay teachers was involved, the clergy did not insist on much control. In the face of the basic problem of securing willing teachers and maintaining an organization in their absence, the clergy exercised little or no supervision over the actual lesson material prepared to be presented by an untutored lay person. They depended entirely upon their sermonizing to make sure that theological concepts would be traditional in nature, trusting they could correct any errors made by lay teachers. The concomitant influence of independent publishers is still largely maintained. The clergy, in sticking to its pulpit ministry, taught the confirmation class each year in preparation for the Easter membership drive. They would then make up what their lay people had not been able to cover effectively. No matter how one tries to evaluate it, the Sunday school, for over two hundred years, has essentially remained a stepchild of the church. Essentially, lay Bible teaching is "blessed" by the clergy as a later help but not vitally absorbed at seminary level into the planning that must be depended upon to undergird the "proclamation of the Word." It is my personal opinion that perhaps Protestantism, in the beginning, leaned backwards too rigidly in distancing itself from the Roman Catholic idea of a class of trained professionals, its nuns, as teachers of the common people.

A very concrete example of this at the upper level is presented by some theological seminaries. A School of Christian Education may be found in close proximity on the same campus or nearby, but they are essentially organized with separate faculties, presidents, officers, and business staffs, although there may be some cooperation and overlapping in the matter of the faculty and teaching assignments. For some reason, the Protestant Church clerical hierarchy has not been the amoeba it should have been, throwing its arms out around the stepchild and absorbing it totally into its sustaining self. It would appear most sensible if such seminaries and such Schools of Christian Education were to become one integrated organization within each denomination. The ministerials would all be required to take basic courses in Christian education, including basic pedagogy and psychology.

Instructing a confirmation class, suggesting the effective ways of making intramembership home visitations during a church canvas, enlarging the duties and mission of an elder or deacon, counseling a couple planning marriage or abandoning a current marriage, assuming responsibility as a pastoral segment of Hospice programs—these activities are just as much part of a church's Christian education program as specifically advising Mrs. A how to teach a sixth-grade class in presenting the story of the manner in which a scheming, rascally Jacob was converted into God's national leader, marked with a lame leg. The Raikes syndrome is going to remain with us as a blockage to good, effective Christian nurture just as long as the seminaries condone the old traditional idea that "to educate" is equivalent to storing facts picked up in a formal class. When folks in the community of faith still insist that the word "educate" means transferring facts of Bible stories into a mind as computer-stored inventory, believing that somehow with the miraculous power of God this is going to be fed into the active, existential, living conditions of our Space Age lives, we are missing the high hope of God's expectancy. It does not really matter whether we call the neophyte pastor/minister the Master Proclaimer, or Master Teacher, or Master *Agape* Lover, for essentially they mean the same. Let us all admit that the end goal, the one we believe God sets before us, is the extending of loving relationships to all others, which Jesus tried so completely to exemplify and show us.

The preceding paragraph makes it clear that we are approaching our conclusion: It will be up to the ordained clergy to snuff out the

99

remaining die-hard traces of the Robert Raikes syndrome. This is the subject of the next section of this chapter, but I believe that we first need to recognize that in the recent decades of our Christian education there is an underlying change in the meaning of terms used to describe the goal we are seeking. The first term is the word "school," as used in the public school sense. No matter how an individual may have changed his ideas of what he wishes the public school to do with his child, there is a tradition-bound link between the words, "class," "teacher," "text-books," and "quiz" (or examination). Later on in this chapter I describe such a procedure as carried out by a college research team in upper New York State. One is not actually upset to discover that they found that studying a series of facts as told by others about spiritual living does not a Christian make, which is another way of stating that the student who was consistent in putting down the "right" answers for his string of A grades could turn out to be the lowest-grade, meanest kid in the class.

In other words, we Christians know intuitively that understanding the facts is not equivalent to their motivation and execution. The spiritual life demands something more. But we are slothful in our attempt to do something about it. You are expecting me to tell you somewhere in these pages how this can be accomplished. I am sorry I cannot be of more help. You and I are both alike as we read about Paul's experience. We have very good ideas about our Christian life now and then, but probably because Paul's teachings would revolutionize our own lives, *we do not follow them.* Paul says it for all of us: *I know what is right but I do not do it. I deliberately do the opposite.* That is why the public school teacher is not automatically an effective Christian teacher. Proper approach, pedagogically, makes the public school teacher feel at ease in the educational programs of his/her church, but it is not a guarantee that John and Mary are being nurtured into the Kingdom of God. We are now asking ourselves why we do not do more deliberate planning in the direction of sharing projects. I cite our citizenry being attracted to the American Heritage program. In the same way Christian adults can share in the revitalization of Christ's Church. A good example: the Methodist men and women who volunteer each year and man the construction crews going into the West Indies and Latin America in the spirit of God in Christ. We sometimes forget that nurturing Christian loving in such projects is just as important and just as enjoyable for adults as with the young members of the faith. Nor does the sharing action have to be limited to building churches and parsonages in a distant spot. Our communities have sick people, handicapped people, poor people to be taken care of. We like to talk, talk, talk, as we proclaim from the pulpit and from the leader of the study class. Now let us match the loving talk with some *doing*. Surely it means actually sacrificing of ourselves. Is not that what Jesus' life meant?

In preparation for the discussion immediately following on the place of the ordained clergy, allow me to fire a warning shot. All too many church members use the term "Christian education" only for those actions we take on Sunday mornings in the gathered community. God forbid that we retain the notion that a minister or director of church education works *only* on a program on which is plotted an hour at church on Sunday morning and in many instances does not mentally and spiritually connect it with the second hour of worship with its central preaching. It is my opinion that when pulpit preaching in the regular local worship service comes to be firmly held as an integral part of Christian education, we will have arrived at the millennium of Godly expectations.

Also, a second warning shot: No church should hire an "education-al" leader to be in charge of the total church education program who is not an ordained theologian. Nor should the senior minister fail to act in a real supervisory capacity over the total educational endeavor as its dean of instruction. The modern Protestant Church in America has not yet decided how best to approach its objective of effective Christian education. We now recognize that the problem is whether to treat the subject as an accumulation of Christian stories, of Bible history, which counts on a skill in educational methodogy directed toward the mind; or shall it be the establishment of an in-church center of *nurture* and *practice* of the faith, directed by and toward the Spirit; or shall it be both? In the meantime, the Robert Raikes syndrome prevails, and this means "Time is Wasting."

Applying Ordained Leadership to Christian Education as the Cure for the Lingering Syndrome

Let us briefly review the American situation since World War I. When Dr. Paul Vieth received his doctorate from Yale Divinity School, his thesis, "The Objectives of Christian Education," became the classic text for most northern ecumenical teacher training schools in the

CARL A. RUDISILL LIBRARY
LENOIR-RHYNE COLLEGE

church. We set out to master the seven basic objectives, but as always we found that Christian publishers had their own ideas as to how to implement the teaching, which was heavily content oriented. Some relief was provided when the Department of Christian Education of the National Council of Churches was organized and later saw to the establishment of the monthly *Journal of International Christian Education.*

In the thirties, Dr. Ernst Ligon, who ran the psychology department at Union College in Schenectady, New York, established a project in the Westminster Presbyterian Church in nearby Albany, New York. My friend, Miss Dorothy Fritz, well-known Christian educational expert of the time, was its director of Christian education. A number of us in neighboring churches were intensely interested. Exact testing of individual students before and after certain courses was carried out for a number of years. You have probably guessed that the results on the whole substantiated the conclusion of Protestant religious education of children in the first half of the twentieth century in America. *Professional teaching of Christian knowledge, no matter how skilled, is not equivalent to the creation of Christian commitment in a life of faith* within the receiving individual. Westminster Church and its minister remained on its given course. Mere facts do not equal love in action.

With the development of the progressive educational movement in the public school system a bit later, churches began to accept the idea that passive absorption of facts in the classroom had to be altered to one of participation and action in *new types of activities both in and out of the classroom, which establish relationships.* Love cannot be kept alive on a shelf. Christian education must become Christian Nurture. We are all familiar with the saying "Character is not taught, it is caught." In a nutshell it means that the children's division of the church school is absorbing the stories about God and His human family and His appearance in Jesus, always with a thought-provoking question left in the child's mind: *Why and how did people feel?* Feeling is a part of nurture. From the prior two generations there are many memories of an Aunt Bessie and her girls' class forming at a young age and following along the years together until high school graduation broke them up. She did not really *teach* Christianity in the pedagogical sense; her girls caught her loving character from her. She expended herself as Christ's servant. But Miss Bessie's world is now the Space Age and I am sure that we must add something to the training of our group of nomadic fathers and

102

mothers and families in their present anticipation of an effective twenty-first century church. Our TV tries to teach us that life is made up of snapshots of quick action, and not much meditation behind the action. The Space Age Church must not follow in like fashion or fail to put its educational program under theologically *and* pedagogically trained pastors *who can mold the public school teacher in the church community into a Christian activator of nurture.* This activation must be led with special training from the pastor who will educate them in the sharing activities of the Spirit, as they are already trained in the mind.

We have not seen as yet a real program of pastors training the lay educators (as they, the pastors themselves, were trained in the seminary). It ought to be taken for granted that the pastoral job description demands this. At that point church membership should begin to feel the catalytic presence of new power from God. The whole church is a University of Life.[4] The pastor is its dean of nurturing education. He should prevail in having his session, vestry, deacons, administrative board, official board, or whatever the governing body of that church is labeled, retrained to accept the idea that he is the chief officer of the church's school. The entire community of faith is a school. The top priority of that body is to see that the person or persons called into the pastorate be properly equipped professionally to closely supervise the total educational program. This board's *first* thought ought to be not how to raise the annual budget but to insist that the pastor maintain an educational training program within that board. This ought to be much more than the annual two or three sessions with new deacons and elders after the annual elections. *Every* regular monthly meeting of the board ought to devote half the available time to its Christian educational obligation as a nurturing obligation. The pastor sets an example as dean of instruction. *I am absolutely serious about the position of the senior minister.*

Under such a commitment the official board, which can hire but one minister/pastor, must insist that the person have earned a seminary major in Christian education along with his knowledge of theology, psychology, and his Greek, and his Hebrew. It means that in no case shall the board hire a single person to be pastor without the Christian educational major, simply because this candidate in his appearance before the "Search Committee" or a possible trial visit in the pulpit impressed everyone with his eloquence and ready wit. Eloquence and wit will always be plus factors in Christian education too, but if the person does not have the major in Christian education *do not hire him/her* (or arrange for an immediate Continuing Education project so that the deficiency is made up within a few years). What a difference one full generation down the road would make in every loyal segment of Christ's Church. Let this not escape the notice of the larger Church which may be able to support a multiple pastoral staff. The accompanying corollary for this is that no ordained person be hired who has not earned at least a seminary *minor* in Christian education. In brief, the seminaries should look upon their obligation to the churches and take it as a natural assumption that their graduates must earn a minor or a major in Christian education; and at best not in some associated institution but *within its own internal self.* The Robert Raikes Syndrome will tend to remain as long as a secondary source of this training is depended upon.

My young pastor who fully appreciates my melded nurturing-teaching-loving approach has pointed out that probably not very many young pastors/ministers will understand me well enough to accept and apprehend my view that he/she is the chief or Master Teacher in the church's educational program. He tells me that tradition, in the matter of the old definition of terms, holds the pastor/minister quite firmly to his/her original ordination vow to *proclaim the Word* as his chief and holy mission for Christ and His Church. I reiterate my personal view that our seminaries have not done their best in meeting the challenge of proper preparation of the pastors/ministers for the Space Age. They *must* enlarge their sense of mission beyond that within which tradition has entrapped them. Such a mandatory enlargement of mission must include defining the word "educating" to mean "loving." Putting it another way, the new pastor/minister's need to proclaim the Word must be matched and melded into his aim to be on the constant alert to teach by conduct as well as by precept, not only in his personal life, but by new sharing projects throughout the church and community. The proclaiming and the loving are as one, therefore, in executing the church's nurturing program. The pastor/minister in brief, is the chief *agape* lover. He must show others how to do it. The chief teacher/lover may not formally teach a regular Sunday school class, but he must personally see to it that his elders (the official board) are undergoing training during a portion of most regular meetings. He insists upon and personally shares in the athletic program of fellowship and fun as well as worship in the church camp periods. He sees that the unchurched of the community are searched out and nurtured into a caring relationship instead of being left in limbo as statistics. The coming new age pastor/minister, in my opinion, is going to lead his community of faith to certain spiritual death if he insists on the predominance of eloquence and dramatics in the pulpit and keeps preaching words as his only number one aim. I am sure God will expect improvement in the interpretation of the ordination vow once preaching is placed in the proper relation in support of loving and nurturing *action*.

It appears that our seminaries have taken a laissez-faire stance from way back. They have assumed that determining the substance of theology is their sole high calling. And since for Christian theology the Bible is the chief source of the revelation of God, the languages of J and P and Jesus and Paul are studied in thorough detail. Contemporary communication between professors, and between professors and students, carried out in basic English with American idiom, is also influenced by the incorporation of ideas of foreign theologians. This language dealing with God can be perceived as moving in two strata. There is one on an elevated plane for discussion and written communication among the professional theological experts and a lower, less technical and precise, which becomes the basis for sermonizing in the local pulpit. One sees this reflected in the two types of theological doctoral degrees; the Ph.D. in Theology and the more recent D.M., Doctor of Ministry, which a few seminaries are now initiating. But our congregations are mixed groups. Misapprehension of sermon terminology will result and even though the preacher may repeat his verbal exposition in various approaches, he must devise working models within the membership and demonstrate what he means by helping to *do* it.

The seminary appears to present the world's best sermons as the basis of a study of Homiletics, i.e., the "art" of preaching, but shuns the instruction of the neophyte in possible ways of setting up the equally important loving, nurturing program of daily life that follows. The seminary does not set up nurturing projects, which one might call "lab work" comparable to what the physical science candidate expects. Thus, training in how to put the words of a sermon into practice is left in limbo. Expecting the seminary student to test the temperature of the water in a summer assignment to a church of his choice merely confuses the issue. The summertime activities do not reflect the average tempo and quality of a total yearly program in either substance or personnel.

I would suggest that for one full academic year, the student be assigned to a carefully selected church situation as an integral part of his course work. He would remain in close communication with his seminary base professor, who would counsel him in special study, analysis, and allowable execution of changes in approach. Bringing these experiences back to the seminary would strengthen both the student and the professor in their understanding of what is going on out there. There need be little increase in a three-calendar-year approach to the doctor's or master's degree if one where willing to consider a *year* as twelve full months of successive academic work instead of the traditional eight or nine.

The difference between the theology student and the physical science student is obvious. From day one, whether he begins in high school or college, the physical science student faces the actual environmental operation of some mechanical equipment and apparatus. His language involves what he himself has actually seen, heard, smelled, felt, or under observation may have carefully tasted. In college he will generally have been taught by a Ph.D. in his particular science. In the university he may be taught by a doctoral candidate under the supervision of his research mentor for the laboratory work and occasionally also in the full class work. Such younger "teachers" will be watched sharply by the older person in charge. By a trial-and-error approach the doctoral candidate who is finally granted his degree is rather sure that teaching is for him. He may add a postdoctoral year to his experience to confirm this before leaving the university. He will have selected teaching as preferable to going into industry or government service as a laboratory research scientist. The teacher will then make up for most of the lacking formal pedagogy by attending worships at the homes of his peers in his specific branch of science. They are rather constantly trading ideas of approach. After chemical reactions have taken place, the recorded data thereon are discussed, and in seminars or class discussion, possible new angles of approach are studied. Perhaps atoms and molecules are diagrammed on the board or given 3-D perspective by constructing models. The point we are making here is that, quite unlike that of theology, the physical science vocabulary and resultant understanding is easier to comprehend because all five senses are being combined in the process of transferring ideas from mind number one into mind number two and back again as each reinfluences the other. About the only place where pure pedagogy comes into play is in the matter of which phase of the subject follows in the best sequence so as to lead quickly to full understanding. For example: do we start with the subject of inorganic (minerals), or organic (carbon) materials; or do we construct models of atoms and molecules that make up our universe's one hundred basic building blocks. Or we might add a pinch of interdisciplinary physics and start with chemical examples of the three states of matter, i.e., solids, liquids, and gases. We may attempt to confuse the beginner by starting with a description of the energy that holds things together and responds to temperature and pressure. The point is that by trial-and-error experimentation and a recording of results, we eventually justify our choice of a future method.

The professional Christian theologian who is placed in charge of a community of faith as its pastor/minister has no such handy framework of experimental results. Tradition tends to keep him in a tight grip. "You cannot do that to the inviolate human mind and soul." So he preaches, i.e., proclaims the Word of God as he sees it revealed in Jesus Christ, and then lies back, rather helplessly it seems, awaiting the miracle of God to do the actual work. If little happens, "Do not be discouraged, He *will* answer you." So he continues to preach and wait. Of course he talks love and tries to make sure that his family lives as an example of that love. Examples sometimes take a very long time. Paul may be faulted for helping establish the tradition that in some miraculous way one can explain Christ's love and the Word will convict and draw the sinner into the fold. In his famous book of theology, Romans, 11:11 and 11:25–26 (NIV), he sets forth the view that in due time the fine examples that the Christians have set before the world will automatically convince his fellow Hebrews to the extent that they will capitulate and willingly fall into Christ's embrace. Were Paul here today, could he explain why his plan is not working so well? We recognize now that coincidental with Constantine's conversion in the early fourth century something vital was lost in the Christian message. As noble as no doubt he felt his act to be, the moment he by proclamation made Christ's Church the "in thing" for acceptable society, Paul's forecast flew out the window. Human deviltry is just too much. The beautiful lives of some saints from that day to this stand out as poignant examples of what could have been if professional theologians had been more effective and taught us to live as we talk. In brief, contemporary theologians ought to be doing lab work as well as talking.

How do we produce more Bonnhoeffers and Mother Theresas?

107

Under the impulse and demand of this fast moving age, it seems as though our seminaries should be straining to set up new ways of demonstrating that proclaimed Word, thus equipping and showing their students how to be Nurturers of the Word, i.e., DOING the Word as well as proclaiming it. *To train others to be chief lover, chief nurturer, chief educator, as well as chief proclaimer, seems to be the legitimate goal of a seminary* that expects its graduates to be the lighters of the incendiary fellowships that will be required for the age ahead. *When seminaries begin their lab work, the Robert Raikes syndrome will be pronounced dead.* Only then will we be able to set Gandhi's judgment of us aside. Remember, it is 500 years since Luther. It is about time for the Holy Enabler to shake us up again in a holy passion of revolution.

I realize that I have created a problem for that group of dedicated Christians who are graduates of denominational Schools of Christian Education and who are now serving as unordained Directors of Christian Education. I believe that such personnel could be afforded upgrading courses in theology by the seminaries under a continuing education plan; in much the same fashion as current Th.M. pastor/ministers who wish to earn the Doctor of Ministry degree while under active pastoral service may do so. The objective is to provide the unordained person with more substantial authority and special standing in the eyes of the congregation. Another possible answer for the larger churches would be for the pastor/minister qualified to be the overall Master Teacher as described above, to employ the regular unordained person as a main or supervising teacher under the ordained Minister of Education. Such a person would be a straightforward hired teacher yielding to basic planning *executed by the single pastor/minister;* or, in the case of multiple ordained leaders, yielding to that one who is designated as in immediate charge of the Church's educational program. I believe that we have made the point clear that our basic objective is to make the person serving as head of the Church's educational program an ordained pastor with a required Christian education major in his degree. In brief, if a multistaffed church wants to call one of the ordained pastors by the title Director of Christian Education, so be it; *but all churches should abandon the use of this title for unordained teachers.* The bottom line on the above proposal leads quickly to the question of how to recruit and train that hard-core nucleus of faithful Christian laymen and laywomen who are to fill the teaching force from crib to grave. We do not have to guess or grope for the answer. It lies in *ecumenicity.*

A great number of the Protestant churches in the south do not really know yet what ecumenicity means. They have a hazy idea that it is almost entirely made up of a Thanksgiving union meeting; possibly a reformation Martin Luther assembly some years; perhaps a union Easter sunrise meeting in the city park at Easter; and just possibly in the larger cities some abbreviated summer vacation plans, wherein during July and August several churches band together and take turns at leading Sunday worship. Most of these links are lightweight links. They are a facade of Christian activity that does not call for money or any hours of hard labor. Ecumenicity in Christian education is a horse of a different color. The training of lay Christian educators invites organizational input from every voluntary church in the community. It is my opinion that a major stumbling block to the wholehearted ecumenicity that is desirable is that the largest Protestant denomination in the U.S., whose Southern section does not hold its Northern siblings quite acceptable as is, makes its superior stance almost a closed door. We pray to God for yielding hearts and minds in the future, finally leading us into a sharing, fruitful relationship.

Three or four basic denominations ought to be in evidence. At this point these pastor/ministers with the Christian education minors and majors will sit down and survey the needs and wishes presented from such churches. They will select eight to ten weeks at a favorable time of year and will select the courses and teachers. They will find that a couple of those pastors/ministers with a Christian education major are going to want to jump at the chance to show off their wares and they will be eager to teach a community-wide gathering. A terrific advantage of the ecumenical training school is the increased resources available for library reference books. Publishers and book stores will provide displays. Also such a group can command the respect of an outside outstanding Christian leader here and there who may be secured for nominal travel costs and a modest honorarium. Such an approach to teacher training yields high dividends in the sharing, caring aspects across the Christian community. It is a catalyst for a neighborly relationship. It allows denominational differences to dissolve, temporarily at least, and pools the best Christian minds of the local area for the benefit of all.[5] Such a community program enhances and supplements the training ventures of the denominational approaches. Synodical, presbyterial, and associational educational leaders, given a new pair of ecumenical glasses, could better reach everyone in their far-flung borders with a quality program.

Ecumenicity practiced at this level by the main line denominations would (a) save precious operating expense, (b) insure self-policing of evaluations, (c) help secure a higher level of professional leadership, or where the latter is already present, release such leadership from superfluous duties which waste his/her time, and would (d) develop a respect for the united Christian Church's ability to succeed in a unified character-building program which will be recognized as being able to do what it says it can do. It would help refute the Gandhi type critics who say of us, "We love your Christ but we shun 'Christians.' "

At the risk of redundancy, we close this subsection with the following summary. Ordained leadership for the Christian educational nurturing program of the local church must be required, not for just a part of it but all of it. In my opinion, this is absolutely the only way in which the historical Robert Raikes Syndrome can be abolished and forgotten. Christian education must be shed of its stepchild status. Such a goal does not insist on the approach that the entire staff be seminary trained. It points in that direction. But it does call upon the local church, however small, to place its Sunday school and all educational accoutrements under the active, direct control of its session or official board, which will require that the planning and the direction shall be the responsibility of the ordained pastor/minister, or when the size of the church requires it, associate pastors who are qualified in like manner via their seminary training. A spate of new job descriptions all round is surely in order.

SECTION 4. THE CONFIRMATION PROCESS

A Special Moment

We here pause to question the validity of the pressure some churches place upon the sixth grader to "accept Christ as his personal Saviour." I speak from the background of a decade of managing a junior department with an average attendance of about 100 fifth- and sixth-grade pupils. The result is a strong conclusion that the *average* sixth grader is not yet ready for this important step. In those churches favored with a large number of public school teachers on the church school staff, there may be an awareness that perhaps *spiritual* development in a child does not necessarily follow the same pattern as the *mental* development upon which rests public school grade levels. The average sixth grader is just completing a strong storytelling and receiving experience. He is a hero worshiper and is enthralled with biographies with exploits galore. Although the public school teacher may be impressed by some sixth-grade scholars who seem to have good skills in problem solving in math, it is but a glimpse of what the seventh and eighth grader will be able to accomplish. The sixth grader is not a logical thinker. He can play games and assume roles in dramatics with great enthusiasm but he will not yet readily identify with a role he is playing. The sixth grader can love Jesus dearly and help Him but very few at that level can apprehend Him. The seventh grader has begun to think and he can be a distinctly different person, partly due perhaps to his being on the front edge of puberty. He now tends to avoid the dramatics loved the year before because he dislikes a particular character he must try to embrace. In brief, the seventh grader is now in a position where he can love Jesus Christ and then be able to follow through to a personal commitment with some real grounds in mind, however limited, for having made the commitment. He is at the fringe of young adulthood and many church workers in education are coming to the conclusion that junior high grades seven and eight and even ninth grade are the perfect grades at which to emphasize attendance in the confirmation class. Lengthening the whole confirmation opportunity to a full year of preparation *or more*, as the Lutherans now do, is now considered by most denominations very appropriate. However, denominational approval, up to the present at least, does not guarantee that individual pastors, under excuse of time, will not cut the instructions to a brief couple of months prior to Easter.

What is confirmation in a Protestant church? Regardless of when or how baptism has been accomplished, either in infancy or later, the step of teenage confirmation, i.e., being admitted to active membership in a particular church, follows appropriately after a suitable training period. Note that the descriptive term "training" is a specialized term implying *much more than a mere attainment of knowledge*. It is not equivalent to a student's extended time and study, which is capped with final examinations and a diploma, though there are similar elements. Confirmation in our religious sense implies sufficient study and action on the part of the novice to bring him/her to the recognition of the connection between moral and ethical conduct today and the life typified by Jesus so long ago. Through observation, listening, and reading, the student has absorbed considerable amounts of historical and spiritual facts stemming from our Judeo-Christian heritage. In Sunday school and family church these facts carry a special emphasis on Jesus and the first-century church. But this knowledge is of little value toward generating a new, fresher kind of life unless it generates a specific resolve, a *real commitment* to a new thought and new conduct. *Somehow he or she should be brought to at least a faint realization that the prior "good" family Christian life has not proven to be the complete answer to Jesus' expectation of what it should be.*

I feel compelled to take a firm stand in attempting to explain Christian commitment which may be misunderstood as too stubborn traditionalism. We require ample discussion. Let us take the example of a young teenager who has been brought up in the average "good" Christian home, which, we have implied, seems incapable of breaking new ground in the next century. Our teenager has had the usual average Sunday school and church experience. He stands high in his special confirmation class, where his pastor and teachers have reviewed the mighty acts of God with His chosen people, the life and teachings of Jesus, and the trouble Peter had nailing down the concept of God's covenant with the Hebrews as really the whole total human family. At this point of full factual knowledge our student must somehow, inwardly and privately, become a candidate for confirmation. Education in the facts and intelligence as to how these facts fit together is not sufficient. He must self-generate at least a faint first step toward making his life count for God in a special way. He has to become *different* in order to do this. We pray that he would have a consummate experience of newness, of passing through, opening a door to a new room, walking out over the threshold of a front door to fresh air, perhaps stepping out on the patio where Jesus is expecting him with outstretched hands; turning with him to recognize at the gate a group of people among whom are his parents and his friends. They are waiting for Christ to lead them up a new pathway rising toward the hills before them. Carrying a variety of tools the group seems bent on building or repairing and cleaning something ahead. Up to this point, Dear Reader, you and I are in full agreement. The youngster has committed himself to a task under Christ's leadership. But I now interject the traditional element I hinted at above.

Up to this point his *commitment* may consist only of a strengthened desire to do more of the *same* good works his family has been engaged in since his birth. Something, however, is still missing in the scenario. At the moment Jesus and he embrace each other on the doorstep there ought to flood over him a certain sense of unworthiness. He may stop for a moment to realize that he is not as "good" a person as he could be. We adults know that every good teenager is also apt to be an angry, quarrelsome, selfish teenager at times, for he is a "chip off the old block." At the moment of that doorway embrace there ought to be a feeling of wanting to be a better person, perhaps feeling sorry, and a wish to let Jesus know how he feels. We traditionalists feel that "guilt" is a good word for it. In the warmth of the occasion he perceives Jesus saying "I love you, John, and despite what you may have done, I'll stay and help you all the way." You and I, in fully adult terms, might want to insist on the words like "confession" and "forgiveness," but remember: "When I was a child I thought and talked as a child, but now that I am an adult I see more clearly." We cannot impose too much upon the younger mind we are trying to lead into the fullness of life. There can be innumerable shades of meaning in between. The confirmants are infants in the Lord and they can take the first simple step of the infant novice. The spiritual genes should be in place, however, as he takes this first important step in his personal spiritual advancement. The elders can accomplish this if they are true to their own ordinations. (See "Adopt-An-Elder" later on.)

Now is the time for the candidate to appreciate the fact that he may be carrying two dormant diseases that he must be on guard against. They are the Encapsulated Home syndrome and the Milquetoast virus. These debilitating sicknesses are generally not recognized until later on in adult life, but the youngster can be trained and prepared to look beyond the range of early life in the home and set up a defense against them. Let him know what to look for. Elton Trueblood has described his idea of the "incendiary fellowship," which is Christ's Church militant. The implications are all there in the title. We Christians of today have become numb and weary of the disruption of the peace, radicalism, confrontation, and revolution. We would like to lay conflict aside for a bit. Are any churches today red hot blazing centers for getting Christ's work done? In contrast we close our eyes to ease the pain and slip into the easier, middle-of-the-road stance, prone to let George do the larger share of the job. When fathers and mothers of this ilk manage a home, the offspring naturally catch on. Social standing, affluency, and *wants* becoming *needs* and acquisition rather than giving and caring—seem uppermost goals. This is not recognized as a conscious trend. The mood has become ingrained as a natural trait. Thus does the encapsulated home syndrome become the albatross of our future generations. Do you wonder why Trueblood is weeping tears in his teacup? And God also?

The Maladies in Our Churches—Reexamined

The syndrome is apparent when second- and third-generation children have come from "good" Christian homes, regular church and Sunday school attendance and activity in the youth fellowship, and yet seem to have lost the spark of spontaneous combustion when dealing with new ideas. The middle class, middle-of-the-road Christianity they have come by naturally is very pale and does not have any real zip. Unless some family tragedy has occurred, the young people just slide along into easy, unquestioning church membership. They grow up in our pagan, litigious culture, and take their later turn at wondering why Christ's Church, of which they are a part, is not more representative of the biblical A.D. 50 church. Occasionally they go on a retreat to try to reaffirm their faith.

If you will recall our discussions of the Growth Curve in Chapter 2, the Encapsulated Family can be seen as a pertinent illustration of what happens in such a family during three generations. Grandfather was an active saint of the church. He was gung-ho on practically everything his church undertook. Time, talent, and money were all poured out in behalf of Love. He represents the first third of the curve, starting from scratch slowly but quickly thereafter shooting for the stars. His son, well trained in generosity by inheritance, continued as diligent worker for much of the younger period of his life. But he slowly began meeting fewer and fewer travelers on the road to Jericho as compared to his father. He occasionally rested on the laurels of his family's past. The encapsulating skin of self-satisfaction was beginning to form and some of the interest in all parts of the church fell off by degrees. One seldom heard him pray in public anymore. As time went on, he dropped his regular attendance at Bible class due, he said, to his inability to "sit for two hours" on Sunday morning. On the Growth Curve he was already out on the flat plateau, slightly sagging. Grandson was born into considerable luxury. The stories of family life heard in his youth were all pleasant ones. He "knew" he came from a "good" family. He did not need to work for

114

anything, either secularly or spiritually. Of course he went to Sunday school every Sunday. He received his third or fourth grade Bible, but he never read it thereafter except once when he took part in a discussion on the Word of God in his confirmation class. It was natural that he be in that class with the pastor. Remember, he was a good boy from a good family. He slid into church membership thinking he was following in his father's and granddad's shoes. Do you believe he was carrying any kind of torch? Actually he carried the snuffer. On the Growth Curve his position has continued on his dad's plateau but at a decidedly accelerating downward angle. By the time he is forty, unless he gets a jolt when his son reaches his confirmation class, he may well be expected to slip over the cliff to his soul's death. In the twenty-first-century church he is apt to be one of the dead albatrosses hanging from Christ's neck.

The Milquetoast virus which has been carried along with the mild Christian genes develops quite naturally. Most pastors have to put up with a goodly portion of the church suffering with it at one time or another. Sermons just do not do any good. This virus lives up to its name, producing weak-kneed, mushy-backboned, timid, shy characters who are incapable of making tough moral decisions. They find it difficult to take a stand on whether YES means NO or vice versa. This malady is easy to recognize, should you hear one of the following well-worn cliches: "Let George do it, I don't have time," "I live too far away, you guys do it," "I do not know how, and I don't have time to learn," "I can't lead a worship service," "I can't talk in front of people." Milquetoast always keeps quiet when some friend is being criticized or a race is belittled. Milquetoast would not do anything differently than his crowd does it. Peer pressure is his motive for most things to do, or say, or wear. Milquetoast cannot say no to alcohol, drugs, tobacco, or immoral sex (i.e., extramarital). Does peer pressure work in your church in the confirmation class? Does it really *force* persons into your membership who have no intention of doing anything other than going through the motions?

Junior High—Foster Fathers

In a general fashion we have previously discussed Christian education for the Children's Division and left it to the inherent sharing nature of the family, both at church and in the home, to implement the Christian nurture of the young child. The goal was to lead the child toward a more intimate relation with God in the steps of the boy Jesus. Logically, we would next engage our youth of high-school age but instead of meeting their needs head on, let us approach them obliquely through a section of the Adult division that we often neglect. There is a possibility of intermingling the problems of both youth and adults where the resulting intergenerational mix will aid both groups in developing a higher level of spiritual consciousness.

There is probably no such thing as an "average" adult church member. Certainly no statistician could draw a theoretical average church person because practically all the data are in a qualitative rather than a quantitative state. Let me call this person a male, because I am a male and I know that the average church *man* does not measure up to the average church *woman* in several ways:

1. He attends church one Sunday in three. (Remember, Protestant church attendance is officially stated to be in the 33–40 percent range.)
2. He seldom if ever attends church school although he sends his children.
3. He is a good father and wishes to see his children with a better future than his.
4. He believes in God but does not pray much, if at all, outside of listening to the pastor in the church.
5. We conclude that he is a Christian believer but is not fully committed, at least in the sense that the church program is *not his top priority.* He would much rather play golf, watch football, tinker on his car, grow roses, hoe his cabbages and tomatoes, or just loaf in the bosom of his family.

We would hope to discover a new way to try and make use of his latent generational potential in the service of his church family. I can assume that God is not too happy with the picture of his life. I know that his pastor and his church school superintendent (and the finance committee) wish they could give him a shot of spiritual adrenalin. Why is he the subject of this page? He is here because "I have a dream."

I believe in the Community of Faith as a Family. We know that Mr. Average Church Man is a family man too. It is one thing about him that we thank God for. Mr. A. C. Man can be approached by his church through his family. He has a couple of children. Pretty soon one of them is going to become a junior high student as he enters the seventh grade. Now we have A.C.M. in a corner. The bait is his interest in his own child. The church has the trap all set. It has come to the conclusion that that portion of its new membership that feeds directly on its own fruitage, namely the confirmation class from its own church school, needs a lot more parenting love than it has been receiving in the past. Word is getting around, wifie having brought the news of a special course being set up for fathers of the junior highs. It is soon apparent that something new is actually underway.

This September a brand new set of lesson materials covering three whole years of junior-high study will be installed. Every junior high student will take it. There is no beating about the bushes. This new material is going to show how to get along with people, how to choose Christian values for one's future life and conduct in the Space Age. It will deal with temptations, drugs, sex, booze, and in the midst of it, Jesus is going to be there to show the youth that they have a partner and a helper. The seventh grader who probably does not remember the word "disciple" from his sixth-grade work or cannot give a complete definition of it by the time he is a ninth grader can now begin to work on it. He will have an opportunity to make a voluntary declaration that he wants to be one himself. What a dream! Finally, Mr. A.C.M. gets the message. *All* junior high fathers report at the church next ——evening at 7:30. He faints when he finds out that he is expected to be a foster daddy to another child other than his Bobby, but he admits that Hank Brown, his neighbor, can be trusted to pal around a bit with his boy.

But he still questions the new setup. "Why can't I be a good daddy to my own child? Sure, I know he will have a little trouble with some of the teenage behavior tantrums, but I'll handle it all okay." After he and his wife have attended the first session on the Parenting of a Teenager he begins to see some sense in it. He is going to have to talk about some things he realizes would be embarrassing to discuss with Bobby directly. And he trembles for sure when he is told that he must prepare a very short prayer for every visit he makes with his foster son. His wife is tickled to pieces at the turn of events. he distribution of foster fathers among the junior high students, depending on the size of the congregation, may need some special planning. If there is a short supply of foster fathers who already have a junior high student in the family, it would be natural to include willing fathers from younger families or, as a last resort, men who have no family. Current divorce figures provide ready candidates. There is also a bit of a problem in the case of the families who have either spouse as a member of the church's top management board, such as elder, deacon, administrative board member, vestryman, et cetera. We will shortly be discussing the position of fosterelder that is being developed in my present church. The fosterelder is appointed (chosen) for those who have already committed themselves or are about to do so. The fosterelder becomes an active member of the confirmation worship service at which times the teeners actually take on full membership. But more about that later.

In the case of the overall junior high foster relationship the purpose is to activate a section of the rank-and-file membership of the church, which needs to see its place in the New Church of the morrow. It is definitely a two-way program. The work and time put into the parenting class of fathers and mothers is, in my opinion, just as worthwhile as the single path position of fosterelder. The Parenting Class will have to have some outside expert teaching personnel if the church does not have qualified folks in its membership. It is a self-help program for initiating the plan but the teaching leadership deserves to be the finest that can be procured. Certain of the theological points being driven home in the morning church-school class will naturally come into focus in the Parenting Class, which incidentally could just as well be held on Sunday morning as well as a weekday night, or on alternating weekday nights and Sunday mornings, to favor the moms. This class also fortifies the foster fathers for their intimate visits with their foster pupils. Topics for discussion will rise naturally for both the foster parent and the teenager.

In line with my personal inclination to see things in a little sketch or outline, I will summarize what we have just been through, using brief headings and short phrases:

The Foster Father Program As Applied to Junior High Youth

Objectives overall:

1. Wake up the average middle-of-the-road church parent by reenergizing the Man of the house (Mother follows suit).
2. Establish intergenerational values of the religious life for the junior

high student as he comes in contact with others outside his own home.

3. Recognize the growing problem of family separation and single-parent situations; the teenager needs both male and female parenting.

Meeting and Classes:

1. The Parenting class should plan on a minimum of six one-hour sessions. A suggested schedule: monthly September through February. Be sure the teaching is at least half by professionals (or semi-).

2. Foster father meets with his foster teen monthly during the school year. This can be anywhere convenient. It should be private. The meeting should be closed with a very brief prayer. The father should try to get across the idea that a good Christian has to talk *to God* as well as *about God*.

3. It is suggested that abstracts of the weekly class material in the morning church school be prepared and distributed at the Parenting class, or placed on posters and/or newsprint paper on an easel. As the children's sermon message in a senior worship service often does more "good" among the adults in the congregation, just so that foster teen's father will be getting the gist of the Church curriculum for junior high students at a level where it should catch on easily on his own personal inner video tape. He has been reenrolled in church school and does not know it. He is being reconciled with God to whom he made his own membership vows of commitment and membership many years before.

Further Delineation of the Junior High School Student

See comments again on pages 86–88 as to the differences between sixth and seventh graders. The latter is really beginning to think. Grades seven through nine may be considered the most difficult level in which to guide Christian development, but the way the modern church operates today it is also the most important recruitment area for the church of tomorrow. For over a half century we have done very little to solve the inherent problems which pursue the teenager. This has to be the place of hope for the future. Were I an unseen author drawing a sketch of the possible church of A.D. 2000 (please allow my fantasy full play, with some exaggeration of mind and spirit) this would be my sample church program of the future:

A special three-year CONFIRMATION CURRICULUM, not unlike the new 1988 AFFIRM curriculum of the Lutheran Church, is taken by all junior high students.[6] Just prior to the September organization every rising seventh grader will have been assigned as a foster Christian to a foster father (and backup mother). A foster father and mother may be two single parents. A backup foster family is named at the same time so that the student does not fall between the adult cracks of sickness, out-of-town assignments, and "acts of God." There is no excuse—this student is a foster member of an active foster family. The foster family has already been to several sessions of know-how discussion so that they will be on their toes waiting. The foster father sets up a visiting schedule. It is not less than once a month, September through May, and at least once during the summer. The foster father takes responsibility for seeing that times and events are adjusted to meet the schedule of the student. The student cannot be expected to follow the vagaries of the foster father. The latter has pledged in these visits to take up in any fashion they wish these important topics: his childhood and early days in the church, especially his becoming a church member, a discussion of his biggest problem as a teenager and what the church did, if anything, to help solve it. He will pray with the student at each visit. The prayer is by the foster father. *Each student will choose a project for the year.* The foster father will be a consultative partner in carrying out the project. The following are only by way of illustration: visitation to shut-ins, building an article for the church or youth center, distribution of Sunday church bulletins to selected people, doing chores for elderly such as checking out of and delivering library books, running errands, et cetera.

An Actual Experiment in Confirmation to Church Membership

The scene is a Presbyterian church in the upper North Carolina Piedmont.[7] The membership has reached very near the five-hundred mark. It is in a county seat, which, together with a contiguous town, makes them, in a sense, an outlying suburban area of the adjacent city with its population of approximately 45,000. Textiles, furniture, and farms abound. This church, though organized and built in the latter part of the eighteenth century and having been rebuilt in the nineteenth century into a substantial, sturdy, brick one, made no spectacular growth in numbers. Slowly developing, it had made only minor improvements in dining and kindergarten facilities until, in the early 1980s, under the energetic leadership of a new young minister, it undertook an expansion beyond its sanctuary space, which more than doubled the physical plant. This construction was long overdue. Such a long-range and sizable planning project was justified within the laudable Christian objective of establishing a *seven-day* working agency for Christian service to the entire community. It would be enabled to expand in an outreach service to the communal citizenry of the area. An associate pastor has been added to the professional staff and the operating budget has jumped from $135,000 in 1983 to $268,000 for 1990 during a period in which there was no slacking off in financial support while the remaining expansion pledges were being paid off. The keen observer reading the above summary will rightly conclude that the congregation as a whole is vitally alive and, if it can successfully fill its seven-day-week schedule, will have taken a giant step towards preparing for the Space Age in the twenty-first century.

This church realizes that in justifying the consumption of such a sizable portion of the Lord's money for local objectives, it cannot afford to slacken the emphasis on long-range planning. It is natural that this church enjoys a considerable share of younger families with a growing number of children. These candidates for future church membership are not sought merely to sustain the organizational life of the church but, under the urging and leading of the Holy Spirit, are being sought as a way of (1) overcoming the Encapsulated Family Syndrome, (2) building the spiritual reserve of its share of the body of Christ so that it can kill off all vestiges of the Milquetoast virus, (3) becoming a more significant, effective aid in support of the Parenting of Children with special emphasis on the teenager as he emerges into independent adulthood, (4) causing the creation of generally improved family life via stronger beliefs regarding the value of sacred marital sex as the best way to meet the rising tide of promiscuousness which seems to be accelerating our cultural downhill slide, and (5) enabling the younger adult section of the twenty-first-century church as an "incendiary fellowship" to carry the Christian Torch in a tremendous revival of creative spiritual sensitivity and consequent action which will rival the Reformation of the Church of the sixteenth century or—in brief—to create new varieties of Christian mustard seed and to develop new processes for the growth and full nurture and distribution of Christian leaven.

121

Now to the specifics of my church's experimental program for the preparation of the confirmation training and rites. Experimentation for Christ's sake is something the average Christian educator shuns whenever he can. His excuse is that he does not feel empowered to tinker with the inviolate God-given personality which he equates with his solid tradition. He wants a clean-cut curriculum with lesson helps and a guide all laid out in detail. But experimentation in this contemporary sense is not aimless fiddling around mixed in with some daydreaming. Experimentation has an objective. It wishes to proceed from here to there. Experimentation says there are several ways to go from here to there. Which one is the preferred one for us to try?

This takes communal consultation within the community of faith, and in this church the pastor is going to live up to his obligation of being the chief experimenter. His official board, the session of elders, is going to look at every possible detail, but my pastor/minister is going to lead the charge along a carefully laid out path. There just may happen to be an "inviolate" character or two to bargain with, but this pastor will pray the obstruction out of the way. The adult parents of the young prospects for confirmation want the experience to be meaningful, elders wish the church to grow both in number and quality, church-school leaders want to know how to adapt even the new curriculum materials to fit this specific church situation, and so there is a *truly united effort*.

Intuitively, these persons knew that an extra stint of study and preparation would be required. And they would not stop at study; they would act it, really *do* it. The preliminary study was intensely carried out for the session by its Commission on Christian education. Past and present leaders of youth and representatives of youth themselves had all been freely consulted. The highlight goals and plans were examined and confirmed by the session. Thus the complete package had been democratically determined under the leadership of the pastor and had deliberately enrolled as many supporting adults as possible in addition to the actual leaders/teachers. I believe we can say that education was beginning to be nurtured on a communal scale.

Step 1—The skeleton outline of the nurturing project is determined. This includes plans concerning timing, the public school grades to be involved, adult leadership, and the basic curricular material to be secured. The confirmants' class would begin in September and run through to the climax service on Pentecost Sunday. Since the regular church-school class was a consolidated class of several grades, this confirmants' class would become the junior-high class for the year.

Step 2—Under guidance of the pastor, a committee puts together a specialized course of study and action. The solid study portion included Scripture, personal and church history, ethical and moral issues involving choices, Presbyterian beliefs, and denominational differences, making faith a very personal and real thing. Appropriate passages for memorization were selected as a basic meditation kit for daily Christian life and prayer.

Step 3—It is determined that there will be a close integration of the morning class and the evening youth fellowship. All those in the morning class taught by lay leaders and occasionally by the pastor will be expected to be present in the evening. This fellowship will receive intergenerational input from a selected team of elders led by the pastor.

Step 4—As the year progresses each candidate intending to continue into church membership chooses an elder as his special buddy for the remainder of the year. He/she is an ADOPTED ELDER.

Step 5—The commission on Christian education with the advice of the pastor prepares a list of instructions on how to serve as this special ADOPTED ELDER. Upon compilation and final approval by the session, this list is sent *to every active and inactive elder in the church*. Depending on the size of the group wishing to finalize their confirmation to church membership, only a portion of the elders in the church will be ADOPTED, but the remaining elders upon receiving the instructions will be encouraged to reaffirm their own personal commitment. The teacher or teachers of the morning class will see that basic outlines of the course are prepared for the ADOPTED ELDERS so that they will have an overall view of what the classwork is attempting to cover. Basic instructions for the ADOPTED ELDER include: create a personal relationship with your confirmant, get his/her reaction to the classwork and reinforce its strong points, show details of how the session committees fit into the church's mission. The youth expects you to share your Faith, so take the initiative. Be prepared to affirm him/her at Pentecost. Afterward, pass on your creative experience to the session (your own or his/hers). Keep your sense of responsibility as an elder. Pass on something that is positive. Keep in mind your session is performing one of its major functions, outreach and in-gathering. *Pray constantly for the one who adopted you.*

Step 6—Youth Performance; the other side of the coin:

- Regular attendance at class and youth fellowship.
- Consistent attendance at church worship should match faithful attendance at class. This is heavily emphasized because in many church families the teenager is not pressured to remain for the congregational worship. During the year, visits should be made to worship services differing from the students' own, such as those of other denominations, a synagogue, and/or services of various racial or ethnic groups.
- Observing the church at work. Trips are planned for visiting national headquarters in Louisville and the local presbytery office. The candidate should be taken to a regular presbytery meeting and, with his ADOPTED ELDER, should attend a meeting of each of the important local session committees. His public school obligations may prevent a full attendance, all round.

Step 7— A trip to Montreal during the regular youth week.[8] Visitation should also be planned to include one of the church's shut-ins, a resident of a nursing home, and the Salvation Army.

Step 8—Spring WEEKEND RETREAT for junior high students and their ADOPTED ELDERS held at the church camp.

Elders will have prepared discussions of various aspects of our Christian beliefs. There will be several small group discussions of theological questions brought into focus by the pastor, dealing with, for instance, use of their everyday school life and home events to serve as examples of faith, trust, and acceptance and with worship and looking ahead in their lives, all this in a happy atmosphere of relaxation and good fun. If parental commitment and support has not yet been secured by those choosing to be confirmants, the pastor now sees that this is accomplished.

Step 9—Final visits at home: Confirmants and Adopted Elders.

Perhaps not every student will decide to make the public step at this time. He/She will have another year or two to be inoculated by the Spirit. Those who are finally committed will still have personal questions of faith and what will be expected of them on Pentecost. They will wish to clear these up with their older companion. The Adopted Elder will also by his/her experience to date with his/her friend probably see a missing link or two that ought to be ad-

124

dressed. This could be a final highlight for both of them. They will be expected to have a share in the dedication-confirmation service on Pentecost Sunday and will want to discuss last-minute arrangements for that service.

Step 10—Confirmation at Pentecost.

The Holy Spirit is certainly expected to descend upon each participant. In his/her public declaration of commitment, his/her elder will add personalized remarks and appropriate Scripture. In a clear sense, the elder at this point is representing the church and charging the neophyte in the coming new life among them. There are warm congregational greetings and the trust that each new young saint goes home to a congratulatory family dinner in his/her honor.

Christian Nurture of Senior High Students

We have so far left out direct reference to what might be taking place in the evening youth fellowship for senior high students. Church-school leadership has never forthrightly attempted to describe the ideal relationship which should characterize the smooth integration of the work of the morning class and the evening youth fellowship for both juniors and seniors. To say that the morning class is a study and discussion session and that the evening fellowship is more of an informal activity period, many times with the serving of a meal or refreshments and usually with a boy-girl courting element, is an oversimplification that overlooks much lost motion. Coupled with it is the matter of the adult couple or couples who act as monitor/leaders in the evening. These vary widely in concept of their leadership, some considering themselves merely as chaperones for acceptable conduct. In many cases true educational leadership is evident and the religious themes discussed directly reflect a concern for preparation for marriage, higher education, vocational choices, teenage temptations, and deep ethical and moral values. It would appear almost mandatory that the morning adult teaching and the evening counseling leadership ought to sit down together and arrive at a mutual agreement on what goes on in each time section. At least for a minimum time period, the two leaderships should get together on a quarterly basis or whenever there is a break between units of study. I have never heard of a workshop covering such an integrated approach. The progress of each individual member toward adulthood ought to be discussed by both leaderships in common.

Although it appears that we may be emphasizing junior high more than senior high fellowship, this has only reflected the emphasis we place on the early teens as the appropriate place for the foster father and foster elder relationship described as the important step of commitment to Christ and His church membership. Assuming that a three-year curriculum centering on confirmation during the junior-high years is now completed, we are challenged by the worrisome problems of the remaining youth period—tenth through twelfth grades. Statistics today in most churches show a sharp decline in church, church-school, and youth fellowship attendance. Whether such decline is the cause of, or the result of, the lack of any one ingredient is not clear.

What can be done to provide a more challenging church assignment for the youth of senior high school age? The constitution of such groups indicates a growing loosening of cohesiveness within them as graduation approaches. There are those who are now "confirmed" members of the church; those who chose not to be confirmed either with or without the wishes of their parents; and in city churches particularly, a group of uncertain character at youth fellowship—they represent one person in a boy-girl courting situation. In the latter situation, the stranger is most apt to be the boy who comes with one of the local church girls. A hidden factor, also, is the fact that some "confirmed" members will continue in morning church-school class and may disdain the evening youth fellowship. The free-will choices of life are now in operation and parental influence becomes less and less. This is youth in conversion to voting adulthood in our citizenry. One day we see a warmly yielding child, the next a violently independent anarchist who insists he is able to take to the airways alone.

In the past, responsible church boards have looked at their youth situation, clucked sadly with serious mien, and then have settled back and done little or nothing. They have, of course, urged that the adult leadership in the evening group be improved, but seeing that this can be done is another matter. Our communities of faith lose hold upon the young person but resolve to try one more angle before giving up. They hire a new young associate pastor as a "youth program" leader, give a sigh of relief, and immediately put the matter on the back burner, trusting that the next annual report will tell them all is well. Have any of our seminaries to date demonstrated that they can turn out young curricular reformers ready to lead senior youth to a loving adults (children) of God? The trainers of our pastor/ministers have witnessed the problem for a generation or more and seem to take little notice. The basic line in expecting the new young associate to have some of the answers is the fact of his own comparable youth. He/she were there themselves some seven years ago and perhaps will therefore have the magic touch of the spiritual lodestone, which will give these youngsters new insight before they totally give up the nest. At this point I must strongly reinsert my insistence that, although the young ordained minister is a proper immediate agent, the senior pastor/minister is the president of that University of Life and must see that the entire staff, including himself and congregation, are mobilized as one in the nurturing campaign aimed at reconciling its youth to the ideal that life has a spiritual profile after all. The senior professional head of his community of faith will know that even his young, enthusiastic, and able associate is still on a mid-point of his/her own ascending personal growth curve and will still have some challenging new experiences of his/her own.

I believe that we adult members have almost never recognized the necessity of following up the confirmation rites with a commissioning assignment that fits the age and limited experience of the young persons. Trying to make a capable church usher out of a boy is a waste of time. Perhaps more fruitful is drawing the girls into the teacher's aide assignments in the elementary church-school classes. But this only adds to the problem of the continuing high school Christian education wherein we should be concentrating on church history, Christian citizenship, marriage, vocational counseling, and supplying the religious element left out of the public school program on alcohol, drugs, and sex. I would recommend trial runs of youth social services programs, each with an elder advisor from the appropriate official board committees, thus immediately putting them to work where they can see and feel results. The elder will need to assign projects and follow through in consultative companionship. The result might mean senior high students be attached as *working* members in each session committee, assigned to special youth projects. In all cases, regardless, young confirmed members should be appointed to *all* committees and boards. They should be asked to give at least quarterly reports on these activities to other peers in either church-school or youth fellowship. The program would deal with real problems of our society where the situation calling for the necessary presence of Christ is strong. Good Samaritan projects will always appeal to young people, including some summer trips away from home on rebuilding and repair projects among the less fortunate. Do not forget regular visitation to nursing homes and retirement villages. Opportunities can be found everywhere.

There are two overwhelming problems requiring the finest, highest level of controlling and counseling oversight: the matter of preparation for sexual adulthood and, second, determining, if one can, the potential end point of formalized cultural education of both himself and the individual youth he is counseling. For a comment on the aspect of sexuality, I am absolutely traditional. Our man Moses got it straight from the Power and Source of all wisdom. Cut out all premarital sex and remain absolutely faithful to your current spouse. I am sorry that the word "current" had to be inserted. Our culture of the world has contaminated the community of faith as regards the strength of our marriage pledge of constancy despite the normal ups and downs of life. Divorce has become so commonplace. Our Space Age young people are not yet committed to the valid claim that *real effort* has to be expended in building a good continuing marriage. Are we well enough equipped for marriage counseling in the church?

The problem of higher education beyond high school is a many-faceted one. Currently our culture says that our children must receive the equivalency of a high school education to be culturally literate. But this is not to say that high school is the end of education. This lower level of cultural literacy can be built upon by a program of continuing education. There are both vocational and avocational demands for this. The prerequisites for vocational preparation are self-evident after the proper choice has been made. Depending upon one's socio-economic level, the demand for avocational education is more problematical. What was once held to be avocational in the individual's life may well develop into the vocational goal.

The American system of state-supported community colleges has developed to fill the need for preparation for life of a great indeterminate class of young (or older) people. Intuitively, the American culture has recognized that the high school level of formal education needs to be raised. It also recognizes that the one-time tendency toward using high school years for training in the trades could only be temporary or spasmodic. It robbed the student of the hours of overall general knowledge necessary for minimum standards of a good life. In making the community college curriculum widely adaptable to the needs of the citizenry and therefore worthy of taxation for its major support, it has developed curricula to meet the desires of a wide range of applicants. There is a large body of high school graduates who have no thought of college, who, in fact, as far as their academic grades are concerned, are insufficiently qualified for college entry. This group will include many ambitious young people of both sexes who are seeking vocational preparation for employment in a multitude of the newer type openings in this advancing age. From them will come thousands of nurses, medical aides of all types, computer and business machine operators, and engineers and mechanics for the trades from electronics to automobile machine tools to construction. A third group comprises a mixed collection of reawakened folks who for one reason or another have slipped through the cracks of high school years as dropouts. They have regained a grip on life and work hard to make up the deficiency and earn their equivalency diploma. The beauty of this arrangement is that a number of young people, not too sure of themselves or what they would like as life's work, can (a) test the educational waters and in college preparatory subjects may be able to qualify and enter a four-year school as high as the junior level, or (b) make entry into a trade.

I suspect that the church is not yet awake to its responsibility in this area of vocational testing, guidance, and counseling. A few on a denominational basis are taking first steps[9] but the real push is going to have to come from the local church. Again I question, does a seminary teach only theology to its young pastors? Local churches are still asleep in the face of the demands of this swiftly changing Space Age. We are working at better CONFIRMATION techniques. In the meantime, senior high students remain neglected. Perhaps ordained ministers of education will be the answer.

SECTION 5. RESOURCES FOR CURRICULA BUILDING

This subchapter required more time and effort in marshalling the original line of thought and in writing and rewriting the material than any other portion of this book. The writer still senses inadequacy in this final form. What must we do to simultaneously challenge a half dozen mainstream educational curricular departments to come out from their denominational dugouts and join in the greatest feat of cooperative lesson writing that Protestantism has ever experienced?

As a card-carrying, inside working member of four denominations,[10] I am aware that they all attempt special approaches to the pedagogical problems in the nurture of persons into the Christian faith. Perhaps they can be forgiven for feeling that they have a unique denominational touch which must be preserved at all cost. Let me assure you that from the inside looking out, except for a very few minor differences, 99 percent of the church curricular material for children could proceed out of the editorial office of an overriding ecumenical headquarters. In the case of the youth division which, of course, covers the age of confirming membership, one concedes that the originating history of each specific denomination is entitled to some special attention. However, we trust that denominational pride does prevent us from realizing that *we ought to pool our best talent from each denomination for the sake of all.* In my lifelong experience I have never known personally of an instance where a person has changed denominations because of a theological reason. Lay persons do not become Cardinal Newmans. They do not read and study enough for that. I dare say that within the membership roll of a single local church of whatever denomination there is a wider individual range of theological views and supposed denominational policies than exist officially among the denominations as a whole.

Every denomination has its expert lesson writers. Why not feel their good influence through a wider segment of Protestantism? Is it not true that Christendom is wasting its potential talent for progressive growth by not enjoying the skills of top notch writers *in whole rather than in part?* Do I err in concluding that the upper echelons of the denominational hierarchies still exhibit too much competitive pride in what they feel is their superior manner in presenting who Jesus was, what He said, and what He stood for? The proper answer is for Protestantism to become more ecumenical in the basic faith. What are we trying to prove, anyway? If some fine points and denominational theological niceties demand some extra attention at confirmation, this is easily supplied by securing appropriate supplementary reference material. Prior mention of especially equipped writers, such as Isabel Rogers and Albert Winn, has been made. Why should not such able Christian educational leaders be writing for a basic church membership of 30 to 35 million instead of the 1 million they did actually labor for?

Do denominational higher-ups continue to feel that they are serving the needs of Christendom best by their lonely struggle in the face of Space Age marriages, sex, family life, and discipleship of Christ in the street?—not to mention the fermenting areas of industrial production and commercial trade. Topping the picture is the stranglehold of financial empire building, which in the last decade reveals a streak of sinister disregard for the small-time investor via inside trading. Christendom is called upon to do a better job in the face of the avaricious greed of political lobbying interests, else even a Supreme Court will be unable to maintain wholesomeness of the democratic and revolutionary flavor of our Declaration of Independence and our 1787 Constitution. Consider how that Court still wrestles with the visages left in the wake of its one blemish before God, the sin of slavery. It is the moment now for an epochal change and improvement in the way we Christians ought to try to work as one. It would appear that unless something is done better in creating a strong unity in the next century, we believers will not be able to match the development of scientific, technological advance in the mind of humanity with a parallel development in our reconciliation with the Spirit. If we hold that Man is an organism, three-dimensional in body, mind, and Spirit, as we have noted elsewhere, it will have little effect on total culture unless we can more effectively integrate the combined resources of Christian church education. It must be more than mere proclamation.

May I draw a rough sketch of an educational scenario I have in mind? Securing the combined efforts of our best minds and spirits is an easy platitude. We accept the nice sound of unity it expresses, but it is apt to end there. There is no blood, sweat, and tears, which must result from real soul-searching in a common approach to the evaluation of what we already have. May I risk laying bare my naivete before the professional educators by suggesting a simple approach?

In the book *A Colloquy on Christian Education* (edited by John H. Westerhoff, III), published some seventeen years ago, a chapter is contributed by D. Campbell Wychoff. It is entitled "Finding Resources" and is appropriately placed near the end of the book to serve as a springboard from which the reader may leap into those resources without having to hunt. I submit the strong recommendation that such a chapter should not be consigned to history as merely a bypassed signpost list of titles. The later Shared Approach material and the Covenant Life Curriculum of the Presbyterians of the United States should be added to it. Further, Christian nurture in action ought to have this wealth of material *thoroughly analyzed* in detail, so that the average church's planning persons can see light being thrown on the answers to some of their needs. *I add this by way of slipping in a challenge for an evaluation group to perform for a share of Protestantism.* The analysis of this material should be classified by a neutral examining board in terms of an ecumenically established set of objectives. The actual lesson writers should not be members of the board of examining experts. They should remain apart from it but upon call be ready to explain and defend their individual productions. Were actual writers to be working members of the board, objectivity and unbiased dispassionate discussion would be next to impossible to obtain.

How to set up such an examining and evaluating group, which would be recognizable as to competency and impartiality, at least to a fair majority of mainstream Protestantism? It ought also to include minority members representing Roman Catholics and Evangelicals. The latter group presumably believes their church-school curriculum and its support materials to be quite sufficient unto themselves, but in the interest of fairness, representatives should be invited for their input. Inclusiveness rather than exclusiveness should prevail.

Again, let me repeat my belief that during the course of the evaluation, the actual appraisals written down in full and then rated from "superior" to "lesser" will automatically be erecting in the mind of the board a skeleton outline of what the most superior grade should look like. What is actually now on hand and rated as superior could prove to be less superior than it ought to be. By the same token the board might discover whole areas or themes of what ought to be found in a complete curriculum of Christian nurture but which is completely lacking in the material to date (i.e., programmed *actions* to supplement *content*). The full report of the findings thus becomes a Guide for Christian Nurture, because the weaker or missing themes would immediately incubate attempts to fill in the deficiency. At least I believe Christian writers would jump at the opportunity, knowing from the start that the offerings would be in demand. My scenario follows in several important actions:

First of all, God calls a special leader with broad Christian educational motive and experience. Such a person does not just pop up out of nowhere. He or she is a pastor skewed toward a Christian education major and is not past the age of willing experimentation. He/she may be a college president who is more interested and equipped in educational curricular aspects than in management and fund raising. Or he/she may be a high-ranking faculty member of a seminary that is generally recognized as interdenominational.

This leader, before going public, takes it upon himself to become acquainted with the top personnel in the Christian education division of a number of denominations known for past capacity and willingness for working together. Included will be some members of seminary faculties who are known to be particularly interested in Christian educational nurture.

The leader, having made the above acquaintance with personnel, invites selected persons to a powwow. If he feels secure enough he will add invitations to a few listening scouts from a couple of major denominations. If not, then he plans for this extra inclusion at a later meeting at which he may have more definite and optimistic plans. He needs to build a sympathetic nucleus and would look at a number of seminaries and make sure that the Division of Christian Education of the National Council of Churches is represented. In the case of recently united bodies such as the Lutherans and Presbyterians, the major component parts could well be represented. Such wider representation may reflect special understanding as to age groupings. We must remember that the curriculum outline we are preparing should be intergenerational, i.e., from cradle to grave, or more accurately a differential equation between the limits of zero and one hundred.

We have now arrived at a most important stage. The number one originator and kingpin will now preside over the formation of the exact procedure to be followed in the program of evaluation of present Christian education resources. To meet the needs of the Twenty-first Century, certain ground rules should be established. I strongly suggest that this evaluation be set up with emphasis on the future. Experimentation is kept in mind. This cannot be merely an evaluation of current resources, which, in the presence of very dim crystal balls, merely washes out as more of the same old stuff. Do not misunderstand me. A good deal of the "old stuff" will carry through as the raison d'être, a necessary backbone for the working tool for the new century. But before such selection can be recommended this evaluation group must become a long-range planning group. Objectives for church educational nurture for A.D. 2050 and beyond must be established against which the evaluation is measured. *It must be prophetic.* It ought to be evident that my vocabulary has already set the forward look at a new angle. The objective now is Nurture, synonymous with Action. "Christian," "church," and "educational" are modifying adjectives. We are after faith, character, and conduct. Content will be a necessary foundation block but it will serve as a means to an end, not the end in itself per se. Action and a working relationship in love are the objectives. Thus I see the main hurdle over which each studied resource must spread its wings in attempting to see if it contains a full approach to nurture for each major age grouping in our communities of faith.

The Traditionalist will note the report of the Resource Evaluation and, perhaps, choose more of the same, but if the advice of the board is followed it will not be exactly the same. He will find the resource materials already on the market and carefully judged and commented upon in terms of how well they meet the needs of Christian life and conduct. He will not order blindly from his usual publication source, but he may now select material for varied age groups with the specific needs of *his* church in mind. The idea of Nurture in the family of faith will be uppermost. The Traditionalist will have an opportunity of studying some material he never knew to be in existence.

The Progressive, on the other hand, will probably wish to try something his neighbor would actually consider too revolutionary. Many would feel inclined to follow closely the board's evaluation but would know that they may have a serious problem the current material did not seem to fit. Nothing in the available resources seems to quite answer the need for the youth one works with. Let this church experiment with a plan of its own concoction. Of course, no one individual below the pastor would make this important decision alone, but the concerned one may spearhead the search and bring the group and the pastor to a good conclusion. Another specialized concrete example is the idea of an "open school" for the children's division.[11] This would certainly require consensus of a sizable group, but the content of the nurture approach can still depend on some fine current resource material. Here and there may be a completely revolutionary type who says, "Throw out the whole works. Let's start over from scratch." So a whole roster of experiments are undertaken up and down the entire line. Even with this stance the report of the board as indicated above will have discussed the OBJECTIVES of Christian Educational Nurture so thoroughly that the revolting group cannot afford to pass up sampling a section of it. Experimentation may run the whole gamut of open-door rooms, family clusters, sharing groups,[12] work camps, social welfare projects, Christian citizenship, more evangelistic activity, attention to shut-ins, care of aging adults, Old Testament history, Old Testament prophets, Covenant Faith, and laic theology.

Paul left everything to governmental authority because he was in a hurry to get to heaven so that he might return soon with Christ. But today the strategies of peaceful resistance to that governmental authority should be studied, for it is mandatory that the Christian learn how to handle the situation whenever he is aware that God's law is above man's law and is not discovered via the ballot box. He may be pleased to compromise for a time but there will come a moment when he must be prepared to literally lay down his life for his Lord.

I cannot refrain at this point from focusing on one specific approach to new Adult study and action. This experience reflects one of the chief faults of present-day adult classes: all talk and no action. The Christian folks involved were a suburban group of warmhearted Methodist men and women who were forward-looking to the extent that they felt Bible study could be more than an inward study of Scripture dealing with situations 2,000 years ago. So a quite large and continuously interested Christian Citizenship Class developed. They looked at and studied the numerous aspects of what was going on in city, state, and national government. They tried to suggest ways in which laws and regulations could come closer to the Christian ideal. They were not adept at attending legislative and other governmental hearings and asking embarrassing questions. They never conceived of a public demonstration or even staging a public protest meeting. They looked at civil rights from the viewpoint of their comfortable chairs. It would have been abhorrent to write letters to the county commissioners complaining about the poor welfare service or writing a hot letter to the editor on this or that aspect of life that was not pleasing Christ. The goal of personal cleanliness and purity is clear and brightly shining, but the Christian who does not do anything about it in action, sometimes abrasive action, is indeed Mr. or Mrs. Milquetoast. Christianity, because of its perfect template in Christ, is embraced by contemporary mortal man who then hedges at the threshold of final, full commitment. We talk about a faith we place at the center of our prayers to Almighty God, but we shrink from the possibility of making ourselves vulnerable and keep away from the brink of utter conviction that we ought to be performing consistently with our talk.

So the work of the evaluation board consists of laying out such a learning and practicing program of Christian action based on a potpourri

135

of choices. Some will work better in your church than in mine. We will experiment together and perhaps our endeavor will bear fruitage in the way of newly published resources, How wonderful to anticipate successive decade meetings in the ecumenical evolution of Christian practice. The new track record could help put the church back on the upward swing of the century's Growth Curve.

The Evaluation Board that has succeeded in accomplishing the task outlined above will already have generated ideas as to how best communicate its findings to the supportive ecumenical communities. One would wish that at least an initial volume could be prepared and made widely available. Actual testing in the field may be desirable for the newer material. The board may wish to set up some simple machinery for (a) asking for reader reaction and (b) later asking for reports from those actually putting the guide into practice. Also, there might be some psychology of Christian education beamed to public school teachers, pointing out that fine pedagogy as a method of transmitting knowledge may not necessarily be Christian nurture. This century has already demonstrated that as a fact of life.

Another interesting question would be to determine if it would be an advantage to show some typical lesson plans for various age groups, in those specific cases where an idea being studied is definitely not completed without relating to other persons as an action in sharing love. A number of such projects could be spelled out, giving the teacher/leader an example of how an idea becomes a possible action. High school youth is a special area for which such examples of *doing* needs more attention and creativity. The report of the board will pay special attention to the meager accomplishments in development of our youth and lay out a challenge for competent writers to become creative. Youth needs to learn how to meet people apart from their peers and how to work with them in helpful projects, which are basically social betterment. The projects should emphasize actual contact with people outside the Encapsulated Family and the Encapsulated Church. The activities must cut across racial lines, ethnic cultures, and socio-economic boundaries.

Recently in 1980 there has appeared a brand new resource, which I must go out of my way to promote. It is John C. L. Gibson's *Daily Study Bible Series* (Westminster) and it will surely compare favorably to Barclay's series on the New Testament. I suspect that Gibson's work on the long-neglected Old Testament will meet some resistance from teachers who expect old-fashioned noncontroversial Bible themes. Nobody prior to Gibson seems to have had the intestinal fortitude to throw Ussher's Ancient Chronology into the garbage. I speak specifically of Gibson's two volumes on Genesis. Not only does he open up some of the first 464 pages of Volume I of the *Interpreter's Bible*, but he makes it as fascinating as an old-time Western. His Volume I deals specifically with the first eleven chapters of Genesis. Every Christian, young and old, should have read it by 1990. It leaves the literal, inerrancy theory of the fundamentalists lying out in the backwoods where it belongs. He makes Creation as a spiritual event real, powerful, honest, and thrilling to read about. He calls it by its right name, a "religious myth," but adopts the earlier term, "story," for common usage, because he wants it read by people who do not understand what this kind of myth is. (My words: A religious myth, in this case a Judeo-Christian myth, is a spiritual myth which describes God as a Person whom we cannot really describe, except to relate our experience with a faint perception of his mysterious attributes.) Gibson cuts the original J-1 and J-2 down to J and describes how editors J and P tell the early stories of these Semitic clans. He speaks of the "audience" assembled around the campfires on special religious celebrations, on the desert or in mountain glen, to enjoy the dramatic presentation of the story of the Garden of Eden. It is a command repeat performance and no doubt the Talking Snake, next to the voice of God, is the most important actor on the outdoor stage. Gibson speaks of the certainty with which the audience "knows" of the prior "epochal periods" of time in their history, of which they did not know the details of the beginning, but to which they attributed the power of their Yahweh, many generations before Abraham. Yes, by all means, add Gibson's contribution to the list of resources.

Finally, the Evaluation Board may find it helpful to choose a title for its report that is acceptable all around. If it is called a Guide, then the board has been successful in defining end goals and standards toward which such a guide leads. If, as hoped, it is truly a curriculum guide, then the high standards of our spiritual goal have been met by a very high type of melding of both content and sharing action. Would that it could be the new *Curriculum and resource guide for Christian education and nurture*. Should the board not see itself able to fulfill this total commitment, it may well suggest the formation of an auxiliary body to complete certain aspects of a total job. Or the supplementary body may be suggested to receive reports on progress made and become the evaluating committee of A.D. 2000 (see below).

It would be unfair of me not to answer a question that some of my readers will have raised at the beginning of this section: Where do I visualize the creation of the ecumenical Evaluation Board? Why did I neglect the existence of the Division of Christian Education of the National Churches of Christ in America? The answer is quite simple. This book was written after retirement, for which event we moved our home from the north to the south. The church people I became associated with in the south are not really antagonistic toward the National Churches of Christ, but a laissez-faire attitude is quite prevalent. People here, having a problem with their Christian education program, never think of phoning or writing to it as a headquarters or source of help. Everything seems so strictly denominational. A major hurdle here, in my opinion, is that the largest denomination in the south, with some ten million members, has remained under an ultraconservative elected leadership. Any definition of ecumenicity here is quite perfunctory. The professional men of the cloth maintain warm clerical contacts, but the regular Mr. and Mrs. Joe Doakes of the community do not get together on church-school problems.

The term Curriculum Guide would remind a few old timers of the first such guide in North America Christendom. In the 1920s and '30s, we lugged a thick, mimeographed 8 1/2-by-11-inch, two-pound paper-backed Guide to all church-school ecumenical meetings in the north. It was essentially Paul Vieth's doctoral thesis from Yale Divinity School. It was the document that introduced the National Council of Churches to the northeast and the midwest. In our churches in the area of Albany, New York, it was the guide the ecumenical Albany School of Religion thought to implement in its public school program of released-time Christian education and its mid-winter training sessions for church-school teachers and personnel. The first three goal-oriented sections were a study under the three titles of "God the Father," "Christ the Son," and "The Holy Spirit."

The Guide helped lesson writers of Sunday school materials prepare their denominational approaches during the first half of the century. It was good because it was a first for both writers and lay teachers. It was exclusively *Bible*.

The materializing and secularizing of American culture following World War II was the testing environment of its effectiveness. Whether considered as a cause or an effect of the failure of Christian education to stem the tide of falling church membership, the results were quite clear. Teaching Bible content and traditional formal theology was not drawing persons into the communities of Faith, nor was it making evangelistic disciples out of our lazy laissez-faire membership within. In brief, proclaiming the Word was not enough. The reader already knows what my reaction has been throughout this book. Our third-person religion, now prevailing, *must* become second and first person. There must be practice and laboratory work in the *doing* of the Word as well as the absorption of content beyond the present inventory of knowledge.

Thus the metamorphosis of the old Guide into a new Guide ought to be of immediate concern to our clergy. The new Guide envisioned in this section of the Christian education chapter must therefore include brand new elements of controlled sharing projects that involve physical effort, i.e., carrying out coordinated serving projects, alongside abstract mentality. Is it not appropriate that in the recruitment of new church membership via the Confirmation Class the professional ordained theologian should become the lesson writer for the youth curriculum? It hungers for immediate attention. Lutheran AFFIRM shows new study. Now let's add new ACTION projects, demonstrating the leadership of professional theologians.

A Benediction: Dear Father-God: Trusting in the Enabling Spirit for guidance, make this a powerful ecumenical effort toward upgrading our current church educational resources in the light of Christian nurture, thus helping us attempt to fulfill God's law, which is Love in Action. The individual is not a full-fledged Christian until he loves his fellows in all conditions of life—in his home, in his church, in his outside labor, and in the enjoyment of his environment. God, grant us the power to turn the tide of the evil we began so long ago. Amen.

SECTION 6. SPECIAL CHALLENGE TO LESSON WRITERS OF THEMES FROM THE EARLY OLD TESTAMENT

The timely publication of the Miller-Hayes *History of Ancient Israel and Judah* refocuses attention on the origin of our faith. When the *Interpreter's Bible* was first issued, the 464-page introduction in *Volume I—Genesis* was somewhat formidable reading for us laymen. The exegesis and exposition of the Scripture text itself was all-engrossing. As time has worn on I have found more opportunity to delve into the cultural and historical background of the Judeo portion of our faith. I began to notice that preachers would differentiate in terms used in referring to Scripture, sometimes saying, "the Word of God" and at other times, "Let us turn to what the Bible says." Most often the "Word of God" phrase was restricted to quotes from Jesus or the New Testament, plus the Ten Commandments portion of the Mosaic Law and the prophets in the Old Testament. The "let us turn to what the Bible says" appeared to cover all the other sections, and with it the word "story" has become very prominent.

I do not believe a great many of our church-school teachers have caught on to this, and since in the younger grades they are telling Bible stories constantly, the possible farther reach of this differentiation has not been given much attention. I consider our theologians to be very negligent and not very forthright for not issuing instructions needed by our lay people. They have seemed to shy away from the historicity of the Hebrew origins, at least until Miller and Hayes came along with their new book. We owe a great deal to these two theology professors for their volume. *The History of Ancient Israel and Judah* (Westminster Press, 1984). They frankly refer "to the staged, composited" manuscripts having been put together by many early editors (not just J, E, and P) and they conclude that not until we get to the period of the Judges do we have a reliable picture of our Old Testament spiritual forbearers. The following is a quote from their comments concerning P: "In brief, the Pentateuch is a filled in essay preconceived and laid out by writers who were doing their best to reduce an oral folk story to a written language form."

With this new material from Miller and Hayes, we are encouraged to go back to the mid-century publication of the classic *Interpreter's Bible*. In the article submitted by Cuthbert A. Simpson and Walter Russell Bowie, pages 442–43, Volume I, we are informed about the probable origin of Abraham, Isaac, and Jacob. It appears that the three patriarchs were clan leaders of Semitic clans or tribes and were far ranging in the Palestine area on both sides of the Jordan. Thus the patriarchs were somewhat geographically separated, each patronizing his own shrine for worship. They were related only via the overall tribal ties and did not belong to one specific family blood line. *They were probably not really blood grandfather, son, and grandson.* If this be true, then the Sarah episode wherein she bears a child at ninety years of

140

age probably is a fable and the "mess of pottage for his birthright" deal by Jacob is just a good story. The loss of these two important episodes, however, is not as bad, in my opinion, as the concomitant loss of the picture of Jacob's reconciliation with Esau. Mercy, love, and forgiveness between men is so important and the flavor of that meeting with presents stacked up on the trail behind should be caught and stored in the spiritual inventory of every Christian. Perhaps that story can remain as a true story of reconciliation if an unknown cause of the breech between the brothers is implied and left to the imagination. The birthright story was so vital and so lifelong that its cancellation does leave a real void. It loses something vital when viewed merely as an imaginary wrong being righted by the God-favored deed.

While I am at this point, speaking directly to lesson writers of the ancient Bible stories, I would like to reemphasize the necessity for being honest about the geological time of creation. The demand for intelligence makes many Christians appear as backward ignoramuses. It's time they got the matter of creation during seven twenty-four-hour days back in 4004 B.C. completely cleared out of their mental computers. This brings us back to the elementary chemistry and physics by which rocks and artifacts from archaeological diggings are dated. The ignorant think this is all guesswork but, the "literately cultural" will recognize the fact of determining time via radioactive analysis. You may still disagree with what I refer to as God's evolution but you cannot argue about the age of a rock beyond an error of a modest percentage (see chapter 9).

Lesson writers may profit by an appendage here dealing with a slightly different aspect of the Garden of Eden beyond that touched upon in other portions of this book. As you may already have gathered, I hold the Garden of Eden story to be without comparison; equal spiritually to any portion of the scripture, except the Incarnation of God in Christ. Give the Oriental, sensitive, poetic mind its due. Those storytellers faced a tremendous mental and spiritual challenge. And do not forget that they sat immersed in environmental polytheism and a Baalic cult worship touching all phases of life. They had to stretch symbolic language to the limit. They dreamed up an imaginary situation because they had no actual data except themselves. This imagery was God-stuff. Call it a special brand of inspiration if you will. They felt compelled to describe the most awesome, powerful Being, He who was in charge of the world. He was someone behind the world, they saw—

and heard, and felt, and smelled, and tasted—some One who had the power and the vision to do whatever He wanted to do spiritually and supernaturally. He had made such a beautiful world and He must have wanted someone to live in it and take care of it for Him. God one day was perceived to have sent forth a mighty surge of spiritual energy and the writers began to write. Their spiritual receiving sets were turned on at full power. Let's try to follow them as they unravel the mystery.

In your reading of the prior portions of this book you may have followed a hit-and-miss plan by selecting portions on the basis of the chapter outline presented in the first few pages. To make sure that you now confront the earlier meditation in the area of our spiritual beginnings, please turn back to chapter 4, pages 79–82. There are listed the series of steps which the lesson writer should review. There is a chance, of course, that they may not appeal to you personally. So you, Dear Lesson Writer, can construct some revised form representing your own experience in the matter of spiritual inspiration and divine revelation. Folks have various ideas as to how God speaks to humans, especially when the topic is of the origins of the human race and God's expectations of His people. I trust that you do not begin as some literalists may, by assuming that God *somehow* wrote a *script*, on *something* permanent, in a language that did not exist in written form, and then hid it in a safe place for J-1, E, and P to find thousands of years later. Slightly more sophisticated is the approach made by others who draw a picture of a specialized saint with sensitive soul who sits at his parchment, ink and pen in hand and in rapt attention, by turns listening to God and then writing down the straightforward action. God does not have a physical vocal chord and listening to God is via the spirit only.

Some problems seem to be overlooked in such a simplistic process. The first is that of the origin of human language as a specific Hebrew accomplishment. We must remember that a part of God's family over in China had a vital civilization underway by 10,000 B.C. I am sure God's spiritual communication in code was being beamed to the Chinese segment of His family earlier than in the Palestine location, which was under what was later referred to as the Sumerian civilization. I daresay we may even conclude that God began communicating with humanity even before there was a spoken language, as witness the communicative spirit of music and painting. An indeterminate period of oral folklore preceded written language. We even feel justified in believing that God never speaks in an audible, humanlike voice like ours. God may speak via His spiritual code to any human anywhere and the receiving party will translate it into the prevailing language of that recipient. Thus the picture of a scribe scribbling as God dictates gives one a false idea of a truly spiritual God. Our God is all spirit. And remember, early storytellers could not write, they could only talk about Him in their everyday languages, and so they gave Him a full slate of human characteristics. Later the writers and editors could show some restraint as a result of their advancing culture and literacy. Though they perceived they were writing about a Spiritual Presence, their writing retained an anthropomorphic character. Today our theologians and philosophers apply new analogies and more highly developed concepts via the mind, but we can only stumble along. Again, *God is all Spirit.* The mysterious Mind and Heart of God seeks our response. We respond as we are able via His gifts to us of Extrasensory Perception (ESP) operating through intuition and conscience.

Secondly, the primal concept of direct physical dictation of the exact and only allowable phrases as promoted by the Literalist overlooks entirely the now well-known fact that the translation of the oral folk story has been the result of many successive editorial revisions. Bible scholars have delineated the handiwork of J-1, J-2, J, E, P and various other Redactors. Contemporary lesson writers who are tackling the Eden episode for background inspiration need to reassess the language they employ, especially in children's stories. I plead for updating our Bible-telling media so that they present the basic traditional truth in a language vehicle that reflects the modern idiom. The engineer riding his supercharge of ammonium perchlorate into outer space must be approached via different language than that of his primal, agriculturally based counterpart who limped on foot or rode his household donkey out to the edge of the family's garden spot. In this same vein we may conclude that the A.D. 2000 lesson writer would have some chemistry and physics in his background academic B.A. and have read the introduction of the *Interpreter's Bible*, duNoüy's *Human Destiny* and Miller-Hayes's *History of Israel and Judah*. (Apropos the reference to the donkey and the garden plot above, even that is open to revision. More correctly, man in the beginning went out to milk the she-goats of his nomadic herds.)

Some of you readers may have already guessed at my rather hard conclusion. It is quite simple, but it does call for real effort and a very open mind. There are approximately 500 pages in the introduction section of the *Interpreter's Bible*, Volume I. I have concluded that until the lesson writer has prayerfully studied through this material and then capped it with a study of the Miller-Hayes *History of Ancient Israel and Judah*, he does not fully qualify as a member of the Nurturing Staff that Christ's Church demands for the Space Age.

Here is the stupendous hurdle these two seminary scholars face us with. After their tremendously diligent study they cannot find any trace of a physical or secular group of nomads who are recognized by other kings and pharaohs as a coherent Hebrew people prior to the period of the wars between the city-states, which subsided at the time of the Judges, approximately 1200 B.C. How will you tell the story of Sarah's birth experience of Isaac (at age 90–100), the Jacob mess-of-pottage story, and the birth and life of that famous lawgiver, the mighty man of morals, Moses? With this introduction we are now prepared to quote from *The History of Ancient Israel and Judah* (Westminster, 1984), Miller and Hayes, page 78.

> The evidence, or lack of evidence, is such that a confident treatment of the origins of Israel and Judah in terms of historiography is, in our opinion, simply impossible. . . . Specifically, we hold that the main story line of Genesis-Joshua creation, pre-flood patriarch, great flood, second patriarchal age, entrance into Egypt, twelve tribes descended from twelve brothers, escape from Egypt, complete collection of laws and religious instructions handed down at Mt. Sinai, forty years of wandering in the wilderness, miraculous conquest of Canaan, assignment of tribal territories, establishment of the priestly order and cities of refuge—is an artificial and theologically influenced literary construct. . . . It is our impression . . . that the early clans and tribes that formed the basis of the Kingdom of Israel and Judah derived from diverse backgrounds and origins. They too, at least to a certain degree, represented a "melting pot." . . . Again there is probably no single explanation to be given for the origins of Israel and Judah; there are many explanations!!!

Having been reeducated in the matter of the lack of secular historicity of ancient Israel and Judah we will probably have to employ further examples of symbolic language. Dear Lesson Writer, you are further advised by Gibson (Genesis, Vol. I) to use care in your choice of terms. Gibson addresses the use of the word "myth" but does not like it for general use because the average person misinterprets it, as follows: "It [myth] can thus be applied equally to, for instance, the Hebrew story of the flood in Genesis, Chapter 6–9, and to the Babylonian story of the flood in the eleventh tablet of the Gilgamesh epic cycle, whatever difference there may be between these stories is a spiritual insight. To the man in the street, however, 'myth' is a loaded word. It almost invariably suggests an opinion word. It almost invariably suggests an opinion or a belief that is incredible or insincere or tendentious or even downright harmful . . . as long as there is a danger of this popular rather than the academic sense being read into the word, we are well advised to stay clear of it as much as we can."

I close this chapter on Christian church education with an attempt to assuage my disturbed feelings after studying Miller-Hayes. From a group of many Bible characters which we remember from our days in church-school we select two extremely important ones. The full details of their busy and important lives seem now brutally assaulted, but in the interest of complete honesty, real transformations may be required. Perhaps Joseph was in reality the doorkeeper of the one granary nearest the palace, rather than Egypt's prime minister. Perhaps Moses, that stalwart man of God, the lawgiver of his people, was a revolutionary foreman over a section of the forced labor gang. During an off-season on the Pharaoh's calendar when he and his chieftains were busy celebrating the dedication of the most recent pyramid, Moses ran off with a dozen families and made it across the marshes safely to the wilderness. He could still be the trustworthy right arm of God whose earthly nation of chosen people came into being, slowly, under his guidance, out of the melting pot of Palestine.

One wonders if the Miller-Hayes investigation was able to gain complete access to all the Jewish rabbinical writings dating back to this early period. The Jewish men of the cloth are certainly intelligent. We wonder how they react to the historical blank?

SECTION 7. AN ABSTRACT

Part I   Definition and Curricula
            Christian Education in the church is human relationships working towards a goal.
            FAMILY is the role model for Christian education in that family is love in action.
            We look at the nurturing teacher.
            Steps to faith (seven) listed.
            Retraining the teacher will be as important as adding action to our abstraction. This will demand new working relations,

laboratory work for the student as well as the teacher.

The one-sentence conclusion is the definition of this chapter; review it.

Part II   Nurture is Loving

We can learn to love the unlovely.

Jesus is the supreme example of love as it works among humans.

Paul's thirteenth chapter of Romans says it all.

"Educating is loving." It transforms abstraction into action.

Part III   The Robert Raikes Syndrome

Identifying its lingering traces in our churches.

History from 1754 England to contemporary America.

Importance in colonial, frontier America.

Seminaries are still separated from Schools of Religion thus Christian education is still a stepchild.

Closing the gap between pastor and lay faculty in the church.

Pastor becomes dean of religious instruction in the University of Life. He takes charge of Nurture.

Applying ordained leadership to Christian education as the final cure for the syndrome.

The professional theologian in charge of the nurturing aspects of a church's life must accept responsibility for seeing that new activities and relationships are established. The public school teacher must be retrained as a theological trainee and executor of the pastor who is dean. The official board is in charge via the pastor but new activities of nurturing will only be as good as the seminary which, both pedagogically and theologically, has been able to furnish the seed. Again, we are reminded that "proclaiming the Word" makes a good excuse for a lazy pastor/minister. He tends to shun the necessary lab work of trial and error.

Part IV   The Confirmation Process—A Special Experience for Youth

Junior-high-age students now considered most appropriate for becoming a voting member of the church. The student should be able to think. He should advance beyond the Hero Worship characteristic of the sixth grade. He is called upon to make a decision during the three years. We hope he makes it a real commitment for Christ.

The maladies in our churches:

The Encapsulated Family makes for the Encapsulated Church.
Discipleship and spirituality had faded to a weak shadow.
We wear a facade of "goodness."

The Milquetoast virus is generated by these Encapsulations.
The Milquetoast fears to be different.

We want the new Christian recruit to have a goal which conflicts vigorously with present culture. No Milquetoast will make the grade.

Junior High Foster Fathers

A new approach at waking up middle-of-the-road fathers. An intergenerational program which attempts to revitalize the Confirmation Class product and goal. It puts the father and his family back in church school and starts him praying. We pray that his son or daughter makes a potent decision for Christ. Rough details are given for:

An actual experiment in confirmation to church membership—A North Carolina Presbyterian Church experiments in the 1980s. Christian Nurture of Senior High students

Our forgotten young people—how can we keep them on the Growth Curve? How can we keep them in touch? We offer no panacea, but the professional pedagogical theologian ought to be doing more and publicizing it. The church seems to be doing very little in the whole area of youth counseling for life, vocation, marriage, spiritual values. *WHY?*

Part V   Resources of Curriculum Building

A plea for a truly ecumenical analysis and evaluation of our current lesson literature and associated materials. In the course of this analysis, a curriculum Guide could be created. Steps in setting up such a Guide are suggested. The idea of experimentation, the lab work, is again emphasized. Search out new materials not previously listed, such as the former Covenant Life Curriculum of the southern Presbyterians, also Dr. John C. L. Gibson's new series on the Old Testament.

Part VI   Special Challenge to Lesson Writers of Themes from the Old Testament

This section is a demand for every Christian educational worker, lay or professional theologian, to read the first 500 pages of the Volume I of the *Interpreter's Bible* and *The History of Ancient Israel and Judah,* a recent volume by Miller and Hayes. This pilgrim has seen no direct reference to the *Interpreter's* prelude section since its publication in the midforties. Is my answer correct? "No guts," either lay or pastoral. Read it; formulate your own concluding paragraph to chapter 5.

Chapter VI

Taking Risks for God's Sake

SORTIE NUMBER ONE. CINCINNATI IN 1970

It may be helpful to you, Dear Reader, to open up chapter 4 again for a recheck of my definition of a modern Christian pilgrim. Listed there are the six sorties into strange and entirely unexpected situations, compelling me into actions and study, which I consider now as among life's crowning features. Every one of them still daily contributes to the feeling that God helps me turn a fresh page each day with a suggestion of what He still waits for me to do. But, in retrospect, perhaps these spiritual sorties in the maturer portion of life were really inculcated and incubated by a special introductory sortie at the very beginning of full adult life.

It began on that long-ago Sunday morning in Cambridge, Massachusetts, when the minister, the chairman of the board of deacons, and the Sunday school superintendent, retiring after ten years, persuaded me to take the latter's place. If I had any Christian armor to put on, I could not have named it. Perhaps youthful self-confidence was about all. And I was scared to death of the size of the membership. Imagine a country boy used to a couple of small, scattered classes sitting in preempted corners of a little church now suddenly engulfed in a strange metropolitan mix of eight hundred enrollees in a church of about twelve hundred members. And I was only halfway through my graduate research at the Institute. God must have felt sorry for me, for only He kept me from going under. Those many wearying, questioning hours did pay off in many subsequent years of church-school work. Chapter 6 was born in that earliest sortie into the unknown. So, now on to Cincinnati.

We had been retired just a year when in 1970 the Presbyterians of this land of all shades of color and subdenominational bent were challenged to come and spend a week together at Cincinnati. With practically no program particulars, the gathering had been promoted under the theme "The Celebration of Evangelism." The title itself no doubt scared off some traditional Presbyterians. With no real program particulars one wondered a bit. At least we got a vague notion there were to be some high quality addresses, some very special worship, and a lot of open-ended afternoon workshop possibilities. A few names were dropped in the promotional literature, and because a couple of them, like Bruce Larsen and Lloyd Ogilvie, sounded good, my wife and I decided to live it up for a week in this second year of our retirement. Maybe the Lord would have a message for us. Another younger couple in our church, he an elder, joined in, and soon the Spirit tapped our first woman elder. Then He generously nudged the senior minister and our brand new associate. *Most strangely it developed that the seven of us represented the one and only church in our entire presbytery which had any attendee in that assembly.*

There were three thousand plus of us when we assembled, and in the first five minutes of a brief opening devotional, we experienced a real wakening. For myself, I refer to it as the *orientation* of the latter third of my life. First, we were complimented for having responded so faithfully to such a vague program. Of course we probably all developed a warm glow of self-righteousness when the project leaders called us that special portion of Presbyterians who had to possess some extra-special spiritual intuition to have responded by actually coming in person. We were the Presbyterians "willing to take a risk for God's sake." The atmosphere was charged with a spiritual tension I had never before experienced. There I was, a retiree of sixty-six, and except for my full-time gardening avocation, ready to roll along at an even pace in church responsibilities for the remainder of the mortal time God would allow me. That week made it possible for many of the ideas expressed in this book to be conceived and incubated.

The afternoon workshops awakened me to the fact that my conception of an objective, third-person God, whom we *talk about* and *talk for*, was widely missing the mark I should have been aiming for. Under the Spirit's nudging I had to allow Him to pull me into a first-person relationship with Himself. An I-You relationship, as the theological experts call it, had to be built. I hope I shall still be building it until the day it can be consummated in His presence. That close relationship demands prayer—direct, earnest, hesitant, fumbling, humbling prayer. After Cincinnati I had Dr. George Buttrick's *So We Believe So We Pray* at home to help bolster my new resolve. Some years later I found a copy of his first book, *Prayer*, which would have been even better. (See chapter 11.)

The real payoff for both me and the Lord was that my former idea of genteel, quiet retirement flew out the window; I saw it was literally for the birds. Now that I was learning to talk to God a little I found that there was plenty of unfinished work left in His Church. He was telling me to pick up on the action which had to follow the talking. In this period came a brand new concept: how to define the word "sharing," as in "Sharing Group." Sortie number two, the section that follows in this chapter, began with a coal carried from the fire at Cincinnati. I was willing to take some small step for Christ's sake. *Careful there now, fellow*, I had to caution myself. *Do not get to feeling too good or He might just have to cut the power off to bring you back to earth.*

Specific highlights of the week's action must be related. They, of course, may tend to be a bit exaggerated by time. They were specifics that will never have a duplicate. There was the reenactment of Jesus' washing of the feet of His disciples. The group of ministers on the platform, some seven or eight persons, represent special interests of the larger community of Christian faith. Mrs. Stair,* wife of the president of Union Seminary in Richmond, and a black minister were in the group. Nothing was said about the matter from the podium but the very fact that this demonstration of unity was taking place was a seed being planted by God toward His wish for the eventual union of the northern and southern segments of His Church. (An amusing sidelight: No one could tell if Mrs. Stair had been tipped off ahead of time. Ladies near us wondered via whispers as to whether she still had her pantyhose on or had had an opportunity for removal ahead of time. It turned out that indeed she did wear her pantyhose through the whole service, and the man washing her feet did so with quiet dignity and aplomb.)

We experienced some religious interpretive dancing. Five or six beautiful female dancers in black leotards from toe to neckline did a very graceful dance of the Lord's Prayer. As to its completely soulful and spiritual nature, that was perhaps not so near 100 percent as the director saw it in her mind. Actually, almost 50 percent of the attendant viewers were male bodies. I doubt if every trace of eroticism could have been shunted off, even though we tried.

*Mrs. Fred. R. Stair, Jr.

151

Cincinnati 1970 will never be forgotten if for no other experience than the serving and partaking of our Lord's Supper simultaneously in that immense audience. The preparatory planning must have been so precise and extensive. At the end of every row of partakers, from front to rear, left and right, stood a server with half a broken loaf and an oversized tumbler of grape juice. Thus the actual serving of the elements took less time than is usually the case in one's small church congregation. Though this worship service was held during daylight hours—toward mid-afternoon, as I recall—the auditorium was completely closed to outside light. Spotlights focused on a symbolic altar table in the foreground and gave light for the accompanying readers of the Scripture. In the semidarkness of that vastness, people could not see the tears of a neighbor. The elements being served were not distinguishable in the hands of the servers at each aisle-side place. The act of taking off a piece of the loaf and taking a sip of the common cup, all so different from prior experience, made for a new common bond. In the semidarkness, a sense of utter privacy was melded into the powerful communality of that moment.

I cherish the hope that any person who holds the view that anyone can fully and effectually worship in solitude outside a gathered congregation could be inserted into such an experience as we had there. Synergism of the most high order is the apt term to describe the interaction between God's Spirit and ours, both individually and communally. One perceived a person-to-person bonding as well as, with God all within, a warming and expanding sense of power. You felt alone with Christ but simultaneously you were aware of the throbbing Spirit of a like-minded throng. Persons could savor the atmosphere, which caused more than myself to proclaim inwardly, *I love you, Lord Jesus. Even though I fail you every day, help me to be your more able disciple.* Even though some of the more mystically minded in that audience may have seen the Dove descending, those of us not endowed with such a vision knew in our hearts that the Presence had descended and was in the midst of us. God blesses us continually in that precious memory.

Several afternoon workshops were open-ended informalities on a scale I had never before experienced in a religious assembly. The subjects discussed reflected the will of the group in spontaneous spirit but the drift and conclusions were in the able hands of him who was both moderator and teacher. This was the occasion during which a number of us had an opportunity of personally becoming acquainted with Dr.

Bruce Larson, of Faith at Work fame, back in Columbia, Maryland. Resuming the regular pastorate, he transferred to the West Coast and now heads up an ordained staff of five at the University Presbyterian Church in Seattle, Washington. Were you to meet him you would understand the broad theological expertise and jovial good humor of the leader I chose to follow that week of weeks. To sample a bit of that leadership, go to your library and borrow a copy of his little volume, *Thirty Days to a New You*. A solid month of daily contacts with the Holy Spirit is guaranteed. You will then know why God preserved him from accidental drowning off the coast of the islands of Sanibel and Captiva while he was winter vacationing.[1]

With a highlight experience of this sort, how does one report to his home congregation? The Teutonic, Nordic, and British mixed therein have developed cool cultures. They were reflected in the faces before us on the following Sunday morning as the minister invited us to report as a group just prior to the benediction. Perhaps minds focused on Sunday dinners had some effect. Our own enthusiasm was abundant but after the service was over it was apparent that we had not succeeded in piercing the veneer of staid formality worn by the vast majority. We had involved them in some physical action, moving in the aisles, holding hands, singing some strange sounding lullabies certainly not found in the hymnal. Later, private comments from a few, who actually felt uncomfortable and disturbed, centered around the theme that they felt outward emotion in religious services was suspect. We tried to make Love the name of the game that day but we did not do so well at attempting to light new fires. For this pilgrim the fire lit in Cincinnati burns brightly to this day.

SORTIE NUMBER TWO. SHARING GROUPS IN THE LOCAL CHURCH[2]

During the seventies, a movement within a number of churches in the east and mid-south developed under the labels "sharing group" and "small group movement." It never seemed to have the overt blessing of the clergy in our general area, perhaps for the several reasons following: Early references to the small group activities did not seem to stress their spiritual aspects. Perhaps the negative reception was influenced by the confrontational group therapy in general psychological practice. Such an approach is still practiced in institutional environments where the cost of professional psychiatry on a one-to-one basis would be an impossible financial burden.

There is, however, a picture of positive gain in the use of group therapy under leadership sufficiently skilled to develop a working rapport among the participants, recognized as peer pressure. Such peer pressure, when kept within orderly procedure under professional leadership, continues to be a useful tool in creating commitment toward improved levels of behavior. There were, of course, also some tales of catastrophe, where freewheeling groups became judgmental in tearing down the individual worth and dignity of the victim who had made himself vulnerable under deep confession of wrongdoing. When church members talked to their pastors about the possibility of beginning a small group program the first reaction would be negative for the pastor could envision the cliché warfare. Pastors generally tended to feel that without closer supervision more harm than good would be the outcome. The negativism was more pronounced when the small-group movement within the communities of faith became a field of promotion in the Christian education area. In the general advice section for its promotion, it was recommended that the clergy of the local church not be regular working members of such a group. I am sure pastors looked with suspicion upon this apparent limitation of their presence.

From personal experience, I can illustrate what took place under one pastor's guidance. My wife and I looked forward to association within the *koinonia* group of a medium-sized church of about five hundred members we belonged to a few years before retiring. The young, well-liked pastor wished to see what could be accomplished within his understanding of the movement, which he had been reading about. It was a group of the right size, attendance being eight to twelve and meetings held on a weekly evening time schedule. We were not retired but the group was well matured. As I recall, the "study" was set up for about ten weeks. This turned out to be pretty much of a traditional Bible class. It was a very fine Bible class, for the minister prepared himself diligently and his leadership was much appreciated. But the *koinonia* aspect, that of sharing deep, personal, Christian convictions and raising serious spiritual questions, was no more in evidence than it is in the usual Sunday morning Bible class. To be sure, several of us in the group who had been or still were active Christian education teachers or leaders expounded some personal views with vigor and considerable

154

verbiage. As in the preponderance of our church activities we were busy *talking about* God and a little about ourselves at times, but always under that rather sedate facade of good decent English grammar, syntax, and formality. The personal illustrations were near the surface and safely exposed. That minister and that particular group of the church's saints were studying the Word but leaving each session at about the level of spiritual function with which they had arrived two hours before. We were wiser, to be sure; we had learned more about some two-thousand-year-old truth; but I believe it is safe to say that private commitment to the Spirit of Christ and the love between participants was about the same after as before. Only sound growth in knowledge had taken place.

With that bit of background orientation we may now define more accurately what we mean by the small sharing group as a tool toward broadening and deepening the spiritual environment and active commit-ment of the local church. It calls for voluntary self-commitment of a small group of Christians who meet together for a covenanted, predeter-mined number of weekly meetings, usually not less than ten sessions. The publicity preceding the effort invites personal sharing of private Christian experience. It promises an opportunity to raise questions and doubts about and within one's Christian faith: the troubles that beset a contemporary Christian parent in the training of children, et cetera. Every person has his own special definition of sin; he hopes desperately at times to understand how his friend knows he can be reconciled with God. During the agreed-upon number of meetings there will be no excuses for absence except sickness or severe accident. In the promo-tional materials it is made clear that persons are attending as in-dividuals. Married couples will be among those at the first meeting but they should decide as individuals whether they wholeheartedly support the project. This pilgrim's experience in three groups was that couples accounted for approximately half of the attendance. Input is expected from each. Within this broad parameter, let us discuss a number of necessary details.

Forming a Christian Sharing Group

Size of group: The experts tell us not to try to set up a group with less than six regular attendees. My own experience tells us there is a sound reason for this. Keep in mind that in a mixed group the physical,

155

mental, and spiritual rhythms are not always in phase as between individuals. See our comments on the "quiet waters" theme in the Twenty-third Psalm (see sortie number three). It may well be that in a given meeting a couple of individuals may not be in the mood for outward warm expression of their thought or feeling. In a group of six, this leaves, we'll say, only four active, effective participants. With the group that small the chances are that the give-and-take on a current topic may not be sufficient to furnish a strong experience background. In the very small group there are also likely to be some who, though very interested in the given topic and animatedly talking about it, may not have had sufficient prior experience to furnish valid data for the rest of the group. Their intake is greater than their output. In other words, there may not be sufficient background data in the group to actually have a convincing effect; the picture remains too incomplete on that particular subject. On the other hand, when the number of participants exceeds ten or twelve, several things are apt to develop. There is great tendency for small sections of several to get carried away in an intimate discussion, which tends to leave the others as bystanders. There is also the possibility that several small clusters then start to talk at once, again dulling the edge for conclusions as a group. Another happening in the larger group is that several more-timid souls hold back in the face of the abundant verbiage and do not attempt to participate verbally at all. We have had the experience of instances where the quiet retiring "mouse" in such a group will finally break forth and contribute a real gem of the evening, but this is not always forthcoming.

The Group Leader is not a teacher, nor is he or she the main talker, except now and then when his individual personal experience is being expounded. Two words describe his best function. He is *the starter*. A good starter is both *prepared* and *unprepared*. He has kept close track of the prior topic of discourse and in his own mind concludes that such-and-such a new area should be added to what has been said before. To introduce this into the discussion he has perhaps previously selected a verse of Scripture or has hunted up an author from whom he can make a brief quote. As an unprepared starter he listens to small talk as the group is assembling and, with a sharp ear and a sensitive spirit, picks up some remark that a mother has made about the kids; or about spouse-to-spouse family retort; or notes an incomer in very high spirits or one who seems to be downcast and in low spirits and privately has asked them the question, "What kind of day did you have, Jim, or Mary?" In brief, he is quick to size up and to seize the quickening of the Holy Comforter, God's Spirit into which they are aware they are immersing themselves for the evening. If one of the group has felt led to begin that session with a prayer, the unprepared starter will listen very carefully for any particular theme appearing in that prayer for it probably contains a matter of utmost concern to that individual. At that moment the leader/starter seizes it as his entree for starting the evening's discussion.

The leader is always a catalyst as well as an active starter. A catalyst in a physical sense is a material, the presence of a very small amount of which, introduced in the given situation, initiates a reaction, a procedure. An example may be a molecule or two of copper out in your backyard garden soil that on a given day makes the color of your row of beets a little bit darker than they were yesterday. The catalyst is not used up itself but is ready to repeat this good influence at the next opportunity. Another example of a catalyst of a different kind is the person who coming into a lackadaisical group of folks seems to spark speech and action immediately. The important thing about a catalyst is that he repeats his function without being dissipated or used up himself. The leader as a catalyst in a sharing group is present throughout the discussion to see that when it shows signs of bogging down or having run its course, a new route can be suggested, say, picking up a side issue of the problem that has been overlooked. If he perceives that that topic seems to have run its course he may ask one of the participants to give what he thinks is an abstract or summary of any conclusions within the group. The catalyst does not allow the subject to drag too long and throws a new log on the fire via his prior preparations. Do not overlook the point that it is the leader's responsibility also to see that dates and times of meetings are set. He notes possible changes of place and accounts for any other details of the actual meeting arrangements and everyone is given the information.

Getting Acquainted: There are two stages in getting acquainted. A general notice has been posted in the church bulletins so that the congregation is aware of what is to be undertaken. Do not try to be completely explicit in this announcement but do stress the idea of personal sharing of experiences that you think are peculiar to you. *Also stress very strongly that the group is not a class taught by a teacher.* This is to differentiate it from the adult Bible class syndrome. Do include the use of the Bible, however, as a resource, as well as other books, papers, articles, and contacts with outstanding Christians. *Do not mention the spiritual autobiography* aspect, as that comes in the second meeting when the most earnest ones predominate. Timid souls will be frightened off if this is mentioned in the original promotion.

Procedure in a Sharing Group Meeting

The first meeting must be handled with care. There will be the curious and those who just want to know what's going on. This first meeting must provide a dignified exit for those who feel they do not wish to continue. The leader will have heard the general reaction among his peers after the first notice has gone up and he will perceive that he knows one or two of the people who are planning to come regardless. These assisting starters may be given a specified subject to get the ball rolling, but if they are already known to be pretty much self-starting, just this acceptance of their initial role may be sufficient. The following activities are vital for that first meeting:

The leader and assisting starters have among themselves set up a rough schedule for the conduct of this session. The following suggestions are only brief examples of what might be expected to take place. A main objective is to allay individual anxieties and any suspicion of abnormal behavior.

The leader opens with a brief but significant prayer, touching on the desirability of each one learning to make a better response to God and seeking guidance in the midst of our human mistakes and inability to carry out Christ's chief concern: that we learn to love our neighbor in more effective, caring ways.

Each one is asked to give a brief historical autobiography: names, addresses, phone numbers, vocation, hobby interests, other churches and places of residence; also such voluntary comments the candidate may care to share about members of his/her family's life, and church activities in general. Please proceed informally through this getting-acquainted period. Keep it low level. This is not the time for trying to promote the spiritual autobiography. It will be introduced in the second session after the merely curious and the uninterested have decided to drop out of the group. The leader, however, is taking mental notes and he is keenly aware of possible topics for later discussion lying just below the surface.

Stress the covenant idea of high priority for the successive meet-

ings for the stated planned number of sessions. People are expected to appear promptly at the sessions except if affected by sickness and emergencies.

Stress the sharing aspect of the group. The leader emphasizes that there must be *input* if the individuals anticipate *output*, i.e., the communal group is going to have to generate the atmosphere of the Divine Presence within itself. It is hoped that two months hence the dispersing neighbors will be carrying new strength out into new life. The person needing and seeking help initially feels down and out, the low member on the totem pole. The leader stresses the fact that in many cases the seemingly deficient one has already in his own life discovered elements of power via the Holy Spirit of God, as Savior, Comforter, and Enabler, and in sharing his weakness is unaware that he is already loving and supplying strength and guidance to the seemingly self-assertive neighbor who privately now recognizes his own deficiency.

Thus, in the process of listening to and mentally succoring the neighbor, we others are being fed spiritually by him/her. It is a bit like Jesus' example of eating together. The master and the slave at the same table are on equal footing. They both give and they both take. Perhaps you, the reader, might consider this a sketchy sermonette on sharing titled: "Why Are We Here?" Such a sermonette need not be over five or ten minutes and is most informal, not pontifical.

Stress the informality of dress and speech. Make it as near "family style" as possible. There is not a preset procedure. Interruptions with questions and repetition are in order. There will be no professional theologians in the following sessions, except upon occasion when one may be invited to clarify Biblical controversy. (An example of this: A mother wondered why having a baby never gave her the inspiration to speak like Mary did in her Magnificat. One of the pastors attended next session and held forth upon the time gap between Jesus' birth and the fifty-year period following His crucifixion, during which witnesses' memories could fail and editors could write Magnificats.) In the informality of the getting-acquainted session, refreshments may be served. The assistant starter poses a question about one of the points in the pastor's sermon of the previous Sunday and there is a decided spirit of pro and con developed while participants enjoy a bite. The meeting closes with prayer by the leader making an earnest plea for mutual Christian sharing and fellowship. After dismissal he sits back and wonders how many will show up the second time.

The second meeting will reveal that the weeding-out process has now reduced the attendance to those who can be counted on. They will be the covenanted fellowship of the continuing group. The leader seals the pact by circulating the sheet for their signatures. This covenant being signed, it is blessed by prayer, perhaps by the assistant starter who has been tipped off beforehand. The leader now lays out the broad outlines of what is actually the basic foundation of the discussions throughout the remainder of the "experiment." It is the enlargement of each person's "Christian autobiography" so that he/she may come to enjoy a fulfilled "spiritual autobiography" hopefully a bit more in line with what God intended for each. Each participant will be expected to give and take and must be willing to reveal intimate details in order that the sharing experience be made a valid one. The idea of good communication is stressed, as is the difficulty of being understood unless there are repetitions and reexplanations made as a crossover. In brief, repetition of the idea is enhanced by using changes of vocabulary. Examples of this will be remembered from chapter 1, on analogies.

One way to start a session of "spiritual autobiography" is to ask each member to think back over his/her life for the single most joyful or enlightening experience he ever had. Suggest to the others that they react verbally to any point that has been made, interrupting as need be. After this has been talked through the person may be asked in contrast to share his/her most difficult hassle with life. This may well range from the aftermath of having committed an overt trespass against God and conscience with a feeling of deep guilt; being rejected in some church relationship; failure to keep a spouse going straight; inability to pray at all, let alone pray in public; finding oneself in the wrong life vocation; plus a thousand more, as you may well imagine.

It is well again to mention the object of such a Christian undertaking. The loving and caring can be frank and deeply probing without becoming so harshly critical and judgmental as to wound those confessing beyond repair. At no time in my personal experience have I witnessed the type of severe confrontational condemnation that is implied in some literature on the subject. It is at this point that pastors may not feel confident that the sharing group will always be willing to behave itself. Of course, each group varies in makeup and in the event that an individual is "unloading himself," the extent of his private hurt he may make public will depend upon how love has prevailed. In some cases this unveiling is prohibited by a natural reticence due to feeling that

160

"people will talk" outside the group. Larger family connections are involved. Personal matters are shared in the confidence that it will be kept within the group.

I will always remember the case of a middle-aged lady with a family whom we knew was hurting badly. Several months after the group sessions were over her husband left her for another. We had not suspected the truly deep nature of the family's difficulty. Her quiet manner, with no expression of judgment against anyone, spoke volumes in behalf of her loving Christian character. She always referred to her sharing group with high praises for its caring support.

Persons in the community of faith, and perhaps ministers especially, do wonder just what those Sharing Group people are talking about. They realize there is no preset program and it is easy for the naturally suspicious to dub the whole business merely as another gossip party. As this pilgrim goes back over his own experience, many many topics come to mind. Listing some of them may be a way of reassurance that after all Christ, as the Master, prevails. Probing and serious study have taken up such ideas as *Who is God? Do I know Him? How will I ever really know? Does He or did He ever speak in a vocal manner? What is actual prayer? Can it really be two-way communication? How do I know that God answers prayer? Perhaps it is only happenstance? Was Jesus a son or a SON? How real was the body of His resurrection? Is the devil a real person?* (Much enjoyment of C. S. Lewis on that.) *What is mysticism? Am I spiritual or mystical?* (Consider Rufus Jones as a Quaker mystic.) *I have animal passions; am I an animal? Did I ever steal? I don't like the word "justification"; isn't there a better word? What is the Holy Ghost? How do I know He has anything to do with me? Do husbands and wives really forgive one another? When is divorce in order, if ever? My teenager is the family anarchist, how do I deal with him? How about that list keeping one busy for a few months?* Enough said.

Sharing groups do not grow naturally in our churches. A large church in a neighboring state with about 2,000 members was at one time supporting some sixteen small groups similar to the above. We invited the layman, a physician at that church, who appeared to be the leading spirit, to visit our session's annual retreat and tell us how to do it. We, in a church about half the size, ran such a group for three months during two years, holding winter sessions in the evening, followed by one group for another two years for retirees, people somewhat older in age,

161

which met on a weekday in mid-forenoon.

A few holdovers attended both years. I was a member and leader of two of these groups during this four-year period and am led to state as emphatically as I can that I consider them to have been the most exhilarating and motivating spiritual force of my entire church life. The brother-sister rapport developed in this church group was warm and forgiving and understanding. I learned to really know fifteen people out of a membership of one thousand.

The real answer as to our failure to have more effect and to advance throughout the church rests with God. But in the interest of you readers I will propose one or two possible reasons. The church had a very high percentage of nomadic, northern, affluent retirees. They became relatively active in the organizational form of the church but the combination of age and affluency raises a laissez-faire wall between them and the kind of close personal contact the sharing group must thrive on. They were at the age and condition of life at which they had already "shot their wad." But I do fault the ministers for not interviewing the individual participating members of our groups afterwards with a view to ascertaining new values. Perhaps they honestly saw no difference in those of us who had participated in the groups and so felt they would not bother. We participating members may have been at fault in other ways. We did not continue to urge session support and interest, though a number of us were elders. We carried too little of the missionary spirit, perhaps, and we stopped working at it. We were essentially selfish. Basically a contributing error was that each group should run for just one season; recruiting the second year's group in each case should have involved a completely new set of faces and experiences. In the face of these statements I challenge you, Dear Reader, to consult the bibliography and select reading material, hoping you may venture and experiment in your own church.

Chapter VII

Plowing Deeper Furrows in Our Tradition

In the prior chapter, the Pilgrim has made two sorties into new and challenging Christian action as a member of larger groups. In this chapter, as a Pilgrim, I make sortie number three and sortie number four as an individual dissatisfied with the limited, strictly traditional way in which two areas of Christian belief have been previously portrayed. These sorties were actually self-*prospecting* safaris. I traveled well-mapped territory but I believe I have found some new nuggets. At least in my own display case they greatly appeal to me, and I now share them with you. The first one is:

SORTIE NUMBER THREE. LEARNING TO SING A NEW MARCHING SONG: TWENTY-THIRD PSALM

In the opening 1980s there appeared an adult Bible study lesson in the Shared Approach material, decidedly out of the ordinary. The study unit that season had been written by a minister who had an extraordinary interest in old rabbinical Hebrew writings. This was appropriate to the quarter's theme, which had to do with prime literary and poetical selections of Scripture. The studies in the old rabbinical reference opened up new windows for traditional Christians. The material dealing with the Twenty-third Psalm was so new and different that it made a lasting spiritual impression of the Babylonian exile experience. This Pilgrim, in his third sortie, tries to bring his appreciation of the psalm into harmony with our daily lives in the Space Age.

As an initial step it will add theological interest in the old Hebrew ideas of eternity and life in the hereafter. I present here the psalm as it appears in *Good News*, the New English Version.

163

The Lord is my shepherd;
    I have everything I need.
He lets me rest in fields of green grass
    and leads me to quiet pools of fresh water.
He gives me new strength.
He guides me in the right paths,
    as He has promised.
Even if I go through the deepest darkness,
I will not be afraid, Lord,
    for you are with me.
Your shepherd's rod and staff protect me.

You prepare a banquet for me,
    where all my enemies can see me;
You welcome me as an honored guest
    and fill my cup to the brim.
I know that your goodness and love
    will be with me all my life;
and your house will be my home
    as long as I live.

Look at this version very carefully and, if you are over twenty years of age, you will note at least a half-dozen places where important new concepts in this pastoral hymn are presented. At the moment, I wish only to direct your attention to the last four lines, which reveal the limitations of the ancient Hebrew idea of mortal life as compared to the Christian faith, which places the fulfillment of total life, both secular and sacred, eternally in the presence of God. It seems quite clear that the exile on the way back to Jerusalem from Babylon was engrossed in getting his mortal, secular, flesh-and-bone body safely back home. It is evident that the phrases, "all my life," and "as long as I live," are mortally oriented. The exile was returning to the House of God, the restored temple, and would be at home there until he drew his last breath. Christian theologians have generally agreed that the early Hebrews were not clear about what happened to souls after death. An indefinite picture developed, the emergence of a third, lower level, i.e., Sheol, under the primeval two-level world of firmament and earth prepared for the Garden of Eden. The author of the psalm apparently thought little of what the far future meant to his soul. He was anxious to arrive in Jerusalem safely and alive. With this prologue, we turn now to the psalm in our Revised Standard Version.

If we can say that taxes and death are everlasting, perhaps it is as true that the Twenty-third Psalm is the basic meditative resource for practically all Christians. It says it all and it is everlasting. Can you remember a funeral service where the psalm was not introduced in one way or another? It seems to fit so perfectly. When the Persians (Babylonians) decided to allow the exiles to begin returning to Judah in 535 B.C., these now well cared for people faced an ordeal that their leaders knew was not for the faint hearted. Seven or eight hundred miles of rough travel, mostly on foot, beset by brigands of various intent, would be a real testing of physical endurance and loyal faith in God. Scholars believe that Isaiah III near the end of the exile was the author of this original *marching hymn*. This was a hymn for a crusader, a returning pilgrim eager to take up a difficult and different life again, a soldier for God prepared to resist all opposition. I personally took the Twenty-third Psalm out of the funeral service, and made it my most repetitive private prayer. Against the Lord's Prayer it probably scores at least two to one in my list of personal power tools. (See chapter 11.) Speaking of power tools, the fulfillment of the Old Testament law and prophecy was the infinite power contributed to this psalm when Christ demonstrated God's contribution of His pledge of eternal life. Thus the temple, the former "home" at Jerusalem, was translated into "heaven" and the eternity of spirituality in His presence.

Shepherds do not seem to have very much in common with an interstate highway system. Nor does the morass of evil stemming from the greedy struggle for power, private and international, which makes most treacherous ground for the march of men and women made in God's image as they surge on into the new century. Billions of the world's inhabitants, however, are still close to Mother Earth and not far removed from pastoral life. As long as a pertinent book or a picture can stir a primal nerve we can easily visualize and apply the analogy that has brought peace and spiritual understanding to generation upon generation. It can continue to do so. The twenty-first century will depict a seeming sophistication, but will not outgrow the need for sheep and a shepherd.

Bible scholars date the original psalm near the close of the Babylonian exile. Next to the Lord's Prayer, it is the most often-quoted selection of Scripture. Every Sunday-school child in America to the present, upon its use or mention of the title, draws a picture from his mental file. This picture is a replica of the painting or drawing held in hand, or standing on a chart before the class, picturing Christ with a shepherd's crook in one hand and holding a lamb at His breast with the other. Generally the words "I am the good Shepherd" will appear prominently. Some portion of a beautiful rural landscape may be in evidence. It is a tender and compelling picture and we, as children, generally begin our movement toward church membership at that point. The natural care of a child for his pet provides his entry into initial understanding of the psalm.

"The Lord Is My Shepherd"

For the Old Testament period of the mid–sixth century before Christ, the title Lord was equivalent to the word God. He was the Creator and Sustainer of a three-level flat universe consisting of the heaven, His dwelling place, with Sun, Moon, and Stars; a lower level of Earth where His human family dwelt; and a third, still lower, indefinite place called Sheol, a dark and dreary place where wandered the dead in a state not too clearly defined. In the prior millennium, God had been a stern God of law and righteousness, the author of the Covenant with Abraham. Moses had added details of a stern discipline for the chosen people as he led them out of slavery in Egypt.

But following the glory of David and Solomon, the nation had gone to seed. They sinned mightily and this stern and just God used a couple of foreign nations as His agents to punish them. They were exiled to these other lands during two time periods, and Jerusalem was sacked and burned. It seemed at one point that God was ready to wash them down the drain to oblivion. In their new humbleness the people were ministered to in their misery by special prophetic leaders who received special insight from God. Prophets like Hosea could actually use the word "love" to denote God's affection for His chosen people. God would even gather them up and see that they got back to Jerusalem where they could rebuild their temple and their nation. Thus to God's original power as a creator, a stern but just lawgiver, was added the attribute of forgiving love. Now His people, and the psalmist in particular, could address Him as a shepherd. The tribe had grown up from

166

the beginning as shepherds, caring day and night for their most valuable possession next to God Himself. Their sheep and goats were their very basis for maintaining life and commerce with each other. What a world of meaning and deep emotion and two-way devotion was denoted by the choice of the metaphor "The Lord Is My Shepherd."

What can we do with this figure of speech in a Space Age? In this country many children have never seen a real sheep. As a matter of fact, we don't like to compare ourselves to dumb sheep today. We do not easily humble ourselves to that category when our egos are clamoring for status and attention. Perhaps one should consider that in order to follow the psalmist's prescription, a period of meditation and prayer for forgiveness should be prerequisite for using the psalm in any way at all. To actually say, "The Lord Is My Shepherd," and mean it, is a tall order to begin with. For the old Hebrew it was a 500-year prelude to "The Lord Is My Savior."

"I Shall Not Want"

There is such latitude in the term translated as "want." It provides inclusiveness of every thing and every situation of relationship to others. In fact the coverage is so broad that for it to mean a tangible, personal something we must approach it from the specific personal condition of the one who is "marching" or "praying" or both. That is to say that a person approaching this terminology from the impersonal, outside, and looking in with curiosity, will find it abstract and almost meaningless. But for the returning, marching exile, on the road from Babylon to Jerusalem with scant food supply and a road bandit lurking behind the big rock at the turn ahead, it was surcharged with specific meaning. Personal safety and the preservation of life was a pressing, constant problem. The fact that the shepherd was close at hand, that he was in the vanguard of the marching line, was reassurance that all was well. He would leave all things today in God's hands and have no fear.

You and I and our neighbors will each have his own immediate condition of fear or hurt, a need for confession. The phrase will mean everything to every person. "My life today, no matter what, is going to work out because He is at my side showing me the way." The New International Version has it: "I shall lack nothing." Today's English Version has it: "I have everything I need."

This latter phraseology gives us a clue within the word "need." It expands the idea of "want" as used in the psalm's initial statement of God's completeness. It immediately cuts the initial use of our "wants" down to size. Do we *need* everything we *want?* Affluent life in many quarters today makes for an exaggerated Santa's list, and our true needs are submerged in greedy wants. One way of interpreting the psalmist is to realize that when I refer to God as my shepherd, I neither *need*, nor *want*, anything but a close relationship with Him. We have established the "I-You" relationship with God, which should be the ultimate in this Space Age as *need* and *want* become identical. We have all we *need*, and all we *want*, in Him.

"You Make Me Lie Down in Green Pastures"

Tired men and women are apt to be short-tempered and very quick on the draw with the sharp retort. Tired men and women do not do good work either mentally or physically and there is no real distinction in this respect between blue- and white-collars. God, with the help of His Hebrew poets, had installed the seven-day week with the work limited to six days topped with a day of rest. But the ingrained daily ritual of bedding down the flock each evening was most important to a nomadic sheep and goat herding people. And though the daily nomadic movement of the tribe had largely disappeared with the establishment of the monarchy, the daily work with animals prevailed for many of the people. God is saying, "You have worked hard today; you have grazed over rough ground; you have met your production schedules; you have settled arguments, gone the extra mile, looked after your neighbor; and now it is time to lie down and allow your physical body to catch up. This is a fine spot I have selected for you, out of the wind and with an abundance of food on hand for tomorrow morning." We are thankful for your care, O Lord; we will rest, and in the morning rise refreshed for new challenges.

Life for most of us is a rhythm of work and rest; we expend and recuperate. Our bodies, our minds, and our souls can profit from our Maker's provision of this rhythm. Our souls are heavy, however, with the thought that millions of God's human family will lie down this night in hunger and despair, not knowing what they will have to sustain bodily life on the morrow. Instead of a green pasture they are lying down in the chill of a bleak desert wilderness. The cement is hard to lie upon. There are not enough warm air vents to go around. The park bench is exposed, rain means crowding under whatever shelters. Several layers of newspaper are no real substitute for underwear. The space under the viaduct is already crowded and a vile stench prevails. Their plight implores our attention and aid. Perhaps we, in our comparative comfort and luxury, feel unable to be much of a good Samaritan, but we do have a resource we must learn to draw upon. We must *pray* for them. We must lift them up to God and ask that the combined strength of the world's minds and spirits and resources be amended to overcome and answer their needs. We ourselves must seek wisdom to learn how we may become one of the answering agents. This will not be light and flimsy prayer; it must be deeply moving and heartfelt. (See chapter 11 on prayer.)

"You Lead Us beside the Still Waters"

Gandhi followed a rigorous daily regimen. He rose at five o'clock and spent one hour in solitude, study, and prayer. Thus, he said, he tried to keep in touch with God. This cannot be done very well in the bustle of the market place or on the production line. Even driving one's car these days does not allow us to safely leave off driving defensively, with a sharp eye ahead and to the rear. God gave us a spiritual receiving set. He expects us to use it. We can learn to modify exterior intrusion, but we do need periods of complete quiet. We believe He expects us to have some sort of meditative concentration each day with Him. We must have quiet waters, a place to drink, or we will slowly shrivel up and die in our spiritual desert. He is constantly beaming a message to us. Do we take time to listen?

I have run across a story from Gandhi's student days in England. He had been reading the New Testament and was ready to inquire about Church membership. Attempting to enter a Christian religious meeting at a church in England, he was turned away by the usher with a brusque "You don't belong in this meeting." Gandhi never again approached the Church Establishment. He was quoted many times as saying, "I love Jesus Christ, but I hate Christians." We hope he was misquoted and probably said "dislike" instead of "hate." Gandhi drank deeply of the living waters in the New Testament. American ministers attest to the fact that he memorized the entire Scripture of Jesus' "spoken words." He was able to lead a whole nation to democratic freedom. He was God's agent.

"You Restore Our Souls and Lead Us in Paths of Righteousness for Your Name's Sake"

No soul means we are dead. But we are often weary and sick of soul. We are wont to say that our spirits are cast down. Life seems to be hard at times and it is difficult to be cheerful about the future. We train and install lifeguards at various swimming centers. They keep a sharp eye on the activities about them. Those who meet with unexpected difficulty in the water are rescued and restored to happiness. Ever since His Creation act, God has had His Rescue Plan in operation. Because it is of the Spirit, there are times we find it difficult to perceive. Our contacts have corroded so that the Holy Comforter is not getting through with His message. We have lost *hope* and we need to realize that only God can restore it. Life's goal grows dim—we may even sit in tears of remorse. Yes, we actually seem at times to be "God forsaken." Very often the catalyst toward improvement is finding someone worse off than we are and then determining to help him out of his situation. Just trying to help once more opens the circuit to God's adrenaline, and we pick up where we left off. That path ahead now seems to have some signposts we did not see before. A verse or two of Scripture comes to mind and we take hold of life again with Hope restored. For His Name's Sake? Of course we are reconciled to *His* plan and purpose.

"Though I Walk through the Shadow of the Valley of Death, I Will Not Fear Because You Are with Me, Your Rod and Your Staff Protect and Care for Me"

This is certainly a very complete sentence. Not only does it indicate life's uncertainties as to length but it contains the antidote. In 500 B.C., the antidote was God; in A.D. 2000 it is *still* God but God in Christ as well.

At this point in the psalm we become aware of what it was originally all about. Rabbinical notes contributed by the American Bible Society

170

several years ago all considered this psalm to have been written as a Marching Song to uplift and bolster the returning exiles as they trudged the eight hundred miles from Babylon to Jerusalem. The dangers on the return trip were very real. Bandits lived off the travelers at every turn and human life was cheap. Some of the group would not reach their destination alive. Nevertheless, they are reminded that their shepherd, God, is present to protect them.

I know we Christians have the freedom to interpret this upon the high level of God in Christ who, because of His personal human life, was easily accepted as the Shepherd figure. He who guarded His flock by day and at night would ward off attackers to the death. Today our vehicular transportation seems to demand an extra measure of care. Every day we drive a car we literally take our lives in hand. We fail to remember that *each year* we kill as many people on our highways as was the loss of American lives in the total span of the Viet Nam War. Over 50 percent of highway statistics are connected directly to beverage alcohol. I pause here only to let 75 percent of my readers know that if they are imbibing Christians, perpetuating the death tolls by the consumer support they give the booze industry, they might consider more carefully whether they continue their one- or two-drink rule. Some accidents, of course, will happen.

One year ago, after we personally learned to know and love our next seatmate in the pew at church, disaster struck. Our friend was a widow of very lovely mien and character, so easy to chat with. Suddenly one Sunday morning she did not appear. She had been in an accident the day before and by Tuesday her remains were laid to rest. In this tragic and temporal life we must stop our daily schedule often and pray for alertness of eye and keenness of mind as we navigate from here to there. *So live today as if it were to be last day of your mortal life!* Do not leave the word of love, the word of thanks and appreciation, the forgiveness of the debt or the trespass for another day. Tomorrow may be too late.

"You Set a Table before Me and Anoint My Head as an Honored Guest"

As with the green grass in the first section we here have another reference to the bread of life and our daily requirement, like the "bread" in the Lord's Prayer. God has treated us generously; we do not deserve anything, but God, out of His goodness and compassion, sees that we are taken care of. But this is no emergency soup kitchen in the slums—we are honored guests receiving the time-honored attention of the Host who anoints us at His head table. How easily it becomes a habit to expect the abundance which surfeits us. Too much of any good thing may become a snare and a temptation. Just as in the assumption of U.S. governmental power in world affairs, we see the tendency of the individual citizen to assume a privilege beyond his fellows. In the super-abundance of this nation's foodstuffs and natural resources, we are tempted to take a superior stance as if it were our right to be so blessed; the sense of stewardship shrivels to the vanishing point.

"Indeed, My Cup Overflows"

God pours the abundance of the "good" things of life into our very private laps and so easily we begin to consider them our right. He is equipping us for a purpose and we fail Him and ourselves when we close our eyes and do not perceive that He means to answer another's need through us as His agents. We too quickly and selfishly assert that the gift is for us to hide under our own selfish bushels. We forget that at God's table we are being commissioned both as a nation and as individuals to do His will in alleviating the hurts of others.

"Surely God's Mercy Will Follow Me All the Days of My Life"

Why should God's mercy continue to be showered upon us day by day? Is the psalmist falling into the same trap we were discussing in the paragraph above? Once again the flow of spiritual goodies just has to keep coming by force of habit or by royal prerogative? Perhaps we have accomplished something on the plus side for God, and this flow of bounty is merely our rightful reward? When Martin Luther finally decoded God's message to him back in the sixteenth century, that question of good works was also studied by the other early Reformers who reinforced the idea that Good Works were never a part of a contractual agreement by which, at the conclusion of the "Good Works," payment was received in full. The reverse was true. One performed good works because it was felt that is what Jesus' way of answering the problem would have been: the action of responsive love. Thus the good work is a by-product rather than a cause, a thank-you for His abiding mercy. The continuous character of God's abiding interest in man was born out by the long centuries of history. By Jewish reckoning God had begun the process of His creation four thousand years before the psalm was written, and had preserved and succored them every day since. The psalmist was proclaiming infinity in the future as the attribute of God's longevity and everlasting power.

"And I Will Live in His House with Him Forever"

The psalmist is again very clear in raising his insignia of Hope for what the condition after death will be. Sadducees of Jesus' time did not believe in life after death, but here we have a saint five hundred years ahead of Him holding out the promise of the eternal life of the spirit joined with God. The spirit is eternal, and within it Hope is consummated. The details of the "house" and the various descriptions of John the Revealer are really so unimportant. It is the Host who is all-important, our Father God.

The change in the use of this psalm in adult worship has been quite marked during this past century. It has practically disappeared from the formal Sabbath service but is almost universally a part of the Christian burial service. Since the funeral service is a celebration of the deceased's entry into God's presence, the last thought expressed in the psalm is a beautiful continuation upon that entry. The Christian, in relating Jesus Christ's promise of eternal life, emphasizes and enhances its use in the funeral service. Nevertheless, I do not feel it amiss to revert to the original motive for creating this psalm as the Hebrews saw it, and presumably they used is as such; namely, it was a marching song for our temporal lives in general.

In my thought about its most effective meditative use, I finally resolved to try it as a personal, individual prayer. This followed directly after reading a theological paper where the establishment of the I-You personal relationship with God becomes one of the most important objectives of life. As you glance back over the psalm you will note that in several of the petitions God, as the Shepherd, is addressed in the third person. Such fashion of address keeps us talking *about* God instead of *to* God. Likewise we should change all first-person plurals to the first-person singular, i.e., I-Me. In brief, when, Dear Reader, you and I talk together as we now are, the direct personal give-and-take is operative. It calls for honest expression and I try to make myself as clear as I can so as not to have you expect too much from me. Please feel challenged to try this experiment with me. First, we write out the psalm with all the pronouns altered as per above. Then we read this chapter over again down to this point. I suggest that you add the proper final sentence of your own composition after you have read the additional thought I used in closing my own personal prayer. The following is my version:

> Dear Father God, My Creator and Sustainer, my Saviour Christ, and my Holy Comforter: you are my shepherd . . . and so I have no need [pause]. . . . You make me lie down in green pastures and lead me beside the still waters [pause]. . . . You restore my soul and lead me in the paths of righteousness for Your name's sake [pause]. . . . I am aware that every day I walk through the valley of the shadow of death [pause] . . . but I will fear nothing because you are with me, your rod and your staff protect and comfort me [pause] . . . you set a table before me in the presence of my enemies [pause] . . . and anoint my head with oil as your honored guest [pause] . . . Indeed my cup overflows [pause] . . . surely your Goodness and Mercy will follow me all the days of my life [pause] . . . and I will live with you in your house forever [pause] . . . not by means of merit, but because I claim the promise of your good news as you spoke to us about eternal life through the life and resurrection of Jesus Christ. In your name I pray. Amen.

The word "guarantee" is pretty strong, but let me surmise that once you have prayed several times to the point where the terminology comes forth spontaneously you will be surprised at the way in which the "peace of mind" you sought is now wonderfully exceeded by the "Peace of God."

In the closing chapter on Prayer, I discuss the necessity of taking sufficient time during each praying episode to add strength to the I-You relationship. One does not expect God to immediately effect an answer, but in a meditative mood we ought to be as receptive as we are able. A part of the mood can be one of coming completely clean with enough mental concentration flowing out of our total reservoir of experience to let God know we really mean business. Rushing through a prayer with words tumbling out pell-mell in an attempt to save time actually wastes the very substance of prayer itself. It would seem that nowhere in our spiritual activities is the well-worn cliché that haste makes waste more applicable. As you read the comments above on using the psalm as a prayer, did you actually wonder what was intended by the use of the "pause" after each major phrase? During the two years this manuscript progressed through the first four drafts, I made no move toward changing that word. I felt that the ultimate reaction of any reader would be a right one—the flooding in of the actual personal daily life experience of the one praying. However, as we approached the final typing of the last draft, I thought better of it and have inserted some examples of my own pauses. They are camouflaged to some extent but plain enough to alert all readers to their own possibilities. Indeed, it becomes an introductory pathway to my final chapter, and I suggest that when you arrive there you turn back and reread the psalm as your introductory example of real prayer.

You have often heard the remarks of a person who has had a traumatic life experience just short of death, such as being about to drown or upon a mountain slope emergency. In the "twinkling of an eye" there flashes across his mind's eye a kaleidoscope of his entire life. It exists for only a moment, but high resolves are born therein. The *pause* indicated above in praying the Twenty-third Psalm is not a *stop* by any means. It is a few seconds during which your own experiences in the particular subject of the pertinent phrase flash before you.

For example, let us consider pause one. As you address God, you are instantly aware of the years it has taken to really make the ONE-NESS of God seem real, and you are sorry before Him for having taken so long. The Great I-AM, the Monotheistic Presence, encompasses us. He made us all for a purpose. Do I fit in? We instantly see Him in His three aspects as One Powerful Presence. (Remember the example of the high-school student back in my analogy section.) He MADE everything. He was in Christ our Saviour, and He is the Holy Spirit, the daily Enabler, all wrapped up in the concept of a single Person, the SPIRIT— to whom I owe everything I am and everything I have. The strength of the Trinity gives me an instant warmth as I recognize the far-reaching God, the God on the cross, and God in my heart and at my elbow making ready to clasp me into His Spiritual Field of Force not unlike a magnetic field of force.

God, with an access like this to You, I just do not need anything more. Is that too much for ten seconds? Then start with part of it at two or three seconds. Now, pause two: *I am tired. I feel exhausted today. I need the rhythm of work and rest. Let me lie right at your feet and go to sleep. I will be safe. Let me wake up tomorrow morning with a thought of thanks to you and your wish for me rather than my own self-interest. I have not worked very hard for You lately, Father. Tomorrow I shall*

175

work for you until I drop. Remind me in the morning. I sip a bit of the cool Living Water tonight as did the woman at the well. Thank you for John Gibson and his new book. He is your man 100 percent. Help me to read and appreciate him. Pause three: *At times I lose heart and hope for I am discouraged over my state of health or over the health of my spouse. There has been a loss of life in our family from severe illness or mishap. There seems to be little sign of relief. My job is going downhill. Pick me up, Lord, and restore me to a happy frame of mind. I used to blame you for letting such things happen, but I know that is very wrong of me. Help me with my choices each day. Forgive me for straying from your side.* Pause four: *What a close call I had today. That chap turned his car right across my clear path—he must have been going eighty. You had him swerve just in time. I am so grateful. Dear God, help me in turn to show courtesy on the road. Keep me from changing my kind disposition when I climb into our family car. Courtesy comes with difficulty then, and I need your special help. Dear God, I long with all my heart to act today, as all days, as if it were the last day you allotted me.*

Having read these flashing vignettes, lest you become discouraged or confused, let me remind you again that the object I am striving for is the establishing of a mood. Such a mood is an orientation of one's thought and spirit toward a state of humility, complete dependence on the largess of God, and the abject position of any human in the presence of the shining, overwhelming glory of God. One cannot hope to cover the vast detail of his life's total experiences in a few seconds, but remember that the playback apparatus of one's spiritual videoscope seems limitless. The above details of life, Dear Reader, may not fit you except in minimal aspects. But I challenge you to place yourself in God's presence and you and He will slowly build a prayer relationship which will be yours alone.

Dear Father-God: You are my Creator, my Saviour, and the Holy Comforter guiding me in my daily life. Thank you for the special gift your servant prepared in Babylon so long ago. You completed his psalm when You came to us within the person of Jesus. We become humble in the midst of the reality of your limitless person of Jesus. We become humble in the midst of the reality of your limitless love and concern for us, your erring children. We pray that we may continue to grow in the warmth and the depth and breadth and height of that relationship.

In Your name in Christ, Amen.

SORTIE NUMBER FOUR. THE APOSTLES' CREED FOR THE SPACE AGE

(Before reading this section, please turn back and review the analogies in chapter 1.)

The Pilgrim has made it through the three previous sorties in comparatively pleasant circumstances. He kept putting off this trip because, though traveling in well-marked territory, he was well aware that he would be disturbing many others in the faith. He saw many of their prominently placed warning signs: KEEP OUT. And others: DO NOT BLASPHEME THE NATURE OF ALMIGHTY GOD. And still others: THE SAINTS WHOM WE ADORE HAVE SPOKEN; TO CRITICIZE THEM MEANS YOU DISOWN CHRIST. Finally, a real bad one: TRESPASSERS FORBIDDEN TO ENTER UNDER ANY PRETENSE—KEEP OUT. A complete negative like that last one always stirred up the pilgrim's objection to being criticized for what he personally defined as his basic honesty and right of investigation. If there was really nothing to hide, he could come to that conclusion too. He could tell others what he had found.

As a member of a churchgoing family I realized in early high-school days the Apostles' Creed was something a Christian knew by heart so that at an appropriate point in the worship service, he could repeat it and keep in tune with the rest of the congregation. Upon being received into church membership at seventeen, my sense of its hidden value began to develop so very slowly. To be sure, an elementary concept of the Trinity had entered my consciousness, and when we spoke of God the Father, Christ the Son came simultaneously to mind. But there was a mystery situation when at the later Pentecost sermons, the rushing wind was supposed to be God's way of showing that a third person had to be reckoned with. He, however, remained a rather neutral, hazy figure of speech. My one year of church history at college finally filled in some of the missing background and I conceded the high mark attained by the Church Fathers when they got together in A.D. 385 and finally agreed on the word-by-word composition. There must have been a great many arguments in that meeting, for final *action had to represent a compromise* between strong minds. How very interesting a verbatim record would have been, similar to what Bill Moyers did for our Founding Fathers of 1787. (During the 1987 TV broadcasts of the daily proceedings of the 1787 Constitutional Convention in Philadelphia, many controversial views at times became so strongly insisted upon that that august body was on one occasion at the point of dissolution. We saw and heard Thomas Jefferson defend the morality of the abolition of slavery. He failed, and the compromise set the stage for the Civil War seventy-four years later.) I wonder how much Almighty God lost in the concluding compromise of that gathering back in A.D. 385. The experience within the Constitutional Convention should teach us that not all wrongs are righted in such human assemblies. Can you blame me for wishing to pry out the truth behind the A.D. 385 edition of the Saints? I am sure God says, "Go to it, but even if I help you, you will make a few mistakes yourself."

I had accepted the third person of the Trinity as a somewhat neutral segment of my faith. The Holy Comforter was not denied; He was merely not counted as much. At that point some of Rufus Jones's Quaker mysticism rubbed off on me and I began to realize that I was daily immersed in God's Spirit and *didn't know it*. I had remained ignorant for a half century that my Holy Comforter, the Enabler, was God's Spirit—was in me and around me every minute of the day.

The year is A.D. 2000. The fall season is approaching and the church's session and its pastor have gone on a weekend retreat. The pastor had promoted this special retreat as the direct result of the question raised by one of his parishioners. The man had been affronted by the remarks of a colleague at their place of employment. The church member upon inviting the newcomer to attend weekly worship was met with this rebuff: "You know, Jim, the other day I picked up one of Judy's Sunday-school papers. It carried a reference to Christian belief. The Apostles' Creed was there in print. I read it with real astonishment and aversion. Presumably people who call themselves Christian say this is their statement of belief. It is your Creed. As you may know, I have never attended church. We have allowed Judy to go to Sunday school with your daughter on the basis of their friendship. I read your statement of belief through again and again, and yet again. As a member of the church you no doubt have sworn allegiance to that statement. Jim, it is such a crude, primal statement that it turns me off completely. How can you really swear to a thing like that? I am not really an atheist, but my agnosticism is in no way challenged to search behind the church's stance of polytheism and the implication that one God is the son of another, further that there is some sort of throne up there above us with a side seat for a second God; and what in the world is this Sheol? I guess it is not really Hell, or is it? Then there is the astonishing reference to a Ghost. Is the church a ghost story after all? The term passes so quickly and without any phrasing to give it substance. Jim, you could not get me into a worship service using that Creed. I'll come to your men's dinner next week, but I hope the preacher is not the main speaker."

There you have it. The direct rebuttal from a Space Age scientist. And even if we are not all scientists, we at least, during our entire lives, seem to reflect a natural show-me spirit. Do you really believe that some oblique reference to the poetic license that allows latitude in symbolic language is sufficient to explain it all? The discussion at the weekend retreat did not resolve the matter, but presumably, as the pastor prepared his coming year's Continuing Education program, he proposed to spend some time talking to the science staff at the denomination's church-related college. He put in an item covering the cost of an elementary science textbook.

Every Christian seminarian, as stressed in my chapter on Christian education, should be advised to include a science minor in his B.A. college work. This is the other side of the coin that calls for a science major to provide for minors in social studies if he is to be culturally literate, i.e., an educated person. How can the future theologian/pastor hope to cope with the age ahead if he does not also understand how his probable adversary ticks?

We can hope, pray, and labor hard to overcome the current state of high school illiteracy. Any definition conceivable for the high school graduate of the twenty-first century must surely require the universal instruction reflected by a minimum of one year in chemistry and one year of physics. Thus, coincident with his teenage experience in his Christian confirmation class, he will have a slightly higher comprehension of the makeup of the natural world about him. His vocabulary to describe that natural world will have some terms and concepts within it quite unlike those in the vocabularies of his grandfather and great-grandfather.

Our young friend knows that the water in his glass is a compound made up of still further, smaller components called chemical elements. He knows that God included some one hundred of these elements when He made the earth. He knows that two of these elements, hydrogen and oxygen, when combined in the proper proportions, i.e., sixteen grams of oxygen and two grams of hydrogen, form water, which is hydrogen oxide. Further, our candidate knows some vocabulary describing this water, this chemical compound that is necessary to the existence of life. He knows that it exists in three states or physical conditions, i.e., as a liquid, as a solid, and as a gas or vapor. He appreciates the fact that all three states are chemically identical, *the same substance*. He knows that this is a natural expectation of a number of compounds. These compounds have characteristic melting points. They may also have boiling point temperatures at which the liquid becomes a gas. The boiling point temperature can be influenced by the existing atmospheric pressure. It is necessary to include this in the following statement. Under the proper conditions of temperature and pressure all three states can exist in equilibrium with each other. One does not have to heat water to the boiling point to produce the gas. Water spilled on a table at room temperature will all evaporate into gas, given time. Thus we may make the correct statement that at 32° F (0° C) and under atmospheric pressure, all three states of H_2O exist in equilibrium with each other. Thus the young mind with this simple technical fact in focus can begin reading about the Christian Trinity and almost instantaneously is able to grasp the concept that beyond this launch pad of certainty, he can now attempt to leap into the mystery of the spiritual Kingdom. *Absolute spiritual identity exists in all three.* God the Creator, Christ the Savior, and the Holy Spirit, the COMFORTER, are composed of the same identical spiritual substance or God-stuff. Truly defining spiritual substance is beyond our mortal minds, but we do arrive at its Oneness, its Unity of parts.

While he is still in high school, the young student is able to explain to his family and to his pastor how he knows in his heart that God, Christ, and the Holy Spirit are identical, just like the Bible says they are. He can now speak of the One God to others and know what he means. Christ was God entering the human person of Jesus of Nazareth. *No high school teenager should be "graduated" out of his communicant class into full active membership in the church without getting this ANALOGY DOWN PAT.* We are now prepared to go the final mile and develop anew the Space Age Apostles' Creed. Let us once more carefully run over the Creed word by word, as it has come down to us from its Constantinian age.

The Apostles' Creed (A.D. 385)

I believe in God, the Father Almighty, maker of heaven and earth, and in Jesus Christ, His only begotten Son; who was conceived by the Holy Spirit [Ghost] and borne of the virgin Mary; He suffered under Pontius Pilate, was crucified, died, and was buried; He descended into Sheol. The third day He rose again from the dead and ascended into heaven where He sitteth at the right hand of God the Father; from whence He will come to judge the quick and the dead.

I believe in the Holy Spirit [Ghost], the Holy catholic church, the communion of saints, the forgiveness of sin, the resurrection of the body, and the life everlasting.

But now our teenager becomes disturbed. Christ at various times in His ministry referred to God as His Father. And especially during those excruciating hours of the Crucifixion, the term "Father" came naturally to His lips. Our young candidate for Christian life remembers the sermons and prayers in his congregation in which the natural reference to Father and Son is prominent and he begins to wonder how this term of familiar family life gets in the way of his new Trinity concepts. He goes back to the Old Testament and finds that in the origins of his faith, spiritually minded poets and writers had to use the anthropomorphic vocabulary they had at the time. Things were phrased in such a way that the imagination could have free play, but the words were very limiting just the same. An example is given here:

Rabbinical comments indicate that every Israelite king following David and Solomon was crowned as Son of God, even though he did not turn out to be the Messiah they believed was coming. In brief, in Jewish theology, it was apparent that the sexual origin and close family tie of ordinary mortal life was not in evidence. "Son of," in Hebrew, carries the significance of the inheritance of a covenant, a commission from a prior generation or a total of such generations.

Our candidate now turns to the detailed Apostles' Creed. He rightly concludes that this statement, written by the church fathers several hundred years after the mortal life of Jesus, is sadly in need of revision. What is this strange reference to the primal Hebrew three-level world with heaven and the firmament above, the flat earth spread out below, and finally, in the dark dreary depths below that, a Sheol, was not very well defined? "How," the young candidate wonders, "can such language and beliefs be allowed to weigh us down in the new century? Christ is not sitting on a throne at the right side of God. He is God. And why tuck the Holy Spirit off in a secondary paragraph?" For He is also God.

Is there any question about the need of sitting down and attempting to bring the Apostles' Creed up to date? How do we expect to exert any persuasive influence on the scientific mind of the twenty-first century as long as we retain such outlandish symbolic language? The agnostic or the half-believing neighbor looks on in amazement. A few, no doubt, already consider us Christians suitable candidates for institutional incarceration, or perhaps worse, in God's light, as harmless passé cultists, not worthy of further notice.

Let us look at the language of monotheism as used by a renouned modern theologian. A few years ago, the theological surveys edited by Patterson (Word) reached the volume on Karl Barth. Only a very brief portion of Dr. Barth's voluminous writings could be discussed. It is fortunate that a portion of his concept of the Trinity could be included. He describes the Trinity as being thought of as "one God in three modes." However, he adds a restriction by saying that at a given instance, one must think of God as momentarily existing in only one of these three modes. One takes this to mean that in a given moment of prayer He is either God our Creator, or Christ the Saviour, or the Holy Spirit, the Comforter. This seems most arbitrary, very confusing, and I consider it to be so abstract as to be meaningless for the usual daily meditation. It overlooks the presence of all three states in equilibrium. No wonder our Jewish brothers look askance at the Christian claim to monotheism when they compare it to the Abrahamic monotheism of 1800 B.C. Are we not guilty of a mild sort of polytheism as we attempt to explain "three persons in the Godhead" to them in *traditional* terms?

The theologian or religionist who has never grasped a technical vocabulary in describing God's physical universe will brush me off with a quick "Don't make God a scientific instrument," but that is much too fast an answer to meet my demand. I am not making God mechanical. I am merely saying that if the religionist wants to get a message through to his scientist friend and technical neighbor, he will succeed by using an analogy that is easily understood by that friend. Refresh your approach to analogies as discussed in chapter 1 and be prepared to digest chapter 9. By accepting my first step as merely attracting the full attention of the hearers or readers you may come up with a better one. The actual substance of the spiritual nature of God is beyond understanding or comprehension. But I do claim that the secularly trained mind can then succeed in apprehending the Spirit via faith, because his prior well-used vocabulary *will bring him to the threshold*. Faith in the Spirit, as the third component of all humans, will be accepted by the scientist who retains some trace of acknowledgement that he is a member of a communal, moral society.

The rather secular example of water, as once used so effectively by Jesus on the woman at the well, became the fully spiritual Water in the *Presence* of God on that occasion. If handled carefully it may also become the stepping stone to the Spirit, in a different culture in A.D. 2000. We have discussed the three states of H_2O (commonly referred to as water) as a solid state, a liquid state, and a gaseous state. Water is capable of existing in all three states simultaneously. We must take our illustration one more step in a demonstration to show that in *whichever state* we encounter it, there exists the *constant identity in all three states*. Though we humans are unable to handle moral and spiritual laws in exactly the same fashion as this illustration, these minds of ours, the gifts of God, can be assumed as capable of grasping the ideas about God at a higher level. Indeed, *God has already endowed us with an extrasensory perception of Himself*. With this in mind I believe the concept of the three states of a substance in equilibrium to be a better starting point than Dr. Barth's "something" in three "modes."

Furthermore, our new concept makes simultaneous existence of the three states a natural assumption, which view Barth appears to wish to avoid. We arrive at the basic concept of the three states of God as Creator, Christ, and the Holy Spirit as ONE SPIRIT. We find it substantiated by both Scripture and the august body of saints who drew up the final form of the Apostles' Creed. We accept what they wrote as a reflection of the state of knowledge of how to put spiritual ideas into words in A.D. 385. What they "knew" then has been exceeded by what we know now.[1] We humbly propose that at the present level of knowledge (and perhaps some God-given wisdom?) of A.D. 2000 we can and should improve on both vocabulary and meaning by restating our basic Creed as follows:

Revised Apostles' Creed

I believe in the Triune God Almighty, Creator of the Universe, my Saviour Christ, and the Holy Spirit my Comforter and Enabler. I believe God dwelt among

His human creatures in Jesus Christ, to personify Love in Action and bring reconciliation between a sinful people and Himself. Thus Jesus was born of Mary under the direction of the Spirit, suffered under Pontius Pilot, was crucified, died, and was buried. He arose from the dead and ascended into God's Spiritual Kingdom, from whence it appears to be God's will to send Himself forth again. I believe in His holy catholic church, the communion of saints, the forgiveness of sin, and the life everlasting.

The traditionalist will immediately note at least two omissions or discrepancies, the choice of critical words being dependent on how fiercely one may wish to cling to the old. The new statement avoids direct insistence on a virgin birth. I may be accused of using "weasel" words, but does it actually make any difference whether Joseph's semen was involved or not? Humans are "made in God's image." He, who is totally spiritual, implants a part of Himself as the spiritual nature of every man and woman. In the case of Jesus Christ, I believe that although He was all man and human in His fleshly parts, God profoundly implanted such a dominating degree of Himself in Jesus that the boy at twelve years began to feel the power of His mission and His execution of it. In my personal meditation I hold *Jesus* as the baby and child, and *Jesus Christ* as the revelation of God during His three-year mission, and *Christ* as one of the three states of God's nature, finally returning to the Godhead.

Secondly, my suggested revision deliberately omits "the resurrection of the body" in the last line. This has always been authoritatively interpreted as referring to the revival of the bodies of all the dead saints at the time of Christ's second coming. I can see no teaching of Jesus Christ that substantiates the resurrection of the bodies of the saints at a future date. Were this to take place it will have to be 100 percent spiritual bodies of a sort that must remain God's secret, else He would run short of construction material. Chemically, we are already recycled bodies. Are the saints not already existing in their eternal bodies with God? At this moment, life on earth decrees that the chemical substances of old bodies are constantly being recycled into new bodies. Your high-school-aged son or daughter will tell you how this takes place.

A third item can be mentioned. How it ever became a part of the official canon is beyond me. The reference to descent into Sheol, an A.D. 2000 aberration, seems needless and was probably included at the last moment to prove to people that Jesus had actually died, that He was completely humanly dead. No one could continue to believe, as some did, that He was merely in a temporary trance.

The place of the Holy Spirit as a portion of our Triune God has always been so difficult for the average layman in the non-Pentacostal churches to comprehend that for many believers, the Trinity shrinks to the dual family term of Father and Son. This is most unfortunate for the adverse effect it has on the idea of the power of the Immanence of God, which is so important in our ever-present daily contact with His healing power and Comfort. Recall how the God of the Old Testament, in carrying out His covenant relationship with His chosen people, went through patient episode after episode until "in the fullness of time" He entered into closer relationship with His human family and implemented His Incarnation, a formal basic step in His ongoing Rescue Plan. Christ, who always had been identical with God before Creation, now was brought out into human experiential encounter. We did not know it in the humanity of incarnation, but near the conclusion of His earthly human visit, He unveiled the third state of His person. Early writers referred to this Pentecostal experience as the appearance of the Holy Ghost as the replacement of Christ's close immanent daily presence and ministration. The English word Ghost was replaced by the word Spirit as more appropriate, and we are also told in the Pentecostal visitation that He was to be the Holy Comforter. This is a most important improvement in the vocabulary for it helps emphasize the daily closeness of God, His Immanence. It helps to bring the far out, infinite, all-powerful, awful, and mighty person of God down from outer space into the midst of my family and into my study and my bedroom. I am immersed constantly in the Enabler's Field of Force just as we are all in the magnetic field of force.

As we have already discussed in chapter 1, the idea of the presence of God as analogous to the force of a magnetic field that envelopes the earth constantly makes it easier for us to realize that the Holy Comforter and Enabler is "closer than hands or feet; nearer than breathing." He is in us and around us, anxious at all times for us to turn on our spiritual receiving set and communicate with Him. Some folks will feel a strangeness when at first they accomplish the thought of God's spirit being housed within their physical bodies. Our faith tells us our spiritual nature is kin to the spirit of God, but just because our lesser spirit is bathed within God's greater spirit, that does not mean that we automatically have the two-way communication we desire. God's Spirit waits for our spirits to exercise the gift of free will. As the magnet of the compass needle responds to the force of the magnetic field in which it is immersed, so must we cause our consciences to make the connection with God. This spiritual connection we cannot explain, but we know that when we admit our mistakes to Him and sincerely ask Him for forgiveness and reviving strength, we experience a restoration and reaction which we call the "peace of God." Do not be disappointed if God the Comforter, the Holy Enabler, does not answer immediately. During our sleep, if we have previously turned on the spiritual receiver, His Spirit may speak to our spirits (through our unconscious or subconscious selves—let the psychologist label which), and when we wake in the morning He has clearly resolved the matter. We must not expect to have a 100 percent system, for we ourselves are so imperfect and we are so ignorant of the extent of the mystery of God's spirit. Then, too, it may be that God's delay is a part of the answer. I submit that more often than not He is using other people as the agent to carry the message to us. I would refer you to the final chapter of this book on prayer for a further discussion on this point. Through unexpected sources and contacts we perceive that the Holy Enabler is at work on our behalf. See, at the close of this chapter, a list of suitable references.

We cannot conclude these comments on the immanence of God as expressed through our ever-present contact with Him as the Enabler without specifically raising the new question of how God maintains the equilibrium between His three states (i.e., Creator, Redeemer, Enabler). For Christians, according to our New Testament, come to God only through Christ, the Redeemer. Does God reconcile mankind to Himself through Christ and then turn the task of our "becoming," which is our "sanctification," over to the Holy Spirit? In some manner and within this vastness of His power, God is able to listen to the confusion of earth's five billion plus souls and amidst their clamor and His infinite involvement in running the Universe, remain personally aware of the small speck that I am. My whole being is flooded with warmth as I perceive that all along He has been so infinitely great as to have Himself as Holy Comforter and Enabler flowing in, around, and over all five billion of us individuals. While busy with His expanding galaxy upon galaxy, He has spared a portion of Himself to engulf me and be my daily companion. Once again Jesus' reference to the sparrows takes on new meaning after a lifetime of groping and questioning.

At the risk of redundancy we repeat the final admonition. I must of *my own will* flick the spiritual decoding switch of *my* conscience. He empowers us only as we take the first step by clearing the lines and turning our spiritual antennas toward Him. *I must learn to pray.*

Holy Spirit

Rather than refer the reader to a detached reference in the appendix which may imply slightly less sense of urgency, I have chosen to conclude this sortie with a biblical reference taken from the *Interpreter's Bible*, Volume XII, pages 753-754.

Should this set of heavy tomes not be conveniently close by, you, as a minimum, may, with your personal Bible, check out the direct references to the Holy Spirit. Volume XII concludes with an index of subjects. Please note that the references under "Holy Spirit" are arranged in an interesting alphabetical fashion. You will probably feel cheated when you discover that only a few are specific scriptural chapters and verses. The majority refer to a discussion of the immanent scholarship of the expositor (or exegete).

Several of the references under the alphabetical approach actually overlap. As an example, the only reference in the Old Testament is: "activity of, and gift of, 4; 690 (b)." One finds this discussion of the very short One Hundred Thirty-third Psalm a quite hazy connection with the idea of the Holy Spirit as we have discussed Him in this sortie. However, we concede that such modern theological discussion may well afford acknowledgement of professionalism which we laymen find difficult to follow. Please note again that the original list does not include the actual scriptural references which I have inserted.

Holy Spirit:
activity of, 4; 690 b
blasphemy against, 8; 224/d/f/Luke 12:11
Christianity and, 12; 9/a
Colossians concept of, 11; 144/b/f/148/b
"democratized," 7; 9/a/f
as 'dynamis,' 7; 8/b
fellowship of, 10; 425/a/f
gift of, 4; 690/b 11; 610/a/f/ Hebrews 2:4
inspiration and, 12; 338 f
Johnannine concept of, 8; 443/a

John, in his fourteenth chapter, gives a fine first-century interpretation of the Trinity in verses 1–17. You will find it very pertinent in your twenty-first century study of Love and Energy in three spiritual states. Read it now, in several versions, not overlooking Phillips, and then join me in the following prayer;

Our dear Father-God: Infinite Maker and Giver of all things, Redeemer and Enabler "closer than breathing," we are grateful for this study period we have had this day. We have come to feel that this Truth of Your Spirit, Christ's Spirit, and the Holy Spirit are ONE: magnificent, mysterious, all-powerful, which is what our Christian faith is all about. As we meditate and pray upon this in the days to come, lead us into a fuller realization that the Three Spirits are, after all, YOU. You, our God, approach us in many different ways, but they are ONE, they are YOU, bearing to us the gift of Your love and mercy. We know we cannot comprehend your all-powerful gracious Presence until death of our mortal flesh will have brought us into Your presence. Dismiss us now with Your blessing—in Your Name in Christ. Amen.

Chapter VIII

Science and Religion—Still Skirmish?

The first half of the twentieth century provided the stage for what the journalists and the religionists were wont to tag "the war between science and religion." Such a label was a misnomer of the highest order. The true scientist never did recognize in his theories or by the material outcome of his laboratory research that he was an active combatant against religion. The second and third generation of von Liebigs, Faradays, Thompsons, and Pasteurs were too busy putting in long hours doing what came naturally. To be sure, they were laying the foundation of the materialistic culture that is now upon us in the second half of this century, but I believe this came by default on the part of theologians rather than by any deliberate plan to oppose or defeat. Science egged it on with a laissez-faire attitude toward religion and our spiritual natures. The traditional scientist saw little in religion to attract him in comparison with the molecules of secular stuff he was taking apart and putting back together into such interesting things, which, wonder of wonders, his compatriot employers were willing to pay him for. Other scientists dug into the rock heaps and the garbage dumps of prior millenniums and found skeletons of animals rivaling our ability to imagine, or other skeletons that came to look suspiciously like our own. Such scientists were probably considered by the religionist to have been the front lines of an attacking enemy.

Religion (not true spirituality) chose to see it as war and first called Darwin the devil's general. A perfectly good word, evolution, became so restricted and closely attached to Darwin's work that it generated the battle cry of the Bible literalists who had lost touch with the imagination and spiritual literary skill of authors J-1 and J-2, E, P, and a continuous line of redactors. The religionist thought he saw his Bible desecrated but failed to understand that the humans who *wrote* the story of Creation long after Abraham's time were somewhat like himself. They did the best they could with the very human language they spoke and were then learning to write.

While these one-sided polemical threats were being hatched on the part of the religionists, a devastating second enemy had risen within the Church's own ranks. What is known as liberalism became a two-edged sword. The traditionalist in religion calls liberal anyone who differs from his own self-imposed literal rigidity. But the tag of "liberalism" was also to be applied to an even more serious theological fault, the loss of God himself. I suggest that the reader acquaint himself with portions of the writings of Reinhold Niebuhr dealing with the No God movement.[1] He was against it mightily. In a word, it meant that many theologians in the Church were becoming enamored with the idea of the goodness of Man in his own self-progression toward Heaven's ideal, the perfect Man. It seems that such persons did not need God except as an emergency prop, a resident in the wings who might be called forth to help in times of real disaster.

Summing up the first half of the twentieth century, scientific progress puts us on the moon. Suddenly it was possible for the people of the world to be able to commit suicide within hours and days. There was created an acquisitive, materialistic culture which, in its present mood, does not really know if it ought to feed the hungry and bind up the wounded or build more weaponry. The scientist can be faulted for his unwillingness to concede any responsibility for the misappropriation of the results of research. He is only now beginning to think as an employer about his part in polluting the air we all breathe and the water we all drink and the soil that grows our food. The religionist camp fell down on the job, first by getting distracted and sidetracked by arguments over evolution and then by losing its initiative and clarity of vision in the face of the "God is dead" humanist philosophy.

In some fashion, religion and Christian spiritual force as representative of the extension of God's spiritual power failed to present to society generally, and to the scientists specifically, moral and ethical extensions of God's law. Clearly, to me, it would appear that Dr. Buttrick, whose scholarship I admire, overlooks his own limited view and that of compatriot men of the cloth. He did not recognize their lack of effectiveness in taking the results of science into the shelter of their faith. If the two parties were to be brought to the point of equal confessions of guilt, we might regain hope that the future will reflect a picture more in keeping with God's promises. The scientist can say, "I did not stop to consider all the results"; the religionist can say, "I am sorry I did not see my neighbor in trouble until it was too late." Monday morning quarterbacking comes so naturally.

Being an educational product of the scientific method myself I do not accept the full indictment of science unless we separate the problem into (a) its origin and method and (b) the exploitation of the results. What theologians see as the pure scientist is a rather cold-blooded, intellectual person in whom finding out how the physical universe works is so ingrained that he has little or no time to evaluate his work in terms of its contribution to his communal culture. There is also a real danger that, concomitantly, the scientist may become so ego oriented that God is pushed aside or more probably merely overlooked or tagged surplus baggage. But the scientific method per se must be considered a noble one, originally blessed by God Himself. In His gift of a thinking brain God told Mankind to subdue the physical universe, or at least to "command it." In a lifetime period in this century the scientist has done a stupendous job in this respect. Theologians should acclaim this and applaud. However, it is in the exploitation of the associate research results that the matter of ethics and morality comes into combatant focus. We have an Environmental Preservation Act in our land of law today for the reason that many of America's big corporations engaged in supplying the outward amenities of modern life based on scientific research have failed to take into account the corresponding evil buildup of by-product waste. This was let loose into the atmosphere or hidden in the underground water system. In many cases the health of the laborer does not receive proper attention. The exploitation of the results of research is fostered and vigorously supported by the acquisitive economic business interest that is the basis of industry. The business ethics of the corporation as an institution tend to override the concerns of any one individual employee. Hence the composite "we" in a corporation is a hard nut to crack; and Christ's Church to date has not had much outward success. It is noted, however, that within the past decade at least one scientific society[2] has been editorializing on the obligation and responsibility for control of industrial actions that impinge on the communal citizenry and environment. Perhaps the church, even though hiding behind the veil of separation of church and state, ought to be examining what it can do to help clean the air we breathe and the water we drink as well as feeding and clothing the poor and the hungry. Is it possible that science has a foot-dragging, impassive, impersonal adversary in religion, which has actually become one of its handmaidens? Has there been a complete reversal of roles? I submit that America is coming under the judgment of God and our spiritual leadership ought to be doing something about it.

For a moment, let us look more closely at a few men of science. Perhaps the preacher and theologian will find them surprisingly amenable to spiritual influence after all. Let us first meet Jonas Salk, M.D., the discoverer of polio vaccine and winner of a Nobel Prize for his work in that field of medicine. The impressions we present here are based on Dr. Salk's answer to questions posed by interviewer Stassinopoulous as reported in the *Parade* magazine.[3] He reveals himself as a warmhearted individual and he vigorously expounds a personal philosophy of caring and sharing with others. He does not hesitate to use the terms "love" and "loving" as his personal goals. In his words, he is adding "to a plan of evolution of his love," whereby he resolves to be a better lover of mankind next year than he was this year. Presumably if he were to live long enough the art of his loving would be perfected as his end objective. Of course the Christian is struck by such use of some of God's language without any reference to God Himself. Dr. Salk appears to be a scientist operating within a humanistic society totally without concern or awareness of the divine. I suspect that the Doctor is in God's hands, however, and doesn't know it; and that the church community of faith could use him as the example of the need for continued and fervent prayers with increased voltage and amperage.

Sir John Eccless, M.D., is a Nobel Prize winner. He has been concerned about the manner in which the human brain functions. What happens physically and chemically in the seat of the thought process? When the man on the street or the patient waiting in the clinic hears a reference to brain scan or CAT scan, he reflects respect for this British scientist. The brain scan is an important contemporary tool of the neurologist. In an interview as reported in the Charlotte, North Carolina, *Observer* of 1970, Dr. Eccless was confronted with the problem of how thought originates. He very carefully referred to a basic process of evolution by which the animal kingdom probably developed. He did not specifically refer to the actual point at which Homo erectus became Homo sapiens, but dwelt on the fact that material was being assembled into a mechanical structure, the brain, in a manner not unlike the construction of a computer. Up to this point evolution had presented a machine for a possible Divine Power to actually furnish the input. One is quite sure he was referring not to the mechanics of the key punch operator or a key board operator seeking information but to the Master Programmer who adds will and purpose.

Father Pierre Teilhard de Chardin was a French Jesuit priest who had served as a noncombatant in the trenches of World War I, an interruption of his collegiate work in Rome. After being ordained he went to England and earned his Ph.D. in geology as a fulfillment of his childhood rock-hound days. Later, he began digging and researching as a paleontologist. Engaged in such an undertaking in China, he was cut off from the Western world and submerged with a group of Chinese professionals who found and evaluated Peking Man during the years of the communist takeover in China. It appears that for many years he followed a Gandhi-type daily regimen of early rising for spiritual meditation and writing. The latter was as voluminous as his scientific notes of the remainder of the day. His religious work could not be published with Papal Imprimatur; in fact his French friends kept him out of Rome and away from the immediate dislike of the Pope. Publication was taken care of, surreptitiously, by those friends in France and England. The world acclaimed Teilhard de Chardin's scientific work on the Peking Man; one more possible world site had been added to the previous four possible locations of an original *adamah*. Prior to his death in this country, he lectured here and in Europe as a religious scientist, a qualified Christian evolutionist. I am not qualified to present his theological view in detail. Suffice it to say that one of his weaker points was that his view of God, a deity he considered powerful enough to be in total charge of all creation, did not appear to present Christ as a warm, personally involved Saviour. Some fellow Christians called him a pantheist. He could pick up a rock and discourse on its formation via the power of God. He could see and feel God in the physical aspect of the universe even to the first grain of sand.

Dr. Paul Tournier is now a retired French Swiss physician in his late seventies. As a young man of medicine, he hung out his shingle as a general practitioner. He was personally a devout practicing Christian. He felt aligned with Christ in the healing art. He became involved in the inner, personal lives of his patient community. He discovered that dispensing prescriptions for drugs and general medication for the ills of his community was answering only a small part of their difficulties. He began to perceive them as fellow children of God. They needed help for their minds and hearts as much as for their physical bodies. After serious consultation with his wife, for he knew his financial income would be reduced, he began letting people know that he preferred cases wherein he diagnosed mental and relational problems as the area in need of healing. He referred the mundane cases of sprains, belly aches, and mutilations of the physical body to his medical colleagues. Basically, he perceived man as having three natures, physical, mental, and spiritual, not separately but in total functioning harmony. He still wrote prescriptions where needed, but he also prayed with his patients and for them and spent long hours privately with them in their homes. He became a practitioner of medicine for the WHOLE PERSON. He established an annual summer vacation week for his medical colleagues, now a well-known European medical retreat at which physicians of sympathetic views get together to present their successes and failures in healing.[4] He personally continued to contribute daily Bible study during these retreats. See the volumes listed in the bibliography and perceive him as a bridge between science and total human life.

The chief purpose of presenting these examples of real science is to reassure our members of the faith that these flesh-and-blood characters are capable of being powerful fellow members and allies. They encourage us in enlisting divine help in molding a higher level of committed service in Christ's Church for the century ahead.

Let us return to the specific challenge that science presents to a church so far unwilling to spread a special net for such practitioners. One difficulty in dealing with scientists who are trained to measure, weigh, look at, and examine matter in the three natural states (liquid, solid, and vapor) is that they do not perceive themselves to be able to be experts in any other area of life. They represent only a portion of what life is all about. They deliberately restrict their outlook and interests. They know the labor involved in their own educational fine tuning and expect others worthy of communication with to understand them. The average scientist may develop a self-satisfied opinion of his upper-level status and can easily shrug off any feeling of cultural responsibility for humanity as a whole. He thus is a more negative-minded prospect for the Church to deal with. However, looked at positively, the scientist will not be satisfied with merely the spoken word, no matter how polished and eloquently the preacher and the theologian may present it. He will be looking at the backup evidence of performance. "Let me see some tangible results" will be his retort. Thus he puts the same challenge to the contemporary Church that Jesus insisted upon presenting to his fellow Israelites. "Put your performance squarely in support of your mouths."

Turn aside and take time from your own day and spend real effort and money in seeing that the wounds are dressed; talk bravely but be sure you actually lay your vulnerable life on the line. The man of the spirit must more earnestly learn to pray that the actual present daily power of the Spirit be responsive to his petition—and then go out and lead the charge of his flock in hard projects, calling for tough commitments. God expects us to work at helping Him answer our prayers. The Roman Catholic bishops are to be applauded for the stand they have taken in the leadership of the Church and its influence on the objectives of good government.

It is about time historically for another spiritual breakthrough. Historical chunks of time in five-hundred-year units seem to be the rough time slots for the Mighty Acts of God. Let's say it took five hundred years for Abraham's clan to get down to slavery in Egypt, get led out by Moses, and put in forty years' training before entering the Promised Land. Let us say it took five hundred years for Solomon's eclectic sons and wives to start wrecking the monarchy and have Israel wind up as a remnant of the remnants, struggling back from Persia to Jerusalem and a restored temple. And of course it took another five hundred years before God felt that the fullness of time had arrived for His personal entry upon the human scene. We pause only briefly at A.D. 500 for the complete eradication of the Roman empire and establishment of the papacy, and at A.D. 1000 for closing the period of the rise of Mohammed with the crusades—each with mixed emotions. However, God's hand was very clear at the A.D. 1500 benchmark with the invention of the printing press; how fast and how far flew God's word, thus fortifying the great Reform begun by Luther and Associates. Here we are at A.D. 2000, having, within a lifetime, experienced entry into the Space Age. Secular knowledge and technology is at an all-time high: man walks on the moon, robots at men's fingertips probe planets millions of light years away. How will God's will be made manifest? Dear Theologians, is it not now your time to perform and show the scientist and technologist that you can lead us on into a BETTER WAY? Or will it be by an event as humble as the Babe's birth and not discerned by the RELIGIOUS ESTABLISHMENT until long after?

There remains in this area of discussion a question that we have so far avoided. Specifically, should the individual scientist respond affirmatively to any project for which his government wishes to hire him? There is a corollary: Shall an individual investigate the product line of a so-called reputable company and decide to be employed by such on the basis of his private ethical and moral code? Hidden within these questions there is the basic one: When should man-made laws and regulated culture give way to God's law? The theologian who is critical of the evil application of the results of scientific research may have legitimate grounds for his criticism when the end use is considered to be for an immoral purpose.

There was a difference of opinion among the staff of scientists solicited by the government to work on the Manhattan Project. The atom bomb was being precisely designed for the murder of men, women, and children of a noncombatant segment of the enemy population. It was to represent a sudden reversal of a basic rule of warfare that civilization had previously woven tightly around the sanctity of the "innocent" civilian population. Guilty feelings by us, the aggressor, were somewhat assuaged when we learned how the threat of its use was preannounced to the Japanese war lords. Two successive secret contacts were made with them and to that powerful figure, the emperor. Twice the threat was rejected. I wonder if the double thrust was, in good faith, sufficient? Under a strict surveillance of a truce would it have been possible to have staged an actual demonstration in one of our Western deserts, the results of which could have been conveyed by motion pictures taken by escorted Japanese photographers themselves? or even not impossible to have invited the emperor and General Tojo to view it with their own eyes? It is probably true that the cultural psychosis of the Japanese military mind made it practically impossible for the general to have made peace on the basis of a threat in the absence of his emperor. If the two had considered the threat mutually in a private conference and then had made the on-site observation, we may have had an end to the war without the mass murder of the innocent population in two cities.

Unlocking the power of the atom revolutionized our ideas of sources of power for the use of world of the Space Age. It is far from having been acclaimed an unmitigated blessing. We seem to have opened a Pandora's box of continuing problems that are never finitely solved. Relative safety is not finite safety. We cannot contaminate the atmosphere and poison the ground with high radioactive fallout, for no

196

one has the final answer to sealing off such waste. Sinking it in lead drums in the deepest part of the ocean seems to be bottom line at the moment. But who can foretell the absolute quiescence of the earth's crust at any given point? To return to individual justice, we allow certain types of noncombatant service for the young man in the military who is a conscientious objector; so also the professional scientist may feel obliged to decline certain support research, in which decision he follows what he feels to be God's choice. By the same token, in peacetime, conscience may well play an important part in the choice of a place of employment. I may choose not to work for a tobacco company, or a concern producing alcoholic beverages or munitions, even though I may be destitute in the face of job scarcity. The theologian observing this scene must not be guilty of hypocrisy. Can he put forth the equal effort to set God's spiritual power to work in negating evil with both sweat and prayer as earnestly as the scientist has applied himself to his education and his particular work? Spirit and Mind must cooperate, and although the Spirit will prevail because He is God, He will not command ultimate obedience by virtue of His supreme Power but by virtue of His Love and Mercy. Our faith and hope remain that we all eventually concede His mastery and lordship.

We are compelled, on the basis of Christian faith, to prepare new lines of communication between science and religion. New vocabulary and analogies are demanded: these must appeal to the scientist and technocrat as individuals in the pew. I respectfully refer you to a rereading of the section on analogies (section 3 of chapter 1) and chapter 9 on evolution. The professional theologian will gain his leadership in the "conflict," if so one wishes to label it, i.e., "the overcoming of evil by good," by making himself understood by the modern materialist and secularist. The mystery of the Spirit will remain a mystery, else God is not God, but that mystery can be couched in the more persuasive language demanded by the Space Age. It may reflect use of more common terms of technology but will not be any less of the Spirit.

In concluding this chapter with the view that some scientists can also be simultaneously *agape* lovers, we are encouraged to add a brief section pointing out that science and religion, after all is said and done, actually spring from a common source, *God as Love*. It would appear that world view and culture prevailing now will tend toward continuing intense scientific study and the resultant technocracy. Christians will find it mandatory to stop criticizing the scientific endeavor as such and come to realize that they must concentrate on the battle against greedy, secular exploitation of the results of scientific research. At this point, I wish to plant a seed for your meditation hoping that by the time we make it into sortie number five in chapter 9 you may have put on more of the full armor of God.

We believers wholeheartedly declare that God is *Love*. We also know that *Love is not* until *action has demonstrated it*. God made the Universe as an abode for His human family. Love has therefore come into irrepressible existence according to His will. Without being too theological about it at this point, let us say that God is Spirit and the only thing we recognize about Him as being human is His Mind. God thinks kindly about us. In this abode, planet Earth, He wishes us to behave like Him and learn to love Him and each other. He made LOVE primary and thus Social Sciences were born in the Garden of Eden. Mind as our connecting link had turned first to behavior. But let us not forget that God also gave his human family the task of using Earth physically. For a long time it was primarily a source of survival. Then Mind revealed the presence of metals and from copper and iron we advanced through Alchemy to about A.D. 1800, when the physical sciences were born and took off in a rush. Thus via that linkage of Mind. Love begat Science. LOVE is parent of science! Shall we not add, Religion in therefore the parent of Science? In chapter 9 we will discover that Divine Energy is the connecting link.

Of course things became more complicated when among the scientists there arose the physicists who began to talk about energy. It took Energy to be the kind of a lover God is, and the physicist made energy very usable as a power to do work. He even coined a name for its unit: "the erg."[5] God worked with real energy when He made the Universe. He must be the Source of the energy. As we say in chapter 9, God is not abstract Love. He is Love in purposeful motion, which is work requiring expenditure of energy. God is the author of at least two kinds or energy: Spiritual energy and secular work energy; but remember they both have God as their source. In praise and acclamation of His Omniscience, we can declare that *God is Love and God is Energy*. Love via its energy gives rise to the Social Sciences and via the same source gives rise to the Physical Sciences. See chapter 9. The simple sketch on page 199 may help you clarify some phases of the relationship.

If true Religion and Science at times act as enemies, it can be only as a cantankerous teenager rebels against a parent. Religion can mend its vocabulary to attract Science and Science can take measures to restrict immoral exploitation of the products of its research.

Spiritual energy NURTURE of people via social action	SPIRITUAL Field of Force
Social Sciences	
GOD—LOVE True Religion	
Physical Sciences	
Nature's energy, analogous to our body's "sympathetic nervous system"	MAGNETIC Field of Force
Active Energy from the Sun and in the Earth	Radiation and Electric transmission

Chapter IX

God's Process of Evolution—
Sortie Number Five

SECTION 1. STUDYING THE ENERGY OF GOD

There it was at last, in black and white, before the Pilgrim's very eyes. On page 34 of the *Leader's Guide for Unit 3*, Search Bible studies, the Evangelical Lutheran Church said it strong and clear, "The biblical creation accounts can be harmonized with an evolutionary theory of the origin of the human species. It is possible to take the position of 'theistic evolution' which holds that the Bible tells who created, and the evolutionary explanation attempts to clarify the matter of 'how' things came into being."[1] One hundred and thirty-four years after Darwin made his famous sea voyage and wrote his book, a denomination of Christ's Church had finally worked up enough courage to say it out loud. Yes, the God of Abraham, the God of Moses, the God who entered His human world in Jesus Christ, probably carried out His mighty act of Creation in a fashion which could be best described by the suspect word, EVOLUTION! Some Christian fundamentalists, however, may still consider it obscene.

It was most significant that the Lutherans stated this view in their strengthened approach to the confirmation process, that important step by which teenagers enter into full voting membership in the church. (Recall chapter 5.) The meaning of discipleship in Christ's Church will be significantly enhanced in the face of the modern world view of crass materialism which tends to obliterate God. In a real sense, the Lutherans would now lead us all into the greater challenge of the evolution of spirituality, which can be demonstrated as theology absorbing and performing as the parent of all science. It seems to me that was what God

200

had intended from the beginning. I commend the Lutherans who are putting the finishing touches on the forward-looking union of their three main denominational groups. It will be interesting to see how Lutheran theologians in their seminary subject matter will support this step. I am hoping that published educational literature will attempt to supply the lay leader/teacher, as well as the seminary graduate, with ample curricular background material. Suffice it to say at this point that every Christian who does not have ready access to Lecomte duNoüy's *Human Destiny* beg or borrow a copy. Christian publication houses should be encouraged to bring out this 1946 book in suitable format for the layman. Every neophyte pastor/minister ought to have studied it in the original. (See appendix for a brief summary of the belief of this Christian scientist).[2]

At this point, I feel a bit let down by my Presbyterian (U.S.A.) consorts. Our denomination has always been inclined to tout a bit its being in the forefront, educationally speaking, in regard to its high-ranking pulpit intelligence and leadership. They have missed the boat here (or I may have missed finding it). You, the reader, now can surmise why the pilgrim's sortie number five is a challenging sortie of a special kind. This Pilgrim subconsciously realized that the most perplexing and troublesome problem in his modern spiritual life would have to be dealt with forthrightly. Else this account of life's experience would be so incomplete as to cause the reader, whatever his degree of sophistication, to wonder why I still wore self-imposed blinders. Did I avoid the subject on an open public basis because I actually feared to risk a so-called reputation as a Christian? So now in this chapter, I perceive my duty is to risk it for God's sake. I pray constantly for the leading of His Enabling Spirit. Only a feeling that I am wearing His armor leads me to undertake this sortie.

The major difficulty before the modern student in his attempt at becoming more intelligent about the creation of the physical environment in which he finds himself is to be able to distinguish between actual new contemporary facts and the various developing theories that attempt to explain them. His *beginning* includes his own physical body, i.e., his concept of being a vertebrate, a mammal with a *special* brain forged by God. Within that organ lies his complication. He finds that above and beyond mere animal instinct, his brain's function, in addition to overseeing the sympathetic nervous system, which keeps his physical continuity in effect, is to produce thought.

201

He is experienced enough to recognize that his thoughts fall into two main categories. He knows that he remembers what he did last year in a given circumstance. He remembers not only *what* he did but *why* he did certain things. They are the facts *as he sees them*. He discusses some of these things with his neighbor in detail and is surprised to learn that the language of communication they are using is so variable, that Jack holds a view so different from John's of what and why certain things happened that they now find themselves in full 180° opposite stance. It is quite evident that there are several sources of thought; one is concretely describable, the other is abstract and not so definitely and easily expressed. One deals with hard physical matter, the other deals with ideas and suppositions. Thus, our thoughts are a mixture of fact and fancy.

We now introduce a third category of thought. John and Jack depend on their brains to operate their physical vocal cords and produce what we say are the spoken vocal sounds of a specific language. But the spoken and/or written form of a language is not the only way in which we humans communicate. A very important feature of our human association is the widespread enjoyment and appreciation (one might say apprehension), of music and art. This can be definite communication without any vocal language. Using this simple analogy it is easy to take a further step by faith in which we couple God into our thoughts. We perceive at times the messages to be more than merely mental stimuli and we rightly interpret the intuition of our entry into the Spiritual Presence. The pure materialist will of course not have this and may continue to hold that we are in the land of make-believe. So be it. We pray that he may yet have a revelatory experience.

There is a fourth category of thought, that which is known as *symbolic* language. We believers may still have in our midst a number of sincere literalists who hold that God once had to speak out loud, vocally, just as we do today; they always call a spade a spade and allow no symbolism at all. They must have a 100 percent anthropomorphic concept for all communication between God and Man. I feel sorry for them and I would think God does too. I am far from being a professional theologian and so I turn such persons over to Dr. John C. L. Gibson who is editor of the new work on daily Bible studies in the Old Testament. He is attempting to make this work comparable in spiritual insight to Dr. William Barclay's New Testament studies. Let the Christian buy the first two volumes, which cover Genesis. The description he gives of the symbolic language, which authors J, E, and P employed in translating the original oral folklore into a written form, is extremely fascinating. It is enlightening to observe God's human agents struggling with the interpretation of vocabulary describing the ways of the Spirit. Of course the agents had different ideas of the proper approach. Sometimes they settled their argument by putting both versions into the final Word. In brief, differences as to the best expression and their disagreements indicate the difficulty—as is very common in our life when two witnesses before a court are trying to tell a true story. Some stray clay of human fallacy tags along. Fully describing the Spirit is absolutely impossible, else it is not the Spirit. We often say that but we do not fully act upon it. We are weighed down by the fault of our individual receiving sets, our consciences. And do not all of us practically "keep out of practice" by not attending to its fine tuning via Prayer?

At this point, I flatly proclaim that any Christian wishing to understand more of God's procedure of Creation, which we call evolution, owes it to himself and all within his community of faith to read, study, and digest the little volume by Lecomte duNoüy, which he entitled *Human Destiny*. This book was published immediately after World War II and is now out of print, but you will locate it in some public libraries and in a few scattered younger pastor's studies. The Lutherans whom I commended in the first paragraph of this chapter will do well to have their theological lesson writers adapt portions of it to teenage terminology so that it becomes a basic section of the curricular material used by each yearly Confirmation Class.

But before reading *Human Destiny* and Gibson's *Genesis*, Volumes I and II, it will be absolutely necessary for the reader to accept one of the new, modern, contemporary *facts* we referred to a moment ago. It is this: measured in man's TIME, this planet Earth on which we reside is about four billion years old, give or take a little; and actual life upon it began about two billion years ago.[3] We do not have to be physical chemists with radioactive measuring tools applied to rocks and fossils or specially prepared devout Christian biologists to learn and accept this fact. It may take another generation or two before we can step into any public school and find it being taken for granted, i.e., a casually known, working fact for everyone. The student will then not have to contend with any parental backwash subconsciously slipping in from the discarded Ussher chronology of the Hebrew development prior to the entry into the Promised Land. He will accept the fact that the Chinese had a thriving, vital, dynasty, Zhou, going by 10,000 B.C., probably pushing the Egyptians from first place by a millennium or two.

You will recall in chapter 8, dealing with science and religion, generally, I took the stance that "war" was actually a misnomer for the conflict between science and religion. The "war" is mostly on the part of the fundamental literal religionists who appear to equate biological evolution with the whole of physical sciences and then, finally, equate science with atheism. We can quickly challenge their placing science in a position of negativism or actual evil by going back to beginnings, when God was in charge of everything, everywhere. All believers agree that in Creation, God charged *adamah*, i.e., humanity, with using His gifts of Spirit and Mind. He gave His human partner the care and oversight of His universe. Humanity, was given the express order to "take command." God thus unmistakably revealed himself as the God in charge of two kinds of science in which *adamah* was to grow and perfect its responsibility. The Bible stresses the one group of sciences by dwelling almost exclusively on personal relationships: relationships between humans and the relationship between humans and God Himself. God, thus, was the Father of Social Science. From the basic family unit, relationship grew through clan and tribe, town or city, the fortified city-state, small kingdom, major kingdom, monarchy. Discontent and revolution were followed by a variety of new national civil governments. We name Political Science as the large total area of concern but we recognize a whole group of related branches, all of which serve Social Science. We list the major ones as Psychology, Paleontology, Anthropology, Government or Civics, Education, and Health. In the latter case, medicine bridges the gap between this group and the Physical Sciences. A physician is a biochemist who treats both the fleshly body and/or the mind. Remember that Paul Tournier practiced the medicine of the whole three-dimensional body, which embraced spirit as well.

In addition to this aspect of personal relationships and the study and perfecting of the Social Sciences, God the Creator also charged *adamah* with "keeping house" throughout His physical universe. This meant making use of water and wind power, building shelters, and taking care of animals, not merely those domesticated for Man's direct use, but employing a long-term view toward seeing that the balance of wild species was maintained. Later, conservation was a word coined to express his responsibility for both life and the inventoried resources growing upon the earth or buried in it. Man proved to be very much more proficient in developing the physical aspects of the Universe than he was in conserving them, and a major result is the selfish greed engendered by geographical chance. We easily overlook our stewardship under God. Science grew faster than, and generally away from, the moral code.

His exploitation of his physical surroundings proceeded quite logically because God's provision of an expanding mind led from challenge to challenge. Overnight results were readily observable. God taught His man-child about fire via His lightning strikes in nature. From fire as a natural start, there followed the invention of the lever, the wheel, the hinge, the block and tackle, all making good use of the water and wind power. Then man became really ingenious; metallurgy was born as he became a practical chemist. Soon he made gunpowder, and at that point, personal relationships took a sharp dive. Alchemy introduced the world of physical science generally speaking. Mechanical engineering, having already been introduced in the experience of all kinds of construction centered around problems of habitation, road making, bridge building, boat design and production, and the making of war, expanded under the development of chemistry, physics and higher mathematics, which grew simultaneously with astronomy, electronics, and, more recently, nuclear engineering. So much for nature and the inanimate framework in which we dwell.

Man had always been intuitively aware that God had given him command over a plant kingdom and an animal kingdom. He had begun as a food gatherer of what God's nature had concomitantly provided. As nomads, man had entered the Promised Land; taking up farming with their Canaanite neighbors they became agriculturists. They learned to select and breed better plant food. The matter of food for their subsistence naturally brought the animal kingdom into focus. In the animal kingdom domestication came naturally among certain species. The dog, chosen to assist in managing the grazing herd, became in the family a valued member of the intimate life therein. Depending upon geographical location, the other selected quadrupeds, the horse or the camel, the donkey or elephant, and later the hybrid mule, all carried man or man's burden. Man himself, representing the top level of organic, proteinic composition, finally began to examine his own body. Thus we note the remainder of the physical sciences shaping up: botany, zoology, animal breeding depending on end use, physiology, medicine, and organ transplanting. It appears that medicine, i.e., the research sustaining it, is able to point quite clearly to the most important component of Creation: ENERGY. We know now that the brain and our bodies operate in a mysterious field of electronics. Thought and electric currents are intimately interconnected. SCANS of the body are now regular features of diagnosis. We speak not only of brain scans; we now introduce the whole human body into a precisely controlled magnetic field and under the title of nuclear magnetic resonance (NMR) study bodily structure and functions. The intimate partnership of God and Man can be perceived in the pathway of energy. It may be helpfully illustrated by the two following diagrams.

Most Christian theologians and lay persons are united in the body of faith which says that God is LOVE. In our attempt to enlarge our comprehension of Him let me add another attribute not yet appreciated by classical or traditional scholars. God is the source of energy with which He formed the Universe. He furnished the building blocks, the chemical elements, which formed secular power from His original mightier spiritual Power. This will be more thoroughly discussed in the next sections. Radiation, a word from Space Age technology, shows how power and energy are transferred from one system to another. This chapter as a whole attempts to explain that in addition to being LOVE, God is also powerful, radiating ENERGY.

Planet Earth (and the total physical system of Suns, Satellites and Planets) is immersed in the larger, limitless scope of God's Spiritual Field of Force. The central core of the figure represents the lines of the magnetic field that surrounds us now. This magnetic field of force, attested to by the action of a compass needle, is overshadowed by God's infinite energy and power of radiation, which surrounds it.

The reader who has not had any physics in high school or college will be helped in his meditation and perusal of the basic fundamental aspects of man and his habitation by studying contemporary dictionary descriptions of "power" and "energy." The unabridged edition of Random House is the source of the following definitions. We begin with the general term "power." The definitions of power run the gamut from systems of material machines, legal and governmental systems, and man's mind to divinity. There are twenty-six numbered statements that show where such a term may be rightfully used. From them we glean three ideas applicable to the act of Creation of the Universe and humans.

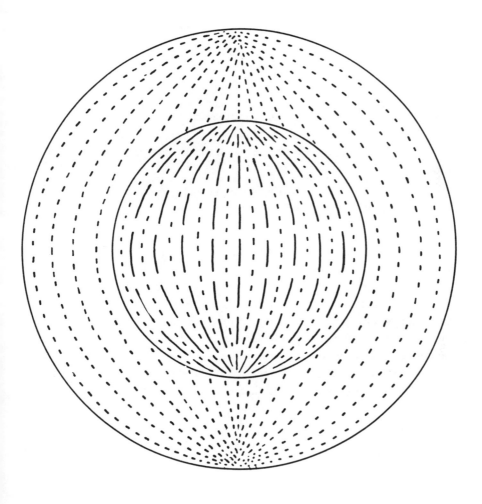

Spirit totally envelops the Earth (representing total Universe)
Note: This and the following diagram are perhaps misleading in the
sense that the outer circle is a solid line. The Spirit is not so limited.
To indicate its infinite nature there should be no outer limit whatsoever. This is a map-maker's problem.

Power is the ability to do or act; capability of doing or accomplishing something. When work is done or energy is transferred, power can be mathematically expressed as the amount of such energy, used or transferred per unit of time.

Energy is a) the capacity for vigorous activity, available power; b) a feeling of tension caused or seeming to be caused by an excess of such power; c) the habit of vigorous activity; vigor as a characteristic; d) the ability to act, lead others, effect, etc., forcibly; e) forcefulness of expression; f) (physics) capacity to do work, transfer of energy from one system to another.

Radiation is a) (physics) the process in which energy is emitted as particles or waves; b) *the complete process in which energy is emitted by one body, transmitted through an intervening medium or space, and absorbed by another body**; c) the act or process of radiating; d) something that is radiated; e) a radical arrangement of parts, a glittering, shining.

Taking into account my own experience as influenced by the nature of the requirements for scientific training, the reader may initially be repulsed by the idea that energy is usually associated with doing work with a machine. One contemplating the creating God in the use of power and energy may thus tend to make Him a mechanical God. This is a very biased and limiting viewpoint. Consider that *the power to act* is represented specifically in the location of one body of water higher than another. Stored energy resides in the higher water level. God the Creator caused that energy to be stored therein. I hold that there must have been a plan to act, to create, which was the Love of God, God who preceded any actual "thing." The secular materialist who says this was merely *chance* cannot be with it if he considers that something had to be *done before* the condition of *chance* could exist. That something was the Love of God, which preceded all matter. My personal theory dealing with this in some detail is presented in section two ahead. Even though you may decide to skip that section for the present, I would appreciate your continued consideration of the idea, the quite obvious conclusion for the Christian, that the God of Love and the God of Energy are one and the same. Furthermore, a study of diagram number two clarifies the concept that God's love is the parent of the material universe, the habitation of His human family.

The broken and light dash boundary as shown in a portion of the outer circle enclosing the Spirit of God is not a true boundary. It helps maintain the idea that the Spirit closely and warmly surrounds us, but at the same time is infinitely present out there.

*Italics are mine.

208

CREATOR-LOVE-GOD-ENERGY-SUSTAINER-COMFORTER-SPIRIT-ENABLER-REDEEMER-CHRIST-SAVIOR

GOD
LOVE and ENERGY

Love and Energy coexisted within God, Himself. Love took command and set the Goal, an abode for His eventual human family. He assigned a portion of His Energy to an evolutionary process by which the physical Universe was formed, one planet being Earth. He reserved Energy with which to establish Nature so as to keep things running automatically; (See p. 218) He stocked Earth with the Animal and Plant kingdoms and when His animal design reached fulfillment, His mutant, spiritual touch gave birth to adamah; crowned with the gifts of causative memory, conscience, and ESP attuned to Himself, -Matt 5:48. He appointed adamah, General Manager, "to command and subdue," His creation, -1:26-30. Earth proved to be a tremendous warehouse of resources bearing on daily life. Adamah did little with it except to scratch out a living until about 1800 AD. when he began to work seriously. Meanwhile, God as Love had been busy building personal relationships to replace the trace of remaining animal instincts. The underlying problem is managing the conflict between GOOD and EVIL which adamah had created the moment he realized he had a free will. Love, which had been the basis of the SOCIAL SCIENCES (from Anthropology to Theology) now disclosed the establishment of God's Rescue Plan. The SOCIAL SCIENCES seemingly climaxed in the Political science area but have not yet reached a foolproof code of action for the mixed families of the world. Meanwhile the Physical sciences, Chemistry, Physics, Geology, Math, Medicine, and the associated Engineering disciplines, have made astonishing advances in their academic fields but so far have shown more skill in exploitation as over against conservation. The question is: What is happening to Christianity's leaven? Love, being the ancient parent of science, ought to be asserting itself. More equitable distribution of natural resources in God's original gift, has not as yet, reached a serious talking stage. Lecomte du Noüy's, *Human Destiny*, third section, shows what remains to be done in advancing the character of Man toward the goal of perfection in Christ.

I II III IV V

The small circles at the lower point represent what I term the five major categories of contemporary humanity. I have attempted to so intertwine Love and Energy as the spiritual attributes inherited by us humans that even the ignorant, the agnostic, and the total atheist must respond in some fashion. It attempts to show that the traditional materialistic Nature about us is an integral portion of Love. My comments under each grouping can only be partial and suggestive. They are presented as they are because each has its distinctive reaction to the idea of Evolution as God's procedure. The number of persons in each group must be considered as in constant flux. We are sure that God's purpose for our discipleship is to improve the spiritual life in groups one and two by diligent effort and prayer. He likewise points to the abundant harvest He hopes to help us gather in group three.

Group one—Humans with the highest degree of spirituality as sensed in daily practice. It is easy to fall into the trap of automatically placing all pastors/ministers and seminary faculty members in this group. We suspect that not all such persons *perform* equally as well in daily life as they *speak* about LOVE to others. A number of senior saints in the communities of faith will also be humbly struggling at their side. This group in the Space Age ought to be leading a bolder, more effective campaign of improved means of communication. It has not kept pace with the new vocabulary of a more technical culture. In places it appears to have lost a sharp evangelistic cutting edge. I believe the outstanding examples of Christly living are the "foreign" missionaries. They are committed to a barely subsistence-level monetary income and, under severe living conditions, demonstrate an ambassador relationship for Christ that puts them very far above the average political leadership of all our nations. Perhaps one of the basic reasons for the high marks of the so-called foreign missionary is that his old traditional Bible vocabulary matches that of the still more primitive developing country he works in. Once the average citizen of the Third World has reached the goal he sees reflected each day on his TV screen, i.e., has gained "the good life" of wealth and ample food and has garnered his supply of mechanical gadgets, he will be as tough a customer to convince that a real Spiritual goal remains as is his Western counterpart.

Group two—Humans who have actually caught a vision of the example of the life Christ portrayed. They do their utmost to expand their practice of love, though in the face of baser animal instincts, they realize they are not too successful at it. We expect that the bulk of our church membership, ordinary practicing Christians, are group two material. They must continue to repeat mistakes and depend upon group one for guidance and example.

Group three—Millions of souls who represent the "fields of the harvest" (John 4:35 and Luke 10:2). Most of them may intuitively feel that there is a God, somewhere, somehow, but he seems to be no reality in daily life. Some are aware of conscience, but it is a dull instrument. They end up with GOOD and EVIL in confusion, skewed in the direction of Evil via instincts of survival selfishness. "I" and "ME" are most important. Millions are awaking. They say, "Come and help me out of my misery."

Group four—Generally very intelligent humanists, philosophers, and accomplished secular materialistic scientists who admit no allegiance to the Spirit of God. If pressured, they will admit to an Unknown God, but he is not available for private consultation and certainly is not involved in our daily lives. World culture is drifting in this direction today. It is aided and abetted by writing and producing personnel heading up our entertainment world and TV news media. A recent poll indicates that less than 15 percent of such leadership with daily impact are really practicing Christians who testify to church support and attendance.

Group five—A mixture of the remainder: ignorant pagans, those totally depraved with a high level of remaining animal instincts, and overt anti-God persons. They resort to violent force in the settlement of all differences of opinion. They laugh at the idea of God as a daily Enabler.

The flow of this preliminary discussion before dealing with the more technical aspects of God as Energy now opens the optional approach hinted at above. Beginning with section 2 ahead, we project the theoretical possibility of identifying God with energy at the initiation of His Creation. Those several pages of section 2 are admittedly theory, and had they been introduced earlier, reader interest may have been so weakened and confused as to cancel out the value of this whole sortie for others. Placing Energy in the diagram so that it is seen to be equal to Love helps prepare the reader's mind with a more traditional vocabulary. LOVE becomes a more active, energizing, creating Love. I will not mind the interruption if you now skip to page 230, but I pray that a second and third reading with meditation may lead you to your own adapted symbolism of the mighty power of our Omniscient Almighty God. In our modern world culture, I still feel no better term than ENERGY puts God in a working relationship with His technically oriented family. LOVE supplies the motivation and care, the searching out of the hidden ills and hurts, but ENERGY is required to do anything about them. We may be tempted to call it *our* energy, but the energy for performing the impossible has to be energy from God; for God set the goal and activates the attracting strength of Spiritual Force that draws us to Himself. Love induces the current of energy from its original source in Him and *sees us through.*

SECTION 2. PHYSICS AND CREATION

Perhaps no word in the English language has experienced such a metamorphosis of meaning and kindled more fires of fierce discussion as evolution. Almost deleted from common usage is its meaning as the record on any many-faceted procedure that produces a result, such as a machine, an idea, a social or business practice, or a new wrinkle in the governing of a nation. Whether it is spelled with a divine capital letter or not, most persons instantaneously reflect the absorbed modifying adjective "biological" as essential. Thus, in Darwinian terms, it was defined as genetic changes in living tissue due to environment, but duNoüy shows this definition to be totally inadequate. As is now well known, the switch of emphasis to "biological evolution" was the result of a five-year sea voyage in the mid-nineteenth century by the naturalist Charles Darwin. He wrote a book which blazed its way through the literate Western culture. *The Origin of Species* has been assaulted by both scientists and religionists. Today it is only one of a number of theories of evolution.

The common man is not interested in the man-controlled breeding by which wild horses, cattle, and swine evolved into our present domestic breeds and types. That does not count, he says. He is confronted by the probability that his own body is the result of the evolution of a single living cell whose prototype began life, say, two billion years ago, after the physical world had been shaping up during the prior two billion. When he turns to some authority for fuller explanation, he finds that the two sources who ought to provide it are in sharp disagreement. The theologian and the secular biologist are at opposite poles in an ideological combat. Later biological scientists have pointed out that though Darwin's observations definitely helped to establish an evolutionary framework for the development of the animal kingdom, he did not account for the death and disappearance of species and definitely seemed to have no place for mutations, those sudden changes in genetic rearrangement and development of new species with no so-called "missing links" being required. Many persons today are still, mindwise, back in the biological era of Darwin's book. The old scare words "man's descension from a monkey," show a total misconception of the probable facts of the progression from the first single cell in primitive sea water to the more-or-less completed structure of physical man today two billion years later.[4]

The Christian says, *"We must insist that God has been in charge since infinite time. He had and still has a plan of Creation which remains to be completed."* The secular scientist says, "Bosh, I deal only with what I dig out of the earth. I deal with concrete facts." The physical universe since its beginning has been in flux and change. Life upon it, at least on planet Earth, has changed with it. "CHANCE," says the scientist, "not God, prevails." He admits no spiritual nature of man related to a divine mastermind. Such a scientist is ideologically a complete humanist who holds that the mind is the super force; his stance insists evolution produced Man and his brain entirely under its own power. Perhaps there is a dialectic inner force in need of neither God nor man's mind. He does not discuss the source of that inner power (nor did Karl Marx, who used this argument to uphold Communism).

The approach such a secular biologist makes to lessen his need for God is to start with the physical universe basically in place at two billion years ago, after a prior two billion years of flux and readjustment. He approaches this with an agnostic observation that he can leave the prior physical universe to his friends the theoretical physicists and the chemist who may wish to theorize on how things started in the first place. He himself will start at the origin of life itself. We Christians cannot be satisfied with this. We intuitively accept the Spirit of God as the prime mover of both the Universe and our human lives. We have mentioned elsewhere that a human is a three-dimensional being.[5] Tournier: "His mind is fed by the Spirit." Let us attempt to build a bridge between the secular biologist and physicist on the one hand and us with our Christian faith on the other. This attempt at bridge building will lead you, the reader into a theoretical discussion that you may not fully appreciate. As noted above, in all honesty you may not be favorably impressed. There is nothing wrong if you will skip a few pages and join us again at the layman's sermon on pages 230–240.

During this theoretical discussion it will help if we keep two questions in mind. First, what was infinite reality before the creation of the universe with its planets, including Earth, revolving around our SUN among many such suns? In brief, what were the original building blocks? Second, can we use more than one analogy for meditation about the nature of God? Medieval theologians writing in Latin coined the phrase *ex nihilo*. They said, "God made the universe and all within it ex nihilo." The direct literal translation of the Latin phrase *ex nihilo* is "out of nothing." This term presents us with a new and strange "chicken or egg" situation. The folks originating that Latin phrase really did not have the new true physical facts we have today. Such facts had existed but the known world view and culture of that period had not yet developed the scientific methods and knowledge of a Space Age. It took sixteen hundred years more for the world to perceive that there was indeed *"something"* present.

Let us humbly, at this point, recognize that we today do not know it all, either. What do you suppose God has in store for us sixteen hundred years hence? It is quite likely that Christians of that future time will read of today's exploits and descriptions thereof and remark, "What simpletons those primitive folks of A.D. 2000 turned out to be." Yes, those Latin writers had said God made the Universe out of nothing. The important thing about that sentence is its beginning and its ending. God we cannot actually define. He is infinite and beyond all human descriptive word languages of any kind. Our faith establishes Him as a *supernatural person*, though we know there are "Christian" theologians who may sell Him short as a person by speaking of "natural theism." We cannot actually prove His existence by our ontological, cosmological, and our teleological arguments.[6] They are very strong statements but not really proofs. So we come back to the position that our faith, strongly confirmed by the later appearance of Jesus of Nazareth, holds that God was the Creator of the Universe and is its Sustainer. If some theologian tries to make out that God was merely the number one associate in Creation, I would hold him as simply a Philosopher attempting to negotiate some compromise settlement between opposing new concepts stemming from our secular and humanistic culture.

The end of the sentence in question has to do with the definition of the word NOTHING. Did the Latin author of the term *ex nihilo* really know what he was talking about? He, no doubt, limited his definition of "nothing" to mean that which his five senses, called to testify to, would merely report negatively, i.e., no sense of matter or stuff with which to build. Their senses presented Truth in A.D. 385 to the extent of their sensual experience of the physical phenomena prior to the use of that term. His "nothing" did not accord with the definition of "nothing" as it is today in the Space Age at A.D. 1990.

Navigators of the ocean, who first depended on the stars and sun, later experienced the fact that the whole world was immersed in a magnetic field of force. A piece of lodestone would react to it and eventually the compass needle was born. It would appear that in such a phenomenon God had given us an analogy by which we may apprehend Him. God's Spirit can be thought of as occupying that portion of space which is outside the physical realm of humankind. Everything and everybody is bathed, i.e., immersed, in His Spirit. We recognize His presence as a force, as a power. We say this power affects the way we think and how we conduct ourselves. Teilhard de Chardin would not stop at the term "immersion" as I have used it. He would say that the Spirit was *actually inside us* even in a more intimate way; that residing within our brain tissue or coursing in our blood stream, God's spirit is actually residing in every single cell of the body. He is that vital force which builds additional cells as a child adds stature to become an adult, or mends a surgical damage and builds a new cell to replace the old one every seven years. Whence comes this tremendous power? Can we know more about its mysterious nature?

Dear Reader, in my attempt to throw further light on the Creative Power of God, and perhaps to aid in our constant daily probing and testing of His communication with us, I set forth some ideas which I feel quite comfortable with in His presence and which I share with you. Yes, we will admit they are theory. It can be your choice to reject them or to build upon them as you can. We direct our attention to a scientific development of the midpoint of this century that has opened the door to the Space Age. Einstein's mathematics and associated investigators have arrived at a formula that reveals a relationship between *matter* and *energy*. In your more serious reading you may have already run across it. It is expressed as an equation, $E=Mc^2$, where E is energy, a force that can perform work, and M is mass, i.e., a substance (solid, liquid, gas) that can be perceived to be in existence via our humanly five senses. M has weight. The requirement is that the objective mass must be traveling at the speed of light, which is 186,380 miles per second. If you picked up a baseball and could throw it that fast it would no longer be a baseball, but a "blip" of energy way out there. It could not be seen, heard, smelled, felt, i.e., detected by our senses. To the high-school boy or girl who did not have the elementary chemistry or physics that he should have taken, it would be as if it were nonexistent. It had disappeared. It would have become "nothing" unless you could perceive the energy. We may simplify what we have just said by concluding that this simple-looking equation, produced by scientific minds, has helped build a bridge between the physical and spiritual worlds. The analogy appears to be most intimate and helpful, quite beyond preceding ideas of the similarity of the two bases of reality. We have transferred our thought from *something* we know as a physical *something* to *something* which is *nothing* when defined in physical senses but is *everything* when defined in terms of the Spirit. Of course, the nucleus of this analogy, by which Nothing is shown to be really be *something*, resides in the projected similarity of Energy and Force derived physically and the Energy and the Spirit of God. Bear in mind that at this point in our meditation we have not said that they are actually identical. But they come very close. That which the scientist can only describe as Energy that can do physical work is now like unto Energy that does spiritual work.

Now really stretch your imagination. Assume that "In the Beginning," the true beginning with God, there was no physical structure whatsoever. There was *nothing* physically formed, *everything* was gathered together as Energy. God had charge of it. (Teilhard de Chardin might even say that this total accumulated Energy was God Himself.) Bear in mind that in this accumulation of Energy in some place in a space we cannot define, we have the equivalent of all of the components of the physical universe. This accumulation of Energy preceded electrons, neutrons, protons, atoms, and molecules, which had not yet been formed and which would be necessary for forming the 100 chemical elements, the desired building blocks we are looking for. God's combined spiritual and physical energy, representing the first step in subatomic creation, was probably the origin of the suns, God's mammoth laboratories and manufacturing plants for the establishment of His universe.

Beginning, therefore, with the *nothing* (*ex nihilo*), so defined because Energy per se cannot be felt, smelled, seen, heard, or weighed,

God's Energy, operating under His plan, was transformed into the Mass which became the physical structure for our planets and all the rest. In this sentence is reflected the *initial unity of physical and spiritual energy*; the supremacy and majesty of our Father-God as a supernatural person; and the establishment of the sense of His Love and Mercy as He formed first the habitation for His humankind some four billion years ago, and then gave us single-cell birth about two billion years later. The scientist who would disavow this view generally would do so on the basis of the time it took. If God really exists and is so extremely powerful perhaps he should have created His Universe and us in the twinkling of an eye, like Peter Pan in a Walt Disney movie who, with her wand, touches some indistinct figure that explodes into a shower of sparks and a beautifully new situation. Such a concept, however, over-looks the view we hold that *God is timeless*. It was Man in his im-patience who invented time. God will not be denigrated by a man-made device. Man as a later arriving co-creator was given certain freedoms by the Master Spiritual Creator and so has made some mistakes. He in-vented the clock and the calendar for his own mundane minutiae of existence but he ought not to limit God to his own human devices.

God's creation act, having arrived at the level of advancement represented by Homo erectus, or two-legged upright humanoid mammal with a somewhat enlarged brain capacity, awaited the moment when God would touch off the mutant reactions resulting in Homo sapiens, a wise man. In ascribing wisdom to God's human creature, there is a difference of opinion as to whether "wisdom" denotes the presence of some spirituality in addition to the physical, chemical performance of the mind. At this point the secular scientist denies any contribution by God and declares wisdom to be the attribute of super self-mindedness. Our Christian faith, on the other hand, testifies to the triple God-given gift the human creature enjoys, namely a causative logical memory, a conscience knowing right and wrong (i.e., a moral code), and a built-in ESP oriented to God Himself, the Creator. This is what we mean when we say we are created in God's image. Some of that spiritual God-stuff is in every one of us.

Above, we have noted that there is a close relationship of the nature of energy as a physical force and energy as a spiritual force and power. Can we not likewise come to a perception of the relationship of our minds and God's spirit? Words may fail but let us try by saying that our mind and God's spirit are capable of melding into each other at least to some degree. He gave us each a bit of His infinite Self as that part of us which is spiritual. Is it blasphemous to say that in Humankind God enters via His Holy Spirit and remains as a trace of His incarnate Self in each of us? The difference between us and the man Jesus, perhaps, may be that whereas our mind is 99.9 percent physical and 0.1 percent Holy Spirit, Jesus' mind could be said to have been fifty-fifty at the time He began His three-year ministry. By the time of the Crucifixion week, God's incarnation had become complete to the extent that Jesus could forthrightly state, "I and the Father are *One*." Our general conclusion is that the hidden unity of energy and matter makes reasonable the concept of Humankind being formed from God's Spirit and therefore being endowed with the three active components of flesh, mind, and spirit. Man has not reached the fullness of His creation at God's hands until, within that triangle, the prior dominance of the fleshly body (animal instinct) has receded to the point where the Spirit is conceded by the mind to be in charge as Number One.

Since God controls the total process of Creation, we imply that, His control of both material energy and spiritual energy thus becoming one in the person of God, He would wisely direct that part of it be earmarked for suns and planets, plants and animals, and part would be assigned to Homo sapiens babies. They would receive some special quanta of energy of His special brand. Dear Reader, I challenge you to reread this chapter very carefully, realizing that my story is, in some respects, theoretical and imaginative. I do not have any of God's answers to our questions. I continue to seek them as you do; but perhaps your efforts will make up for part of my deficiency. We will, however, always continue to know Him only in limited part, for He is God.

We must not overlook a very important part in any theory of creation. That is the establishment of Nature. We are wont to personify it as a parent, Mother Nature. The inexhaustible source of all energy, God Himself, solves this problem very handily. Just as our physical bodies are physiologically maintained by sympathetic nervous systems which automatically superintend our breathing, digestion, and the replacement of worn-out cells with new ones, so may we perceive Nature as a sort of automatic operator of the physical apparatus and its concomitant environment, the Universe. With His total supply of energy God could have started by earmarking a certain portion of it for the special case of Nature. Such ENERGY He may have placed largely within the SUNS of His creation, for they are His power laboratories.

Within the area of space filled with water vapor and the elemental gases comprising the atmosphere, He could have set up a sort of automatic operation like unto our sympathetic bodily controls. When *adamah*, planned by God, later appeared and with that wonderful gift from God, his brain, looked out upon his environment in wonder, awe, fear, and thankfulness, he/they could call it NATURE. Such a provision allowed God to be concerned with other details and provided a nursery in which He could start with a pool of water, the ocean, and therein nurture the first protein cell. During the first two billion man-years it had taken to do this God had had His weather working on the hard crust of planet Earth so as to provide some rooting and growing medium for the state of His PLANT KINGDOM. According to our biological scientists, God had His nature operating the marine water nursery quite some extended period of time before He put the land portion of the nursery in operation to originate and nurture His PLANT kingdom.

We interrupt at this point to give the reader a quick thought about his own beginning. Many Space Age scientists apparently agree with duNouy that the sea worms inhabiting the marine nursery were the initiating human stock at the base of the evolution tree. The sketchy blueprint, scientists have assembled, shows physical man emerging at the top of a central core of evolutionary forms. At various stages side shoots of this central core break out into the various phyla, genera, and species. Mother Nature apparently made a few mistakes and the species withered away. Likewise, drastic weather conditions led to environments to which the animal could not adjust. So came the furry little mammal who ate the monster's eggs, and so disappeared the dinosaurs. At various levels the ascending evolutive core gave rise to the various side shoots ending in the array of our animals. Thus, we did not *descend* from any animal. We *ascended* from the sea worm, but as we rose, God picked out the various specimens from the side shoots. We *did not descend from monkeys*, we only "make monkeys of ourselves." Finally, the center core of evolution reached the two-legged humanoid with a larger space provided for a bigger brain. We believers feel that at this point God, with His hand on the mutation control, chose to install a causative, logical memory; a conscience by which man was given the knowledge of right and wrong and the power to choose between them; and, third, an extrasensory perception oriented toward God Himself.

The stance of the secular scientist regarding the inner urge for perfection, which we intuitively refer to as the ultimate object of evolution, is not too difficult to explain. Since he shuns the idea of God as a supernatural force, one perceives that he is giving "man of dust," with his mind, a sort of built-in "soul of all matter." I am not a philosopher but it almost appears that there is therein something like Karl Marx's state of mind when he dialectically set up constant revolt and turmoil as self-continuing until perfection is obtained, i.e., equality of man as Communism describes it. Of course the Christian shrugs this off as the stance of atheism. Our God, on the other hand, wishes higher levels for His creation and is the Master Planner with a goal. Biological evolution as presented in the high schools and colleges of our land creates problems in the area of our curriculum of Christian education. As mentioned at several points in this book, a first necessary step is to realize that our high school graduates and our B.A. graduates entering the seminary are culturally illiterate if they have not obtained academic credits in elementary chemistry and physics. If we are to proclaim the Word and nurture beginners in Faith, *we must present it to the world culture in a language the latter uses when it speaks about today's life operations*. The real Space Age vocabulary is a must if one is to succeed in opening up Christ to a secular scientist or engineer and his family.

Whether the Christian family fully appreciates it or not, its support of the public school system would appear to be a God-given assignment. The authoritative, tax supported, educational system under our constitutional governmental system should be recognized as a useful common tool of citizenship. The Christian family in the Space Age must further be instructed through Christ's Church on how to educate its young and at the same time preserve God's spiritual values in personal life. Despite some agnostic or atheistic teachers, whom our children will be found sitting under in biological science classrooms, it behooves wise Christian parents to see to it that *God is also the God of science as well as God of the hearth*. The Church must provide instruction in parenting to strengthen the faith of the teenager in his belief that God used an evolutionary procedure in producing not only mankind but everything else in His Universe. The students' stance in the classroom will become an instance of His testimony for God. He will support a study of God's evolutionary method by his questioning and by his insistence that his teacher distinguish between facts and various theories different today from those of yesterday and continually changing. There should be no repetition of the sad mistake of a college freshman who, back in 1922, parroted in a quiz the details of Dr. Ussher's chronology taught to the class by a Missouri-synod trained minister-professor. That freshman had his eye on his academic grade and refrained from asking the questions that were troubling him.

Naturally, if Christian parenting and the curriculum of Christian education in the church is to assume its rightful leadership, those who write lessons about Christian goals and values and prepare the skeletal basis of Christian nurture had better be about their job. I may have missed it but in my long-time search for examples prior to 1988 for lessons on Creation that are more than a slight facade of the literal Bible story I have been disappointed. We have been so cowardly in our search for Truth. Wonder of wonders came to view in 1988 when, as related in the opening paragraph of this chapter, the new Lutheran AFFIRM material appeared. One wishes that the individual student and the teacher will see this subject matter develop to a point of real classroom give-and-take. I know of no other denominational courage matching the Lutherans' in this respect.

To give you an instance of another denomination's reaction, I share with you a letter and reply in which I am the only identifiable person, in courtesy to the person addressed.

September 22, 1986

Dear Mr. Editor:

My assignment as teacher of our Men's Bible Class concluded with the quarter ending August 31, but I looked ahead because I also teach a Bible class here at Abernethy Village the second Friday of each month. When I saw that the writer of the Noah lesson for September 14 was willing to "tell it like it was" I was overjoyed. For twenty-five years I have been wondering when the Adult lesson writers would get beyond the traditional "retired minister's" statements of the old *Literalist* line on the first eleven chapters of Genesis. I have taught the transformation of the Old Sumerian 'Noah,' into the Hebrew system of theology by spiritually minded storytellers who did their best to make him over into a monotheistic farmer with a mission for his God. Ninety percent of the class generally gave me cool stares but a few always saw the light. Congratulate your writer for me. Too bad he did not come straight out and call the first eleven chapters of Genesis the *symbolic* language of Hebrew spiritualists (i.e., prophets) handicapped by an anthropomorphic vocabulary in describing what took place billions of years ago . . . In the creation story of September 7, the writer could have honestly admitted that God's geology of this century has resolved a timetable which throws out the seven twenty-four hour days in a human week. If the writer of that creation lesson did not wish 'to spoil' his good text on the image of God, he should at least have had a brief footnote (even if in fine print) covering some of the highlights of *Interpreter's Bible* Introduction to Volume I. We adapted a pagan year-end carousal as our Christ's birthday—why can't we adapt an old pagan Babylonian myth and put it in spiritual clothes honoring our indescribable monotheistic Lord of Lords? The writer of lesson material for Youth and Young Adults for September 14 comes very near to it and needs to be congratulated; albeit he could have clarified his statement on page 17, paragraph 3, in the *Leader's Guide*. Instead of the two views on creation there are really three, and I suggest that they are as follows:

(1) First, there is the literalist view that total creation historically took place in God's hands during a one week period in the fall of 4004 B.C. as described in Genesis.

(2) Directly opposed is the non-believers' view that science accounts for a biological evolution of the plant and animal kingdoms from an original single cell over an extended period during which CHANCE prevailed. At the top of the evolutionary chain, Homo erectus became Homo sapiens through *its* (not his) brain development. All is scientific emphasis on the 'how.' 'Why' is avoided and can be left to the religious student.

(3) An acceptable spiritual view is that God is in charge of His universe and has been since He started with (nothing) but Himself. He superintended an evolutionary process, still being studied by science, which resulted in the plant and animal kingdoms. When His animal chain reached the final stages of Homo erectus, He transformed His creation into Homo sapiens, His human family, by virtue of His gift of causative memory, a conscience, and an ESP (extrasensory perception) oriented toward Himself. God's purpose is the motivating power behind every step of His process. I subscribe to this view.

Looking forward to your comments.
Sincerely,
Fred Ebersole

The reply I received from the Editor was a three-line letter stating that he found my letter "interesting" and that he had passed it on to his assistant editors, who "may wish to comment." There was absolutely no recognition of any problem. It was a brusque brush-off. There was no further response. I cannot refrain from adding some words spoken by God, via Revelations 3:15 as recorded and translated by Philips and addressed "to the complacent church": "I know what you have done and that you are neither hot or cold, I could wish that you were either cold or hot. But since you are lukewarm and neither hot or cold, I intend to spit you out of my mouth."[7]

To conclude this chapter I have added my layman's sermon delivered at Browson Memorial Presbyterian Church in Southern Pines in September 1983. The reason for presenting it under this chapter title is both explicit and implicit. It is important that the implication of the message of establishing the perfection of God in Christ as a legitimate and challenging goal for us human creatures be driven home. I suspect that among some "Christians" there may reside a semi-unitarian view that Jesus, merely an exceptionally good man, was a bit ahead of the moral mix of His times. Such theology appears to me to be a travesty, dishonoring God who is Creator, Sustainer, Savior, Holy Comforter, and Enabling Spirit. God's goal for us is more than a manifestation of "natural theism," a sort of halfway station. God Himself was in Christ, and makes clear that His evolutionary advancement of mortal children, if they choose, will finally join their souls with Him.

Consistent with the foregoing discussion the sermon points out that the perfection as of God is the goal we unlikely clay mortals, imperfect but cooperative partners in creation, are *hoping* for.* We are harnessed to a spiritual resource we cannot fathom, which guarantees success, perhaps not in this mortal earthly existence, but at the moment God accepts and receives our soul into the inner soul of His Kingdom. It will have been a glorious evolutionary pilgrimage risked for God's sake.

SECTION 3. HUMAN DESTINY FOR CONFIRMATION CLASSES

LeComte duNoüy's view of God creative act in evolution is an ideal source of auxiliary ideas about God and His Spirituality for beginners in church membership for several reasons. He was a devout Christian, sufficiently so that he elicited the acclaim of some America churchmen. Secondly, he was a reputable biological scientist who recognized that his religious and spiritual views were not acceptable to a group of secular, materialistic, fellow scientists. He could be quoted as saying that almost everyone these days believes in evolution (1946) but was realistic enough to know that many would not agree that the evolution of God's human family did not stop at the appearance of physical man with his enlarged brain. Our evolution is still actively in full force today and continues to develop towards the goal, which is the attainment of the template found in the Perfection of Christ. Man continues to shed his inherited animal instincts, becoming the fully Spiritual Man

---

*Originally this sentence was written with the word "working" in the place of the word "hoping." I felt that the term "working for" is still misunderstood in many Christian circles. Love, grace, and mercy as the gifts of God "bestowed upon us while we were yet sinners," disclaim the ordinary concept of working for merit. On the other hand, our working for God is synonymous with a thank-you, the grateful response to our Sustainer and Restorer of our souls; therefore, the word "hoping," which includes the promise of eternal life.

ready to enter the realm of the eternal life. It may require X millennia to reach that goal as man's time becomes God's Timelessness.

The young high-school student need not be confronted with the higher math treatment of the laws of probability, which comprises the first of three sections into which *Human Destiny* is divided. Sufficient to say that the adult writer of lesson material for youth need only be convinced that these laws, via the method of higher mathematics, demonstrates the improbability, if not the impossibility, of mere CHANCE accounting for formulating the chemical composition of the first cell of biological life. The protein molecule is very complex.

The second division of the book covers the origin of life in the primitive fresh-water ocean pools and follows the establishment of the animal and plant kingdoms to the point where the materialistic scientist notes the appearance of Homo sapiens; he is intelligent man because of the enlarged brain. DuNoüy, however, defines Man as not only intelligent, but *endowed with Conscience* and the ability to produce abstract thought, which requires logical Memory. It is important for the young student grasping the basics of human evolution to realize that the secular scientist leaves God, the spiritual force, completely out of the picture. Having arrived at Homo sapiens by CHANCE, the currently secular world view holds that man's power to develop is all within his own brain, self-developed, and so, HUMANISM rules in all future development. Such latter view is secular evolution. The young person of today who grows into and develops his acceptance of evolution as God's spiritual process must point out to his fellows that the evolution of God's human family is only partially completed by the initial gift bestowal of conscience (i.e., a moral code). We believers will hold that in God's act of mutation upon man's completed physical framework, He entered into the thinking process of man with a powerful force of Energy, which man will continue to feed upon as one of his energy sources. Man's thought process may be comprehended today as involving chemical reactions and an electronic field of force, but *they are the result of, not the cause of,* the process of thought. We hold that God's Spiritual Field of Force existed in its priority and that His spiritual power was the parent of what we call the power of energy whether it be called spiritual energy or physical energy. His Field of Force induces in man's mind and Spirit a working reflection of God's energy. To the extent that man can tune his receiving set to God's wavelength, so will he receive commendation, condemnation, admonition, or critical directions for the future. Thus God's energy prepares humanity in the pursuit of life's joys and sorrows. However weak, man's brain power is a reflection of God's power. The wholly materialistic scientist forgets that God gave that man-brain the gift of free-will decision. Through bad choices man has created evil and has made a mess in a number of directions. He must call in God to straighten things out and start afresh. God's goal will not be abandoned.

The process of evolution must continue under God until we have become like unto Christ Himself. This goal can be reached only by extreme conscientious effort, at times with "blood, sweat, and tears," in answer to God's magnetic drawing power. No doubt polemical contests will debate this upon the mistaken basis that they think they are debating the same common set of facts. The young Christian student must realize that an agnostic teacher can be reminded that his projection of science is only physical. The student is able to point out that when man receives his conscience from the source outside himself, God, the giver, continues to energize that conscience, and it grows in the ability to discern right and wrong. We know that man *never* actually performs as well as his conscience demands. How could he then have developed his own? On the basis of self-interest, greed and lust, and expanding ego? Hardly!

Actually the pastor and his confirmation class will quickly discern that the third and final section of *Human Destiny* deals with what he might rightly label "the sanctification of man," to borrow the biblical term which notes the growth of the religious person who daily draws nearer to his Creator and is simultaneously drawn into the heart of God by the magnetism and power of His Spirit. One only needs to turn to the appendix in this book and note the chapter titles beginning at duNoüy's chapter 13, "Religion—True Religion is in the Heart," and following through to chapter 17, "Intellectual or Moral Development," to realize that they would make up quite a profound slate of sermon titles. They cover a tremendous area of spiritual development which, if the secular materialist considers them at all attractive or desirable end goals, will, no doubt, smugly declare that man's will and mind alone will scale the heights entirely on their own. Such would be pure humanism, finally flowering and fruiting as the epitome of its own brain power. Such a view by the materialist sometimes concludes with the pronouncement that "After all, humans can depend upon Common Sense to see them through." DuNoüy has a very cogent paragraph on the subject of common sense, which I quote here in full: It begins: "Besides the scientific attitude, which is the privilege of a few and has led some of the greatest minds of all times to admit the necessity of God; besides religious and spiritual thinking, which have made their roots in the deeper aspirations of man, there is only one mediocre and misleading approach left—an approach sadly bereft of beauty, namely [common sense]." (Italics mine.) DuNoüy goes on to say:

> Alas, common sense will not suffice to catalyze, to accelerate, the spiritual evolution in which man is engaged. However, common sense has never been a tool of evolution. It is a practical, selfish notion without value for human progress. Not only does it frequently lead us astray scientifically, as we have seen, but as it is often based on empirical facts and superficial human logic, it suffers from the same weaknesses as the elements which serve as its foundation. It is not suspectible of development it itself, outside of experience. This is rather fortunate, for if common sense were universal, it would mean the end of the spiritual development of man, the end of evolution. It would prevent us from improving ourselves, from striving toward an ideal, from acting in a way opposed to our immediate interest; *it would forbid our ever taking a chance.* Common sense is never back of a heroic deed; if it were carried to an extreme, virtues would not have many occasions to shine. It almost looks as if God had taken care of this sad eventuality by distributing common sense, parsimoniously. A certain amount of common sense is necessary, as is salt in our food, but its absence is more fruitful than its excess.

Note that I have emphasized "it would forbid our ever taking a chance." Let us dwell upon this for a moment. One must eventually come to the conclusion that he cannot become spiritually fulfilling if he must fall back on his own full will and reason. There must be a prior reconciliation with the Power around and above us and a reliance on the strength there from that we cannot fully understand. As disciples of Christ, certain objectives are discerned as very desirable but without any clear pathway among many difficulties. In such cases, the Christian must "take risks for Christ's sake." Do you have the courage to skate out on thin ice to risk your reputation, or your money, or your influence over a pet personal project, all for Christ's sake? Are you ready for martyrdom?

A question may have arisen in your mind as to why duNoüy did not get around to considering God the source of *all energy* as we discussed it in the prior portions of this chapter. Perhaps his death in 1946 may well have occurred before he had the opportunity of personally meeting with Einstein, who was at Princeton. The equivalency of Energy and Matter in that basic equation was being formulated at that time but may not yet have caught his full attention. Although duNoüy in his *Human Destiny* refers in a general fashion to the energy of God implied in His Omniscience, he does not conceive it as a possible integral forerunner of Matter itself. On the other hand, Teilhard de Chardin, a contemporary Jesuit scientist, wrote about such matters in letters to his friends behind the pope's back. He was able to pick up a rock and discourse on the nature of God revealed in it in such a manner as to indicate of God's presence in the physical, inanimate portion of His creation. I have previously referred to Teilhard de Chardin as discussed in the Patterson (Word) series on modern theology. I found him difficult to understand. Suffice it to say at this point that some Christian theologists consider him to be a full-blown pantheist. It may merely reflect their lack of appreciation of any basic knowledge of science's contribution to theology. In my own meditation I have come very close to a pantheistic stance on the supposition that the energy present in the intramolecular being of the rock is energy originally from the substance of God Himself.

Having done my best to promote the study of *Human Destiny* in our confirmation classes,[8] I now summarize this brief section by listing the successive paragraph themes the foregoing discussion has followed. These themes may be handy opening statements for any number of class sessions. You may turn back and review them as follows:

1. Introduce duNoüy to youth who should realize God's process of evolution is still ongoing.
2. Set duNoüy's section I of *Human Destiny* dealing with the laws of probability aside for the average group of high school students (especially junior high students).
3. The origin of life begins as a process of development which is both spiritual and physical. The gift of Conscience labels the active beginning of humanity's spirituality.
4. God's plan for Man's continual growth of his spiritual and mental qualities is a continuous infusion of energy into Man from God and is essential in the thought process. God's concomitant gift of Free Will allowed man a choice of action that allowed him to create evil. Under *pure* Humanism, the Evil cannot be eradicated.
5. The "sanctification of man," i.e., his approach to the template in Christ, is not a matter of materialistic common sense; see duNoüy's quotation on common sense.

6. Impossibility of risking oneself for God without tuning in on Spiritual power: "Tuning in means reconciliation and recommitment."
7. DuNoüy, in *Human Destiny*, did not progress to the point where he could feel the equivalency of energy and matter. He knew that God had existed before neutrons, protons, and electrons. He stopped short of Teilhard de Chardin's view of God's energy being in molecules in every inanimate object.

At the beginning of this chapter you have perceived my imaginary concept of what could have been the situation *before* matter was created and the suns and planets appeared. This is a quite private view of what $E=Mc^2$ means to me at this point. The equation, spiritually defined, says that the spiritual Power of God resides in a directing supernatural Person existing above, around, and all-inclusively, prior to ANYTHING else. That Power is transferred to us in this, His physical Universe, via radiation, not unlike the manner by which we label materialistic energy transference by radiation from one system to another. Space may be filled with numberless radiations of energy either as particles or waves in a quantum, which physicists now speak about. The radiation of God's spiritual energy must certainly overbalance and precede the so-called secular energy that fuels the Space Age. I invite all my young friends to examine my explanation of how *all* energy in the beginning may have been gathered together in one "place" and became the flowing source of both material energy and spiritual energy, the whole procedure being in and of God Himself. And remember, we have said above in unmistakable fashion that God is LOVE. At the same time God is ENERGY. Above and beyond the Energy of God that flowed into the physical structure of His Universe we call nature, we are unaware of what could be the vast, unfathomable, inexhaustible reserve of Energy in God Himself. Even after the energy He apportioned to Nature has, under the laws of thermodynamics, wound down to cold, stillness, and utter darkness, leaving a residue of unusable energy in Entropy, we can still maintain our faith in a merciful Creator-God who is able to direct his remaining inexhaustible supply of both spiritual and physical Energy into a totally new divine plan we are utterly unable to grasp imaginatively.

SECTION 4. BE YE PERFECT—A SERMON

Prologue:

This discourse is a personal Christian testimony. It has been in formulation for several decades. Active fermentation has occurred since coming to Brownson in 1969 and now we release some of the inner pressure before moving on to a new church home. I truly believe God has helped me prepare this sharing session over the years. Its format may require a bit of explanation. We begin in the middle of a story with the Scripture from Jesus' lips as reported by Matthew. Thereafter you will recognize my Christian education background as we start at the origin of the physical Universe and wind up in the spiritual domain— eternal life in Heaven. Thus, it is hopefully a lesson in evolution, all in God's hand. Its language centers on two words, Perfection and Happiness, each with new twists, and members of the Young Adult Class of five or six years ago will recall some faint strains of past discussions. The action: Getting on God's escalator of perfection and feeling happy about it.

The Good News:

Jesus held His version of a summer camp-meeting on the mountain 2,000 years ago, and after spelling out a list of objectives that His followers ought to be giving high priority to in the conduct of their daily lives, He concluded with a very strange statement, as recorded in Matthew 5:48—"Be ye therefore perfect as your Father in heaven is perfect." Never has there been a command surpassing that command. Being that perfect is a tall order, an impossibility as humanity sees it. Perhaps we call it a divine carrot and since we mortals do not serve very well as receptacles for divine amperage and voltage, we lay it aside for the fireside and a rainy day. We never really tackle it. "Oh, well, that was just the idealism of an eloquent preacher closing with his peak punch line. He doesn't really mean that I take Him seriously."

Now Jesus was not talking through His hat! His plain Aramaean idioms were addressed to ordinary Cohens, Strausses, and Silbers, alias Smiths, Johnsons, and McDonalds: the butcher, the baker, the candlestick maker, the landlords of the inns and vineyard, the day laborer, the craftsmen of all ilk; and the women of every reputation. Of course these plainfolk at that moment had not yet suspected Him as being the Messiah. What did Jesus know that these people did not know and comprehend about the idea of becoming perfect? John, of course, came to know, for he says in his first five verses that Jesus Christ, the Word, was with God and within God (from the very beginning). He was there before the Creation of the Universe. He helped plan and guide the very nature of our being. It had a planned and terribly exciting beginning and an overwhelming ending. (In that ending we were to be like God and be drawn into Him.) Yes, God's plan for Creation was a plan calling for perfection at its end. It was not an experiment in His mind, the way we perceive it now. It would be an experiment only for the mortals. They would have a free-will choice of taking a sip of the living water and spitting it out in a spirit of rebellion. Now, God seems to have brought the physical Universe to a fair state of completeness, but in the spiritual arena, where he was counting on us to be his hard-laboring co-creationists, we have let Him down! In the face of our slackness, how long will the perfecting process still take? Our answer lies with God, of course, but we know that in the interim we are challenged to get ourselves back into a pattern of individual spiritual growth. Our faith must involve more doing beyond the hearing and the saying. God's plan of Creation is continuous growth: an evolution requiring our commitment to responsibility for our share of the action. Let's get aboard.

Let us return to the physical beginning of things for a moment by looking at the life of a French Jesuit priest and scientist, Teilhard de Chardin. Halfway through his preparation for the priesthood in Rome, he entered the Italian army and served as a noncombatant medical corpsman, sustaining nineteen "over the top" combat charges in the trench warfare of World War I. He went back to Rome, completed his theological studies, and was ordained. He went to England and earned his Ph.D. in geology, and since Jesuits are teachers, he taught and engaged in digging into God's earth. As he taught and dug he also wrote, and when what he dug began to reveal a history of God's human family, he became a renowned paleontologist. Behind the scenes of the communization of China he helped diagnose the meaning of the skeleton of Peking man. Could China have been the birthplace of an Adam and were other Adams brought forth in Java or South Africa or mid-central Europe?

Teilhard de Chardin wrote theological notes each day in his early morning devotions. His theological papers were almost as numerous as his scientific papers. To be sure the Pope's imprimatur never okayed them for publication through the papal print shop, but his Jesuit friends back in his native France saw that they were printed and widely distributed. Father Teilhard de Chardin knew that God had used millions of man's years to bring our universe and its people into being. But he maintained that God, not chance, was in charge; and so Christ came at the proper time to be the Divine Answer to man's problems of conscience and prideful self-assertion. As God led the spiritual side of evolution toward perfection there would come the time of Parousia and God would make all things clear. He raised the question, "Why can't Christians let God be the God of evolution?" Teilhard's evolution in the physical world was climaxed by evolution of our spiritual nature as an integral part of God's plan. The divine milieu would end in a fulfilled Parousia.

I believe that the church of today is dragging a heavy anchor of deserved disrespect in intelligent minds, both pagan and Christian. Is it not time that we introduce our children to the real wonders of the physical Universe and ask our church-school lesson writers to quit shadow boxing? Why not tell the boy and girl searching for wives for Cain, Abel, and Seth the truth? Whatever the evolutionary details of God's plan, there came a point in the formation of the top-level vertebrate candidates wherein God implanted His divine gifts of causative memory, a conscience, and an ESP oriented toward Him, the Creator.

We do not know what these first men called themselves when they learned to talk. The Hebrews in their oral culture and tradition used a word from their Semitic background language. *Adamah* with a small "a" meant human or humankind. It is possible that God brought forth humankind in four or five likely places on the face of the planet Earth. Timing of this act? Well, Dr. Ussher, the Bible literalist, claimed his Adam appeared in 4004 B.C. He did not know that the Zhou Dynasty was a viable going concern in China by the year 10,000 B.C. How futile to count the generations between *adamah* and Abraham over the millions of years involved.

When the nomadic Semites under Abraham finally finished their 400 years of Egyptian servitude and were enrolled in the Mount Sinai School of Correction under Headmaster Moses, they still needed a few hundred years in which to subdue the Promised Land and learn to write spiritually. We have no original scraps of papyrus, but Bible scholars can point out the traces of beginnings. Groups of Samuel-type persons representing a special function like the priesthood, or living geographically near a spot where the more sensitive, poetic types congregated, did their bit. One such group referred to God as Yahweh, another called him Elohim. The two stories of creation reflect the work of these two groups.

As the reign of David was ushered in at 1000 B.C. and the nomadic way of life was replaced by a sedentary culture, the scribe became a most important person. But what to write? Instinctively they knew that the spiritual nature of their oral culture must be handled in a very special way. After all, they were the chosen people. God had already favored them beyond measure. The mind set of the Middle East was Oriental, not Occidental. That meant that imagery in words flowed naturally and easily. A story, an allegory, had to be set up which would convince fellow Israelites what God expected of them as special agents of His will. It would have to be honest about sinning and rebellion and it would have to present God's moral code in unmistakable fashion. With no eyewitnesses of Creation and no pre-Abramic people they could fully trust for evidence, they forged under the nudging of the Holy Spirit the most wonderful story the human family has today.

Of course, we know this tremendous spiritual history contains some secular and technical errors. God's own rock calendar now reveals that instead of six twenty-four hour days for Creation, we have to substitute millions of years. Abraham's heritage of the Noah story no doubt was based on the Sumerian Noah who had been written up a couple thousand years previously and, of course, the chosen people had to rework the Sumerian Noah into a Hebrew character. They had to appropriate the heathen hero and make him a true agent of God. Some of God's messages to the consciences of His earliest people had already broken through here and there. Three of God's commandments had their first edition as far as we know in Hammurabi's legal code of 2000 B.C.: Do not kill; do not steal; do not lie. We Christians do not forget that we have appropriated other pagan values and have upgraded them. We took a Bacchanalian year-end carousal and changed it into Christ's birthday.

The punch line behind this Old Testament writing: Abraham proved to be God's dependable listener and doer and the first monotheist and so his family became the vehicle for transmitting God's blessing to the whole earth. God's acts of creation and perfecting continued down the stream of history. Prophets discovered that in addition to being a God of law and justice, Jehovah was also a God of love, a God of forgiving grace. God's people learned very slowly in the midst of ups and downs: apostasy on the part of ten of the original tribes; exile

232

and temple demolition for the other two.

In the fullness of time, He decided that His human family was ready to receive Him in a form more readily apprehended, a part of Himself who would live elbow to elbow with humanity; and in the mundane world of farming, fishing, building and trading, demonstrate what love really was when applied to all relationships. In this demonstration of love He would reveal more of His perfecting procedure, His rescue plan, so that His sinning and rebellious people would reestablish the lines of communication with their Father-God and Perfecter. His master plan must continue toward the perfect ending, so again we pick up at His camp meeting.

You have in your program folders the summary He delivered that day. Why "happy" in the place of "blessed"? Because that is what He really said. Every time a new word replaces a traditional one, our minds and hearts are activated. God thus challenged us when a Rabbi helping on this translation for the American Bible Society claimed that blessed was not the best meaning for the Aramaean word used by Jesus. It should be more like our word "happy." Now that Dr. Phillips followed suit in his version, what does the word "happy" and the condition of happiness mean to you?

And again, we have to thank a Hebrew for our enlightenment. A few years ago, a session of the McNeil-Lehrer Report was devoted to the theme of happiness. Mr. Lehrer presided over a trio comprised of a lady psychologist, a male psychologist, and Mr. Harry Golden, our eminent Jewish brother of Winston-Salem. The lady chose the mental state of the animal as her most perfect example of happiness—plenty of food, water, shade, relative safety, and protection. The other psychologist followed somewhat the same line, although he did allow that association with other agreeable and kindly human creatures made the happiness perhaps more meaningful and substantive. When Mr. Golden entered the fray he demolished the entire premise they had set up. Even Mr. Lehrer gasped. Mr. Golden completely eliminated the animal nature as an example. He immediately pointed out that since man's creation had placed him in a different and higher category, then happiness would have to be described in terms of that higher nature. The punch line of his very lively dissertation, as I remember it, was something like this: "True happiness is the realization by a person that he or she has made some growth on a scale of moral values." What an example of our Judeo-Christian heritage: a Jewish writer and publisher, with a Rabbi, helping the American Bible Society explain what Jesus was getting at in that 2,000-year-old sermon.

To attain happiness one must be growing, progressing toward the perfection of the Divine Creation. Actually, the word "blessed" implies a somewhat completed, or arrived-at state. It is a bit like a pat on the head for a series of good works. One may be tempted to become passive or too self-satisfied when he is "blessed." Jesus didn't want that to prevail, did he? He was admonishing us to continue our evolution, our perfecting process, our creation partnership with the Father. As Matthew says it: "Be ye therefore perfect as your Father in heaven is perfect."

A necessary step in that procedure is our mortal physical death—for our completed spiritual goal can only be attained as we shed the limitations of our flesh. God's creative act of perfecting us as individuals and as a society ends in the planned goal—the ingathering of all the children of the world, past and present, into the perfected divine family. This Parousia or fulfillment of Christ's Kingdom in the last days is beyond our mortal ability to describe or comprehend. John, the Revealer, tried it in what we have as the last book of the Scriptures. He does not tackle the problem of how all non-Christian pagans who have gone on before will be presented at the court of God through the person of Jesus Christ. The chosen-people concept was still too fresh and exclusive for Him to try. Suffice it to mention at this point that our Mother Church may have a thing going for it in the concept of purgatory as the anteroom to heaven. All nonbelievers, pagans, and backslidden Christians may be given a final last chance, a crash course in the diagnosis of sin, the act of repentance, and the forgiving love of God.

Postlude:

Breaking up the road to perfection into successive, shorter-term goals, which can be specifically defined, would appear to be mandatory. Such immediate goals or steps will give a sharpness to our individual creative daily efforts and provide the resulting happiness of accomplishment which will motivate us for undertaking the next step. As creating, perfecting partners with God, we have time only to present three intermediate goals for A.D. 2000. They are community goals, not purely individual goals. A fourth one we can only list in passing: Restore the validity of the family as described in the aforementioned Mount Sinai School of Correction.

Item 1—O! happy day! when the first church-school curriculum materials for the junior department will appear with a special unit of study embellished with a picture of a nice fat dinosaur and an article discussing God's rock calendar and how scientists read it, perhaps with a simple explanation of the working conditions of the writers of Genesis—how they became fatigued when they worked six twenty-four hour days and felt that God would too—and that they did not have a chemist on hand to advise them about the age of the earth. Other interesting geological discussions of fossils will be included throughout the succeeding junior high and senior high materials; and upon completing the twelfth grade the graduate will be given the opportunity of handing in a personal, private paper to his pastor entitled "God's Creation and My Part in It," subtitle: "I Believe Christ Will Be Perfecting Me throughout My Life, If I Work with Him"!

Item 2—Problem: What to do about beverage alcohol? It is the Space Age dilemma. Alcohol began as an ingredient of culture in the dawn of settled agrarian life. In the push-button Space Age wherein technology creates a new culture, alcohol becomes an outlawed beverage except under a doctor's care. What blind hypocrites we Christians are. We turn a president out of office because a war he fell heir to was wantonly killing thousands of our young men. *Yet each year* alcohol officially murders over 50 percent of the number losing their lives in the whole ten years of that war. Statistically, 65–75 percent of Americans drink some form of alcohol; increasingly, it is reported as a major high-school problem. A goodly number of church members, upon leaving cocktail parties, climb into their high-powered projectiles and potentially become their neighbor's killers. We slough this off by claiming one drink never impaired the driving, but we are untruthful. After thirty-seven years of industrial life, having witnessed many situations, I swear there is no such thing as a one-drink person. Do we realize that booze costs—in work loss, rehabilitation, and health care generally—more than the total cost of our primary and secondary education? Yet we continue to act as if there were no problem. The technical control of our daily lives will demand some better answers as we enter the twenty-first century. How easy to push the red button, start World War III and our demise. Five million Mormons already have one good answer. Keep away from it. Keep it in the medicine closet and administer only under a doctor's prescription.

Item 3—An astounding Christian experience is taking place in the world today. We see the beginning of the move to outlaw nuclear war.

We speak of peace in ways the Church has never had the courage to preach before. In the past, Christians prayed for peace in a passive, polite way. God was asked for a gift but not shown much real effort on the part of the supplicant. Today we pray for peace with fervency, with a demand of the Holy Spirit to gird us with armor and to give us backbones and longer arms to reach out to all other people. The year 2000 ought to see nuclear warfare put to rest for good—and how wonderful that Mother Church's hierarchy can take such a strong united stand. Thus Christianity seems integrated, as one, as never before. If President Eisenhower had never pronounced any other presidential opinion, his public reference to the necessity of saving the world's peoples and the planet by abolishing all nuclear weaponry places him on a pedestal as a statesman and a military leader above all others. We pray that there will be other leaders like him to have the same courage of outspoken conviction. His challenge to us points up another Space Age dilemma: not enough spirituality to balance and control the material advancements of science and technology.

Dear God, help us to catch up in your process of perfecting!

Dear God and Father—Maker of us all: We, your people, have come into this sanctuary yearning beyond measure to come into your Presence. But! we do not even know how to address you. It sometimes seems that we deliberately search for just the right name that will somehow unlock the barrier that we have erected between You and us. We anxiously address this point so that like grasping a straw of magic, we might press the proper key of the spiritual computer under which your universe operates: the One God, Creator of the Universe, Giver of Life, Ruler of the Universe, Father, Lord, Master, Jesus the Christ, Spirit of God, Holy Comforter and Enabler. *We test each name in turn and most of the time we become discouraged because no instant flash of recognition flows over and within us. You have called us your children, but we see no real person as we peer from the cloudy windows of our soul. Nor coming up the front walk to the door of our hearts, nor as we attempt to more sharply fine tune the fuzzy image and jangled sounds of our private TV set we call the conscience. In our frantic search we finally fall back on your saint, Rufus Jones, who constantly said, "You, God, are everywhere. We, your people, are immersed in You." Some of your Being actually penetrates the hard crust of the facade of our self-righteousness. You are nearer than hands and feet. You are in us.*

Dear Father-God, help us to be truly sensitive to your Presence. May we break the code of your constant messages to each of us; not only in these moments of congregational worship but in the heat and the burden of our daily lives.

You have called us to work toward perfection in the conduct of our lives. You have instructed us to become like your human self, Jesus. We have shied away from this responsibility because the present gap between us seems such a wide, boundless chasm. Intuitively, we have called this wideness our alibi. We are pitiful in our unworthiness. We fail to recognize the inevitability of your persistent and every-continuing evolutionary process. We thought we had to accomplish the drawing near under our own poor power. We have failed to keep clearly in mind that though we must supply our Will, You will supply the drawing energy.

A sense of understanding floods us as you gently turn our attention to Jesus. You constantly reveal yourself in Him. You walked with us in Him. You even allowed us in our wickedness to inflict a horrible physical torture upon You in Him. Father, forgive us if You will. Each one of us shall see You as the God of love in Him. Jesus showed us how to travel on our Jericho roads: how to search out others who are hurting and to give such aid as we can. Jesus showed us by His daily living that we cannot be fulfilling Your purpose for us when we so exclusively devote ourselves to the production of our widgets; gloating over the black ink of our personal accounts, involved in total concern for our own children and the long list of worries that beset us. Yes, even now at this instant, we are preoccupied with the menu for Sunday dinner and the afternoon ball game.

Jesus, pausing, saw a lame man in the shadow and healed him. Jesus, pausing at that ancient water cooler for a drink, met the promiscuous woman and reversed her life-style. Later He said, "Come to me, you who are sick and tired and overburdened. I can give you rest." Gradually a bright light does dawn upon and before us. You are defining real LOVE. *You loved us in Him and You love us now in spite of our mischief, more than we can ever comprehend. And more—You set, in Him, the pattern for our love of neighbor. A second great light shines forth: that we can return our gratitude to you by trying to be loving neighbors ourselves. Our love in this area is so imperfect, but we pledge our best attempt.*

How very much this world, which You gave to us to run, needs Love today. We perceive that Your love has to come dramatically, as a flash of lightning from heaven, but that it will be as the slow persistence of leaven. You will work through each one of us. So we pray for strength of persistence in loving all strange people who talk differently, and have such antagonizing customs. We pray earnestly for your wisdom to prevail at the peace-keeping our pastor is attending this weekend. Bless his endeavor. May our whole church be enlightened and charged to begin preparing for this leadership in loving, as never before. You have asked us to love the unlovely, one of our most difficult tasks. Teach us to differentiate between the behavior of unlovely governments and nations and their true inner hearts and minds and spirits as individuals. Let us will to love these supposed enemies of the peace in such fashion that they and we together can arrive at the common goals, acceptance of our brotherhood. We know how difficult it is to love the sinner while hating his sin, because sinners reflect ourselves. We know we cannot accomplish this by our human effort alone, for our egos blind us as we skew things in our favor.

Dear God, make us fit channels of Your love as it flows through us to all others.

Hear these petitions we pray, in Your name, in Christ.
Amen.

Chapter X

Potpourri

During the writing of this book, the skeleton form of the six sorties was always in focus. However, as can well be imagined, a variety of Christian experiences kept knocking at the door of this Pilgrim's consciousness. During cyclic pauses in writing and reediting, scribbled notes on various subjects developed. They went into a folder labeled "Potpourri." Whether that term means a mixed meat stew in the kitchen or a jar of dried fragrant leaves on your wife's dresser, the Century dictionary also allows it to be applied to a "musical medley; a literary medley; or collection of literary extracts." The last word is quite appropriate. And, hopefully, this collection of extracts of my experience will attempt to be as literary as the record of the pilgrimages. There are six subtitles as follows:

1. The Reading Church
2. Intelligence and the Christian
3. Ecumenicity as Seen through the Pilgrim's Eyes
4. Fail-Safe Reality in Christ
5. Beverage Alcohol in the Space Age
6. The University of Life*— A Final Challenge of the Space Age to Pastors and Local Theologians

---

*'The University of Life"—Christ's Church
Reverently and lovingly, I recall my association with the Reverend Dr. Leon M. Adkins, who, during the '30s was the pastor of the Methodist Church in Delmar, New York, a suburb of Albany. This village also became my family's hometown. He and I served happily for a number of years as fellow instructors in the ten-week winter terms of the ecumenical Albany School of Religion maintained by the Albany Council of Churches. Of course he taught Bible classes while I taught church-school administration. Though I was a Baptist and attended church in the city, as our children became a part of the local public school life, we joined Leon's University of Life. We were intrigued by the yearly catalog following a format based on the usual college catalog style. Every activity was

1. THE READING CHURCH

In the spring of 1986, our home television gave out. The question of immediate repair, uppermost in our minds for a week, easily slipped out of focus into oblivion before we were aware of how well we had adjusted to life without it. I had previously joined the ranks of the weekly *Time* and Sunday newspaper readers, so that more permanent significant history was quite well recorded. Actually, our only TV regret was missing McNeil-Lehrer and Bill Cosby and *This Week in Washington*. This experience automatically reestablished the importance of libraries and book reading. It brought to mind the church reading program my wife was responsible for back in the '30s in a little church in upper New York State. It seemed that more people knew how to read then than now. We sighted Christians currently do not read a great deal, or at least we do not conversationally refer to our reading. We do not read THE Book that we profess to be the Book of books, except for the few who participate in a weekly Bible class, and even there too many of us (especially the men) slide into an easy habit of leaving the lesson helps lying around the house because the teacher on Sunday will try to bring us up to date anyway. We sin because we are truly card-carrying members of the Priesthood of Believers who ought to be studying the basic source of that faith.

But I am not limiting book reading to the Bible. I am referring to the growing neglect of books generally in our lives. Am I mistaken in the view that trashy TV entertainment and athletic games on end now become our chief diversion of leisure time? As regards athletic games, I am thoroughly confused. I thought colleges and universities still depended on considerable book reading and digestion of them. And professors who are proficient and skilled in the interpretation of those books receive minuscule incomes compared to the salaries in the

described as a course in Christian Living, with title, instructor, and aids, with meeting places and scheduled hours. *All* leaders in the church program, whether as menu maker in the kitchen or those who cut the grass and repaired the building were listed as members of the University faculty. I have a little packet of these catalogs laid away in my guarded treasures.

This kind, generous, and talented man was slated for higher places. The District Superintendent soon snatched him for a larger, more prestigious church and shortly thereafter they took him to Nashville as the capitol of the new United Methodist Church. There he served the remainder of his active life as that great denomination's director of Christian education. He carried a brightly lighted torch for his Christ. For him, Christ's Church was, indeed, the University of Life.

"muscle and beef" departments. Are we, perchance, repeating the opening scenes of the Roman games of 2,000 years ago?

But let us go back to reading books in the Christian congregation. The church library is no longer the catchall, odd closet, or attic space filled with the congregation's castoffs. It enjoys official board recognition as a sizable specific item in the annual budget of Christian educational planning and is managed by educators who know how to order a new book, how to classify and list it, and how to open a book fresh from the printer. The library management members also know how to promote their wares among their customers from age zero to age 100. Their repertoire of subjects will include not only the standby inventory of the active, current Christian education curriculum but will keep abreast of trends and advanced guard research in that field.

Basic reference works in the biblical category will show the standards like the *Interpreter's Bible* and its five-volume dictionary and a half-dozen well-known translations. Incidentally, there ought to be a duplicate set of the twelve-volume *Interpreter's Bible* so that one of them can be checked out by teachers while one set remains inviolate and complete on the reference book shelf. Included will be Barclay's well-known Daily Bible Study readings for the New Testament, now joined by Gibson's similar work on the Old Testament. In the general section will be pictures and story books for very young children followed by a variety of browsing table materials on up to the youth classification, Christian adventure, Christian autobiographies and biographies, Christian morals and ethics, and Christian parenting for youth of a quality that Dr. Albert Winn and his peers put into the high school under the former Covenant Life Curriculum. For the adult section, autobiographies and biographies of outstanding Christian characters are a must, for the simple reason that, however much we read of the philosophy or reasoning behind our faith, it is the actual living of that faith that makes it comprehensible and therefore apprehensible for one's self. Church history from the time of Christ has been neglected by almost all Christians except those who may have attended a church-related college that required this credit among other religious themes. In the recent past there has been a fair amount of literature also referring to the rise of the foreign National Churches in which Christian faith is being brought forth at grass roots. Who knows when their interpretation of Christian life and conduct will be coming back in a reverse direction to the home base in America? Both Protestant and Roman Catholic authors should be read. Good fiction on Christian themes should be available; also worldwide evangelistic developments both from our current missionary effort and the growth of Third World national churches should be included.

I make a special plea for books of theology written for the layman, such as the Word Book series covering such authors as Barth, Bonhoeffer, Buber, Bultmann, Niebuhr and others.[1] Such books of theology present wonderful possibilities for making meaningful book club discussions or special Christian theme studies. In my opinion, pastors would do well to give adult reading assignments to those entering the church by transfer of letter. In reviewing these with his elders, deacons, or other official board members, he could initiate further discussion throughout the congregation. Many Christians have so far missed the chance to read the challenging books of authors of reputation, such as C. S. Lewis and Paul Tournier. As a test case, Dear Reader, read a few pages of Bonhoeffer's theme of "Cheap Grace."[2] He put his life where his mouth and mind were; he gave it as he had risked it, for Christ's sake.

2. INTELLIGENCE AND THE CHRISTIAN

The theme of this exploratory section is one that is never heard discussed directly from the pulpit. Reduced to its fundamental terms, it is simply this. Does the level of learning acquired by the Christian, both self-acquired and academically earned, more or less guarantee the *quality* of our Christian life, or, more crassly, does the level of academic experience reflect the quality of our Christian life? On a general basis, what is the relation of *intelligence*, knowledge, and wisdom to the moral and ethical quality of actual Christian performance? And hiding out behind the group of trees posed by the above question is another. What is the Christian faith of the great mass of illiterates in America today? This also brings into focus the poor soul who is born in a retarded mental state.

Perhaps we should define the three levels of learning referred to above. *Intelligence* is perhaps synonymous with mental ability. The readiness with which one comprehends is looked upon generally as intelligence, but one must be careful not to equate "animal" intelligence with "human" intelligence. Our animal nature and our spiritual nature blend toward each other in forming initial human nature. When speciation produced Homo sapiens from Homo understock, God added the logical mind, i.e., causative memory and conscience. There is recognition of degrees of intelligence in man. There is "native" intelligence in Homo sapiens to which is added acquired intelligence. "When I was a child, I thought as a child, but when I became a man [adult], I put away childish things." It is on this Pauline experience that Christian educators are now coming to the view that the traditional move toward church membership, i.e., confirmation, should be delayed for at least a year, perhaps from the sixth grade to the seventh grade level or more. The entire junior high school group from seventh to ninth grades would be considered ready for recruitment. The child should be beginning to think with at least elemental logic before the idea of his commitment to a life like Jesus Christ's become really meaningful (see chapter 5). We were "Children of God" in varying degree in our early lives. In early Sunday church-school we had acquired many stories from the Bible along with the elementary use of the three Rs in the public school. Knowledge acquirement in education and our culture demands that education be an important goal throughout our mortal lives. The rate at which we grow in knowledge can be seen as we inspect our Growth Curve (see chapter 2). We note that continual growth is necessary or we may soon "go to pot." Our ability to think with the knowledge we have accumulated wanes and withers and the facts lower to such dimness as to be almost worthless. Those of us who are older know that retirement raises the question of what to do about this. We know we can remain truly active in our areas of interest. We take steps to enforce this.

The term "knowledge" is often blurred because we fail to make a distinction between two aspects of it. The mere storage of facts in the brain's computer is sometimes assumed to be equivalent to knowledge. This limits knowledge to being merely an inventory of the facts. The college graduate who goes on to earn a string of academic degrees may be burdened with factual knowledge and yet be unhappy because he fails to accomplish anything with it. Hidden in the word "accomplish" is that second aspect of true knowledge, purpose. We organize the whole word "knowledge" when we introduce the end point, the goal, we are aiming at. When the goal is missing, the Growth Curve tends to turn down and we stagnate. When the process is Christian commitment and

Jesus Christ is the template, we soon find that being a Christian is a lot more than storing facts about God and His chosen people and the beginning of His Church in Christ's resurrection. It is living with each other in a reactive relationship by which we nurture one another in the faith; love becomes the new power stemming from such knowledge. See again, chapter 5, page 92, where Loving is identified as nurture.

Purpose directly influences the type of knowledge we strive to attain. With most of us Americans, we look toward preparation for a job in a specific field of activity, all the way from A for atomic to Z for zoophilous. Most American universities expect the student to have chosen a field for his major by the time he is well into his sophomore year. There will continue to be controversy, especially in liberal arts colleges, as to the degree of broad cultural background knowledge to be acquired as a supplement to the specialization or avocationally tuned courses one takes. After all, there are just so many hours during which to accomplish this, so say we very busy Americans. And we certainly must not overlook the horrendous problem with the mass of people who just managed to get through high school. The tremendous growth of our two-year community college system, largely state supported, is seen as one avenue by which our culture seems to call for an advance beyond the high-school level of knowledge attainment. Much of the additional study is avocational training as well as college training, all in the interest of getting a better job. I suggest that there is still a residual problem greater than we are willing to confess. There must be thousands upon thousands of our people who are just below or barely above the so-called cultural literacy line. Working within the power of the Spirit of God, what is our obligation toward them? Many of these youngsters are willful dropouts. Most of them do not know what self-discipline is. Many of them are poorly prepared by lack of home resources and support. Many of them are poor. The public school system seems to have failed them. What in the world can the Church of Christ now do to succor them and bring them a hope for the future, restoring confidence that our citizenry can once more react in a fulfilling democratic manner?

Christians seem very confused at times when they try to connect the young innocence of the child with the wisdom exemplified by Paul. Picking up a little child in His arms, Jesus said to the crowd, "Truly, I say to you, whoever does not receive the Kingdom of God like a child shall not enter it" (Mark 10:15). Jesus here was emphasizing the quality of faith to be reflected by the new disciple's entry into the kingdom. No strings are attached; he is humble; he is openly trusting, just as the child is towards its parents. Jesus at that occasion was not referring to the expectation that the later growth of the child would entail expanding knowledge of life and a development of his ability to perceive spirituality. Paul, in I Corinthians 13:11–12, was saying that when a young person begins to be thoughtful about life his first ideas are quite likely to be very rudimentary. As he grows in experience and knowledge he should arrive at adult versions consistent with the reality of life as properly adjusted in the spirit of people's love for each other and God. Paul, in a sentence, was sketching a path for the Christian development of each individual from point zero to eternity. Jesus, on the other hand, was speaking of a child at point zero; what he said had to do entirely with the quality of faith when first experienced as commitment. Jesus was essentially saying, "Look, even if you are an old man (say as old as Nicodemus) and you are meeting God in Me for the first time and are so moved as to wish to be my man, you do not logically reason yourself into a position of discipleship. A great light has flamed up in your soul and you say yes to Me. You grasp the prize of God with the same certainty as the faith this little child has in its daddy or mother who will provide everything, will do everything, and will be everything in life for an indefinite period of time." But, as the wise Paul then instructs, "Do not forget to step on your spiritual Growth Line and keep it curving upward. You now have a purpose toward which your intelligence and your knowledge and your wisdom in choosing values to live by will make you a full-grown man or woman, the type God desires to see all His disciples become."

Can we attempt to sum it all up in one encompassing sentence? The call and magnetism of God in Christ is so powerful and accommodating. Upon entering the spiritual life at the lowest level of childishness, each disciple has placed before him a plan and purpose demanding a constant effort of love to attain it, and above and beyond any level of intelligence, knowledge, and wisdom of entry, there exists unlimited room for growth, even unto the genius which is Christ Himself. In the plain language of the street, God says to everyone, "No matter how smart you are, with my support, you must continue to grow and assume responsibility in the spiritual kingdom of which you are now ignorant."

3. ECUMENICITY TODAY—THE PILGRIM'S EXPERIENCE

The following is a brief outline of the *denominational* aspects of the author's religious experience. In the list below I have broken up my total church membership into five sections of time and have attempted to roughly estimate the duration of each one by the year in which the change was made. Please note that the yearly total in each is inclusive of the yearly date given.

Period I—Birth to the second year of high school, cradled by Methodism Circuit Rider (via a branch of the Great Northern Railroad in North Dakota, rather than by saddle horse) prior to World War I, 1903–18.

Period II—Baptist (Northern Convention) 1919–1938, twenty years; this period included four years at Saint Olaf, a Lutheran college in Minnesota where I had three years of required religion courses in Bible, church history, and contemporary Christianity.

Period III—Methodist—1939–1956, eighteen years; New York and New Jersey.

Period IV—Congregational—1957–1966, ten years, now known as United Church of Christ; New Jersey.

Period V—Presbyterian—1967–1990. This is at present twenty-four years and still going strong; New Jersey and North Carolina.

This was not a matter of search and check and evaluate by joining various denominations. It was a case of doing what comes naturally as a result of living in seven different home localities and following the public-school life of our children as supportive parents. As an introduction one must refer to the three yearly courses in religion at Saint Olaf College. The one year of Bible, one year of Church History, one year of Christianity and contemporary religion gave me a background I would wish for every Christian. This was academic Lutheranism with no real church congregational aspects for me, who as a non-Lutheran attended his own church. Nevertheless, these three-year courses plus daily chapel five times a week for four school years gave me a certain plus feeling about Lutheranism, especially as regards the professional standing of

Lutheran pastors. This may not be true of the denomination today and would require further checking out. But there is one very distinct aspect I have always carried with me. It is that the Lutheran ordained ministry carried with it a definite authority and leadership on the part of the pastor never quite duplicated in any of my other extended denominational contacts. I may be in error as to the situation today, but I hope not, for it carries a plus factor that I did not experience with the other four. A theologian by training is an expert in the spiritual field (or ought to be becoming one). Though he may not command the obedience of his flock in the manner of an M.D. who is prescribing medication for the physical ills of a patient, a pastor/minister knows more theology, should understand Christian commitment more thoroughly, and should indicate lines of progress facing his fold with his supportive suggestions. Perhaps some of my faulting of the other denominations may rest on the observation that they spend so much extra time on what is justified as democratic teamwork in the investigation and discussion from which the church educational leaders are to pick and decide what they want to do. Most of the time I did not see a pastor who was really leading in the Christian educational field until I joined my present church. I rather favor the more authoritarian leadership of the Lutheran pastor. He may be loosening up a bit currently, but I would hope not too much so.

When our family moved from North Dakota into southern Minnesota, my parents reactivated their early life allegiance to the Baptist Church (Northern Convention). I was baptized in the Baptist fashion and experienced what I consider the highlight of my early spiritual life. I, upon my own consent, joined the Priesthood of Believers. I have always rejected infant baptism as a sacramental rite, and feel that the adoption of a family dedication service as is done by many American Baptists is the better way to incubate the nurturing support of the community of faith. It reserves real baptism to a period of consciousness where the experience can become subjectively overwhelming for the idealistic teenager. I wonder if any confirmation class, no matter how well developed, could ever quite match the miracle of this act of adult conversion. Skinny-dipping jokes on baptism are blasphemous. I am broad-minded in this respect toward others. Such a church is honor bound to accept a transfer of church membership by letter from any other recognized denomination where infant baptism has been followed by a teenage confirmation class.

The Methodism experience of the boyhood Sunday school period in primitive Dakota prior to World War I was enhanced by the association with one of the finest church-school teachers I have ever met.[3] The warmth of that association seemed to follow me into mid-life in the late '30s and into the '50s when I, in turn, sat on the other end of the log. The Bishop and his district superintendent seemed not to have much to do with it after all. This inner warmth of Methodism, I believe, included the relationship with the black race in the top church denominational structure later on. The black Methodist Central Jurisdiction had its own Bishopric and District Superintendents and when the United Methodist Church was later put together, the new church served as an example for all Christiandom. Black District Superintendents were indiscriminately assigned throughout the white northern constituency and most were well received. Our greater New York suburban New Jersey church received such an assignment in the '70s and did its share of racial reconciliation. I believe that the Methodists have set a fine example for all denominations in this area of our common brotherhood.

Congregationalism followed in the democratic steps of the Baptists and indeed, in our decade there, the church we attended was ministered unto by an ex-Baptist preacher. Area Associations formed the guiding supervision of the denominational program. An outstanding trait of the Congregationalist Church (now United Church of Christ), seems to be one of eagerness to do a good job in Christian education for the rank and file. Perhaps I was greatly influenced by the local General Superintendent for the public school of our area, who was a fellow church member and preceded me as Chairman of the church's board of Christian education. In chapter 5 on Christian education in this book, we discussed the long-term effect of the Robert Raikes Syndrome. Perhaps the Congregationalists, more than any other denomination, are melding the ordained and lay educational ministry into a single coordinated effort.

Finally we reached the Presbyterians. Selling our home two years before retirement and moving to a new community made it easy to become United Presbyterians and, upon moving finally to North Carolina, it was a simple step to continue as Southern Presbyterians. The brand new concept of church organization via the local presbytery and in general the whole system of representative government was a welcome addition to our idea of a church. We became aware of some of the roots of colonial heritage that issued into the basic form of the government of our United States. We found that well-touted concept of educated ministry easy to support, but, alas, also that this did not necessarily mean any less evidence of Robert Raikes Syndrome. Indeed, in our historical reading the upper-crust Presbyterian minister tended to nourish the syndrome. The younger ministerial ranks today are waking to the need to shake the syndrome completely. I want to take this opportunity to brag about the qualifications of our current young pastor in the field of Christian education and again emphasize his contribution in the creation of an approach to the confirmation curriculum for the junior high students in our church.[4]

I rejoice in my Presbyterian connection as it reaffirms the historicity of a united north and south. The sore has been healed after two centuries as we now become a single serving agent of the Spirit of God. I trust that the alternate election of black preachers to the position of moderator and other high offices will continue ad infinitum. Traditional white southerners who may have originally shied away from using the term "United," because it looked like they were joining a black denomination, must realize what a friendly overture was made by the northern whites when the latter gave up their descriptive adjective "United." Perhaps someday the Presbyterians (America) will drop some of their extreme fundamentalism and we can then create a truly United Church again. The north demonstrated an overwhelming force for union since it had twice the democratic votes to begin with. Choosing a neutral city for the new church's headquarters appears as God's will for a rebuilt, newly committed member of God's family.

My Statement of Ecumenicalism

Except for the matter of baptism these "denominational" emphases did not make for any fundamental theological conflict. They, in total, increased mightily the depth of the definition of "neighbor" and increased the hope that together we can tackle the twenty-first century with good heart and spirits. My theological concepts have heightened considerably over the past twenty years, but I believe it only incidental that it has taken place in a Presbyterian environment.

4. FAIL-SAFE WARRANTY IN JESUS CHRIST

The Jonathan Sea Gull philosophy of "practice makes perfect," may allow one to embrace illusory goals that are so far out of nature that failure must follow. The other side of that coin is that the goal may be very clearly defined but the means of obtaining it are so meager and problematical. The resiliency of human nature either under physical duress or mental and psychic aberrations is wonderful to behold. Of course we believers readily add God to the picture and ascribe success to His power and love. Even in cases where the recipient may not acknowledge the presence of the Spirit, we may say that God's unsolicited love is in charge via the prayers of friends and even unknown neighbors.

I treasure these two experiences of the '80s: The first is the story of a man who became a personal friend after the main event had taken place. He had been a business executive, a vice president of a national corporation. So far as he knew his future industrial and business life was mapped out on fairly normal lines of expectancy. But unexpected merger and consolidation developed and suddenly he was without employment. Fortunately, the financial settlement was very liberal. He had always been a practicing Christian and he turned to Christ for strength and guidance. Seminaries in his area made for convenience and he threw himself into a concentrated theological program qualifying him for the pastorate. He added sufficient extra credit to earn his Doctor of Ministry degree. I came to know him just before he was ordained as the associate pastor of the church we attended during the winter months in the south. Of course this man does not consider the term "failure" in any way applicable to him.

The second story is gleaned from a newspaper editor who was impressed by the tenacious grip on life held by a young lawyer he had interviewed in depth. The young man's brother had died of cancer. Seven years later, at fourteen, he lost a leg due to bone cancer. The incident was followed shortly by the death of his younger brother and his father, both of cancer. After completion of his law school work he had a bout with a brain tumor. Fortunately, the doctors performing this delicate operation pronounced the tumor benign. The newsman paid homage to the mother's faith and quoted her as follows: "I admire my family. They were strong, brave, and never negative. I know our story is very sad but I don't feel sad. In fact, I feel very lucky. My sons and husband have been very special people; full of love, happiness, and never with any self-pity." And then came her crowning statement: "There must be a reason for what has happened in our lives. Maybe it's

250

to help others." And there was the concluding quote from the young man himself. "I made up my mind that I had not lived enough of life to give up. What's more important, surviving with the ones you love, or giving up?" I believe that God wishes me to add a footnote to the second case for the sake of those many persons who, due to sickness or catastrophe, must depend on extensive surgical/medical repair to their bodies. My M.D. friend, quoted in chapter 2, emphasizes that the actual mending of the body tissue, after the surgeon reestablished arterial blood supply, is from the heart of God.

Looking back at these two accounts I hope everyone will perceive and laud the tremendous willpower and sense of commitment that canceled out the word "failure." I feel certain that it was God who supplied the spiritual adrenalin and, to this day, is outlining to each of them the goals he has in mind for these two souls. No sense of mere humanism with clear working minds is sufficient, for God, the healing Spirit, has been in charge all along.

In this technical age of gadgetry and mechanical equipment, everything from lawn mowers to nuclear power plants is designed with the idea of safety to the operator. If, in a procedure depending upon a potentially dangerous tool or device, a malfunction should occur, a shut-down function is automatically triggered to protect both personnel and environment. These fail-safe devices are especially important in procedures that operate continuously on twenty-four-hour days. These safety devices are an acknowledgement that failure does in fact face us in the technical, secular world, and we try to minimize or negate them entirely. I submit that a fail-safe device that works in the secular-mental level of humanism gives us a very appropriate analogy for God's message to us in the spiritual realm. God's mission for each of us is apt to experience blowups and reversals resulting from the fallibility of our poor personal resources. When human self-interest interjects itself and our seemingly noble projects are on the verge of failure, is there a fail-safe device for us—perhaps on a less spectacular scale than that represented by the two stories with which we began this section? How do we shut down the negative and magnify the positive when trouble erupts?

God's fail-safe system works today in the Space Age as it did some four thousand years ago. It is built about God's LOVE. LOVE was why he came to us later on in the person of Jesus. The time required to make this fail-safe procedure available was the time it took God's people to

251

understand just what God meant by that term. God's Hebrew spiritualists, the prophets, had to work on the theme mightily to give it birth. Hosea introduced the idea of love as a communal attribute, Jeremiah tried to give it individualistic and personal application when he began to preach about writing God's message on individual hearts. Isaiah I and II forecast the love gift of Jesus, God Incarnate, and meanwhile Isaiah III wrote the marching song, the Twenty-third Psalm, that we discussed in Chapter 7. The shepherd psalm put loving care and concern in God's shepherding of the millions and billions of souls.

God, realizing that His family was at times stubborn and bullheaded and overflowing with pride and greed, knew that He would finally enter human society personally and show them what He meant. First He demonstrated that the fail-safe device was for EVERYONE, no matter what their artificial social caste. For him who had no material goods whatsoever, there still were God's LOVE and a purpose for the future. The gift was not one of acknowledgement of merit for us; it was love willing to lay down mortal life as a sacrifice on behalf of us immoral, sinning people who need a specific moral direction. They had to be convinced that LOVE was real.

We go a step farther. This love assurance is life insurance. Though our project, which we thought was blessed by God, seemingly has failed, He asks us to put on our spiritual glasses and survey things again. We definitely must learn from our failures that He is present to help pick up the pieces. Love is powerful medicine. You will be receiving it *from God* through your neighbors.

The daily communication with God must not be missed. One must stop to tell Him about that day's slippage, the angry word, the behind-the-back slur, the sly lobbying of self-interest, one's blindness on the daily road to Jericho. Plead complete responsibility and confession and feel His overwhelming love as He says He will pick you up and love you as much tomorrow morning as He did yesterday. He is going to stick to you if you will allow Him to. Then if what looks like disaster or failure appears, the rescue harness is already in place to pluck you out and save you for a better end. Do I hear some of you say, "Mr. Author, that is a pretty glib story." My reply: "Brother, come round and visit me some day and I will tell you MY story."

5. BEVERAGE ALCOHOL IN THE SPACE AGE

Our modern secular culture has moved ethyl alcohol from the jurisdiction of the pharmacy prescription counter, where narcotics belong, to the abundant and open shelves of the supermarket grocery store where, though direct purchase is restricted by age, the entire family, with infants sprawled among its containers in the shopping cart, is exposed to the acceptability of abusive drinking. By allowing this, our culture has exposed and promoted the most extensive, blatant hypocrisy in the present era of Christendom. The picture even includes the worldly way of some clergy who may serve alcohol in the home or, on an occasional convivial outing of the men's club, join in for a can of beer. We can praise God for the appearance of some opposing public leadership in such articles as that published in the *Fort Myers News-Press* of January 7, 1989, by Professor Donald L. Mosher of the University of Connecticut. We quote it here in its entirety. Please allow for full significant mental penetration of steps eleven and twelve in his twelve-step procedure recommended for the control of the alcohol problem. The equivalent kindergarten Christian term is commitment.

As a psychologist, I make a portion of my living helping people change their drinking habits. Treatment is no magic bullet; it merely means helping people resolve to change their lifestyles.

No matter how many problem drinkers I help, I know that social norms, the macho mystique and $2 billion in liquor advertising ensure my financial future. But I don't want this heartsick future.

The drinking problem is neither defined nor bounded by alcoholism. As a society, we create the drinking problem—by both permitting and encouraging drinking. What is the recipe for a problem drinker? Take one social drinker and add stress.

If we continue treating drunks without preventing problem drinking, the alcohol industry that gets them drunk—and the medical professionals who dry them out—will continue to earn healthy profits at the expense of the American public. The cost of problem drinking is estimated to be $100 billion a year.

Treating alcoholics will never solve the drinking problem. From a public health perspective, the only solution to problem drinking is prevention.

To control the prevalence of problem drinking, the incidences of heavy drinking must be controlled. Heavy drinking is defined as drinking two or more drinks a day. Problem drinking is defined either by a sense of dependence on alcohol to sedate worrying, nervousness or depression, or by incidents of impaired performance on or off the job.

We must stop soothing our consciences by believing alcoholism is a disease.

The American Psychiatric Association and other organizations have assured us this is true—even that the problem is genetic. But if the problem is in the person, we feel no need to control the environment that promotes drinking. Who dares whisper: You can't become a drunk without getting drunk; you can't become drunk at all without heavy drinking?

Who are the heaviest drinkers? Men in their teens, 20s, and 30s who believe, and have male buddies who believe, that it is manly to drink eight or more drinks on some occasions. These are men I call macho. What is the recipe for a dangerous drunk? Take one macho man and add alcohol.

Macho men watch sports on TV and drink beer. Advertisers understand that macho men believe danger is exciting and real men drink, fight, and fornicate. Alcohol impairs judgment and releases aggression.

But who takes on the alcohol industry? Who dares say alcohol advertising encourages drinking in our youth? Who dares say that some sports heroes encourage boys to drink beer as a symbol of manhood? Who dares say that crimes such as rape are associated with drinking? Who is outraged enough to stop the drinking problem?

The solution to the alcohol problem is prevention. How? Follow these 12 preventive steps: 1) increase alcohol taxes; 2) add warning labels to alcohol; 3) eliminate the tax write-off for alcohol as business entertainment; 4) place the actual percentage of alcohol in a beverage on the label; 5) eliminate the misleading advertising for alcohol; 6) require the liquor industry to pay for equal-time alcohol prevention ads; 7) restrict alcohol advertising on television; 8) restrict time and place of sales of alcohol; 9) enforce the limits on underage purchase and use of alcohol; 10) understand that alcohol is the dirtiest drug of all: end hypocrisy about illegal drugs; 11) stop pushing drinks; stop serving drinks; stop drinking yourself; 12) write your legislators now.*

The very sad commentary is that the American generation following the repeal of the Volstead Act seemed unable to conclude that there was still a moral consideration that our schools and churches should have immediately committed themselves to: namely one of the most intensive educational and nurturing plans that society has ever experienced. Democracy, having concluded that indeed, "morals cannot be legislated" by a conglomerate citizenry, swept everything under the rug and went to sleep. Any Christian leaven left in the upper warming closet was allowed to cool and appeared to die. This Space Age generation now sees a disastrous waste of the $2 billion for advertising and the $100 billion for taking care of the trouble it has cost us, not to mention the terrible wasting of human lives. Does the commercial alcoholic beverage industry have any degree of conscience at all? Must such greed be perpetually tolerated? So, finally a new generation is slowly

*Professor Donald L. Mosher, University of Connecticut, Dept. of Psychology, Fort Meyers, Florida, *News-Press* for January 7, 1989. Used by permission.

awakening to its obligations under God.

There are fair numbers of those in any church congregation who are inclined to fall back on the old ploy of those who take their Bible with a little booze. They make up the "one drink" crowd. They say:

1. God's world of Nature provides the fruit and grain, so enjoy them in any way possible, as long as moderation rules.

2. When the Chosen People entered the Promised Land and transformed themselves from sheep herders into farmers, God blessed the wine making, or so it seems.

3. Jesus drank wine (actually made it for that wedding).

4. Saintly Paul recommended a little nip for the wearing-out body.

5. Many concede that the Bible is right when it comes down on hard liquor or excessive wine, but always a LITTLE wine or beer is all okay.

6. Many churches, both Roman Catholic and Protestant, continue to insist that real wine rather than grape juice is essential for the sacrament of the Lord's Supper.

So why stir up such a moral stew when Paul says we can still be among the *strong* ones? This is why:

Mothers Against Drunk Driving is an organization born a few years ago amidst the grieving consolation of the loss of those mothers' murdered children. Drunk drivers are potential murderers. Our Jurisdictional System tries to shun the term murder in such cases. The easygoing system of plea bargaining with all the "legal" tricks of the trade most often comes up with a slap on the wrist for drunk driving on our streets and highways. Contemporary culture has put the hex on the sixth commandment. The original Hebrew versions made the penalty for it the death of the perpetrator. In the three thousand two hundred years since, humanity has reached the point where murder can be easily considered *accidental* manslaughter, perhaps the murderer sentenced mildly, granted parole on the basis of time—alas! already spent in custody— and turned loose to mix his next drink with gasoline. Mothers and fathers were left to mourn in silence until a nucleus of activist mothers decided enough was enough. But so far we continue to simply define the legal term—murder—out of recognition and look the other way. The drunk has to be taken in hand and taught a hard truth. Alcohol in the bloodstream is more than a loaded gun; it is a gun already firing at random under narcosis. You had better believe it.

With that introduction, let us briefly refute the six so-called Christian views represented by the statements listed above. We will treat items 1 and 2 as one. The organic life upon our planet, within both plant and animal kingdoms, exists as a constantly active recycling system. Living material dies and, under the influence of various enzymes, molds and bacteria, and air, is reduced to its simpler chemical components, chiefly carbon dioxide, water, nitrogen, oxygen, sulfur dioxide and mineral components containing phosphorus, iron, and calcium, with a little sodium and potassium. These are used over and over again in generation after generation of plant and animal life. Remember that in chapter 9 we spoke of God providing His Universe with one hundred such building blocks. Many are used up and wind up in more or less inert conditions, but the basic ones maintaining the plant and animal kingdoms are used over and over.

In a plant's cycle of life, maturity brings fruitage, which may be pulpy—like apples and grapes—or hard and flinty, like the seeds of a grain. The pulpy fruit with the enclosed seeds doing their thing for the perpetuation of the species is usually scattered about by wind and rain. The actual wasting away of the fleshy pulp is not noticed unless a large volume collects in an out-of-the-way place where fermentation (rotting) takes place and odors develop. The food gatherers of a primal civilization discovered that the juice from certain fruits made a very enjoyable drink but it could not be stored away for more than a few days. The preservation of the juice was very uncertain and was easily affected by rising temperatures. It soon turned very sour and became what we know as vinegar. A brief technical lesson is in order. Saccharides (forms of crude sugar), which are concentrated in a desirable fruit, undergo natural fermentation by the enzymes present in nature and the successive steps from the sugar produce alcohol, organic acid (such as vinegar) and finally end up as carbon dioxide and water. Winter temperatures practically stop the process. Summer temperatures accelerate it. Keeping the air (i.e., oxygen) out of the system is the chief method of control.

Observant eyes and minds among primal people had noted that certain wild animals, gorging themselves on rotting fruit, went through clumsy gyrations and then calmed down to normal after sleeping it off. Human minds associated this happening with the change in the flavor of a fermenting fruit juice and it was not long before Man had learned how to interrupt Nature's recycling process and make his own wine and hard cider. He seemed to enjoy the periods of inebriation caused by the narcotic effect of the alcohol and took pains to ingeniously improve the quality and quantity of that step in the process. Thus mankind yoked itself to a narcotic substance that, if not controlled, may yet wreck modern civilization. Left to its own devices it could require much time, but in conjunction with our present store of nuclear armament it could make subatomic mincemeat of us in a few hours. How awfully devastating; a narcosis with a power beyond imagination. (A footnote to the above is here elevated to equal status: The use of a very hard fruit such as a cereal grain like barley was later diverted to beer making and so also deleted from future food inventory. In this case the hard grain saccharides must be heat treated in aqueous suspension before undergoing the fermentation process.)

Jesus, no doubt, in His human life as a young man, followed the universal custom of wine drinking, at least for weddings and special occasions. At this point, we Christians may be troubled by the fact that His cousin John, being an Essene, was therefore a pledged teetotaler. I believe it is reasonable to conclude that in Jesus' day the narcotic effect of alcohol had been factually observed. But we also feel that Joseph's and Mary's household was definitely a sober, well-disciplined one. Jesus did not contemplate what the fast-living world of A.D. 2000 would be like or know of the demand for complete sobriety after the results of scientific research had shown alcohol to become the tool of random murder. He did not perceive that by A.D. 2000, 75 percent of our adult Americans would be imbibing alcohol nor that the "legal" definition of drunkenness depends upon a blood content of 0.10 percent alcohol. He did not foresee the murder of 25,000 persons by drunken drivers each year, officially labeled as due to alcohol. Our physical bodies do not all function precisely the same and one may question the physiological effect in others when such narcotic content was 0.09 percent or 0.08 percent or less. No doubt some bodies will lose normal control with any amount above 0.00 percent.

My private opinion, therefore, leads me to feel that alcohol indeed actually influences the 50 percent death rate on our highways of 25,000 lives annually, but may really account for another 12,500 lives more than the official record shows. Chemists and physicians who analyze the blood for alcohol content realize that 0.10 percent is not a sacred value. Recall the recent Alaskan Valdez episode and you will note that our Coast Guard has set a limit for sobriety at 0.04 percent for marine pilots. Some state legislatures are now considering tightening the limit for the heavy trucking drivers in similar fashion. The North Carolina state legislature this year is working on a plan to reduce the current legal limit of 0.10 percent to 0.08 percent for all general drivers. It is not inconceivable to expect that in our increasingly mechanized culture driving licenses will one day be issued on the basis of 0.00 percent. This is equivalent to saying that any detectable presence of alcohol in the blood could lead to the suspension of driving privileges.

Jesus, as a man, did not contemplate what the fast-living world of A.D. 2000 would be like and that the need for complete sobriety in a power-tooled civilization could not be overlooked. He did not stop to contemplate that alcohol would become the easy tool to random murder. He did not perceive that in America 75 percent of our adult population would be imbibing alcohol. With the new figure of eighteen years as the age of adulthood and the teenage drinking habit widely spread, it seems as if we have become a drinking nation. Jesus, by nature, did not set up a specific list of dos and don'ts! He did, however, have a considerable amount to say about the necessity of learning to love. When self-control gives way to random murder, we know exactly where Jesus stands. He would agree with Professor Mosher. God in Christ holds an infinite Love and Mercy for mankind. He sees our sorry performance. Would He not tell us now, since we have created such complicated machinery of daily living, that *at the very least* we ought to avoid all narcotics when operating any kind of technical gadgetry, thus being kind to ourselves as well as to others?

Production of cough medicine calls for placing a warning label on the bottles or other containers going to the consumer. Why not require a warning on every container of beverage alcohol? Paul's usage of wine quite reasonably falls into the pharmaceutical category. He took it privately and no doubt retired immediately. We can all agree; let the doctor and the pharmacist dispense it.

We finally confront the last item on our list. Lest I be misunderstood, I emphasize that a discussion of the use of wine at the Lord's Table is in no way to be construed as encompassing or affecting the spiritual relation between God in Christ and His human family. At that supper Christ held a cup of the common beverage characteristic of common daily life. It did not have to be purchased as an article of commercial trade. In those cases it was from fruit raised on the home grounds. It may have been pressed and processed in the home or in a local communal winery.

Our Roman Catholic brother may look askance at the suggestion that his doctrine of transubstantiation does not really prevent his priest (or himself) from using 1) the unfermented juice, or 2) the alcohol in its narcotic form, or 3) the resultant vinegar. God's power over His Universe is exerted noncommittally throughout the whole recycling process. But, as we have already stressed, these two thousand years since Christ have, alongside a religious kingdom, produced a crass culture of gross commercialism that annually wastes *billions* of American dollars which should have been devoted to human welfare and that has annually murdered over 25,000 of God's American sons and daughters and sent thousands of families into utter ruin and/or treatment centers at catastrophic expense. We have deliberately conspired to interrupt God's recycling process in Nature and have chosen to make alcoholic narcosis an acceptable social emblem, thereby committing perhaps the greatest sin before God today! You now know why Alcoholics Anonymous and alcoholic abuse treatment centers call for abstinence from communion wine. The Church continuing to serve only wine on its trays may well be sending the unknown alcoholic patient straight back to the Hell he has only recently escaped via his treatment regimen.

Since America has quite conclusively demonstrated that human habits based upon a moral principle cannot be enforced by democratic legal procedure applying to a total cross section of society, we ought to embrace a more thoroughgoing educational effort in all our schools and churches. We ought to continually review the penalties for disobedience of the rules suggested by Professor Mosher. Do not allow Christendom to forget his eleventh rule: *Do not drink any beverage alcohol.*

6. THE UNIVERSITY OF LIFE—A FRESH DEFINITION

This Pilgrim realizes the risk of tiresome redundancy but focuses once more on the subject of updating the vocabulary of spiritual communication. He feels it is absolutely obligatory in the face of the increasing materialistic culture of Western civilization to revert to the old-fashioned triple-pronged dictum for teaching any new fact or idea. The student should *hear* it then *review* it. I, of course, will be mightily disappointed, Dear Reader, if in considering our Christian obligation of discipleship, and having spent some years on this book, you do not burst forth with the next requirement: *demonstrate* it, i.e., *do it.*

One readily grasps the fact that in Christian education, such demonstrations of true example, such Nurture and parenting activity, such actual showing of how it is done was Christ's way. We know by this time that Proclaiming the Word is only the preliminary step. Actually, today, proclaiming the Word primarily means carrying the message of Christ to the Third World. The local preacher in America today cannot afford to stop there. Christianity in its infancy called for a lot of proclaiming; but its adulthood demands a great deal more than verbal proficiency, no matter how erudite and overflowing with Christ's love. When it comes to the pastor/minister doing his complete job, his demonstrating ought to be accompanied by descriptive language, which makes his messages really comprehensible to contemporary Space Age participants. We have referred to the level of scientific understanding of a literate high school graduate in A.D. 2000 with the implication that his pastor will be as well equipped. We have referred to the same point in discussing the upgrading of the Apostles' Creed to fit the reality of the Space Age. We have made other references to the pastor's qualifications as including day-to-day familiarity with his/her technically oriented pew members.

The Pilgrim is not a skillet pointing to a black pot. He is simply reemphasizing the need to improve the vehicle of communication of the love story of God in Christ in influencing twenty-first-century ears. The current scientific era began less than two hundred years ago and has made what most of us term a miraculous spurt in the development of the view of how the physical universe has yielded to man's exploitation, both good and bad. The pastor who, perchance, is reading these words will understand that I am NOT asking for any change whatsoever in the actual substance of Christ's message. I am merely claiming that in the last two hundred years we have changed parts of our daily vocabulary so dramatically and so drastically as to call for the installation of a course at each seminary to add depth and breadth and height to the verbiage employed to tell and demonstrate the story of Jesus.

The theologian (pastor/minister) may be bursting at the seams with good ideas about the God-stuff he is yearning to share with his congregation, but he has to learn to communicate by choosing the proper conveyance for letting it out of his mind and into the heart and mind of his listener. David was effective in his skillful use of the slingshot and got his message across to the Philistines. Prior to wireless we used the telegraph and pigeons. Today, in the process of building a nuclear armament system to suicidal proportions, we, as a concomitant result, have built up a vocabulary that reflects the science and technical engineering that created it.

Let us also realize that Man is carrying out God's command to supervise and manage as much of the physical world as he is able. God's second gift went beyond the mind itself to the exercise of the self-will thereof. This has shown up the moral weak points in humankind. We have dealt out a high percentage of fermenting evil in a developing pagan culture. Instead of being the successful harvesters of the crop Christ charged us with, we are dropping out in the heat of the day.

Now it would seem that professional theology, which could be the sharp cutting tool in getting the effective antidote across, has instead turned out to be rather stubborn. Are we being too harsh with our theologians by blaming them for being a good share of the reason for the widening gap between scientific advancement and the lagging theological advancement? For those who have already turned God off, this lagging behind is out of sight as well. Classical Greek and Hebrew terminology in the Bible is still being handled by most preachers today just as it was during the intervening twenty centuries. Thus theology insists on continuing to use terms, concepts, analogies, and vocabulary of bygone eras. It has not kept pace with the rapidly growing pagan, secular, technocratic world view. In plain talk, classical terms of philosophy and spirituality, using old-timey vocabulary, have lost a good deal of effectiveness in the Space Age. Theologians seem to object to a sort of "scientism" that they do not know how to meet on equal terms.

I realize I run the risk of being run over or merely passed by as the neurotic nut who has his own drum to beat, but I honestly feel that we ought to be studying theology in the pews as laymen. And it ought to command the very latest in means of communication. Because we laymen *do not*, we sin also. We are all members of that technocratic culture and we ought to be building a two-way link between the Church and the world it reaches out to and hopes to affect. Somewhere, we must actually come to grips with evil, but in making that evil understand us, we need not become evil ourselves. It is not evil to work with an eighteen-wheel tractor-trailer in transporting goods between population centers, a job for which we originally hitched up teams of horses and hauled to a warehouse or, if real distance was involved, took to nearby railroad sidings.

Our theologians, and hence our pastors, seem loath to try to change the old language or at least to expand it. The spiritually minded theologian would be well advised to set aside any prejudices against the intrusion of scientific or technical analogies. After all the technical, scientific age is here; let us face it. The laissez-faire attitude such an age has held toward theology during the past half-century has produced no discernible overt action on the part of religion as the foe of the secular nature of our current culture. Does this mean that theologians are simply taking the easy way out by tacitly accepting science as generally good but, withdrawing within a false monastic isolation, then quietly going about their own knitting in the old traditional manner? This, of course, is absolutely contrary to the basic relationship expressed by our discussion of God and Energy and the basic assumption of the diagram on page 211 which claims that the Spirit is the parent of the Mind, and thus the parent of science.

Today the firmament around and over us is filled with a vast array of energy pulsations, radiations, and electronically comprised waves. From here on every communicants' class will be secretly primed with an everyday communication vocabulary that includes terms like radiation, wireless phones, frequencies, currents, resistance, contact, plug-in, quanta or energy, three states of nature, directional beaming, energy potential, playback, static, amplifier, backyard dish, power transmission, work, dynamo, magnetic field, field of force. It adds up to the most *sophisticated communication system that the world has ever known.* Isn't the answer quite obvious? Theology has not tried to join in on the rather simple way that spiritual power and physical power can be interchanged in our explanation as to how they may work together for the good. "Why do we have to change or possibly lose our classic terminology?" My reply is simple. Keep the classic nest egg in private during a generation or two, but for God's sake and the sake of billions of our human family, so redefine the terms and translate them into analogies that the man in the street, or at least the high school student, can appropriate and respond to with a new life reclaimed for God.

Theology today seems to be in danger of talking to itself. The God's truth of the matter is not getting into the consciences of the travelers on the road to Jericho nor to the Woman at the Well. The younger half of our intergenerational communities of Faith are being cheated. Perhaps technology would not have made so many blunders in the husbandry of the world's natural resources if our theologians had been as industrious as our scientists. Why cannot every theologian take a year of chemistry and a year of physics so that he can learn a new language? Remember, it is the scientist who now has the ball. The theologian is responsible for the recovery. Do I actually overstate the case when I say that he/she has remained a "cultural illiterate" in respect to language communication with society at large? It would appear that the severity of the situation is compounded if the man of God continues to feel that he is above reproach as long as he persists in holding to the timeworn way. I pray that our preachers will pick up the necessary vocabulary of new terms and analogies with which they can challenge this age; that they can actually revel in the pulsating, radiating, immanent Power in the Spiritual Field of Force in which we are immersed every minute of the day and night. Our daily Enabler is beaming special confidential messages to each of us. Let us learn how to flick on the lodestones of conscience and under the high impulse of the Spiritual power line decode the messages undergirding our discipleship for this day's mission. May the power of prayer and its daily practice keep all contact points free of rust and grime so that His full potential will be applied to chipping away the hard core of our selfish resistance.

The challenge of the Space Age for our theologians extends beyond the necessary improvement in their manner of communication as discussed above. What shall be the most effective manner of his/her person as he/she goes about heading up the volunteer local crew that makes up his Rescue Team for God, the local community of faith? Shall he/she be a priest, or a prophet, or can he/she succeed in melding both roles in such a fashion as to know pretty precisely when he/she can best bury the dead or bless the marriage union and at the same moment know when it is time to marshal his/her heaviest verbal battery from the pulpit and still know that God may be preparing him/her for the moment when, having mustered his/her complete armor of God, he/she forges out literally into the public way and gets arrested and thrown into jail for perceiving that there are times when God's laws are above the laws of the United States of America? If the reader will readdress that sentence, he is immediately aware that the Pilgrim has sketched the characteristic outline of three types of pastor/minister: (a) the priest: placid, patient, middle of the road, perhaps judged to be best for pastoral counseling; (b) the prophet: definitely speaking for God, projecting the Bible truths of A.D. 50 forcibly into the active, specific situations of today and tomorrow, he does not hesitate to take risks for God's sake; and (c) the

Composite Ideal, who knows God's work can be a stretch of rather mundane, unexciting days, but who is alert for the evil trend, the political compromise that roughs the Christian conscience too strongly, and is ready to give his Godly response in opposition to the School Board, the Housing Authority, the Zoning Board, the Prison Administration, minority unemployment, and anything else he knows God is truly dissatisfied with.

In my youth, in the '20s and '30s, I have a remembrance of more emphatic "thus saith the Lord" pronouncements from the pulpit than I hear today. Please understand that I am not speaking about the "hell fire and brimstone" of a Billy Sunday revival, but God's law, a prophetic voice raised against a current social problem that seems insoluble. There is no mistaking the sense of outrage in the truly prophetic voice as opposed to a priestly approach, which, while sympathetic with misery, points more often in the direction of Psychological Positive Thinking as the cure-all, rather than the cleansing power of acknowledgement of transgressions before God and the healing power of a penitent heart. Positive thinking should be the result of the cleansed, penitent heart, not its prescription.

Seminaries appear to turn out priestly pastors rather than prophets, and one may question whether they are doing their best at developing a theologically professional view, with a polemical stance against evil. My illustration may be dated, but it would be great if the seminary, like the old-fashioned professor as coach of the debate team, helped youngsters in college build up various arguments against the opposition. A more timely illustration might be that of the young lawyer who studies the law but depends upon the expertise of a mature lawyer-teacher who knows the courts inside out. Elsewhere we have referred to the pastor as the president of an academy of Christian life. Although that academy looks proudly at its past, its true focal point is *forward*. We have to learn how to make the Christian tradition applicable to strange new changes which are upon us even as we speak.

I suppose many preachers definitely avoid prophetic leadership because it is the more difficult path. It does not come naturally and no doubt if the pastor is tallying his/her personal successes in terms of the number of bouquets his sermons yield, he/she soon finds the voyage becoming rough. One cannot compose sermons as a Jeremiah and deliver them at the public gate and still maintain a smooth-working, loyal congregation. An Amos avoided the Establishment at City Hall and kept aloof as no pastor can afford to do today. Amos could pit himself against the idolatry of the day and after a week's hassle with the "in" priests and authorities, could retreat to his farm and his Ficus Sycomorus.

Perhaps one way a real live active prophet can be conserved is to promote him/her into the midst of a multistaffed church so that he/she can be shielded by the personal loyalty of his/her ordained associates. In the Methodist setup, a wide-awake bishop or a similarly sharp district superintendent can easily promote such a progression to the right spot. The presbytery executives in my church might not see the total area and be able to move that expeditiously. The only way that a single staff pastor could remain a firebrand for righteousness would be to keep his hammer and thunder clapper in the closet and bring them out only on auspicious occasions. After all, Jesus did not clean out the Temple courtyard every Sabbath. The priest in him will have plenty to keep him busy at more mundane things like marrying, baptizing, visiting the sick, burying the dead and preparing the weekly messages of hope and good-will. Perhaps the average preacher really is trying to be both priest and prophet but never seems to have time for prophesying. However, he can provide a base for extended operations as a prophet by picking the special, more controversial sermon topic from time to time and by writing the special sermonettes for the local press. He may accomplish more outside the pulpit than in it.

Strictly speaking, prophetic preaching, both in the area of educational leadership and in the pulpit preaching, calls for special courage because it means making oneself vulnerable. This applies as forcefully to the inner educational program where the nurturing process may seem to be entirely sheltered from criticism. But here the prophet finds that tradition and the minutiae of how Grandfather did it can be enormous stumbling blocks. It is further complicated by the fact that the very willing and able personnel he is dealing with are among the most dedicated of the flock. Private feelings must be assuaged and much extra praise must be lavished on those who finally see a new light and begin to act upon it. The rock-ribbed tradition that gets in the way of new ideas can make prophetic planning within the church most difficult and it must be met with patience and commitment.

The prophetic pastor/minister in his/her role as presiding officer of his/her local University of Life must actually assume the stance of an experimenter. He/she constantly searches for better ways to nurture the immature into effective Christian adulthood. The Spiritual immaturity of physically adult Christians is consistently recognized as childishness, ingrained through years of stagnation and disuse except in outward, most perfunctory ways. Of course the prophet does not forget that his maturing Christians must meet the hard daily contacts of the secular world and he can expect abrasive reaction from time to time. He/she may not be the ready recipient of handy tomatoes or rotten eggs as the public prophet but can expect disgruntled looks, slowdowns, sit-down strikes, or complete flameouts. The Pilgrim concedes that whether the prophecy proceeds from the pulpit or from the inner sanctum of a church-school class, a certain amount of pastoral pleasantry and a little back-slapping may be needed to maintain good attendance and financial support.

Finally, there is a third area of challenge. The Pilgrim has found but few executives in the industrial field who, as able church members, are willing and able to give the proper interpretation to the problem of management which a pastor/minister faces. The quick retort, "The minister ought to be a better manager," is many times a castigation based on ignorance. Influential business leaders as members of the working church may at times arrange for the attendance of their pastor at a suitable industrial workshop on the theme, hoping to infuse some of the church's business with real efficiency. Such workshop courses may well straighten out some local treasurer's records or computerize the overall bookkeeping, but beyond the sympathetic support from the pastor/minister, they do not touch the heart of the pastor's area of responsibility as a Manager. His management is unique and peculiar. Everyone seems to forget that the title of Manager in business rests on the solid rock of line-executive control of all the jobs involved. These jobs carry a salary as a financial reward. This control is exercised in ranks and the rules made at any level are expected to be followed by the ranks below. A business personnel manager may teach intrahouse courses attempting to show how to *persuade* another to perform under those rules and at the same time preserve relative goodwill and productivity. But no matter how skillfully the word persuasion is employed in these instances, the real persuader is the big stick of executive line control. A job is at stake. Though the word is shielded from actual usage, the implication is that control is *command*. By comparison, the pastor/minister is sheared of all this kind of authority in getting the job of the church done. "How does a church continue to exist?" some business people may ask. Only God really knows. He puts part of the answer in the heart of every single communicant in the community of faith. The pastor prays diligently and earnestly but has no assurance that he has properly decoded the Divine Message. Many times God's advice and help has been offered to the pastor via His lay supporters, who then have let Him down. We fail to contribute our share of the effort. *We* are the sinners and the procrastinators. *We* have neither been diligently praying with the pastor nor for him in our own private closets.

There is a procedure useful in business and industry that we could utilize by adapting some phases of it to our local churches. That is the annual employee evaluation ritual as applied to middle- and upper-class employees. It usually begins at the foreman level. A supervisor of a function grades each of his employees he is responsible for on a set form. It is activated by a private interview with the employee. The performance form is prepared to show such qualities as personal appearance, personal habits on the job, productivity, manner of receiving criticism from a superior, personal relations with fellow employees, support of company goals, et cetera. Ratings may be from poor to excellent on a one-to-five scale. Each employee has an extended, private, and confidential session with his supervisor. He does not see the actual rating but he is aware that what the boss is doing is forming an opinion as to whether he is worthy of a raise in salary or a promotion which might well be outside his immediate department.

In applying this procedure to the church one difference in concept must be recognized at once. A pastor/minister receives his/her paycheck through an official board, but the ordained leaders of that organization far outrank the board in the professionalism of the spiritual Development Program, which is the raison d'être. It boils down to a matter of developing and working within a relationship that is warm, loving, and very understanding. An ideal manner of introducing such a trial run in your church would be to have considerable exploratory conversation with the pastor until he arrives at the point where *he* makes the actual recommendation to the board that it would be wise to undertake it on a trial basis.

We will draw a simplified organization chart of a prototype composite Protestant Church. No attempt is made to indicate the nature of the supervision exercised by the next upper layer of oversight above and outside the local church, for it will differ with each denominational format. An example of common vocabulary is the use of the title "official board." It means the church's Administrative Board, whether it is a

Board of Deacons, Elders, Stewards, a Session, a Vestry, or whatever. They are charged with correcting faults of the ranks of personnel below, awarding them for good performance, largely through affirmation of the leadership training the pastor/minister has set up and supervises.

The oddity of the church management situation is unique in that the lines drawn in such a chart are not the equivalents of the direct-line control in a business organization where the supervisor has a rather powerful influence on actual job security. A business venture handles money or goods, or a production item, a very tangible object, whereas the church is working on the spiritual basis of relationships. The individual, as an agent of God, may be going through standard actions of raising money for charities, preaching the Word, teaching a church school class, and trying to help others. It is hoped that there will be no stagnation of life at any point. Nurturing a Christian is not necessarily happening, though any line in the chart implies that this should be taking place.

The Official Board is made up of a mixture of relationships. It represents the top level of management in a business sense in that it has the physical plant to maintain, sees that the sexton is doing his job and raises an annual budget in which all the members are as individually responsible for underwriting as the regular pew member. The Board, as an agent of the congregation, hires and pays the pastor, but the pastor is hired to train his professional skills on the building of Christian character.

Production skill in this case is not measured in terms of daily output delivered at the shipping dock or stored temporarily in quiescent inventory or reflected on a banker's daily financial statement. Every member indicated on the chart submits himself to the plan the pastor has evolved with the aid of his strongest supporters. Such line supervision as exists can be claimed to be solely based on all members *voluntarily* making the response, "I want to help." They of their own will assume a servant role. It is persuasion and challenge at their best, versus the direct line control of an organized business. Within the church the poorly performing member is worked with for a time but is ultimately delivered to a less-exacting position where a warm, loving fellowship can help him maintain attendance in the pew. Eventually the ultra-senior citizen is the object of home visitation or adult day care programs.

Therefore, as you examine the chart below, bear in mind that the lines between functional levels are not for the purpose of producing widgets, but are power lines branching out from the main spiritual power line from God, which, under the care of the pastor, is carrying the Energy required to operate the nurturing process of Christian faith. Each member of the congregation will also be directly connected to God's power line, but the voltage and amperage will vary according to his private commitment to the Enabling Spirit.

Another anomaly in the church that escapes the attention of secular management is the election of the members of the Official Board, which is nearly always by the nomination and election by ballot from the congregation at large. Actually it is a process of electing the members who man the chief departments of the church and simultaneously creating the current training class under the tutelage of the pastor. He is responsible for seeing that the proper theological goals are understood and mutually accepted. He is actually the coach of a team of Christian nurturers whose skills reflect his own. Since his own humanity is imperfect, he labors also in a continuous plan of professional improvement. His own example should approach a level which is an inspiration for his lay flock. His tools are three: his own example, his power of persuasion, and much praise for the weak cohort. Nevertheless, within the democratic fellowship of the church community he must at times be prepared to speak decidedly for God. Morals and ethics shall not be compromised if he can help it. This brings us full circle to the point where he now leads in the evaluation program.

He does this evaluation with help from his Department of Personnel. A progressive church in the '90s has as one of its departments a Commission on Personnel. Even the smallest church has at least one individual capable of extending real assistance to his pastor. He can maintain a record of years of service each member has had in various offices. He can recommend training sessions and workshops, if not in his own denomination, then ecumenically. With the pastor in personal discussion, he can see that membership on the Official Board is itself a segment of such training. In the larger church, the Personnel Commission can be the agent to prevent each new class, group, or project from pillaging leadership willy-nilly across the congregation. The presence of a sympathetic, widely respected member as a Personnel Chairman becomes an inestimable aid to the pastor in detecting the signs of slack performance and conflicts in the recruitment of leadership from among the newcomers.

Under the volunteer relationships within the church it is still pos-

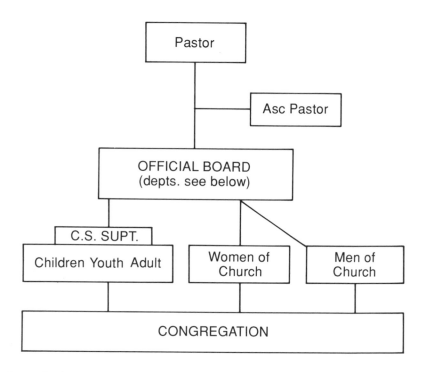

Commissions or departments of the official board: 1—Budget and Finance, 2—property and grounds, 3—worship, 4—Christian education, 5—mission, 6—personnel, and others as a local church sees fit. The commissions will ordinarily be completed by members at large from the congregation.

sible to profit by raising the level of performance by adopting some aspects of the industrial management, i.e., a frank personal confrontation. Just the annual review action necessary to make any evaluation process meaningful is a plus factor for all. At the Official Board level, two approaches should be prepared for as a minimum. Let us consider the more difficult one first. That is the special session of the Board during which the sole agenda deals with the pastor. One may be tempted to say the pastor is subjected to analysis of his performance, but since the pastor's professionalism is far in excess of that of his helpers, he is able to constructively criticize the congregation. What is desired is a session in which the give-and-take is exercised in both directions. The church members have an opening to ask for reasons for his performance and the pastor has the opportunity to have some of his disappointments addressed. In a spirit of respect, love, and hopefulness on all sides the following questions from parishioners could be a good beginning.

1. Are you reasonably happy as our pastor? Be specific in the areas of greatest happiness.

2. Are you unhappy about any aspects of your pastoral relations with us? Have you given the Personnel Commission an opportunity to work on this problem?

3. Is there any pro or con comment you can to make about your salary and housing support? If none, can the Board rest assured that you are reasonably satisfied?

4. As our professional theologian and pastor, please grade the Board by function or department. (Include Men of the Church and Women of the Church since there will be members at large from both groups. See number five following.)

5. As Dean of this University of Life you have aided in the evaluation of our church-school under the general direction of the Commission on Christian Education. Please give us your pastoral summary, directing your attention successively to the Children's, Youth, and Adult Divisions.

The set of questions to be handled by the pastor as moderator of the "official" board may be augmented as desired by board members receiving questions from parishioners. These questions discussed by the board and pastor in preliminary fashion are made the agenda of a special meeting of the board. The pastor as Moderator may prepare his answers before time but should be followed by friendly, though thorough, discussion by all members.

In carrying out the evaluation of others, the pastor will find it helpful to hold a foregoing session with each Board member who is a department head or chairman. Self-help criticism ahead of time in private can be graciously accepted. In a private, meeting the pastor, his Personnel Chairman, and the Board's department heads or chairmen (separately), carefully and lovingly examine the following questions:

1. How satisfied are you with your performance in your present position?

2. Do you feel that you are meeting friendly and helpful personal relationship standards? Can they be improved? How?

3. What independent reading and study have you engaged in? (Very important if no formal training was involved.)

4. Have you attended a training class, workshop, or retreat centering on your present position in the church's plan?

5. What do you feel is your highest accomplishment experienced so far?

6. What is your most difficult leadership problem? Do you feel any disappointment over the past year's work?

7. Do you care to share any experience from your private devotional life as it may influence your spiritual servanthood this past year?

For those who have never attempted this approach before, the following grading scale is basic: 1—not acceptable; 2—acceptable; 3—good; 4—better; 5—outstanding.

The reader will understand why I wish to make a final point. If Christian education is to be truly Christian Nurture as discussed in this book, then special attention is demanded in the yearly evaluation of the church-school. In the small church it is conceivable that the church-school superintendent may also be the Chairman of the Christian Education Commission in the Official Board. The traditional experience of many small churches has been that a good Sunday School Superintendent is locked into his position in perpetuity. This is a sad mistake, no matter how fine a Christian job he makes of his position. Sometime in his/her career as Superintendent, he/she is bound by human nature to cross over the top peak of active leadership creativity. Before that period arrives several other persons should be given a trial period at it.

The feelings of the old-timers are carefully assuaged by creating the first-time position of either Personnel Manager or Chairman of the Christian Education Commission within the Official Board of that small church. The former expert will thus remain near at hand to see that the school does not fold simply because he/she is one notch farther away from the details. The broadening of the leadership base extends his/her expertise to additional new connective points in the next generation. He/she thus continues as a coach for Christ in his/her new spot.

Likewise a footnote may be added to the evaluation of the detailed formal educational program as carried out in the Children's and Youth Divisions. The Chairman of the Christian Education Commission, or the Chairman of the Personnel Commission, will make sure that the preevaluation of the leadership in these younger age divisions has been given high priority and will see that suitable awards, dinners, public announcements, et cetera for deserving teaching leadership have all been made.

The test of the presence of the Holy Spirit will be revealed in the atmosphere of mutual love by which the items of the evaluation are established. The Board will bear in mind that it is not taking God's place. Not only does the suggested procedure bring the background of the entire congregation into focus but it gives the pastor an opportunity to candidly point out some of the lack of performance on the part of the membership. In a real sense, the pastor can now act as a helpful physician by dealing forthrightly with some ills of his church family. It would probably follow that the full actual minutes maintained in the files of the Official Board be abbreviated and written in less personal fashion for actual general publicity throughout the church. Consistent with the view that the right of privacy is sacred, the pastor may profit by maintaining his own private personnel file. The entire congregation could be placed on cards. Every year the pastor, in checking over the progress of his members toward a more fulfilled Christlike living, as he sees it, will in essence be jotting down the progress of each individual on the way. It would indicate that more active consultation in some areas is called for. This file is not a calendar schedule of mere calling but would aim at being a private Growth Curve Record of the individual. (See chapter 2.) Consistent attention to the least active fringe membership would keep that group to the minimum.

Chapter XI

Prayer—the Most Important Sortie: Number Six

In a life of seven decades within the membership rolls of Christ's Church, I must confess to a much-delayed realization that the single most important duty and privileged responsibility of those of us who try to practice the Christian faith is prayer. Praying is, in spite of it being a gift of God, the most difficult aspect of our faith by its very nature. Jesus set the example of prayer before His Twelve. Jesus demonstrated this open-line communication with the Creator Spirit. And His followers observed and were impressed. He made it look so very easy at times because it was a habit.

The human creatures of God consist of much clay. We find that clay is not a good conductor of the electric current of spirituality. We have to work exceedingly hard to break through the hard shell of our egos. This human difficulty is substantiation of the goodness of God. To be able to open the door of our private enclosures, we must be ashamed of the fact that we all are such sorry performers. That is what makes praying hard.

I believe penitence is the open Sesame to prayer. Even when we open the door to God's presence on the basis of great love and praise and thankfulness, there is a sense of regret. Why have I not responded to Him much sooner and more frequently? Why do I not respond with joy every day? We tend to justify our self-interests and forget prayer until the backup breaks over the dam. We do not easily humble ourselves for we must admit then that we are not really number one after all. So we avoid actual prayer. We beat about the bushes to search for an excuse. We begin to locate verses of Scripture; we take on an added church committee chairmanship or two; we might even take on a Sunday school class and, in total, become so busy for Christ that we have no quiet time for straightening out things with Him personally. We even join religious book clubs and complain to the local community librarian about the lack of religious titles.

In late mid-life, I thought that joining a religious book club might be a good thing to do to keep me abreast of the change I intuitively felt was taking place in theological thinking. I was not fitted with some of the appropriate vocabulary necessary for complete understanding of the more sophisticated material, and after collecting a few shelves of books over several years I finally let go of the membership. The references in the various sections of these books classified as falling under the topic PRAYER were challenging. If you turn to the bibliography you will see the books of Garret, Ferrier, Scott, Connor, Buttrick, and Casteel.

As one of the too-busy Christians referred to above, I settled into a long-lasting battle to overcome my embarrassment in discovering that prayer, to mean anything, *had to be* the fruitage of the I-You contact in a first-person-singular relationship. Our communal church, class, and committee groups of one kind and another all make prayer seem easier. The "we" of the first person plural is like the editorial "We," which tends to spread the responsibility of the statement among a number of people. "I," as one of the group, thus hid myself within the group. Making a communal prayer with the plural "We" allows the "We" to admit deep sin before the Lord, because the "I," the one vocalizing the prayer, already has his own share of that sin reduced to the minimum. The other fellow is always grosser in rough conduct than I am. So the "We" of the communal prayer does not represent equal guilt and wrongdoing. The others of the "We" are sharing and shouldering 98 percent of the blame; the "I" in the "We" is willing to answer to the other 2 percent just to show membership in the club. It is when we personally and individually enter the I-You relationship that prayer becomes real and honest and very hard and truly cleansing. I suggest that you go back to chapter 7 on the Twenty-third Psalm. I prescribe using it as a practice exercise as a preliminary to this longer section on prayer.

May we turn back to the use of helpful books in learning how to pray? When I received Dr. Buttrick's *So We Believe So We Pray*, published shortly after World War II, I was ignorant of his longer treatise written in the prior decade, which was acclaimed as a masterpiece by a member of the faculty of Union Seminary, New York. I obtained a copy only seven years ago by culling out an old volume from the rejuvenation of another church library. I carried it home as a gift from God. I will present it to a new church library with the recommendation that every member be required to read it and take notes, which I hope the pastor will anonymously evaluate and present at a number of congregational functions. I strongly recommend it as required reading for any new member or any added member via transfer of letter.

Christians often discuss what might prove to be the most effective time of the day for prayer. Since God is a spirit and never sleeps, it would seem rather unimportant what time His children took to pray. It would be quite beside the point to try to prescribe for the other person. You yourself in your particular lifestyle, condition of employment, and possible family arrangements, can best make that appointment. Let me suggest some points in review of previous references in this book. Prayer upon awaking is excellent for "morning people"; the thoughts are clear, more apt to be profound, and flow with greater ease. Such folks probably find the close of the day to be tiresome with details of the day that readily distract them from spiritual thought, and they trail off into sleep, which, after all, is what they need. "Night people," in reverse, are revved up to late action and discussions. They remain fully awake and rightly supplied with spiritual energy. They are in a perfect position to align themselves with St. Paul, who stresses the close of the day as being the perfect opportunity to recount and total up the sins of the day. He made confession and was born again through and in Christ, so as to be able to rise the next day a "new man in Christ." As a matter of fact, Scripture exhorts us to pray constantly, and this should present plenty of opportunities as long as one maintains the safety of his conduct in regard to others (for instance, care should be taken when driving one's car). One must give the full measure of devotion to vocational obligations and respond in a helpful way to others who, as neighbors, may need our help.

A second physical aspect in most effective prayer is the concern that many persons have as to the best position of one's body. It would seem that in private, any stance is good if it gives a good supply of blood to the brain, does not interfere with regular and deep breathing, and does not introduce strain or stress on a muscle or bone and so tend to distract thought. My public speaking professor who monitored us during college days always stressed the fact that a clean-cut upright position with hands and feet free, and belt not too tight, was conducive to creative thinking. Prayer needs all the creative thinking you can muster. Of course, much, if not most, of private prayer may be silent, either out of necessity or by preference. So the position may not be much in question at all. I have at one other point mentioned my pastor uncle who, in family, knelt at his chair. There is no doubt that this contributes to a feeling of humbleness. We do not kneel normally to others except those whom we deeply love; and Love is the name of the game.

I am lying in bed for most of my private prayer and meditation. I am usually wide awake by 5 A.M., as I have been practically every day of my life, and during retirement, especially, I attempt to devote myself to things eternal. The most important thing is to get sin cleared away by a proper accounting to God for my shortcomings. When I have reached the point where I feel His forgiving love present, I proceed with teaching next Sunday's lesson in great detail, recalling memorized verses of Scripture that provide hints of the probable conditions of life hereafter. I pray for my wife who is not physically robust, and for all the members of my family wherever they may be. I pray for my church and its pastor and its enlightenment within God's mission. I even pray for the redemption of the pagan culture of America and trust that the Church's leaven will be sufficient to its task. Most of this book was put into the first draft before breakfast. So it goes. You pray in any position you choose. I am sure God hears.

A third problem with praying blends the physical and the spiritual-mental. This problem is the absence of a definite vibrant mental picture of what God looks like. We so easily overlook the fact that our definition of God as a spirit precludes the possibility of seeing Him physically. We know that the divine communicating party is not physical as humans define the term. Although we use vocal cords and create an actual audible sound or the effect of them in the written or recorded form, the Spirit cannot be so described. We humans also quite naturally engage in body language in addition to the spoken word. When you and I converse it is important that the eyes confirm or deny or modify the spoken word. In addition, the vocal tonal qualities also reflect inner meaning. When we speak of communicating with God, we must try and adjust to the difficult conditions that prevail when the party addressed is not seen by the physical eye or heard by the physical ears. We are consoled by the experiences of other humans, which have become a part of the written record. They have been written for others to meditate upon. Thus we have our Scriptures and other religious tomes. But the neophyte learning to pray realizes that in his case the experiences of others tend to remain secondhand, third-party interpretations. We continue to long for our own deeper first-person experience.

We are subtly aware that other means of communication exist. Blind persons discover that God has given us special means of communication. We are not here qualified to discuss the point at which the fine-tuned physical perception may become the intuition that borders on the spiritual. It appears that Helen Keller was able to make the transition. Likewise, we are securely on spiritual ground when we consider the private confession of the Reverend John Powers, S.J., whom we will meet (on page 298). The very title of his book, *He Touched Me*, is indicative of the influence of the Holy Spirit in our daily comings and doings. We humans commonly say that we feel the presence of God. Wishfulness becomes actuality, or so it seems after some serious laboratory work prompted by that Presence. Perhaps it is not outrageous to suggest that when God chose the human framework of Jesus of Nazareth to be His means of entry into human life as a way of personifying His law of LOVE so we could understand it, He was expecting that the regular members of His human family would fan the little speck of spirituality deposited in each into an everlasting flame. This flame would be evidence of the transfer of the powerful God-energy we draw from Him each morning as we, like Paul, arise to the demands of each new day. The power radiated from God becomes the equivalent of His wireless communication system. The fee for its use is humility, earnest searching, and gratitude to a Father who repeatedly blots out the record of our sinning souls. Thus we employ our human language, realizing that God hears and sees every thought and every action in that mysterious fashion that we cannot understand until the day we stand in His presence. Until then we fall back and rest our case on the communal history of our faith and testimony.

The mystery of what constitutes the Presence while we pray is a real problem. One's anthropomorphic inheritance seems to insist that some form of a human is somehow involved, even as if we were addressing a person who is behind a hanging veil or curtain. Presumably, Christians are most apt to feel this way because they easily call up the picture of the body and face of Jesus, though dimly, as if their higher sense perceives that they must now transform Him into a weightless, nonmaterial Jesus. Even some pastors express uncertainty about it. I discussed this once with a pastor who was consoling us upon the death of our young daughter. He candidly admitted to me that he was unable "to think about God as an indefinite GLOB of something up there in the sky."

Do we need to visualize that Spirit as a form or something that borders on the intangible? I share with you some private attempts at what may be labeled nonsense by some, but I insist on trying. In the middle of the night, when having had sufficient sleep to take the edge off the physical tiredness of the preceding day, you suddenly find yourself wide awake. Your body makes no demands and makes no reports of the operations of its sympathetic system. You feel nothing but a kind of warmth, and so you "feel great." You begin to think of His Field of Force in which you know you are immersed. You wonder what spirit-nature is really like. One way I attempt to do this is to consider *what* or *who* I would be if at that very moment my fleshly body were to leave me totally by myself. Would I be just the mental thought then in my mind, and is there a spiritual fraction melded therein? I ask myself that question because if there were no thought, I would either be subconscious or, perhaps, unconscious. At this point I run into difficulty, since if I were unconscious then my brain, the site of thought, would be nonexistent or nonfunctioning. Subconsciously there is a possibility that God-energy is holding me in a quiescent state and supplying a sustaining grace so that I exist in His kingdom. This allows me to feel a force or power but I am now the object of those who criticize by simply saying, "If you resolve that you are now merely a quantum of energy melded somehow with God-energy, are you not merely wishing yourself into some sort of a mechanical, but dumb, machine?" But wonder of wonders, I can immediately reply, "Love willed me to be here. Love set up the plan for me. Love is a 'person.' " The point is that for a few moments a human person has been simultaneously a spiritual person. Communication seemed very real in that speck of time.

When Moses saw the bush on fire and stopped to investigate, he was answering God's knock on the door of his heart. We know that the "fire" was not an example of our human definition of fire, which involves oxidation via the oxygen of the atmosphere, which in that case would be the oxidation of cellulosic fibers converted into carbon dioxide and water. We know this because "the bush was not burned." After Moses went on his way the plant and the environment was as before. We cannot say what the fire was. Besides Moses, there was no other witness. In some mysterious fashion the radiation of God's almighty energy and powerful Field of Force caused Moses to perceive a brilliance about the bush, which he tried to describe later to his family. Perhaps, as we note with the succeeding prophets of God, Moses has a "vision." The Spirit took the initiative in this introduction of Moses to his new job. Moses had demonstrated spiritual sensitivity, the first requirement for the induction of an agent of God. Let us consider further the matter of the Energy and Field of Force Moses was subjected to.

My Recent Comments on the Being of God

Intelligence (i.e., the logical use of knowledge) must arrive at the point of acceptance of the principle of the mutuality (the equivalence) of energy and matter. The equation expressing this relationship was discussed in chapter 9. The high school student with a year of chemistry and a year of physics should be in a position to understand and discuss this relationship in sounder fashion than his parents in the average contemporary home. For fulfilling prayer, we have said that it is helpful, indeed almost mandatory, to have some objective feeling of what the one we pray to (God) *seems to be.* (I almost tricked myself into saying "Looks like!")

Such a high school student recognizes the POWER of LOVE in the personality of Christ and he is wise enough on the basis of his elemental science to conceive of the power of God as Energy. Reading his New Testament, he sees that energy expended in every day of Jesus' human life, especially the very last mortal one. The student recognizes that the physical human body of Jesus was but a temporary conveyance by means of which Love was put into action as an example for us. We conclude that the student who understands something of the elemental concept of radiation and energy is able to draw from this into his mind a "feeling" of the physically unseen Spirit behind that outward Love, which was perceived each time Jesus came in contact with another person.

I am attempting to reassure the Reader that it is possible for a young neophyte Christian, properly prepared, to pray, to communicate with, a Spirit who does not hold a physical form but is radiating a kind of energy into a Spiritual Field of Force in which the young person perceives himself to be immersed. To be sure my idea may be labelled abstract; but I believe it is less abstract and more spiritual than praying to a dim humanoid form up there in the sky. I firmly hold the view that if Dr. Barth had had some modern science in his educational background, he would make a greater impact in his discussion of praying to our Trinitarian God.

We insist that Faith in the unseen, though labelled by some as abstract, must nevertheless include a concept of extrasensory perception of the Spirit. The history of mankind to date testifies that secular thought is generated by the unseen Spirit. When the progressive growth of the thought becomes aware that Perfection will not be attained via mere human effort alone, God, the unseen *but felt*[1] Spirit, must be depended upon *to energize* the unseen human mental process and to direct the efforts made toward attaining a desirable goal.

A stumbling block for the non–technically trained person is to overcome his feeling that a discussion of the energy of God makes Him a sort of cold fish, if you will. He avoids the idea since he feels no warmth of personality as we normally define it. Personality does demand relationships with others to be defined. Personally, I perceive that the LOVE of God (His caring relationship as characteristic of a person,) *existed and preceded* the accountability of Energy as the building block of His universe. The human mind can only assume via Faith that Energy coexisted with Love from the beginning.

Was there a system of Divine energy preexistent to the physical building block energy of the universe? I do not find this a necessary precondition, for I can assume that all energy was in God's Being in the beginning. When he formed the Universe from a portion of His Energy, he earmarked another portion of it for the functioning of Nature, something like the sympathetic nervous system we find in the human body, charged with keeping the operation going somewhat automatically. Our mechanical energy present in the world today characterizes this type of energy. He retains the third portion as His divine or spiritual Energy by which He maintained His Spiritual Field of Force, comparable to the Magnetic Field of Force found in His Natural resource section.

One's faith in God as a God of Energy does not have to depend upon the absolute identity of these different applications of energy but the *analogy of similarity of the two fields of force is very helpful.* Remember that "field of force" means energy to do work, and in these very human words—work and labor—we see things being accomplished in this world that can be interpreted as being accomplished by human hands and minds but that have essentially originated from and been successfully maintained by a flow of Spiritual Energy. How else does God help us "do the impossible"?

The spiritual adrenaline is quite evident. Our young student can thus "visualize" the Power of LOVE. We have already mentioned Jesus as a physical example of the Energy of Love. He can go even further. He can visualize the concept of God being in the very cells of his body and within his thought process, in his brain tissue, which is all-immersed in a Field of Spiritual Force kin to the Magnetic Field of Force. God is present everywhere and in every thing.

And we must remember that though He supplies the energy and ability to support a thought process, mankind has been given the gift of choice. He can choose, and will therefore create Evil as well as Good. How badly God must feel when his family members abuse the gift and divert God's original energy into Evil ends.

By comprehending the Holy Spirit, the daily Enabler, as one state of being for Almighty God, we flesh out further details of His un-fathomable power. The idea of God's far-out infinite reaches as creator, (still creating) is complemented by the intimate, immanent (i.e., here in the real world), close-up connection within our bodies; seeing this expands our vision of the larger dimensions of the Divine Unity. He is our Holy Comforter, our daily Enabler and Advisor. His love and con-cern is sufficient *for any situation*. Thus, five billion souls and all the sparrows become manageable figures in our periods of devotional meditation.

The Lord's Prayer

The Lord's Prayer is probably the most beautiful and important piece of religious literature that God, through Jesus, spoke. But by this same token it has been misused, abused, or reduced to a mere matter of pronouncing words often reduced to an unintelligible mumble. There is that difficulty with the "we," the first person plural, which we have already discussed above.

This "we" is consistent with Jesus' Hebrew vocabulary reflecting the basic relationship between Yahweh and His chosen people as a group. From Abraham until Jeremiah, the communal group was con-sidered the entity dealing with their god. Even Hosea, in the experience with his prostitute wife, describes God's love and Israel's marriage to Him in terms that show us Israel as a communal people; they were dealt with as one. Remember, Jacob equals Israel. Though throughout this early period there were numerous examples of personal conduct singled out for correction, the overall governmental Hebrew theocracy was a covenant between God and a tribe, not between God and an individual.

When we Americans say "We, the People," we also really mean ourselves as individuals. This is significant, for from the day of our birth as a nation, we held individual powers and rights to be paramount. When Jesus used the words "our" and "we" and "us" in this prayer He probably thought of it as an act of worship by a group; it would be natural to use the Hebrew plural. But for us this automatically waters down the sense of personal obligation in our current everyday sense.

My strong advice to others who use the Lord's Prayer in private devotions is that they enhance the feeling of the I-You relationship with God by using the first person singular, thus "our" father becomes "my" father. In "Give us this day our daily bread," of course, "us" is changed to "me," and so on throughout the prayer. When one reaches "forgive me my debt as I forgive others," the plural no longer blankets the sin that I have committed. I must stand before God on my own two feet. Another advantage of using the prayer privately is that one can combine "debts" and "trespasses" as "forgive all my sins, my debts, and trespasses."

Denominations have spent a lot of time justifying a choice of either Matthew's or Luke's selection of words, or at least the *memory work* of the witness(es) who heard them. We, in this Space Age, ought to use both terms and as many more as our private specific case may demand. In this twentieth century we seem to have more ways of sinning and many more neighbors than ever to overlook and to neglect. Use the real "sin" word for your fault, for God already knows what you have done.

The Lord's Prayer can be said (i.e., repeated) without running the words together, in anywhere from twenty to twenty-five seconds. "Saying" the Lord's Prayer may mean only that one has memorized a bit of Scripture. *Praying* the Lord's Prayer, i.e., with a short pause between thoughts or phrases or clauses during which the heart and mind catch a significant reflection of the way Jesus showed us how to live life, will require at least fifty or sixty seconds. More time is appropriate in meditative praying, and the thesis of this prayer may occupy our entire day.

I remember a most interesting example of what I have been saying. Our minister, on a certain Sunday, had preached a most powerful sermon on Forgiveness. The next Sunday in the Lord's Prayer, when the congregation reached "forgive us our debts," we, all of our own accord, as if in unison, by common assent, almost came to a halt while truth took hold of our minds. In a month's time the old rapid cadence had been resumed; the congregation as a group had forgotten anything special about forgiveness. It left individuals in the group wondering what would have been the result if the preacher had run a full eight- to ten-Sunday mini-course by preaching on each successive phrase contained in it? We could have learned to really pray the Lord's Prayer and perhaps exceed sixty seconds if the pastor, by dramatic inflection of a few of the terms, could emphasize some amongst others. The preacher could give a couple of seconds to each of his ten previous Sunday themes, thus allowing time for recall.

Another approach to the Lord's Prayer and praying in general for greater effectiveness is to throw the subject of prayer into the limbering-up period of a sharing group meeting. (See chapter 6.) In the sharing group one can almost blot out the "we" dampener and make it all approach the "I" quality. This is most apt to occur if the group has met enough times to allow persons to become well acquainted. At the point where they do not hesitate to make themselves vulnerable to one another, one will learn more about prayer and its power than ever before. You will learn that your peers have answers and suggestions that you never expected or suspected. Remember what we had to say a good while back? God answers many of our prayers through the mainstream of one's neighbors. Learn to recognize the blessings received via the neighbor as direct from Him.

FACTS: Some Constituents of Prayer

While I was still a college student, a highlight summer experience was my fortunate lot. The Baptist's Young People's Union (the Northern Baptists of America, now the American Baptists) held its national convention in the twin cities, only thirty-five miles from our southern Minnesota home. For a young chap originally from the Dakota prairie and now a member of a small-town church of not over 100 members, this was a week's thrilling adventure. Nationally known preachers, many with worldwide mission experience, honored our youthful idealism and brought it to a very high-level pitch. One address on prayer made such an impression upon me that I have retained a simple rule all my life.

I was very ignorant of the subject of the address and needed all the whys and hows I could find. The speaker made it interesting from the viewpoint of a catchy word-memory trick. His advice: if one wishes to be sure that his prayer life is complete and he has touched bases all around with God, he should remember that the code word—FACTS—sparks his memory. The speaker then carefully, forcefully, and with many personal examples, proceeded to enlarge on the meaning of every letter in the code word. I am glad I do not remember his specific details of that 1920 summer because I wish to convey *today's evaluation* and in *today's vocabulary* and *my today's-adult interpretation,* which follows.

F equals Fellowship.

The fellowship between God and Man can be viewed from two focal points. It may be man searching for and finding God or it may be primarily God's love reaching out to the person and waiting for His human creature to make the move that allows Him in. The ideal fellowship must be frequent and it must be trusting. It is not a fellowship of equals, for God is so far above the nature of man that we are unable to describe Him. His majesty is awful in the highest sense. In such a case true I-You give-and-take is only possible because of the Love and Forebearance of the Greater One. Because of that Love and Forebearance, the humbleness of the lesser does not overwhelm him to the point of inarticulateness. Jesus' own preaching about humbleness as well as His personal actions, which are studied by the family of faith, create a trust on the part of the lesser. God invites even any hesitant approach, knowing that He can gently lead His earthly son or daughter to a more confident state with increasing frequency of the contact.

A equals Adoration.

The verb "adore" may carry too much of a connotation of earthly human affection to be well adapted to express our adoration of God. But to find pleasure in God's presence and to wish to be close to Him as a response to His interest in us would seem to be a supplementary trait of adoration. Perhaps the word "praise" also carries additional expansion of the thought. And, of course, when we arrive at that point of affection toward Him in which we are forgiven, a logical link is made to thankfulness, which we will approach in a moment.

C equals Confession.

This is the epitome of prayer. At this point the humble transgressor and sinner figuratively and/or literally kneels humbly before His Maker and does his best to uncover the dirt that God already knows all about. Do not forget, Dear Reader, that many Christians are able to refrain from outright overt evil during most days, but the insidious sin of the "upright" Christian is his inability to control his self-respect. It so easily becomes self-righteousness. It so easily mushrooms into self-interest, pride, and self-importance, which after all constitutes our most deadly sin. God's Rescue Plan for His human family absolutely depends on the person building up sufficient courage to tell it all and to come clean. Confession is the ticket of entry to the Rescue Plan. Today's psychological preachers of right thinking and positive action, who talk about the "problems" of living, are soft-soaping the sense of sin and confession that are absolutely necessary. Jesus and God have told us so. The answer to confession is God's forgiveness, which we cover under "supplication" below.

T equals Thanksgiving

Thanksgiving without a doubt stands second only to confession. The thankful heart is a happy heart and lays out the pathway to peace of mind, which is the latchkey to the peace of God. In the midst of trials and tribulations there comes that moment at the bottom of the fall when things begin to mend; thankfulness to God then pours out when we sense that things are no worse than they are, thankfulness that hope is born for the morrow, thankfulness that God's spirit surrounds us. We are thankful for God's Rescue Plan in Christ and the chance to get back in step with Him. Let us not, however, forget to thank God for the little things too. Do you notice that this generation is in jeopardy of losing much of the common courtesy of yesterday? Have you noticed this lack of "thank you" and "excuse me" and "may I" or "please" by the kids and young folks particularly? Those things rub off in our new relationship to God, too. Is it too terrible or trifling to thank God for the night's rest, the sunny morning, or for the rain when that is appropriate, for the friend who hugged you yesterday and whispered, "I love you," for the neighbor across the way who comes from her garden with a single flower for you, for your spouse who has prepared hundreds and hundreds of meals for you? And you may give thanks for the occasional driver who waves you on at the intersection or waits with his car while you are putting away your parcels before he drives in next to you and opens his car door.

S equals Supplication, which in turn equals Humble Prayer, Entreaty or Petition.

The dictionary meaning of the word is resorted to here in order to help substantiate a long-held view of what we may "ask" for in a prayer. I am convinced that prayer conjoins our mental secular and spiritual natures and in that inner connection the mental secular nature fights for the first choice. However, the preferred choice of subject matter is brought to God's attention by sloughing off from the list of petitions any references to "things" (objects of our physical senses). Thus we must not pretend to bring materials things under the umbrella of the "humble petition." Such requests as a new model car, a new dress, or a new mechanical widget with which to count our money are quite suspect. In my opinion, I believe that "humble petitions" would not apply to things but to *conditions and relationship*. These involve our relationship with our neighbors—i.e., all other humans—and with God.

At this point, Dear Reader, it may be well to refer ahead to page 293 where we discuss the Eternal Triangle (God-neighbor-I). Of course there are occasions when mundane physical things may become legitimate objects of prayer. You remember the situation in the preacher's home on a Sunday morning when getting to church was pretty important. Where were the car keys he had left on the piano bench just a few minutes before? This end of the county was sparsely settled, no near neighbors and no taxi service. As the temperature rose, a Sunday School teacher, a neighbor living a couple of miles off, happened to drive in. Needless to say she was happily commandeered for him. One of the children had thrown the keys down the toilet and the ultimate answer to prayer was no doubt a locksmith, and/or a plumber. But the preacher always considered the unexpected neighbor's car the "Godsend."

One is pleased and feels fortified when he encounters evidence that his spiritual experience is corroborated by others. The Pilgrim is here following the FACTS code word given by the preacher in 1920. It is evident that Casteel, in his approach a generation later, has used the identical code without actually specifying it as such. Furthermore if the term "Fellowship with God" is used as a synonym for Casteel's description of what he stresses as "communion" with God, we conclude that a "son" has followed in the exact footsteps of a "father." Casteel begins with Adoration, page 21; then the approach to Confession, page 68; followed by Christian Thanksgiving, page 86; and Asking, Petition, Intercession, pages 103-114, the code ACTS is immediately in view. It is further strengthened when we examine his argument supporting prayer in general: He emphasizes the "communion with God" so strongly as to fashion the equivalence of the F for fellowship. Thus he arrives at the previous speaker's code, FACTS à la 1920.

The Family Altar

At the turn of this century there was a considerable effort to promote the adaptation of a family altar in every home. The pulpit and religious literature regularly emphasized the importance of the family group giving loyalty to the practice. The term altar was a figure of speech in most cases, although some plans suggested that a corner of the living room be graced with an appropriate small cross and/or a picture or two. Appropriate seating could be easily arranged. As was the case of my uncle the pastor (before 1950), praying was done on one's knees, and this was usually suggested for general family altar practice. Reading from the Scripture with a brief comment by Father or Mother was in order. Some denominations followed the practice begun early in the century of following with daily readings from a devotional pamphlet like the Methodist *Upper Room*. Similar publications were introduced by others but primarily they seemed beamed at use in private daily devotions, whether in the privacy of one's room, in travel, at leisure, or wherever.

It is questionable whether the use of a family altar was ever a truly functioning, widespread practice for the American home group in the early part of the twentieth century, although it had been during the prior century. It had probably then been more prevalent in the south, but the daily high activity of the American scene in this century tended to play down its usefulness. Exacting schedules of public school hours and economic job schedules of varying cycles tended to disrupt smooth habitual practice of family prayer.

I would assume that my own personal home schedule would be carried out by others in like fashion. My wife and I, between marriage and our first daughter six years later, used daily readings from the *Upper Room* at the evening dinner. Our young children then disrupted the idea from there on, and although training of children was supposed to be the main reward of the practice, we decided to try again when they were both in high school. Evening mealtime did not work out even then. In retrospect I see that the activities of the school days, the parenting care of my wife, all came to a final climax at that evening meal. I was home from the lab and plant after a busy day, and I was tired. This is not an excuse—just a statement of the reason we were not in a restful, quiet mood for a worship period.

After the girls went off to college my wife and I resumed a quiet time at meals on Mondays through Fridays. Church work occupied Saturday and Sunday. Though the timing was changed from the evening to the midday meal, we continued this practice for the next fifteen years of retirement. From then to now it has ceased to be steady daily habit due mainly to the faulty hearing ability of both of us. Thus the record is a human cycle, one of heat and cooling, affirmative and negative.

My deepest regret is my lack of family leadership in this report of family worship during the period when our two children were a vital part of the family. There was one ameliorating activity during a solid ten-year period following the entry of our older daughter into the junior department of the church-school. As with many fathers and mothers who are drawn into the teaching activities of the Sunday church-school, I accepted the appointment as superintendent of that department. Much of our family time at home was occupied with discussion of the details of that job and their execution, and the whole family was involved, including my good helpmate who taught fifth grade for the first five-year period. The girls did have a share in a daddy trying to do his best to keep a family Christian time.

Following the erection of a new educational building, it was possible to expand the traditional one-hour Sunday school into a session running from 9:30 A.M. to 12 noon with two sets of teachers. This afforded me a thirty-minute period in which I functioned as the leading teacher of a group of over 100 fifth and sixth graders in a suburban metropolitan town. Our junior church became a reality.

The Lord both challenged and blessed me and my efforts placed me in some sort of a Christian growth curve. Much was attempted, some mistakes were made, but there was a feeling of progress within this special area of effort. Evaluation by parents and others were helpful. It was during this period that I attempted to demonstrate what prayer and worship were like for children. We learned at least the skeleton activity or outward appearance of sincere prayer in which we loved and praised God and asked His help in establishing our mission in life. I hoped that the children learned to comprehend the view of the importance of knowing how Christ handled life, and that worship with specific prayer in focus was very important.

Answering Prayer

Doctor Buttrick, in his far-reaching volume on Prayer, finally approached the matter of God's answers to prayers. In my humble laic approach and reaction to such a high-level theologian's views of communication with God, I found that the author's discussion of this part of the subject seemed somewhat incomplete. One gathers that he felt most prayers are not recognizably answered. This leaves the average Christian in a deep sea of doubt as to whether the individual believes he is able to actually establish lines of communication with the Divine Power of the Universe.

A "line of communication" implies that in the I-You relationship, which is insisted upon as necessary, there must be a two-way exchange taking place. To be sure, the layman does not expect to ring up God's number on His spiritual telephone and carry on the rapid exchange that two friends make. But on the basis of Scripture generally, and considering the practice of Jesus specifically, today's Christian has every expectation of a response from God in answer to earnest, humble, penitent prayer. Indeed, that response may many times be seemingly as negative as no, but when this is the response there will generally be a future realization as to why the answer is negative. Thus, even when a negative, seemingly dead end results, there is ultimately a Divine response.

Naturally, what appears to be unanswered prayer may not be legitimate prayer to begin with. I feel that we humans are slothful in the cultivation of our spirituality and so impatient that we expect an answer before the day is over—certainly within the month or year ahead. Actually, God may have reasons for insisting that for His answer to some prayers, an entire lifetime may be required, even in the face of constant entreaty on our part. And in some instances, we do not become conscious of the answer until later than we expected because we have been looking for it in the wrong place, or it has come via one whom we thought was an impossible agent.

Thus we may helpfully address, first, the means by which the answer to our prayer is received. Though God is Spirit, we believe He has the attributes of hearing and speaking to us, but not in the same manner as we discuss the TV evening news with a friend. The connection with God is not via the physical aspect of contortions of the vocal cords or the audibility of sound waves striking ear drums. We must simply assume that God absorbs our human words, which our mind, catalyzed by the Spirit, has formed for Him and which have, in turn, been melded into His understanding, wordless, mysterious Spirit. We use the word "meld" to allow for the unknown mystery of the Mind of God, which in some small way is kin to that with which He endowed His humans.

It must also be our realization at the time of prayer that God hears more than the thought words we employ at the moment. He, in His infinite wisdom, receives simultaneously a full representation of our emotional state. The professional psychologist may not like the use of the term "emotional" here but I am referring to the variable stances we take as regards our truth and honesty about the matter we are discussing with God. Are we really thinking and/or saying the whole truth in our prayers? Are we exaggerating? Are we glossing things over? Are we really hiding a disagreeable and probably a very prejudicial fact of the matter? In brief, are we coming across complete and clean?

We must instinctively be aware that at the very moment we introduce a subject to God's attention, He has the instant replay of our spiritual video cassette covering our entire personal history from the moment He blessed us at birth. So there is melded into His mind not only what we are specifically now thinking and saying to Him, but the facts of all our previous conduct are instantly in focus. God, having the whole picture of truth, in His wisdom takes on a loving judgmental disposition toward us. In His care and concern for us He may rightly decide that no answer is best, at least for now. He has other plans for us, which He knows will take a long time (humanly speaking) to materialize. Patient waiting will be best for us.

How does God now "speak" to us on a singularly private matter when His answer is a positive, active affirmative? I do not presume to prescribe for the other person. All I can do is to recount some personal experience and allow you, the reader, to react as you will. There have been times in which I have realized that I have sinned mightily against God's moral, ethical law. With heavy heart I have approached Him, laid everything out in the open, asked Him for forgiveness of my fault, and claimed His reconciliation and continued love. Momentarily I have been flooded with a warmth of mind and physical body that is really indescribable, not unlike the wonderful feeling one has when he lies back in a tub bath and feels the warm water engulf him. I fall asleep instantly thereafter and in the morning I rise to the new day, just as Paul described it in his letters.

For a second point in recognizing answers to prayer we can now turn to the importance of accepting and practicing the Eternal Triangle principle. It is truly love in action, for it involves a third person, the neighbor, with whom one must be interacting. Both speech and conduct are the means of communication with him. Monastic withdrawal from society into the completely singular conditions of privacy cannot be justified except for the limited periods of discipline and training that may be helpful in reestablishing a serving relationship with society. No one who voluntarily chooses to be abandoned permanently on his deserted ocean isle without any means of electronic communication with his world is fulfilling a Christian life. The "social gospel," as over against "private singular gospel," is a misnomer, and philosophical discussion of the difference between the two is really impossible. In brief, the gospel, the good news presented to us by God in Christ, is not realized merely by the cognizance of it in our heart and mind via reading and hearing; the relationship with others is established to make the "good news" of love meaningful; the cognizance is not fully comprehended until a neighbor is brought into the sharing experience. Thus the Eternal Triangle principle may be illustrated by a geometrical plane figure, which eventually, by massing together all humanity, becomes three-dimensional, i.e., a sphere with God at the center.

It is noted immediately that the first triangle formed by God, you, and I, is not an equilateral triangle. This distance is *not* an equilateral triangle. The distance between humans is indicative of the vast differences between the divine and human nature. This distance is *not* a physical, spacial fact but illustrates the difference between spiritual communication and our human vocal speech and conduct. *This is true even though God is closer to us in His spiritual way than are our neighbors.* "His way is closer than hands and feet, and because He is inside our bodies, is closer than breathing." Our communication with Him is prayer no matter when, where, or how; the instant a thought is directed toward Him we are at prayer. We are at prayer whether we are fully reclining, kneeling, standing or sitting in the park, or on the beach, driving the car, or in a church pew. The line between conscious and unconscious prayer is quite hazy and indistinct, and we leave it to the

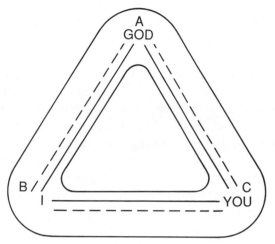

The Eternal Triangle: God, You, and I

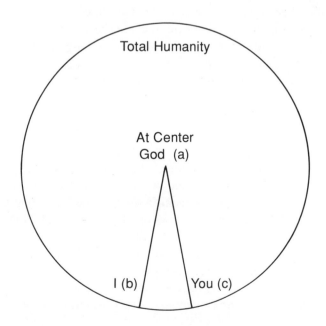

psychologist to fuss over. We may unconsciously receive the prayer answer while asleep and awake to the answer when morning comes.

Above, we have taken pains to make sure that our use of the term "communication" is not limited to comparison with a telephone conversation with actual vocal language flowing in both directions. Our decoding of spiritual insight must include intuition, subconsciousness, wordless meditation such as springs from the impression made by art and music, and the mood of an environment. This is all spiritual language, God's language, and some may say that it includes the sudden appearance of "the light at the end of the tunnel."

A definitive bridge between spirit and mind is encountered. When, in the midst of my private meditation, there suddenly appears a new word or concept and a feeling of comfort and relief is derived, who am I to claim that it was all mind or all God? Can we not compromise? I do not fully understand the theological descriptions of mysticism, but associated therewith I perceive a sort of Quaker inspiration, what is referred to as a "quickening" of the Spirit.

All of these aspects of spiritual communication are indicated in the above diagram by using dotted lines between the three parties as one path of spiritual communication fully as important as the solid line representing the spoken or written everyday mode. Some readers may appreciate further considering that the two lines (i.e., the dotted and solid) are not insulated from one another, but as a matter of fact may be as closely melded together as two strands of wire interwoven so intimately that they become one strand.

In our comment we will call the line AB to mean communication going from A to B and we will call the line BA when communication flows in the opposite direction, i.e., going from B to A. A is God; B is I; C is You, the neighbor.

I pray to God via the line BA and I attempt to discern His response via the line AB. But God's response to me may not be direct. He may well speak to me through you, the neighbor, via line AC. You in turn answer the original request by reaching me via line CB. My ministration to my neighbor via BC may well have originated with God, who has reached me via line ACB.

Our prayers are a mixture of singular and communal objectives. The originating worship or reading, or conversation or physical observation, may likewise be a single personal experience of a communal experience, as in the church sanctuary. Let us attempt a few examples to flesh out the above discussion. They may help generate your meditation upon your own responsibility as an agent of God.

When we pray to God to heal a physical hurt or ailment it seems discourteous to merely ask of God, "Please make me well." One might first ask for a strong perception of His Presence, a comfort, for instance, in somewhat the same expectation as that of a clasp of the hand of a friend given to one on the sick bed. There is a bridge of empathy constructed. This may be followed by a petition that the proper medical practitioner be designated to treat you. (You don't really expect God to step in the moment you finish prayer and miraculously answer in the affirmative, followed by your leaping out of bed well and secure and perhaps immediately forgetful.) Soon the name of a special doctor is brought to our attention. We seek his advice and we are made well.

God's special direct healing of the most drastic cases of physical ailment and disarrangement is however not to be totally disclaimed. That we may not comprehend what we believe our eyes behold is always a possibility. Kathryn Kuhlman will be lovingly remembered by many people who attended her healing sessions in public meetings during the seventies. On one occasion, my wife and I drove down to Atlanta for an overnight stay and attended such a healing session. The Power of God seemed to be in the air. I testify to a perception of strong audience psychological participation. This "on the scene" participation seems impossible when carried out via TV PA broadcasting by others, wherein the timbre of the voice is modified by the electronic transmission and one feels cheated of a vibrant audience participation. In the personal mass demonstration of such a meeting, however, the failure to know the absolute medical details of the illness dampens the effects on some participants. Perhaps our own problem was that despite my dear wife's physical hurts, we may have actually been more observers than supplicants. We saw what was acclaimed as a miracle by God. Some of the healings were said to be permanent, others were not. We witnessed testimony to God's power by others and were intrigued by what we beheld, but faith did not fully accept. Perhaps we must confess a bit of envy of those who were able to make themselves vulnerable to His Presence.

Let us examine another example of answer to prayer wherein a number of facets allow a number of individuals to be involved. Such is the case of our intercessory petitions to God in behalf of another party. Let us further assume that in the intercessory prayer the matter of a physical healing is not obviously involved. We are petitioning God to help a family we know, whose house burned down while the family was away on vacation. The family has only modest financial resources at its command. Intercessory prayer in this instance readily takes on some of the character of Christ's mission pronouncement in reference to feeding, binding up wounds, clothing and nakedness. If the hurting family is already a member of the Christian community of faith, it would be natural to assume that there will be a number of similar intercessory prayers being offered.

How do we who are making the prayer expect our prayer to be answered? We really do not expect to see God appear in the form of an angel driving a big truck containing an unlimited supply of the amenities of life, including a big bag of money, or better yet a cashier's check with the amount to be filled in by the stricken family. It will be quite clear that in this case the answer will be supplied by a group of neighbors who out of mercy and love will be quickened by the Holy Spirit and whose responsive hearts and minds will succor the family.

Was the Divine Power at work in this case or was the help merely the humanistic response of a group of those of goodwill? The agnostic observer will claim there is no evidence of the Divine assistance that the Christian helpers of the family will proclaim. Are we engaging in mere wishful thinking? No! We are emulating the faith of Jesus, whom we observed praying at moments of difficulty, if not constantly. God the Father was there with Him. We as His humans cannot claim the same identical spiritual quality of vision as Jesus in a substantiation of the spiritual power hookup that He was a part of, but we can, in our Christian faith, leap upward from our clay launch pad into the heart of God, which is LOVE. The answer of approval from God we intuitively and absolutely recognize as kin to that spiritual nature of the Good Samaritan. God bids us to be awake on our daily roads to Jericho, keeping our self-interests under control, so that our discerning glance comes into focus upon our fellow creatures who are in distress, those who are bruised by encounters with evil. That bit of us that is in God's image is the connecting power line from God's heart, and we immediately set to work to bind up the wounds of the traveler and get him to the innkeeper. We keep him in our thoughts until he is well, at the hands of the innkeeper. God has answered us with the gift of the spirit of the good Samaritan. God calls all humankind to reconciliation with Him and with each other. The Eternal Triangle means reconciliation and a fresh start for us individually and communally. Such energy-filled reconciliation is never withdrawn on God's part. He awaits your pledge and mine as we join in our best efforts in daily living.

In closing this chapter I must share a prayer experience which came upon me out of the blue. Meditation following the discovery of two little volumes on Prayer demands that some elaboration be made in their favor. I came to feel that God placed these two books in my hands knowing I needed extra help in my pilgrimage. He wished some additional element included which would please Him? A sort of benediction for this chapter, if you will.

I was heavily engrossed in editing and expanding draft number four before typing it to make it the final one, number five. As a return favor for a gift my good wife had given her next-door cousin at our winter quarters, we had received a little paperback, *Power Through Prayer*, by E. M. Bounds. I really had no fit opportunity to look into it. However, one morning later in a mood of uneasiness, which I ascribe to the Spirit, my daily Comforter and Enabler, I picked it up and could not let it go for the next two hours.

The author's foreword challenged me from the beginning. Here was a preacher who had served our Union troops as a chaplain in the Civil War. That was interesting, but what really set off a little bomb in my mind was the date of the publisher's printing. Yes, it was in the '80s, but it had a 19 in front of it instead of an 18. Yes indeed, this message must be really good. In this day of quick purchase and quick trashing, such repeat printing certainly suggested the nugget to be found therein; and I was not disappointed.

Bounds referred to preachers who become so practiced in the pulpit and skilled in the proclamation of the Word but who slip into the habit of letting the praying slacken, not only in length but in intensity with which love and mercy of God in Christ was being implored. One properly deduced that he was referring to the amount of private praying going into the preparation of a sermon as well as his praying in the public worship. I quote a few potent lines. "The preacher who has retired from prayer as a conspicuous and largely prevailing element in his own character has shorn his preaching of its *distinctive life-giving power.*" The italics are mine and are made to remind us that beyond mere proclamation of the Word, the preacher should actually demonstrate how to absorb and apprehend that Word. How is that achieved? Through prayer. And a bit later: "Of two evils, perhaps little praying is worse than no praying. Little praying is a kind of make-believe, a salve for the conscience, a farce and a delusion." These strong words emphasize that praying is absolutely necessary in the proclaiming of the Word. Bounds closes this thought with one of John Wesley's testimonies regarding prayer. "Give me one hundred preachers who fear nothing but sin, and desire nothing but God, and I care not a straw whether they be clergymen *or laymen*, such alone will shake the gates of hell and set up the kingdom of heaven on earth. *God does nothing but in answer to prayer.*"

The second volume appeared even more quietly. My wife and I had made a collection of surplus household and wearable items and had taken them down to the local charitable sales operation of the Catholic Church. After tucking the gift slip for the IRS away for safekeeping, we wandered through the old warehouse-type facilities, examining other families' disposables. I headed for the little corner room stacked high with the literary surplus of the day. It ranged from random paperbacks through condensed Reader's Digest books, maps, broken sets of all types of encyclopedias, How-To pamphlets by the dozen, the usual attic and back shed cleanout inventories. Approaching this room I paused at a rack just outside the entrance on which a scrabble of paperbacks and some children's books were left unassorted. At the near end of the top shelf, on a level with my eye, lay a single small volume of some one hundred pages by itself. I hope it does not offend your sense of reality, but I knew that the Spirit of God, my daily Enabler, had arranged to have that book placed there for me. At the top edge was the author's name, John Powell, S.J. There was the flash of a question, *Is he as good as his brother, Teilhard de Chardin?* (See chapter 8.) My eye fell to the lower edge and the subtitle, *My Pilgrimage of Prayer*, gripped me. I knew this was to be my book. Lastly, in the centered, hazy, darkened, symbolic picture of a wheat plant, was the title, *He Touched Me*. I turned the cover and discovered that I owed a measure of sincere thanks to Marie Larrison, who had owned it before me. Handing over the quarter to the cashier was almost a sacred act. And after lunch I devoured most of it.

In my opinion, Powell's *Pilgrimage* tops the list of those found in the addenda under prayer. The author receives two strong commendations and two constructive criticisms. The outstanding plus is absolutely unique. He had fifteen photographers take pictures that are randomly scattered throughout the book. They are full page or double page and the reader must supply the title. After reading the book, some of the titles your heart and mind first proposed will be changed to more appropriate ones. They are *not* discussed as such in the text. I found them to be communicative paths to God, who is trying to convey a spiritual message from His heart to ours. They are supreme examples of my earlier reference to wordless Art as a real communicative link between persons. The second plus is his strong reiteration of the necessity of subduing our strong self-interests, our ego, our seeming insistence at wishing to be number one. To enter into real prayerful communication with God we must admit all our evil, i.e., we must become open, clean, and very vulnerable. It must be real, not a sham, make-believe performance. I felt that he was adding much support to my discussion of the sharing group in chapter 6 as a way to learn to pray in the presence of others, shedding any tendency toward a facade of artificiality.

Hopefully constructive, on the other side, I must include the author in a fault of all professional theologians as a class, in not advancing in the modification of a spiritual vocabulary that can be more comprehensible in the face of Space Age science and technology. This is not a mere matter of redefining words. A whole new concept of what the universe is and where it originated ought to be a goal for all future theologians. Perhaps this is the underlying reason for the necessity of pointing to a second missing factor. Professor Powell does not seem to embrace any significant constant operation of the neighbor in the Eternal Triangle. He appears to keep communication with God pretty exclusively a two-party system. He does not seem to put much emphasis on those we meet every day on our individual Jericho roads. Let us keep in mind that it is *more often than not that our neighbor bears God's answer to us.*

The paragraph above has just hatched a "dream." Imagine a situation: A young candidate for a doctorate degree is casting about for a suitable field of investigation, compelling grounds for a thesis. Challenge the candidate to study the four diverse characters below via their writing and generally recognized pedigrees. First, Lecomte duNouy, Christian biologist, author of *Human Destiny*, who says Man has not yet completed God's evolutive process. Secondly, Teilhard de Chardin, geologist and anthropologist (discoverer of Peking man), who has been reviewed by American theologians. Those who are not particularly fond of him put him aside by calling him a pantheist, but I could be his kind of pantheist. God is everywhere and in *everything*. Which, of course, adds Albert Einstein to the survey, as theoretical physicist and mathematician who can contribute a description of the equivalency of matter and energy. Now complete the study by adding Professor John Powell, S.J., theologian and psychologist, whose views as to ways in which the communication via prayer between Man and God can be recognized are the only approach by which the Power of God can be fed into the operations of the next century. He will balance some of Teilhard de Chardin's seemingly somewhat impersonal Creator with Powell's reality of the light of the Love and Mercy expressed by God in Jesus Christ, his personification of love.

This Pilgrim is approaching the closing of the mortal portion of his journey. This telling of his movement toward what he perceives to be upper ground with God has been a reward for the longer years his Creator, the Divine Enabler, has granted him. He realizes that a good share of his experience has been expressed in a vocabulary that may be criticized and misunderstood by some. He maintains, however, that it needed to be said as it was. He hopes that lay people will have found in it some seeds of stimulant for themselves and their neighbors as they attempt to help resist the secular world culture of this new age. He also hopes that theologians, pricked by his condemnation of their slowness in responding to the rapid advance that science has made in the last century, will see a challenge they ought not to ignore. They can realize that science is God's science and that they should be about the task of reorganizing their verbal approach and connection to the body of Christ. The church must reflect both love and energy, for God is the God of both theology and science. The Pilgrim invites you to share these several prayers with him:

Neighbors

Dear Father-God, our Creator and Sustainer, Our Saviour Christ, Our Holy Comforter and Enabler: We meet in your presence this morning with praise for your Lordship and a deep sense of gratitude and thanksgiving for Your Gift of Life. We approach Your throne of grace with some timidity, for we realize that as individuals and as communities of faith we are soiled with sin. Though our acts of disobedience may not be overt breaks of Your Holy Decalogue, every one of us is guilty of magnification of our selfish, greedy pride. We are

300

guilty of mixing up our priorities and, in many cases, we have made our egos our god in Your place. We have not heeded the words You placed on the lips of Jesus: "I have come to fulfill the Law, namely to show you how to control yourselves and become spiritual Lovers, so that my neighbor may become number one, and I take the lower position of servant."

Father, forgive us this sin of self-righteousness that we may feel the surge of Your Power picking us up and wiping the slate clean. We pledge to do better next time. Help us each to apply your servant Paul Tournier's simple text under which he operates Your tutorship: "Turn your personal compass 180 degrees from yourself and perceive your neighbor's condition. Know you are succeeding when, as troubles flood in upon humanity, you, through your acquired spiritual nature, think FIRST of that neighbor and lastly of yourself." Dear God, strengthen our will to do likewise.

And when we have really apprehended the importance of making our neighbor number one, may You lead us into an astonishing comprehension of the new nature of our prayer to You. In the midst of our bad hurts we often made a quick direct appeal, "God, I am in an awful fix. Send help at once." It is as if we wanted your reply by six o'clock. And, because we get silence from You, the apparent "No" ends up with our rejection of prayer altogether. As you told Isaiah long ago, "My thoughts are not your thoughts, neither are your ways my ways; for as the heavens are higher than the earth, so are my ways higher than your ways and my thoughts than your thoughts."

As we meditate over this, your Spirit finally gets in its inning and we begin to understand a little of why You place so much emphasis on *neighbor relations* and *loving*. Neighbors become the agents carrying many of your true replies to our prayers. We think back over our lives and it dawns upon us that most of your answers for help come via other fellow mortals. We pray that every member of this community of faith will learn that keeping communication lines open to You means keeping the lines from our neighbors in good operating order. We pray that You will help us keep neighbor lines free of static and power brownouts. We realize good neighbor relations is Your answer to both public and private praying. We know we need to do more than just passively listen. The Yellow Pages tell us where to get secular daily help. Thank You for the neighbors who are spiritual Yellow Pages in your hands.

We are saddened when we realize that there are millions of persons in our land who do not have neighbors, who do not know what the word really means. In our nation we are generally known as being generous to recipients of welfare but we sometimes are tempted to limit our neighborliness to a passive impersonal financial support. Please, Dear God, forbid that we become satisfied with that. The gift is not really complete without a portion of the giver himself. Thus the testimony of Your gift in Christ shows through and the neighbor's load is lightened.

We remember this day all those in need and as we bring them to You, may we be individually empowered to seek those special cases where we can actually be Your Good Samaritans. We pray in Your name in Christ. Amen.

Long-Range Planning

Dear God, Our Father: You have richly blessed this church in the recent OUR BOLD MISSION program and campaign, which raised substantial sums for the expansion of our physical plant. We realize that in giving us this SO-FAR-SO-GOOD blessing You expect this to be only the first step toward full fruition of many types of services, both in our local community and in our world family at large.

We pray that as we serve, so will faith be nurtured. Grant that the pertinent long-range planning committees now earnestly studying the situation will tune their spiritual receiving sets of causative memory and sensitive moral conscience to the frequency of Your Holy Spirit. May we never forget that the code password is LOVE.

We pray, too, that in 1985, many Maggais and Zechariahs and Nehemiahs and Ezras will be raised up in the congregation to see that the job is completed. We know not exactly whether we have an Isaiah or a Jeremiah in our pulpit, but Charles Durham and his beautiful wife certainly are your gift from Heaven. Our pastor, being human, will stub his toe now and then, perhaps may even pull a tendon, but You will bind up the hurts and pour Your reserve strength into any flagging step. Continue to fill him with power and with understanding, with humor, and with humility. Make him some of both Priest and Prophet. Bring to the entire congregation the idea that this church can be expected to become a special agent of performance and creation to all Presbyterians through our pastor. Things we can do here will feed directly into the national Mission Board, of which he is a member. We believe that You saw to it that he was elected to that board. Our church can be on the first page of *Presbyterian News* and we pray the news will reflect Your Power and Your Majesty, not ours.

Father-God, with Your indescribable and inexhaustible Mercy and Grace, we pray that You enter into the hearts of all those whose suffering pain today, be they members of the faith or any pagan on land or sea or in the air. We pray not only for those who suffer physical trouble on beds of pain, but also those who carry heavy burdens of mind and soul; those with ruptured relationships; those sorrowful and those of unbalanced mind; all those whose sufferings seem beyond us. In Your wisdom, heal and restore them to creative use. As we pray the prayer You taught us we will attempt to generate real congregational spirit power. We wish as individuals to consciously feel a common concern for what this church could be doing for You. Hear us, Dear Lord, as we try to go beyond the mere "saying of words."

Our Father, which art in heaven . . . (Above and beyond infinity)
Hallowed be Thy Name . . . (Yes, clean up our daily speech)
Thy kingdom come . . . (We have not been out telling others)
Thy will be done on earth as it is in Heaven . . . (Help us, as
　　　　a church, to seek jobs only Your Church can do)
Give us this day our daily bread . . . (Let us be mindful of the sore
　　　　needs of others)
And forgive us our debts as we forgive our debtors . . . (For as a Church
　　　　our failure to make a mistake may mean we are asleep)
Lead us not into temptation . . . (May our experimentation as a Church
　　　　mean more successes in Your name than failures)
But deliver us from evil . . . (Help us to overcome the human tendency
　　　　to evil whether individual or communal)
For Thine is the Kingdom, the Power, and the Glory forever . . . (You
　　　　spread this holy Benediction over us as we hear the
　　　　Proclamation of Your Word)
We pray in Your name, in Christ. Amen.

Sabbath before Election

Dear God, our Creator, and Donor of our Souls: We humbly approach you this morning, quite immature and very sinful in our selfish actions. We come only upon Your invitation, which is overflowing with Your Love and Grace. We deserve nothing, but we need your Presence in each heart here, brooding over and throughout this, Your sanctuary. You feed our mutual fellowship in this community of faith; and we feel renewed in strength as You answer our prayers through the ministry of our neighbors. Absorbed in our human needs and entanglements we can do very little by ourselves. We beseech You to search us inwardly and help us to sweep out the dirt and tidy up our rooms. We ask this of You each Sabbath and we pledge ourselves to better effort in the week ahead. Help us through the mundane days of the week. Our conscience tells us that we do not measure up to the bright, glowing light of the template Jesus Christ our Savior is; but You have asked us to keep trying. We are grateful for the pardoning of these precious moments when we feel Your Spirit has stepped in to strengthen our wills alongside Your Will and has made straight our twisted, poor judgments.

We pray that You will help us sharpen our sensitivity towards the needs of others. The Good Samaritan had the empathy and sensitivity we wish we could build within our own lives. As Your servant, Paul Tournier, has told us for You, we know we are not Born Again unless our constant first impulse is to see the condition of our neighbor. And our neighbor? Yes, we know, he is all others.

We pray earnestly today
>for those who are under par;
>for the ill—grant respite and loving care; may those who serve them
>>have the power of healing hands and keen minds, warmed and guided by Your Spirit;
>for the lonely—move the heart of a visiting, caring neighbor;
>for the discouraged and poor in Spirit—grant them new hope and a more promising tomorrow;
>for those who sorrow this day—give comfort and courage;
>for the discriminated against, because of race or culture—assert
>>through us Your Fatherhood of the family of all Your people and
>>strike us to the quick should we be guilty of passively standing by.

We pray for our nation in these searching hours of our country's need. Help us to sort through all the verbiage and choose good men and women for the positions of trust. We would hope always that our politicians be of statesmanship calibre. Politics seem to create a seething hotbed of special interests. Some of them therefore directly counter their constituencies' interests; they are very selfish. We know that a common-sense compromise is sought as a working solution, but, Father, get to us when it appears we are about to compromise with the Devil himself. Help us to assert Christian choices and priorities in all our civic transactions, be they of private citizenry or public officials.

We pray that You make Your answer to nuclear war more clear to us, a dumb humanity. Lord, we beseech You to quicken our path to the abandonment of this way to our annihilation, either by catastrophic war or by stealth in the poisoning of Your natural environment. Only You know the right answer to the burdens we have unwittingly taken upon ourselves as we have opened this Pandora's box. We pray for sensitivity of conscience so that we properly decode Your constant advice and concern. We petition You, in Christ. Amen.

Epilogue

A BRIEF SUMMARY OF MY MESSAGE

This book has aimed at adding, in at least a small measure, to some of the vital areas of human life that the Space Age is questioning us about. It is getting late. We attach man's idea of Time to the mighty works of God and realize that five-hundred-year periods have been recognizable between Abraham and our walk on the moon. The Reformation burst forth in 1516 and so reminds us of *Great Expectations*. Will we be able to recognize the cue to the transformation of today's crass materialism in the hands of the Holy Spirit? We do pray so.

We summarize our remarks under five headings:

1. We must develop our appreciation of the more significant use of symbolic language, which the human must fall back upon when he deals with Spirituality past, present, and future. Applying the term "symbolic" to authors J, E, P, R, and the prophets of the Old Testament does not subtract one iota from the authenticity of their Godly message. It sublimes their monotheism. Only comprehending that God personified His Love and Energy in the human body of Jesus do we begin to understand. We may disagree over what he said but we believe we know what He DID. Via His life we reinterpret the Old Testament, and symbolism becomes reality.

2. This book describes the broad outlines of a fresh approach to a Christian concept of the total Creation of the Universe in the hands and at the will of Almighty God. All of it, and us, are of the nature of God Himself. We desecrate or honor at our will His gift of freedom.

3. It charges the professional theologian as being negligent for not keeping our spiritual acumen in the vanguard of the physical sciences. He fails to take the stance that theology and the social sciences are actually the parents of the physical sciences. Theology seems not to care to do its lab work. Honesty, of course, demands our admission that

307

collecting the data in a matter of years instead of days is difficult. But we ought to try.

4. This book calls attention to the danger of failing to develop the childishness of youthful spiritual enthusiasm into a program of adult, laic, theological growth. It reaffirms the commitment aspect of the Confirmation process entered into by junior high youth. Such commitment means that youth accepts a lifelong goal of DOING the Word of God as well as speaking it.

5. And, finally, we conclude that there is a hidden factor in our lives today which we hesitate to share. To act in Fear is our most tragic human failure. We fear to embrace LOVE in its fulfilling power because we must make a complete 180-degree about-face in our self-interest life-style. We look at Christ and fear death as the end for a martyr. Fear keeps a pastor from telling it like it is and demonstrating it in public. Fear keeps the U.S.A. directing inexcusable sums of money to military strategy while people suffer. The only cure for fear is opening up our understanding of how God's energy can be absorbed via spiritual radiation from His spiritual kingdom to the human domain. We are surrounded by His Field of Force, but we do not learn how to tune ourselves into His wavelength so that He can induce a current of vaster power within us.

Dear Father-God, our Maker, our Reconciling Savior, and our Daily Enabler: We pray for your blessing upon everyone of these readers. We pray that a seed therefrom may be empowered by You, to grow into fruitful abundance within the life of each partaker. In Your name in Christ. Amen.

Appendix
DuNoüy's *Human Destiny* in Teenage Confirmation Curricula

This book is of vital importance in assisting the spiritual revival due in this Space Age. See the previous reference to this theme of God's evolution which the Pilgrim has referred to, above pp. 225–230. *Human Destiny* ought to be studied deeply by all Christians so that they may be in a supportive relation to those in the family circles who are entering the adult voting membership of the community of faith. Every pastor conducting his confirmation class should see that it becomes an essential selection in outside reading in support of God's Word in the Scriptures.

THE THREE PARTS OF *HUMAN DESTINY*.

This book was written by a devout Christian biologist at the close of World War II. The theme of the book is the evolutionary process, which accounts for the creation of the Universe with emphasis upon humanity therein. A most important aspect is that man, as a co-partner of God, has only begun the final stage of evolution toward his goal, his perfected likeness in Jesus Christ.

The author divided his discourse into three main sections. The first one is somewhat mathematical and may seem too theoretical and abstract in parts, especially for high school students. Its purpose, however, is to demonstrate that there is an intelligent operating goal behind the creative, evolutive process. Things were not left to mere CHANCE, which is the view of the secular, materialistic scientist. The author attempts to show that mathematically calculating the laws of probability leads one to conclude that a "cause" or "antichance," must have prevailed from the beginning of time.

The second section deals with the probability of how, after the earth had cooled down, there could be habitation in which could begin the simplest form of living matter. From this would develop, over additional millions of years, first the marine animals, followed by the land animals and plant kingdoms. The final stage of animal evolution produced an upright humanoid who, in the next section, becomes true man (Homo sapiens) upon the receipt of conscience. The mind and brain power set him far apart and above others in his ancestral animal chain.

The third section, titled "The Evolution of Man," is a most challenging exposé of the ongoing spiritual evolution of man toward the goal of Christly living. For some Christians, it may emphasize too heavily the part that individual man himself contributes towards this ascendancy in God's preferred plan of human life. I feel that duNouy has placed his finger on the actual weakness of our present church memberships. We remain as children, too timid to assume responsibility for routing out the remaining traces of animal instincts that remain a part of our characters. The sketch of chapter headings in this third section shows the noble quality gained as the mental and spiritual aspects ascend toward God. This is a continuous long-term struggle toward the fullness of human dignity. This section could become a list of sermon titles for any pastor or youth group leader. The number of pages devoted to each of the three sections speaks directly to the importance of each subject: 25 percent to I; 15 percent to II; and 60 percent to III. Thus the greater share of the book is devoted to the current evolution of man, which no one has previously thought of as *Evolution.*

SECTION I—ON THE METHODS

First, a word from the author's introductory preface; "Now what characterizes man or MAN, is precisely the presence in him of abstract ideas, of moral ideas, of spiritual ideas, and it is only of these that he can be proud." It sounds exceedingly challenging. We make a few brief remarks, by chapter.

Chapter I. One should always take into consideration the specific level of reference chosen for making an observation about our universe. DuNouy has a fine illustration of his point: "Mix flour and soot and the white and black powders become a grey mixture in which neither is discernible with the naked eye. Examine it under the microscope and one observes the separate and distinct white specks and black specks." He says, "We will frequently bring in the scale of observation in order to explain apparent contradictions."

Chapter II. "The aim of science is to *foresee*, and not as has often been said, to understand." And again, "Our Scientific laws always derive after the fact and governed by the fact to which they must submit. It is clear that expressions such as 'scientific truth' should be taken in a very limited sense. There is no scientific truth in the absolute sense. Any electrician thinks he understands how an electric battery works, but the best physicists do not share his opinion and admit that even if they foretell exactly how it will function, they do not fully understand, why it functions."

Chapter III. Deals with Probabilities and the Laws of Chance. It is rigidly mathematical. High school students do not need to tarry over the basic law of probability that "order is borne of disorder." Nor is the student at this point required to understand Professor Charles-Eugene Guye's mathematics applied to the probability of molecules being arranged as they are in the protein molecules of egg albumin.

Comment by Pilgrim: I cannot myself comprehend a situation where the calculation of the probable time required for the formation of the protein molecule might require 10 followed by 321 zeroes, as the billions of years required, when only four billion years is the current (Stanley) estimated age of planet Earth. We finally quote duNoüy's conclusion: "We are brought to the conclusion that, actually it is totally impossible to account scientifically for all phenomena pertaining to life, its development and progressive evolution and that unless the foundations of modern science are overthrown, they are unexplainable."

Chapter IV. This chapter makes clear that "the inorganic evolution of the earth itself, is progressing energy wise, on the basis of a slow winddown thus flattening out dyssimilarities. This is in conformity with the second law of thermodynamics which in essence says that in any transfer of energy from one system to another a certain fraction of the energy is irreversibly lost, i.e., goes into a state of entropy which is not available for further use. Theoretically, the planet will finally stop, in total darkness, and it will become very cold. Living things operate upon a different basis, for the evolution of life will tend to produce greater and greater dyssimilarities. This is due to the presence of the human brain, which the 100% materialist will maintain is operating by Chance." The author then flatly states, "An explanation of the evolution of life by chance alone is untenable today." To tie it down firmly with a bit of humor, he quotes Whitehead as follows: "Scientists who spend their life with the purpose that it is purposeless, constitutes an interesting subject of study."

Comment by the Pilgrim: Lesson writers for all ages in the church could pick up the author's example of the microbe living in a crack of the skin of an elephant's ear. This illustrates the necessity of true perspective, the level of our observation. This changes as our brain becomes aware, intuitively, of a CAUSE behind it all. In referring back to the point in time of evolution of atoms and molecules of matter from their precedents, the electrons, protons, and "particles," he does not get back to the prestep in which the electrons and the protons and the particles were themselves formed. It is at that step that this pilgrim takes the leap of adding the missing link, which he perceives the age of Einstein and fellow physicists to have supplied. (See my chapter 9, section 2.)

Let us bear in mind that *Human Destiny* was written during World War II. Einstein had set up domicile at Princeton and was writing and lecturing, reducing the relation of TIME, SPACE, and MATTER into a manageable concept. Perhaps he had not completed this or the publicity had not engulfed duNoüy as yet.

This Pilgrim humbly submits his idea that all Energy was, and is, in the nature of a portion of the substance of God Himself, and that He existed in absolute control of total energy prior to His formation of the electron and the proton. I accept this as the first step of His creation of the Universe and Man. *Thus, the Creator God began everything with nothing but Himself.* We do not know whether Einstein and his fellow scientists had ever discussed this angle. At least I have not discovered anything except a hint that many of his associates did not care for his ready acceptance of the spirituality of his Hebrew book of Genesis.

The author closes his section 1 on methods with a helpful note on the basic conflict of materialism and spiritualism by discussing the reality of Free will by which man can shape his destiny, or at least be a co-partner in the process. Man realizes that he may choose the easy capitulation to his animal instincts or he may choose the conflicting path of pain, "blood, sweat and tears," knowing that is the pathway to the greater happiness and joy. At our present stage of evolution most men

312

appear ready to fall back on their animal instincts, the easy and thoughtless path. A student wise enough to appreciate duNoüy's approach to the ultimate goal of evolution may wonder why the concept of Free will is introduced so early in the introductory discussion of his subject. He sends the reader a strong signal that the future of the human race is being provided for, perhaps millenniums beyond A.D. 2000. There is therein the author's personal stance, which is with the spiritualist as over against the materialist.

SECTION II—"THE EVOLUTION OF LIFE"

The Pilgrim comments: We know that some 10 percent of the one hundred chemical elements making up the material Universe are unstable and have been disintegrating since the beginning into the more stable form as lead and helium. Uranium is the major element in the unstable group. Radon is a small trace of radiating residue still seeping here and there from the ground. It will probably continue to do so X more millions of years. At this moment the majority of geologists and physicists agree that the earth is about four billion years old (Stanley). When fossils and rocks are analyzed for the amount of lead and remaining uranium, the scientist calculates the age of the specimen.

Creation was an inorganic system for about two billion years and then living, i.e., organic, material appeared. Whether it was amorphous or cellular and whether it was animal or plant remains a conjecture. We are further confused when we examine the residue of fossilized life fluids of these earliest living forms: hemoglobin with an atom of iron (animal), and chlorophyl with an atom of magnesium (plant), and now and then a blue algae residue with copper in it. DuNoüy suggests that we may never know which actually came first. It occurred in or along the shores of the primitive, fresh water oceans. No doubt original reproduction occurred via mitosis, i.e., simple cell division, which is indefinitely repeated. Mysteriously, this was replaced by fusion of bodies. Death later enters the picture and the two original cells or masses, now dead, have produced a new individual. At this point, living matter escaped the inorganic world and death returns its elemental residue to the system.

The age of fossils indicates that the marine life began millions of years before plants first appeared growing on dry land. So far the earliest land fossil known comes from the Canadian Gaspé Peninsula. It

313

was discovered about A.D. 1870. A hundred million years after its introduction came the enormous ferns, fifty feet tall, which formed the coal veins we mine today. There are no fossils so far to tell a connected story of the rise of the animal kingdom. Such as we have do indicate that many side shoots have developed and then became extinct, as witness the dinosaurs who left skeletons in our western states. There appear to be no connecting links except in the case of reptiles and the airborne birds. Some paleontologists believe that they have found a skull midway between reptile and mammal. Up to this point there is no definite indication as to where the progression toward human stock fits in.

Chapter VII is somewhat philosophical and the author suggests the reason for expecting evolution to be heading toward a preset final goal. Many variations in animals and plants have taken place but only a portion have actually made it. It is enlightening to include this statement from the chapter: *"Adaptation and natural selection are no longer identified with evolution.* [Italics mine.] The latter is differentiated from the former by its distant goal, which dominates all the species. In this hypothesis, and in opposition to Darwin's thought, the survival of the fittest can no longer be considered in the origin of the evolving strain and the fittest of a certain line can eventually give birth to species destined to disappear or vegetate, for which latter conditions become unsuitable. Let us make this point quite clear, the properties and qualities of living organisms are not attributed to special principles as was done by the old vitalist doctrines, but it is simply assumed that a goal must be attained by means of the most varied methods in conformity with the chemico-physical laws and the ordinary biological laws. Nature often has recourse to chance, to probabilities in living things. Fish lay hundreds of thousands of eggs as if they knew that, under conditions under which the eggs would hatch, ninety percent are destined to be destroyed."

Pilgrim: It is my opinion that experienced lesson writers of teenage church curricula study this chapter very thoroughly. The temptation for the Christian, seeing that he is halfway through the book, is to hastily close off any further attention to the animal kingdom and move on quickly into the third section on the Evolution of Man. With his previous concept that Evolution merely interpreted or explained the origin of Man, the non-Christian students are inclined to view that as the endpoint of the process. They are most apt to refer to the development in life over the past ten or twelve thousand years as purely an *inner human* effort. DuNoüy considers the human brain as part of the material world, and so Humanism as the power in mankind in charge thereafter. The thorough young reader of duNoüy now begins to realize that *Human Destiny* deals with the perfecting of God's child's progress toward the goal found in the template of Christ. This puts the student on firm spiritual ground but he should not fail to meditate on the prior discussion in this chapter. It becomes a real argument for the existence of God, the Author of the "telefinalistic goal," which has been effective during the preceding millenniums, magnetically drawing as it were, the animal strain upward toward the eventual goal, Himself.

SECTION III: "THE NEW ORIENTATION OF EVOLUTION OF MANKIND"—SECOND CHAPTER OF GENESIS

Chapter VIII: "Evolution goes on. The animal shape capable of sheltering the spirit, capable of allowing it to develop, is found. He feels free to accept or reject, the new orders. As an individual, he is conscious of the beginning of a moral code. It is from this memory based on the liberty to choose between the satisfaction of the appetites and the flight toward spirituality, that human dignity is borne. True human personality appeared from the moment speech was developed." (However, at another point duNoüy felt that the humanoid became really human when God gave him a conscience.) "Man revolts against death. He buries the dead with care and ceremony. The 'memories of the animal' are transformed and he now asks of himself, 'Is this right or wrong?' Conscience now exists and the eternal conflict begins. His intelligence has now gained a new quality not enjoyed by his animal forebears."

Comment by the Pilgrim: Contemporary Christians at first reading, at least those with the most sensitive natures, may be dissatisfied that duNoüy does not immediately rush in with news that our Creator, God, was now evident as the Founding Father in charge. One may gain an impression that he allows too much leeway to mere man's individual effort for his ensuing ascendance to the higher levels. But please keep in mind that duNoüy is writing for his effect on fellow scientists, many of whom are not ready nor willing to entertain the idea of Almighty God as a Reality. Be patient, for the author still has a half dozen chapters in which to cover the continuing story. Note that he abruptly opens his Bible to the book of Genesis. The reader may not have expected this

315

quite so soon. We already know that in the symbolism of the Garden of Eden story, duNoüy joins most of us in making God's breathing into man's nostrils the equivalent of gifting him with Life and Conscience. The Pilgrim and our readers at this point breathe a deep and fervent *Amen*. In his description of this event, the author makes clear the beautiful act of God endowing Man with a reflection of Himself and a contract of Partnership in Creation. We quote: "Thus he will fulfill his mission as a man and will contribute to the divine plan which intends to yield a spiritually perfect human. Human progress therefore, is no longer solely dependent upon God, but on the combined efforts made by each man individually." We are now all in warm agreement.

CHAPTER IX—TRADITION, A HUMAN MECHANISM OF EVOLUTION—MORAL IDEAS AND NOTION OF GOOD AND EVIL—THE BELIEF IN GOD AND THE REPRESENTATION OF GOD—THE GOAL.

This chapter is straitforward and should challenge most High School students. There must however, be some caution in classroom discussion, since Tradition is here suggested as a continuing tool of evolution for the *future*. Normally we think of tradition as a looking backward to the stored knowledge of past experience, an examination of what our forefathers did under a given circumstance, i.e., we question what was used as a guiding principle. Elsewhere, the author has stressed that the animal instincts are to be overcome as evolution continues. In other words, a sort of an instinctive pseudo-tradition is to be replaced by a fully human tradition. It should be made quite clear that he is now speaking about the tradition of Man, who is imbued with conscience.

We, Mankind, are just now originating a respect for tradition as over against animal instinct. Here the author is treating what has taken place within that *new* human tradition in the past few thousands of years. It seems to this Pilgrim that the author does not sufficiently stress the need to refurbish and constantly add to a changing, moving, improving tradition. I take it that duNoüy would discuss the ills of a rigid straitjacket tradition after he has established a tradition based on conscience and only recently separated from animal instinct. He is definitely not speaking of tradition as a rigid mold of the way things were done in our great-grandfather's time in the past century. He is speaking of

Man's inexperience with his new gifts of causative memory, a conscience, and the ability to use speech to meld together the composite experience of this new mutant group.

Tradition, new or old, as duNoüy puts it, should not be thought of as a rigid block of past experience, but a dynamic, growing, moving force. To be the latter, it must have a goal. This is a noble concept. The advance toward the goal is by means of the hard work and special effort put forth by the few individuals who rise above the common denominator. The Pilgrim comments, those individuals are changing the tradition.

Though the term "tradition" persists, its composition must change. In the days of commercial sailing vessels, ballast going from A to B might be rock, easily and quickly available at the port of departure. It was changed to sand at port B for the trip to C, where it had monetary value in new construction projects. At C, it was exchanged for grain, which was useful and valuable back home. Tradition is a ballast but it is modified as civilization advances.

Even so there are some elements of tradition that never change. The pilgrim cannot leave this particular theme without referring again to his most satisfying decade of church service: those years in which he managed the extended educational program of a suburban junior church-school department. In those full two-and-a-half-hour sessions, a number of personally led teaching themes were developed in addition to the regular published lesson material.

The examples of modern Stephens, Barnabases, and Pauls centered on the evangelistic lives of the flood of missionaries who carried the gospel and Christine medicine to India, Assam, Burma, China, and Africa in the latter half of the nineteenth century and the early portion of the twentieth. In the history of Christ's church, the tradition of the life-expending service of a Paul and a Barnabas evolved into the tradition of our foreign missionaries.

This tradition as viewed in the Space Age rises to haunt us. Now our world neighbors are only seconds away through TV. Do we recognize the challenge and the problem? The former ambassador of Christ lived his message in the daily lives of his foreign neighbor from morning to night, elbow to elbow. Today, dramatic TV preaching from the upper class trappings of a modern broadcasting stage can be in danger of painting a phony picture of what righteous living really is. The preacher in his well-insulated and culturally protected position cannot appreciate his hearer's hurting experiences and ancient culture. The nurturing aspect of Christian relationship is entirely lacking. Nor can the hypocrisy of the preacher's message and the vision of a wild, rampant American culture viewed that same day in the evening news hour be brushed aside.

Let us return to duNoüy. Dear Lesson Writer, can you strengthen the concept of daily Christian living for the teenage confirmant as God's procedure of ascending evolution? Can you show the teenager's private life as formulating a moral code in the midst of affluency, motivating him toward a church membership for which God has set the goal and is magnetically drawing all persons into Himself as co-partners? DuNoüy speaks: "Good is that which contributes to the course of the ascending evolution and leads us away from the animal toward freedom. *Evil* is that which opposes evolution, and escapes it by regressing toward the ancestral bondage, toward the beast."

He concludes this chapter by calling the attention of his fellow material scientists to the idea that the true God is their "Anti-Chance." Faith undergirds our intuition that He is a Personality akin to our own. "We act as though He existed" and are happy in that thought. Under that influence, God tells us of His mission for us and we find joy and happiness, trying despite our inability to make the grade, for much animal (beast) still remains. We end the chapter with this quote: "Pure intelligence, deprived of moral background, often ends in destructive or in futile discussion, in an intricate and complicated childishness." The Pilgrim ponders his own degree of childishness.

CHAPTER X—"CIVILIZATION"

One of the first points, perhaps the most troublesome in my personal case, is the difference between the races. It is unfortunate that the author does not philosophize upon those differences, since racism in our current age is such a major problem. He does reach back into antiquity by stating that the development of the human brain took place at different rates, thusly: "The development of the human brain did not take place with equal rapidity in the different races." I fear that teenage students coming upon this statement without warning would be inclined to turn it into fuel for the racism conflict which may be considered as today's major psychological shortfall against the Golden Rule. The author expresses no opinion as to the possibility that this difference in the rate of development of the prehistoric brain has any bearing or influence upon racial thought production in A.D. 2000. Perhaps the slower prehistoric one merely caught up in time. Standing on the threshold of a new period of civilization as a world family, is it not possibly a God-idea that racial brains have finally arrived at a state of equal function? Quality rather than early quantity should prevail in the final analysis. In time, the racial brains, having been brought to a commonality of function, would thus equate racial intelligence and morality as having no inborn bias. This would still be consistent with the author's view of the examples of today's remains of aboriginal lines, such as the Australian bushmen and African pygmies, which are simply approaching dead-end vegetative endpoints of species not designated to remain to the mainstream of human society.

Assuming that a common racial development of civilization can now be depended upon, the author realistically points out "that those involved in the advancement of morality and spiritual nature will some day, perhaps sooner than we think, be obliged to take refuge in the desert." By this he infers that the ascending evolution may be meeting what appears to be overwhelming obstacles so that it must escape to further incubation and development in an exiled or isolated place. The Pilgrim would hope that in such a protected enclave, or temporary encapsulation if you prefer, *All* races will be represented. It would seem to be a prerequisite that God would wish all of His people to be represented in the resulting new thrust upward toward His Perfection.

Typing these thoughts in 1989, the Pilgrim wonders if perhaps God, by turning Mr. Gorbachev into one of His own angels, may have decided on a change of plans? The Pilgrim hopes that the human race of the far future is a melded raceless people.

The author proceeds to intrigue us with his two definitions of civilization. The importance of this twin approach is obvious when we note his overwhelming devotion to the idea that progress toward higher moral and spiritual levels will come only through the committed, sacrificial lives of a hard-laboring few. First is "the *static* definition. Civilization is the deceptive inventory of all the modifications, in the moral, esthetic and material conditions of the normal life of man in society, by *the brain alone*. The second is the *dynamic* definition. Civilization is the global outcome of the conflict between the memory of man's anterior evolution which persists in him, and the moral and spiritual ideas which tend to make him forget it." One of course is struck by the total exclusion of material "things" in the second definition. DuNoüy is saying that the "man of things" is not in the same league as "the man of spirit." He swings a heavy one-two at the materialist. "True human progress, that which can be linked to evolution and which prolongs it, can only consist in perfecting and ameliorating man himself and not in improving the tools he employs, nor in increasing his physical well-being. This last attitude is that of the materialist and is insulting to man, because it reflects systematically the noblest human qualities alone capable of assuring him of happiness worthy of him, and superior to that of a ruminating cow. Man can aspire to joys higher than those of his animal ancestors."

The author concludes that it is the purpose of evolutive civilization to overcome the stance of those who do not fully understand human dignity, a costly prize richer in sacrifices than in pleasures. He deplores their return to animality and the midway position of passively "good" folks who put on a semblance of good deportment for fear of their reputation, the deadwood who have no courage to do otherwise. No doubt some such are even found on church membership rolls. At this point the author neglects stressing that God's goal must not be a mere abstraction, but is a magnetic, drawing spiritual attraction of God in Christ and compels man to keep trying in the midst of his difficulties.

There remain eight chapters in *Human Destiny,* as follows:

Chapter XI—Instincts—Societies of Insects—Intelligence—
    Abstract Ideas—The Role of the Individual
Chapter XII—Superstition—Origin and Development
Chapter XIII—Religion—True Religion is in the Heart
Chapter XIV—The Idea of God and Omnipotence
Chapter XV—Education and Instruction
Chapter XVI—The Telefinalist Hypothesis [Summary]—Human
    Destiny
Chapter XVII—Intellectual or Moral Development—The Wake of Man
Chapter XVIII—Universal Thought—The Shrinking Earth—
    Recapitulations and Conclusions

These chapters are more or less self-evident discussions of Christian growth. However, chapter XV, dealing with education, reinforces one of the Pilgrim's lifelong avocations. You will recall a number of allusions to his work as we have travelled together.

Notes

CHAPTER I
ORIENTATION: MAKING A ROAD MAP FOR YOU, THE READER

1. In 1806, five students from Williams College sought refuge in a nearby haystack during a heavy rainstorm which had interrupted their outdoor prayer meeting. Among them were Judson, who went to Burma, and Brigham, who went to Hawaii. *Tongues of Fire*, Keyes F., p. 226.

2. NIV Deut. 4:9. Watch closely so that you do not forget the things your eyes have seen or let them slip from your heart as long as you live. Teach them to your children and to their children after them.

    NIV Deut. 11:19. Teach them to your children, talking about them when you sit at home and when you walk along the road, when you lie down and when you get up. [All biblical quotations marked "NIV" are taken from the Holy Bible: New International Version © 1978 by the New York International Bible Society, used by permission.]

3. The Greeks did not have a word the equivalent of our universal word *love*. Sexual intercourse was erotic, from Eros; and at the highest level was *agape*, used for divine love. In between were *fraternitas, soror, familia* (Latin), terms indicating specific areas of relationship.

4. Mr. Harry Cartzdafner, manager of the Farmers Cooperative Bank at Upham, N.D., Prior to World War I.

5. Dr. Edward R. Cooke, Director of Physical Education, St. Olaf College, Northfield, Minnesota, in pre–World War I and on into the thirties.

6. NIV I Cor. 13:11. When I was child, I talked like a child, I thought like a child, I reasoned like a child. When I became a man, I put childish ways behind me.

7. NIV I Cor. 13:12. Now I see but a poor reflection,* then we shall see face to face. Now I know in part: then I shall know fully, even as I am fully known. (*) No doubt refers to the image reflected by the polished piece of brass carried as a mirror in the Roman soldier's kit.

8. The reader is referred again to the note 3, on *love*.

9. Random House Dictionary.

10. NIV Gen. 1:1. *In the beginning . . . the Spirit of God* was hovering over the waters. John 4:24, *God is Spirit* and his worshippers must worship in spirit and in truth.

11. NIV Ex. 20:4–5. You shall not make for yourself an idol in the form of anything in heaven above or on the earth beneath or in the waters below. You shall not bow down to them or worship them. For I, the Lord your God, am a jealous God . . . (also) 20:23, Do not make any Gods to be alongside me; do not make for yourselves gods of silver or gods of gold.

12. Alfred Lord Tennyson, "Pantheism." See references on pp. 193 and 215.

13. "Rufus Jones Speaks to Our Times," Edited by Harry Emerson Fosdick.

14. *Power* is defined technically in chapter 9. In general, I have used *power* as being the ability (i.e. a force) to act both materially and spiritually.

15. ESP, extrasensory perception, a term used by psychologists. It is intuition of the highest order. This book assumes that God forged and implanted His moral code in humanity, and intuitively, we turn toward the Author.

16. NIV Gen. 1:26–27. Then God said, "Let us make man in our image, in our likeness, and let them rule over the fish of the sea and the birds of the air, over the livestock, over all the earth and over all the creatures that move along the ground." So God created man in his own image.

17. See note 13. One must expand that definition and realize that techni- cally, power, when it exerts itself in action, performs work. The physicist explains that this can be thought of as quantified energy. In chapter 9, we conclude that God, besides being Love, is also Energy, which is more significant than the more general term, *power.*

18. Paul's concluding eleventh chapter of Romans leaves the door wide open for his fellow Jews to enter, via Jesus Christ.

19. *Objectives of Christian Education*, by Paul Vieth, doctoral thesis at

Yale Divinity School, published at the close of World War I, dominated the initiation of modern Christian education in our local churches during the first half of this century.

CHAPTER II
THE GROWTH CURVE

1. The Incendiary Fellowship, Elton Trueblood.
2. The Reader may feel that reference to Death in our search for Faith throws a damper on the conversation. However, the symbolism of the death of the wheat plant is quite apt if we do not limit death merely to the physical structure which holds the seed grain. Paul spoke often of his daily death to sin. In I Cor 15:31, he flatly states, "I die every day." Thus, Paul could die each evening as he retired, but arise each morning a new man in Christ, denoting a constant cycle of life and death. Let you and I not forget that the vehicle by which this cycle is maintained is earnest confessional prayer.

CHAPTER III
TEN LETTERS TO MY GRANDSONS

1. This endnote is for the older, more mature reader who has never made the heroic effort of reading through the roughly five hundred pages of introductory material in Volume I of the twelve-volume set of *Interpreter's Bible*, Abingdon Press, 1954. The *origins*, note the plural, of the earliest writings of the Scriptures, indicate that the historicity of Hebrew tribal and clan life is a matter of conjecture. In the introductory section of the book of Genesis itself, Professor Simpson sketches early life at three centers, Beersheba, Hebron, and Trans-Jordan. It seems that the early, oral storytellers wove the backgrounds of three subtribal units into one united, purposeful family. Thus the actuality of the direct blood relationship of Abraham, Isaac, and Jacob, is very questionable. Such a view has more recently been corroborated in the research findings of Miller and Hayes in their recent volume, *The History of Ancient Israel and*

Judah (1988), see bibliography. This, of course, destroys the veracity of Sarah's miraculous birth of Isaac. Read and taught properly, it does not, however, destroy the monotheistic, convenantal relations of Abraham, God, and His chosen people. Abraham as the head member of a great "family," had many spiritual "sons" to become the blessing to all the earth. We Protestants are "sons" of Abraham. But future lesson writers of Old Testament stories, especially for the children and youth, ought to exhibit honesty and integrity. Lesson writers for the older members of the communities of faith should acknowledge the historical error in the oral folklore and carefully explain it. I hope that new lesson writers have the intestinal fortitude to see that this is done. (My further references to Gibson's Bible Study on Genesis I will assist in this effort.)

2. A teenage boy or girl in confirmation class may not have much of an idea as to what "Abraham's blessing" may consist of, but the older person will have experienced deeper feelings. A full-fledged active Christian of 1990 should be able to proclaim the miracle of the initial belief in monotheism, the working establishment of a moral code (Moses), God's employment of nations as His agents (via the Prophets), the Divine Personification of Love (Christ), formulation of democracies doing away with the divine right of Kings under human aegis, and even the formation of the constitution and government of the United States. Secular humanists will not buy the reference of our government, of course. The Reader at this point in my story has already met my high school student who began to appreciate the Father, Son, and Holy Spirit as three states of the same God-stuff in the Trinity. Check back on analogies in chapter 1. See ahead to chapter 7, "The Revision of the Apostle's Creed for the Space Age."

3. Psychological analysis of the power to think in children indicates that the attraction toward church membership should best be undertaken by a slightly older child than has been traditionally past custom. The hero-worship exhibited by a sixth grader has been the traditional point in urging commitment to Jesus. Attention now seems more effectively applied to the slightly older boy and girl, who within the current generation may become an uncertain, anarchial element. We now generally agree that obtaining the substance of a true, personal commitment to a change in life-style requires more knowledge and the beginning of reasoning ability. Note my recommendation for acceptance of the Evangelical Lutheran AFFIRM material.

4. The Reader should become aware that the older Christian will wish more to be said about the matter of total commitment. See chapter 5: "Christian Education."
5. Sorry to say, the Dr. Spock generation of young people cannot be depended upon to be ready to accept authority of parents, and they certainly do not take kindly to discipline. The young confirmand, who in some cases will have previously behaved as the family anarchist, must decide *upon his own choice* what his course of action will be. It will not be of much help for the distraught parent to merely point to *some* of Paul's advice. He had felt obliged to recognize governmental authority in preference to complete disorder otherwise. The teenager, sooner or later, must arrive at some sense of order as he relates to the OTHER.

CHAPTER IV
FINDING MY OWN IDENTITY

1. Psychologists coined the term ESP, extrasensory perception. We Christians perceive the Presence of God through unlimited channels in addition to the communication via languages. See John Powell, S. J., *He Touched Me*, in the bibliography.
2. Her book detailing her experiences as a missionary in Burma is now in preparation for publication.
3. Scripture references: NIV Luke 5:13, Rom. 7:6, Eph. 2:15, Eph. 4:23–24, Col. 3:10.
4. See *Power* defined more thoroughly in chapter 1, page 14–15 and chapter 9, page 206.
5. NIV, John 13:34. LOVE was the unifying principle.
6. See the whole introductory section of the *Interpreter's Bible,* Volume 1, but especially see the portion within the book of Genesis proper, pp. 440–60, Volume I.
7. NIV Exod. 3:14 and John 8:58.
8. See introductory section, *Interpreter's Bible,* Volume 1.
9. The Noah story is on page 446 of the *Interpreter's Bible.*
10. Dictionary definitions of figures of speech, according to *Random House Dictionary.* These definitions are applicable to the first eleven chapters of Genesis:

allegory: presentation of an abstract or spiritual meaning under concrete or material forms; a symbolic narrative.

metaphor: applying resemblances between things not strictly applicable.

parable: a discourse conveying likeness of comparable action.

simile: directly expressing a resemblance in one or more parts of one thing or another.

11. It appears that the medical profession chose the more ancient occidental Hindu concept of the serpent for its modern symbol. (According to Bill Moyers and John Campbell discussing mythology and religious faith on PBS channel 30 at Ft. Myers, Florida, 7:30 P.M., December 23, 1989.)

12. Old Testament Bible Study Series, Genesis Vol. I John C.L. Gibson, see bibliography.

13. *Interpreter's Bible,* Volume I, Noah story, p. 446.

14. J. Maxwell Miller and John H. Hayes. *A History of Ancient Israel and Judah.* (Philadelphia: Westminister Press, 1986.)

15. John C.L. Gibson, Genesis, Volume I.

CHAPTER V
CHRISTIAN EDUCATION—GEARING UP FOR THE NEXT CENTURY

1. NIV Matt. 19:19, Mark 10:20, John 3:16, 15:57.

2. Toyohiko Kagawa, *Love, the Law of Life,* trans. J. Fullerton Greffett (Philadelphia: John C. Winston Co., 1929.)

3. The Overstreets, a man and wife team, wrote in early midcentury. This quotation is from one of their books: *The Mature Mind.* (New York: W.W. Norton, 1949), page 272.

4. See chapter 10, Potpourri Number 6, "The University of Life," beginning page 239, and page 259.

5. In the decade of the thirties and early forties, the Albany (N.Y.) School of Religion was such a community force. The motivating leadership was centered in Mr. Elmer Yelton, who met an untimely death in 1943.

6. Junior high curriculum, AFFIRM, Augsburg Publishing, Minneapolis, MN, 1988.

7. First Presbyterian Church, Newton-Conover, North Main Avenue, Newton, North Carolina. Budgets: 1983, ca. $135,000; 1990, ca $270,000, now two pastors and ca. 500 members. Newton-Conover is 14,000-person community in the suburban area adjacent to the manufacturing city of Hickory, North Carolina.
8. Montreat is the synod summer retreat center, near Black Mountain, established by the synod of North Carolina. It is now operated by the mid-Atlantic synod of the Presbyterian Church, USA.
9. St. Andrews College, Laurinburg, North Carolina.
10. See chapter 10, Potpourri number 3, Ecumenicity Today—the Pilgrim's Experience.
11. *A Colloquy on Christian Education*, edited by John H. Westerhoff III, section by Frances W. Eastman on "The Open Church School," United Church Press, 1972.
12. A *Colloquy on Christian Education*, total volume.

CHAPTER VI
TAKING RISKS FOR GOD'S SAKE

1. Bruce Larson. "The Lifeline," *Guideposts* (August 1979): pp. 7–9.
2. A brief note for this sharing group section is given here: Leflie, Robert C. *Sharing Groups in the Church*. (Nashville: Abingdon Press, 1970.)

CHAPTER VII
PLOWING DEEPER FURROWS IN OUR TRADITION

1. See chapter 9, "God's Process of Evolution."

CHAPTER VIII
SCIENCE AND RELIGION—STILL SKIRMISH?

1. Bob E. Patterson. *Reinhold Niebuhr* (Waco, TX: Word Book Publishers, 1979.)

2. Michael Heylin is editor of the bimonthly *Chemical and Engineering News*, official magazine of the American Chemical Society.
3. Stassinopoulos, Arriana. "Courage, Love, Forgiveness," *Parade* (November 4, 1984): p. 9. Dr. Jonas Salk's formula for the future.
4. Paul Tournier, *The Medicine of the Whole Person.*
5. An *erg* is the unit of work performed when a mass of one gram has been moved one centimeter in one second. The force (i.e., the force expended) to do this is called a *dyne.*

CHAPTER IX
GOD'S PROCESS OF EVOLUTION: SORTIE NUMBER FIVE

1. SEARCH, weekly Bible studies, Leader's Guide Unit 3, James Limburg, Professor of Old Testament, Lutheran Northwestern Theological Seminary, Minneapolis, Augsburg Publishing House, New York: 1983, Mpls.
2. Lecomte duNoüy. *Human Destiny.* (New York: Longman Green and Co., 1947). Published paperback by New American Library, New York.
3. Steven M. Stanley. *The New Evolutionary Timetable.* (New York: Basic Books, Inc.)
4. See note 3.
5. A favorite expression of Dr. Paul Tournier.
6. Dictionary definitions are as follows:
   ontological: referring to the science of being, the natural essence of being; used theologically, is the intellectual apprehension of God, and is immediate and intuitive.
   cosmological: deals with theory of the cosmos or material universe, its parts, elements, and laws; cause and effect.
   teleological: dealing with the argument for God; doctrine of final cause; shaped and designed by a purpose (commonly referred to as the watch maker argument—Pilgrim).
7. J. B. Phillips. *New Testament in Modern English.* (New York: Macmillan, 1952), Rev. 3:14–16.
8. Lecomte's *Human Destiny* is referred to in several sections of this book. His approach lays a heavy emphasis upon the magnificence of

man's future yet to be in an extended timelessness. He must simply reiterate the goal of man's development as beyond comprehension except in terms of Christ's spirituality and at the moment of our mortal death; thus, the Pilgrim introduces his sermon on Perfection, as we close this chapter.

CHAPTER X
POTPOURRI

1. Titles in *Makers of the Modern Theological Mind,* edited by Bob E. Patterson, published by Word Books, Waco, Texas.

Karl Barth by David L. Mueller	*Reinhold Niebuhr* by Bob E. Patterson
Dietrich Bonhoeffer by Dallas M. Roark	*H. Richard Niebuhr* by Lonnie D. Kliever
Rudolf Bultmann by Morris Ashcraft	*Gerhard Von Rad* by James L. Crenshaw
*Charles Hartshorne by Alan Gragg	*Anders Nygren* by Thor Hall
Wolfhart Pannenberg by Don Olive	*Friedrich Schleiermacher* by C.W. Christian
Teilhard de Chardin by Doran McCarty	*Hans Kung* by John Kiwiet
Emil Brunner by J. Edward Humpgrey	*Carl F. Henry* by Bob E. Patterson
Martin Buber by Stephen M. Panko	**Paul Tillich* by John Newport
Soren Kirkegaard by Elmer M. Duncan	*Ian T. Ramsey* by William Williamson

The Pilgrim has not read those marked with an *.

2. Dietrich Bonhoeffer, "Cheap Grace," partial chapter in *Cost of Discipleship.* (New York: Macmillan, 1949) pp. 43–47.
3. Mr. Harry Cartzdafner, Manager of the local Farmers Cooperative Bank in Upham, North Dakota.
4. See page 000 and note 6 in chapter 5. My church of which Dr. Charles M. Durham was minister until December 1989.

CHAPTER XI
PRAYER—THE MOST IMPORTANT SORTIE: NUMBER SIX

1. The anthropomorphic nature of the terms of ordinary communica-

tion, such as "looking" (i.e., eyes for seeing), "vocally speaking" (i.e., use of vocal cords), and hearing (i.e., eardrums of the receiving person), should prevent us from using theses terms when speaking of communication with the Spirit. We do not stop to realize that such usage is symbolic. We excuse those who may pray to a mental image or form of the mortal face of Christ, or they do not feel they are actually praying. They actually imply that they have not yet programmed themselves to the point where they can "behold" God as all Spirit. It would be most enlightening to have a group of professional theologians varying from age thirty to eighty or ninty participate in what we may term a "Sharing Group" environment. They could be guaranteed anonymity while discussing their concept of the God they pray to, at the point of vulnerability to others in the group, their discussion pro and con being recorded electronically. A skilled literary editor who did not know the participants, either directly or by hearsay, could summarize the discussion. I wonder if any seminary class has tried an experiment like this. I believe such a confidential and factual statement would advance our spiritual understanding greatly. It could open up new avenues to God.

2. I have had other experiences of what I call a "felt" spirit, as a Presence. I have been both the cause and the receiver, depending of circumstances. When a person walks into a room where another is sleeping, the one sleeping becomes aware of the presence of the other and arouses slowly to full consciousness as he becomes aware of the other person. No noise, spoken word, or physical touching has been made. True, this has only occurred with my wife or my children. Perhaps some mystery of the close affection influences, even in a state of subconsciousness or unconsciousness.

Bibliography

Baillie, John. *The Belief in Progress.* New York: Charles Scribner's Sons, 1951.

Bonhoeffer, Dietrich. *The Cost of Discipleship.* Nashville: Abingdon Press.

Bright, John. *The Kingdom of God.* New York, Nashville: Abingdon-Cokesbury Press, 1953.

Buttrick, George A. *Power of Prayer Today.* Waco, Tex.: Word Books, 1979.

———. *Prayer.* Nashville: Abingdon-Cokesbury Press, 1942.

———. *So We Believe, So We Pray.* Nashville: Abingdon Press, 1951.

Casteel, John L. *Rediscovering Prayer.* National Board of Y.M.C.A. Association Press, 1955.

Church of the Brethern, *Curriclulum for Christian Education.*

Coffin, Henry Sloane. *Joy in Believing.* Edited by Walter Russel Bowie. New York: Charles Scribner's Sons, 1956.

Colson, Charles. *Born Again.* Old Tappan, N.J.: Fleming H. Revell Company, 1976.

Day, Albert E. *An Autobiography of Prayer.* New York: Harper Brothers, 1952.

de Lubac, Henri. *The Religion of Teilhard de Chardin.* London: Collins, 1967.

Dubos, Rene. *The Torch of Life from Credo Perspectives.* Edited by Ruth Nanda Aushen. New York: Simon & Schuster, 1970.

duNoüy, Lecomte. *Human Destiny* New York, London, Toronto: Longman Green and Company, 1947.

Emerson, William A. *Sin and the New American Conscience.* New York: Harper & Row, 1974.

Fosdick, Harry Emerson. *Adventurous Religion.* New York, London: Harper & Brothers, 1926.

———. *Rufus Jones Speaks to Our Times.* New York: Macmillan, 1957.

Garrett, Constance. *Growth in Prayer.* New York; Macmillan, 1950.

Gibson, John C.L. *Daily Bible Studies in Old Testament. Genesis II.* Louisville, Ky.: Westminster Press, 1982.

Hale, Joe. "The Spirit of Methodism." *Christian Herald,* December 1984.

Harrold,——. "John Henry Newman." Written at Ohio State University, 1945.

Heschel, Abraham J. *The Prophets.* Philedelphia: Jewish Publications of America, 1962.

Hobe, Phyllis. *The Guideposts Handbook of Prayer.* Old Tappan, N.J.: Guideposts Associates, 1983.

Holmer, Paul L. *C.S. Lewis: The Shape of His Faith and Thought.* New York: Harper & Row, 1976.

Interpreter's Bible, The. 12 vols. Nashville: Abingdon Press, 1952.

Kagawa, Toyohiko. *Love, the Law of Life.* Translated by J. Fullerton Greffett. Philadelphia: John C. Winston Co., 1929.

Larson, Bruce. *Thirty Days to a New You.* Grand Rapids, Mich.: Zondervan, 1974.

Laubach, Frank C. *Prayers.* Old Tappan, N.J.: Fleming H. Revell, 1956.

Leflie, Robert C. *Sharing Groups in the Church.* Nashville: Abingdon Press, 1970.

Lewis, C. S. *The Best of C. S. Lewis.* Iversen-Norman Associates, 1977.

——. *Mere Christianity.* New York: Macmillan, 1945.

——. *The Problem of Pain.* New York: Macmillan, 1962.

Limburg, James. *Search.* Adult Study Evangelical Lutheran Church Curriculum. Minneapolis: Augsburg Publishing, 1984.

Long, Edward Leroy, Jr. *Conscience and Compromise.* Louisville, Ky.: Westminster Press, 1953.

Marshall, Catherine. *Adventures in Prayer.* Old Tappan, N.J.: Chosen Books, 1975.

——. *Prayer, Man's Way to God.* Guideposts Trilogy. Edited by Shoemaker, Marshall, and Peale. Carmel, N.Y.: Guideposts Associates, 1962.

Marty, Martin E., and Dean Pierman. *A Handbook of Christian Theology.* Nashville: Abingdon Press, 1965.

Miller, Maxwell, and John M. Hayes. *A History of Ancient Israel and Judah.* Louisville, Ky.: Westminster Press, 1986.

Nastby, A. Gordon. *Treasury of the Christian World.* Edited and with a foreword by George M. Docherty. New York: Harper & Brothers, 1952.

Nelson, C. Ellis. "Is Church Education Something Particular?" Union Seminary paper presented at the joint 1970 meeting of United and Southern Presbyterians, prior to uniting.

Nouwen, Henri J. *Making All Things New.* Notre Dame, Ind.: Ave Maria Press, 1972.

———. *With Open Hands.* New York: Harper & Row, 1981.

Ogilvie, Lloyd John. *A Life Full of Surprises.* Nashville: Abingdon Press, 1969.

Patterson, Bob E., and Carl F. H. Henry. Waco, Tex.: Word Books. Here are listed the volumes issued to date under their editorship:

Karl Barth, by David L. Mueller	*Reinhold Niebuhr,* by Bob E. Patterson
Dietrich Bonhoeffer, by Dallas M. Roark	*H. Richard Niebuhr* by Lonnie D. Kliever
Rudolf Bultmann, by Morris Ashcraft	*Gerhard Von Rad, by James L. Crenshaw*
Charles Hartshorne, by Alan Gragg	*Anders Nygren,* by Thor Hall
Wolfhart Pannenberg, by Don Olive	*Friedrich Schleiermacher,* by C. W. Christian
Tielhard de Chardin, by Doran McCarty	*Hans Küng,* by John Kiwiet
Emil Brunner, by J. Edward Humphrey	*Ian T. Ramsey* by William Williamson
Martin Buber, by Stephen M. Panko	*Carl F. H. Henry,* by Bob E. Patterson
Sören Kierkegaard, by Elmer H. Duncan	*Paul Tillich,* by John Newport

Peck, Scott. *The Road Less Traveled.* New York: Simon & Schuster, 1978.

Powell, John, S.J. *Prayer, He Touched Me.* Allen, Tex.: Argus Communicatoors-Division of DBM, 1974.

Ringo, Stephen. *AFFIRM.* Evangelical Lutheran Church Teenage curriculum. Minneapolis: Augsburg-Fortress, 1988.

Sayers, Dorothy. *The Whimsical Christian.* New York: Macmillan, 1978.

Scott, E. F. *The Lord's Prayer.* New York: Charles Scribner's Sons, 1951.

Seymor, Jack, and Donald E. Miller. *Contemporary Approaches to Christian Education.* Nashville: Abingdon Press.

Shapiro, Robert. *Origins: The Possibilities of Science for the Genesis of Life Upon Earth. New York: Summit Books, 1985.*

Smith, Huston. *The Religions of Man.* New York: Harper & Row, 1958.

Speight, Robert. *Tielhard de Chardin.* London: Collins, 1967.

Stanley, Steven R. *The New Evolutionary Timetable. New York: Basic Books.*

Taylor, Marvin J. *Changing Patterns of Christian Education*. Nashville: Abingdon Press, 1984.

Tournier, Paul. *Fatigue in Modern Society*. Richmond, John Knox Press, 1977.

————. *The Healing of Persons*. New York: Harper & Row, 1965.

————. *The Person Reborn*.

Trueblood, Elton. *The Incindiary Fellowship*. New York: Harper, 1967.

Uhlig, Herbert E. "Letter to Editor," *Chemical & Engineering News*, September 25, 1989.

Vieth, Paul. "The Objectives of Christian Education." Doctoral thesis, Yale University Divinity School.

Westerhoff, John, III, Ed. *A Colloquy on Christian Education*. New York: Pilgrim Press/United Church Press, 1972.

Willis, David. *Daring Prayer*. Richmond: John Knox Press, 1977.